ENTRÉE TO JUDAISM

Tina Wasserman

ENTRÉE TO JUDAISM

A Culinary Exploration of the Jewish Diaspora

"Eat in Good Health!"

Tina Wasserman

URJ Press
New York, New York

For my husband, Richard
Whose love and encouragement
Make anything possible

Photography by Dave Carlin, Greg Booth and Associates
Food styling by Paige Erin Fletcher and Jane Jarrell
Design by Abbate Design
Cover design by Michael Silber
Composition by Publishing Synthesis, Ltd., New York

Library of Congress Cataloging-in-Publication Data
Wasserman, Tina.
  Entree to Judaism : a culinary exploration of the Jewish diaspora / Tina Wasserman.
    p. cm.
  Includes index.
  ISBN 978-0-8074-1110-0
  1. Jewish cookery. 2. Cookery, International. I. Title.
  TX724.W38 2009
  641.5'676--dc22

                          2009020188

Printed on acid-free paper
Copyright © 2010 by URJ Press
Manufactured in Canada
10 9 8 7 6 5 4 3 2

Do not forget the things you saw with your own eyes,
So that they do not fade from your mind as long as you live.
Make them known to your children and your children's children.

DEUTERONOMY 4:9

CONTENTS

FOREWORD *by Rabbi Debra Robbins* · ix
PREFACE · xi
ACKNOWLEDGMENTS · xiii

COOKING IN THE DIASPORA ᾽ 1
Adaptation and Reclamation

The Levant and Persia · 3
Jews and the Orange Trade · 17
The Maghreb and Africa · 27
Spain · 45
Italy · 57
Turkey and the Ottoman Empire · 73
India · 99
Jewish Traders on the Spice Route · 109
East and Southeast Asia · 117
Russia and Central and Eastern Europe · 129
Western Europe · 143
The New World and Latin America · 169
Jews and the Vanilla and Cacao Trade · 183

CELEBRATION OF THE JEWISH HOLIDAYS THROUGHOUT THE WORLD ᾽ 199

Shabbat · 201
Rosh HaShanah and Yom Kippur · 217
Sukkot · 235
Chanukah · 251
Tu BiSh'vat · 269

LEFT: *Chanukah Chocolate Truffles, pages 190–91*   vii

Purim · 295
Passover · 309
Shavuot · 335

ICONS OF JEWISH COOKING ⁓ 343

Chicken Soup · 345
Knishes, *Borekas*, and Filled Pastries · 357
Gefilte Fish · 383
Eggplant · 393
Cheesecake · 411
Charoset · 419
Apples and Honey · 431
Pickles and Preserving · 447

INDEX · 457

FOREWORD

The Talmud (*Nedarim* 50b) records a story about friends sharing recipes. A man makes a financial arrangement to send his servant to study cooking with a friend who was (or had) an accomplished cook. The agreement is that for a fee, the friend is supposed to teach the servant the one thousand ways he knows to

prepare a certain kind of fig. The servant returns having learned eight hundred of the thousand recipes. The man sues his friend and takes him to court. The rabbi presiding over the court sees the episode as an example of epicurean extravagance. He suggests that in more affluent times *maybe* people knew one thousand ways to prepare a single ingredient, but in their world, to know even eight hundred of a thousand recipes is worthy of celebration.

Imagine the kitchen where one would learn to cook a fig a thousand different ways. Smell the vast array of ingredients—fresh, dried, preserved, grown locally, and gathered from around the globe. Watch the techniques expressing an integration of international culture and style with local custom. Listen to the stories that accompany the preparation, words of wisdom that come from experience, small details about origins and adaptation that make a big difference in the final presentation. Taste the richness and history of the Jewish people making their way in the world and around the world in the foods we cook and share. Tina Wasserman is the friend in our generation with one thousand recipes. With this book she invites us to come into her kitchen-

classroom to learn them. Even if we, like the student in the story, are only able to master eight hundred recipes, what a blessing that will be in our lives.

In Tina's recipes each ingredient tells a story. Each recipe expresses an ethical value, explores an historical event, evokes a memory. To study in Tina's kitchen-classroom is to be in a place of challenges and paradoxes, and this book brings that experience to its readers. To cook with Tina, in her kitchen or in our own, is to encounter the place where precision in technique intersects with culinary creativity, intense concentration gives way to laughter, and our personal lives blend with the historic stories of our ancestors.

This book is a little bit like the Talmud, where the story of the one thousand fig recipes originates. It is a compilation of rules and stories, with real life examples and illustrations, a guide not only for preparing certain recipes but for living Jewish life. In this book there are recipes for Jews by birth embracing the history of our people, Jews by choice compiling scrapbooks of memories, interfaith families shaping new shared traditions, college students celebrating Shabbat on their own for the first time, newly married couples hosting holiday celebrations, families balancing work and school and home looking for ways to share a meal. These are recipes that will nourish and nurture not only our bodies but our hearts and minds and souls. Tina Wasserman is an extraordinary chef, teacher, and hostess. *Entrée to Judaism* is our invitation to join her at the kitchen counter and classroom table, and begin the sacred work of learning one thousand recipes for loving and living Jewish life.

Rabbi Debra Robbins
Temple Emanu-El
Dallas, Texas

Preface

From the time I was twelve, I knew that I wanted to teach people about food and cooking technique. I loved the creative process and learning about other cultures. I grew up in the 1950s, an era when food was becoming more than sustenance. Our world was expanding. Ethnic foods entered the mainstream as soldiers returning

from two theaters of war brought home new tastes they had acquired overseas. "Hawaiian-style" foods with lots of canned pineapple and Americanized Asian dishes that were deemed authentic because they incorporated soy sauce, and canned bean sprouts found their way onto my kitchen table. My father's specialty of Texas hot wieners with Mexican chili on top was a result of his time spent in the Air Force, and curried chicken over rice was my introduction to Indian cuisine. Although most of my parents' relatives got out before the start of the war, news from Eastern Europe and the popularity of Molly Goldberg on television rekindled the family's interest in traditional Jewish cooking, for food was the connection to the cousins left behind. For all recent immigrants to America, food was the bridge between their cultural observances in their new country and the holiday traditions of their ancestry. They adapted the produce available here to replace the fruits and vegetables of their homelands. If tamarind wasn't readily available, then maybe sour lemons or tomatoes would add the acidity required in a dish.

As ethnic communities were established, entrepreneurs opened food carts and restaurants so people could go out to eat the familiar foods of their former homelands. These foods were familiar to some, intriguing to others. As intrepid food explorers came through the doors of these establishments, they

began to learn about the cultures and enjoy the foods of these exotic lands, and they spread the word. More people came, and more people started to experiment with the new tastes in their own homes. I was a teenager, but I was no different.

Curiosity about food always compelled me to explore. My earliest foray into food experimentation took place when I was three and my mother found me on the kitchen floor with a five-pound bag of flour, one dozen eggs, a rolling pin, and a board . . . I was making a pie! After receiving my master's degree in food and fashion merchandising (I was a junior high school home economics teacher at the time), I traveled with my husband to Europe. We were on a tight budget, as all students were at the time. To save money we ate the prix fixe dinners that were offered at restaurants. Our first stop was Rome, and when my first dinner in Italy included ravioli, I cringed, thinking that I would be eating the Italian equivalent of those little pasta pillows in light red sauce from the can. I had an eye-opening experience when that toothsome piece of pasta filled with flavorful cheese and tinged with green flecks of an herb called basil (yes, young readers, there was a time when all those fresh herbs were not readily available!) entered my mouth. Everything was bursting with flavor, and I wanted to re-create it all when I got home.

After many years of teaching cooking— sometimes Jewish, but always kosher—I experienced an epiphany about my food heritage. I was asked to introduce Claudia Roden at a Jewish book fair in Dallas. Those who knew her work excitedly showed up to hear her speak; many only knew that she had written a new cookbook, *The Book of Jewish Food*. What none of us knew at the time was the world that would be opened to us through the portal of Sephardic cooking. The flavors, the textures, the shapes of those foods were just as much a part of our Jewish lineage to Moses and Abraham as gefilte fish or chopped liver. My time with her taught me to look at each and every recipe as a story of our struggle to survive and thrive. She ignited a passion in me to understand each and every story, and that has brought me to the present.

In 2002 I wrote to Rabbi Eric Yoffie, the president of the Union for Reform Judaism, beseeching him to include articles in *Reform Judaism* magazine about Jewish heritage and continuity through food. The editors of that quarterly publication, Aron Hirt-Manheimer and Joy Weinberg, liked the idea and gave me a chance to write one article. That one published article led to a longtime association with them. They nurtured me and supported my passion to disseminate the folklore and history that surround the culinary tradition of Jews in the Diaspora.

Countless hours have gone into learning about the little links in our cultural chain of fifty-six hundred years. There were times in the quest for the origin of a food, cooking technique, or religious allusion that I would find myself reading deep into the Talmud or the original accounts of first-century Jews by the historian Flavius Josephus. While I may not have shared every detail of these readings in this book, I have tried to connect these historical documents to the recipes I've chosen.

Throughout the history of the Jewish people, the two constants in their lives were the celebration of Shabbat and the commitment to keeping the laws of kashrut. These two observances are the foundation of all Jewish cuisine throughout the world. However, you do not have to be Jewish or keep a kosher kitchen to see or taste the history in this book's recipes. Rather than arranging the recipes by appetizer, main dish, and dessert, I hope that the life experiences and contributions of the Jews who lived in the past can be better understood through the recipes arranged by region or topic. Along the way, I hope you will learn some cooking "tidbits" as well.

It is my sincerest wish that this book will transport you back in time to better understand the culinary roots and heritage of the Jewish people and propel you forward to comprehend the culturally diverse world that we live in today and our children and grandchildren will live in tomorrow.

Eat in good health!

ACKNOWLEDGMENTS

Writing a book is like creating a good recipe; if you don't have the highest quality ingredients the finished product will not be the best. The people who worked with me to complete this book can not be showered with enough accolades, but they must be recognized for all their help and support. It is a pleasure to thank them in these pages.

Rabbi Hara Person championed this book and believed strongly in its concept. When she moved to the CCAR as its publisher and the director of its press, she promised she would find an editor for the URJ Press who would carefully and enthusiastically bring this project to fruition. I could not have asked for a better person to guide me, educate me, and nurture my writing skills than my editor, Michael Goldberg. His calm, straight-forward confidence in his approach to this project continuously made me feel like we were on the right track. He let me keep my voice while orchestrating the content to tell a great story. I am also indebted to Debra Hirsch Corman for her painstaking attention to detail in copyediting that caught the missed word or direction that was crucial to the recipe. Her help was immeasurable. Thanks are also due to Victor Ney, Stephen Becker, Rebecca Rosenfeld, Jonathan Levine, Michael Silber, Jessica Katz, and the rest of the staff of URJ Books and Music. My gratitude also goes to Avvennett Gezahan, who assisted me in collating my research for the book and enjoyed learning about Jewish culture.

My thanks go to Aron Hirt-Manheimer and Joy Weinberg, my editors at *Reform Judaism Magazine*, who encouraged me from the very beginning to deeply explore Torah and Mishnah to better understand the origins and roots of our culinary history; to Rabbi Debra Robbins, my friend, my rabbi, and my mentor, who continued to encourage me to pursue the idea for this book once I had obtained my own voice in the world of Jewish cooking; and to my readers who shared their stories, asked me questions, and encouraged me when I had created recipes that rekindled a fond memory. I thank you all.

Many people spent time telling me their stories about growing up Jewish in the Diaspora. Their personal histories and family recipes educated me far better than any didactic pursuit; their recipes contained the added ingredient, love. Thank you to Rachel Bortnick, Edith Baker, June Penkar, Rita Sasso, Rachel Gomel Israel, Debby Luskey, Libby Zucker, Yvette Feiger, Clemence Barkate, Chantal, Kathy, and Jacques Aferiat, Morton Wechsler, Jacques, Sam, and Albert Capsouto, and J.J. Keki for giving me a better understanding of life as a Jew in the world at large.

A good picture can often say more than words and sometimes it says volumes. Dave Carlin made my food come alive, tell a story, and invite the reader to look closer at the recipe. A joy to work with, he and the staff at Gregg Booth were my cheering squad and good taste testers! Paige Erin Fletcher, a great food stylist, taught me many tricks to make my food look as good as it tastes. She made you want to stick a fork right into the food on the page! One of the greatest joys was having my portrait taken for this book. The photographer made me feel totally comfortable in my kitchen despite the hours of shooting and the lights and reflectors positioned throughout the room. Telling stories and seeing the smile on his face behind the camera made it easy to smile; the photographer was my son Jonathan, and he knew me well. It shows.

A very dear friend believed that "if you saw a turtle on a fence post you knew it took a lot of people to get it there." This book would not have been conceived without the nurturing and support of good friends and wonderful family. My thanks to the "Bridge Buttes" for their love, encouragement, and understanding that my focus couldn't always be on the 5–10 rule; to Liz for sampling food, sometimes as early as 6:45 after walking the dogs, and always

lending an ear and words of advice; to Jerry, Arlene, Jerry, Jan, Joyce, and Tony, who patiently prodded me until I could really understand that I was "supposed to" do what I love to do and could do it with confidence; and to Karel Anne and all my students over the years who reminded me weekly why I love to teach and who were my best recipe testers.

No words of thanks are enough for my family, my best taste testers and guinea pigs. My children, Jonathan and Leslie, lived through lots of "experiments" and knew to eat the "ugly" rugelach. But they also knew that every box of rugelach sent halfway around the world or challah right out of the oven sent overnight to camp had one extra ingredient in the recipe, my love. My husband has the patience of Job. I often neglected his culinary needs while researching this book, and he certainly ate his share of unusual dishes. But his patience and scholarly insight into Judaism helped me focus on the intent of this book, and for that I am ever grateful.

ENTRÉE TO JUDAISM

COOKING IN THE DIASPORA
Adaptation and Reclamation

Jewish communities outside the Land of Israel have existed, and sometimes flourished, since ancient times. Jews settled throughout the Roman Empire, working not only as farmers and artisans but as traders and merchants, connecting with fellow Jews along the Silk Road from Europe to the Middle East and all the way to China. The Middle Ages saw important Jewish communities established in Babylonia, Spain, Germany, and beyond. Jewish history is filled with events that led to mass migrations across oceans and continents. Whether seeking economic freedom, fleeing persecution, or simply searching for a better life, Jewish communities spread to the four corners of the world. Wherever Jews settled, they adapted to the customs, tastes, and ingredients available in their new environment, creating our culinary heritage. This story is still being written as Jewish foods change to meet the times and needs of our communities in kitchens from Texas to Tel Aviv today.

THE LEVANT AND PERSIA

The eastern Mediterranean region that encompasses Iraq, Syria, Lebanon, Jordan, Israel, and parts of Egypt is known as the Levant. This moniker, meaning "to rise," was given in the 1920s by the French to describe the region where the sun comes up. The Levant is the land of biblical lore. With a climate similar to that of southern California, the region produces succulent fruits such as citrus fruits, apricots, figs, grapes, and melons in its temperate areas, as well as dates in the more arid areas. The spice caravans rode through this region, and it is the choice of spices more than anything else that differentiates the cuisine from country to country.

⤳ SYRIA ⤲

The first Jew to set foot in this area was Abraham, who was traveling in the Syrian hills on his way to Canaan. Aleppo got its name because Abraham stopped to give some of his goat's milk to the poor of that area, and the Arabic name for the city is Haleb, meaning "he milked." It was the Venetians who adopted the name Aleppo from their transliteration.

Although a Jewish community was said to exist during the time of King David, it was the fall of the First Temple and the Babylonian exile that brought the first major wave of Jewish inhabitants to Aleppo. The trade routes of Byzantium crossed from Asia to the Mediterranean right through the city. Aleppo's Jews didn't benefit from this trade route initially, since the early Christians impeded their financial progress. However, once the Arab Abbasid dynasty was established, and continuing through the rise of the Ottoman Empire, Aleppo and its Jewish merchants benefitted greatly from all of the culture and commerce centered in its midst. Silks, spices, jewels, and aromatics as well as local wheat, pistachios, almonds, and olive oil were traded to Venice and Livorno and then shipped throughout Europe and the New World.

As the Ottoman Empire began to decline, so did the success and personal freedom of the Jews in Syria. The opening of the Suez Canal in 1869 signaled the end of the trade route through Aleppo, and some Jews left to find work in Cairo and Beirut. The next wave of emigration occurred during World War I, when the Ottoman Empire was looking to conscript Jews to fight for its deteriorating empire.

More Jews fled to Europe and the Americas. In 1946, when the French Mandate over the territory ceased, the rise of Arab nationalism and the declaration of 1947 to make Palestine a Jewish state created difficult living conditions for Aleppo Jews. Harsh restrictions and travel bans prevented the Jews from leaving Syria, but in 1992 the ban was lifted and over four thousand Jews living primarily in Aleppo left for the United States and Israel.

Today there are only a handful of Jews left in Syria, but the culinary skills of their women, a prized asset throughout the millennia, live on in Brooklyn and Israel and Europe. Food ingredients from the poorest of poor to the affluent homes of former consuls and merchants have all been incorporated into the cuisine of Aleppo. Whether it is a simple lentil dish or an intricate chickpea dumpling that is encased in a delicately thin bulgur crust, the great reputation of the Jewish cook with Aleppo roots is worldwide.

IRAQ

Iraqi cooking is greatly influenced by its location, agriculture, and prosperity. Turkey to the northwest and Iran to the southeast imparted their culinary proclivities to the Iraqi culinary repertoire. The Turkish love of stuffed vegetables, lamb, rice, and yogurt-based dishes journeyed to Iraq, as did the rice dishes, pickles, and fruit and meat combinations of Persia/Iran.

Hospitality is the hallmark of Iraqi Jews regardless of where they live now. Following the lead of the most famous Iraqi, Abraham, Jews in this region always make more than enough food in case they are visited by unexpected guests.

The Tigris and Euphrates Rivers helped irrigate the surrounding lands and created moist, fertile ground in which to grow an abundance of vegetables. Iraqi dishes containing protein are primarily vegetable-based. Iraq's location on the Persian Gulf put it in direct contact with merchants on the spice trade route. Iraqi cooks use many herbs and spices in their cooking. Thyme, oregano, basil, dill, mint, parsley, and sage are frequently used herbs. Turmeric is used for color, and cardamom, cinnamon, ginger, tamarind concentrate, lemon, and rose water are used as flavoring agents. Even the color of foods plays an active role in menu choices in the Iraqi kitchen, according to Rivka Goldman in her book *Mama Nazima's Jewish-Iraqi Cuisine* (Hippocrene Books, 2006). According to Ms. Goldman, eating yellow vegetables results in laughter and happiness, green fruits or vegetables are considered sources of hope and prosperity, and black vegetables are thought to be unlucky, which is why Iraqis generally peel their eggplants!

ISRAEL

If the foods of the United States are varied because of its vast melting pot of ethnic cuisines, then the food of Israel has multiple personality disorder! Over the last sixty years, Jewish immigrants have come to

Israel from virtually all over the world. They bring with them hopes for the future and cling to culinary traditions from the past. Fusion cuisine takes on new meaning in Israel.

To identify the basis for Israeli cuisine, one need only look in the Bible for the listed seven species. In modern times there is no better example of the use of these wild and domesticated produce than in a meal presented to you by Moshe Basson, the former chef-owner of Eucalyptus Restaurant in Jerusalem. Moshe thrives on the education he gives the patrons of his restaurant every time they sit down to enjoy one of his meals. A history lesson that fills your stomach, mind, and heart all in one forkful is Moshe's best culinary feat. As one of the first participants in the worldwide Slow Food Movement, he strives to initiate people to the wonderful tastes of foods that grow locally in the wild or are cultivated in the region.

The icons of Israeli food in the twenty-first century, falafel, *zatar*, and an abundance of salads, all highlight foods whose roots literally go back thousands of years. Street vendors and small falafel shops sell the crispy little balls of seasoned chickpea flour rolled up with tahini and stuffed into pita pockets with fresh vegetables and even an occasional French fry!

Large semi-rectangular bagels are sold warm from street carts and served with a small cup filled with *zatar* for dipping. *Zatar* is the spice combination of wild thyme, oregano, sumac, salt, and sesame seeds that is used in conjunction with olive oil as a garnish for bread or for marinating meats.

Sit down at many restaurants in Israel and you will be inundated with the small plates of salads placed before you. Carrot salad with cumin, eggplant roasted and then pureed with spices and tahini, pickled beets—the list goes on and on, and each recipe is better than the next! Are they Greek, Bulgarian, Turkish, Syrian, Persian, Baghdadi? Yes, yes, yes!

❧ PERSIA/IRAN ❧

If French cuisine was the platform upon which all fusion cuisines were built in the last three hundred years, then Persian cuisine set the bar very high for the ancient world more than twenty-five hundred years ago. Modern-day Iran is the center of the Old Persian Empire and the seat of its culinary heritage.

The origins of this exquisitely flavored, delicate cuisine go back to the time of Cyrus the Great in the sixth century B.CE. Cyrus was the leader of the Pars tribe (Persians) that conquered vast stretches of land from India to Egypt and north to parts of Turkey and Greece. The Silk Road and the spice trade route that passed through Persia were instrumental in introducing new foods and flavorings to the region. It was through these routes that citrus fruit cultivation, eggplant, and rice were introduced throughout the Middle East.

Persian cuisine is noted for its juxtaposition of sweet and sour tastes in one dish, ground nuts to thicken sauces, and the use of fruits, as well as vegetables, to enhance the flavor of *khoreshes*, stews containing small amounts of lamb or poultry. Marinating and grilling meats as kebabs are also a hallmark of this region. However, Persian cuisine is probably most identified by the many dishes that incorporate rice. Rice is revered whether it is served simply adorned with crisp, golden shreds of fried onion or crowned with prized dried fruits and fragrant almonds. *Chelo*, the crispy base of cooked rice left in the bottom of the pan of properly prepared rice, is a delicacy that is served to special guests or used to garnish the fluffy mound of rice that is presented at table.

The proliferation of fresh herbs in the region coupled with the many spices indigenous to the empire account for the abundance of flavor in Persian cuisine. Basil, chives, dill, parsley, mint, tarragon, and marjoram are some of the many herbs used in Persian cooking to this day. The spice trade route facilitated the inclusion of black pepper, coriander, cardamom, cinnamon, cumin, fenugreek, saffron, sumac, and turmeric into the cuisine as well.

Onions are used in all forms, including scallions and leeks. However, garlic is never used in Persian cooking. That ingredient is left to Persia's surrounding neighbors. Pickles and flatbreads are always served at meals, and meals end with desserts often perfumed with rose water and garnished with bright green pistachio nuts. Diners might find rice offered in this course as well.

Persian Jewish cooks are known for their sumptuous feasts that reflect all of the cooking techniques employed in this region. Because little or no pork is used in Persian cooking and the Persians didn't rely heavily on the use of animal fat in their cooking, the traditions of Persian cuisine are easily adapted to the laws of kashrut.

MILLET PANCAKES WITH FRESH CORN

One-third of the world consumes millet as a staple of their diet; in the United States millet is more familiar as birdseed! High in protein, it is often eaten as a cooked porridge. Here it is briefly soaked to retain some of its crunch. Although these pancakes, with their subtle sweetness, are often served for breakfast with honey or syrup, they are equally at home at a cocktail party served warm with caviar and flavored yogurt or sour cream.

½ cup millet seed
1 cup all-purpose flour
½ cup whole-wheat or corn flour
½ teaspoon baking soda
1 teaspoon baking powder
¼ teaspoon salt
2 large eggs
½ cup fresh or frozen corn kernels
2 tablespoons honey
1 teaspoon vanilla

1½ cups milk plus ½ teaspoon lemon juice or vinegar
2 tablespoons unsalted butter for greasing pan
Honey for topping
  or
¼ cup thick Greek yogurt, sour cream, or crème
  fraiche
¼–½ teaspoon *zatar*
1 teaspoon wildflower honey
Red lumpfish caviar

1. Place millet in a small bowl and cover with hot water. Set aside.

2. Combine the dry ingredients in a medium bowl. Set aside.

3. Beat the eggs in a 1-quart bowl, and add the corn, honey, vanilla, and milk. Set aside.

4. Strain the millet. Place in a 10-inch frying pan over medium heat, and toss until the millet stops steaming and then dries and begins to toast. Rotating the pan gently will allow the millet to toast and "pop" evenly.

5. Add the liquid ingredients to the dry ingredients. Add the toasted millet to the mixture, and stir rapidly but gently until all the ingredients are combined.

6. Heat a nonstick griddle until very hot. Grease with some of the butter and reduce heat to medium. Pour batter into desired size pancakes.

7. When pancakes develop little holes on top, gently flip them over and cook on the other side until golden. Serve with honey or a mixture of the sour cream, *zatar*, and honey topped with a small dollop of red lumpfish caviar.

Yield: 14–20 pancakes, depending on size

TINA'S TIDBITS

- *Corn flour is finely ground cornmeal from the whole kernel of corn (as opposed to cornstarch, which comes only from the endosperm of the kernel).*
- *Adding a little vinegar or lemon juice to milk creates the equivalent of buttermilk.*
- *Use no more than 1 heaping tablespoon of batter if you want to use the pancakes as a base for an hors d'oeuvre.*
- *Zatar is a popular Middle Eastern spice mixture consisting of sesame seeds, sumac berries, thyme, and salt ground together. Often used as a flavoring agent for roasted meats, it is most commonly used in Israel as a seasoning with olive oil to coat the tops of breads.*

GREEN LENTIL AND BULGUR SALAD WITH HAZELNUTS

Bulgur is a culinary staple in the Middle East. Kernels of wheat are steamed, dried, and crushed into coarse, medium, or fine grain. Perhaps the best-known uses of bulgur are in tabbouleh salad and combined with spices and meat for kibbeh. Here the bulgur is paired with small, green French lentils and hazelnuts to create a very elegant and nutritionally balanced dish.

2 large shallots, finely chopped
3 tablespoons tarragon vinegar, divided use
$\frac{1}{2}$ cup green French lentils
Salt and pepper to taste
1 cup medium bulgur
$1\frac{1}{2}$ cups water
1 teaspoon salt

2 stalks of celery cut into $\frac{1}{8}$-inch dice
$\frac{1}{2}$ cup finely shredded carrot (purchased in bags), chopped
2 tablespoons minced fresh tarragon
2 tablespoons hazelnut oil or extra virgin olive oil
$\frac{1}{2}$ cup toasted chopped hazelnuts

1. Combine the shallots and 1 tablespoon of the vinegar in a 1-quart glass bowl. Set aside.

2. Place lentils in a 1-quart saucepan, and cover 2 inches with water. Simmer the lentils for 14–20 minutes or until the lentils are tender but not mushy. Drain well.

3. Add the hot lentils to the shallot mixture, and stir gently to coat the lentils. Season with salt and pepper to taste and set aside to cool.

4. Place the bulgur, water, and salt in a 2-quart saucepan, and simmer covered for 12 minutes or until the water is absorbed. Transfer to a 3-quart serving bowl, and stir to cool (or place **uncovered** in the refrigerator to cool).

5. When the bulgur is cool, add the lentil mixture and the remaining ingredients, and toss to combine. Season with additional salt and pepper if needed.

Yield: About $1\frac{1}{2}$ quarts salad

TINA'S TIDBITS

- *Green lentils are very small, round seeds that are more common in Europe than North America. They are the only lentil sold with their seed coat intact and therefore do not disintegrate during cooking.*
- *To remove the bitter outer skin of the hazelnuts, toast the nuts in a 350°F oven for 7–10 minutes or until they are golden. Immediately encase some of the hot nuts in a terry dish towel and rub firmly. The texture of the towel should remove much of the skin. (I carefully take the towel outside to my herb garden and empty its contents to act as biodegradable mulch!)*

FATTOUSH SALAD

I first tasted this Mediterranean classic at a Lebanese restaurant. Although the main components of the salad are reminiscent of an Israeli salad, the toasted pita chips add a different texture and create a flavorful result. This is a great salad for a Shabbat cold luncheon.

2 large pita breads
1 tablespoon extra virgin olive oil
1 teaspoon *zatar* seasoning (optional)
$\frac{1}{4}$ cup fresh lemon juice
$\frac{1}{3}$ cup olive oil
Kosher salt
Freshly ground black pepper

$\frac{1}{2}$ head romaine lettuce, cut into small pieces
$\frac{2}{3}$ cup coarsely chopped parsley
5 scallions, thinly sliced into rounds
$\frac{1}{2}$ cup coarsely chopped fresh mint
1 cucumber, peeled, seeded, and finely chopped
3 tomatoes, seeded and cut into $\frac{1}{4}$-inch pieces
$\frac{1}{2}$ teaspoon sumac (optional)

1. Brush the tops of the pita bread with the 1 tablespoon olive oil, and sprinkle *zatar* over the tops. Bake at 375°F until golden and crisp. Allow to cool and then break into $\frac{1}{2}$-inch pieces. Set aside.

2. Combine the lemon juice, olive oil, and seasonings in a small, screw-top jar. Adjust seasoning if necessary and set aside.

3. Combine all the vegetables in a serving bowl, and sprinkle with the sumac and pita pieces.

4. Just before serving, toss with the salad dressing.

Yield: 6–8 servings as a side dish

TINA'S TIDBITS

- *Sumac is the small red berry from wild bushes that grow throughout the Levant. Its flavor is suggestive of lemon or a sour candy.*
- *The easiest way to seed a cucumber is to cut it in half lengthwise and run a spoon tip or melon baller down the middle, scraping out the seeds as you go.*
- *To seed a tomato, cut the tomato in half horizontally and gently squeeze each half, cut side down, over the sink. A final shake should release the seeds.*

CHICKEN FESENJAN WITH WALNUTS AND POMEGRANATE SYRUP

This very famous Persian dish is considered a festive dish served for important occasions. Its importance has something to do with the amount of walnuts used to make the rich, flavorful sauce. Although this recipe serves 4-6 people, Persian Jews often served this dish to their extended families, thus requiring significant amounts of walnuts, which were very costly. In the north of Iran the custom is to make this dish with duck or pheasant. Chicken, lamb, and meatballs are also used with this sauce throughout the country.

1 heaping cup of walnut pieces
1 large onion, cut into $\frac{1}{4}$-inch dice (about 2 cups)
3–4 tablespoons extra virgin olive oil
3 tablespoons tomato paste
3 tablespoons pomegranate molasses or syrup
2 tablespoons honey or 3 tablespoons sugar
4 grindings of sea salt or to taste
10 grindings of black pepper

$\frac{3}{4}$ teaspoon cinnamon
1 tablespoon fresh lemon juice
3 tablespoons water
3 chicken breast halves
3 chicken thighs
1 cup of chicken broth or water
2 or more tablespoons lemon juice (as needed)

1. Toast the walnut pieces in a 350°F oven until fragrant (5–6 minutes for large pieces taken from freezer). Remove from oven and cool before finely chopping them in a food processor.

2. Heat a 4-quart Dutch oven for 20 seconds on a cooktop over moderately high heat. Add oil, heat for another 15 seconds, and add diced onion. Sauté for 5–8 minutes or until onions are soft and lightly golden.

3. Add onions to the processor work bowl with the nuts, and pulse the machine on and off for 7 times until a coarse paste is created.

4. In a small glass bowl combine the tomato paste, pomegranate molasses, honey or sugar, spices, and 3 tablespoons of water. Set aside.

5. Remove the skin from the chicken pieces. Rinse and pat dry.

6. Reheat the pan in which you sautéed the onion. If necessary add another tablespoon of oil. Add chicken, meat side down first, and cook for 5 minutes or until slightly browned. Flip meat over and cook for another 5 minutes.

7. Remove chicken from the pan to a platter. Add the onion-walnut mixture to the pot along with the contents from the glass bowl. Add 1 cup water or chicken broth, and stir to combine.

8. Return chicken to the pot, turning pieces so that they are well coated with the walnut mixture. Cover pot and put in 350°F oven for 35–45 minutes or until meat is tender.

9. If necessary, adjust seasonings by adding more sugar or lemon juice to the mixture to get a balanced sweet-and-sour taste. Serve with basmati rice.

Note: This dish tastes even better made 1 day in advance.

Yield: 4–6 servings

TINA'S TIDBITS

- *Because it is hard to skim off fat from this nut-thickened sauce, remove the skin from the poultry before frying to reduce the amount of fat in this already rich dish.*
- *Although tomatoes are not native to the Middle East, many recipes for fesenjan include some tomato paste to slightly thicken the sauce and brighten its color.*

SYRIAN SPICED CHICKEN AND RICE

This is a quicker version of an Iraqi dish that I have created for the busy home cook. You could easily add thin slices of small eggplant, peas, or sautéed cauliflower to the rice mixture before baking for a complete meal.

2 tablespoons extra virgin olive oil
1 medium onion, chopped into ½-inch pieces (about 1½ cups)
1 pound boneless chicken breast or boneless chicken thighs
1 quart chicken stock or two 10.5-ounce cans chicken soup concentrate reconstituted with 2 cans of water

Salt to taste
10 grindings of black pepper or to taste
1 tablespoon extra virgin olive oil
1⅓ cups basmati or jasmine rice
¾ teaspoon ground allspice
½ teaspoon cinnamon
½ teaspoon cardamom
¼ teaspoon turmeric

1. Heat a 3-quart pot over high heat for 20 seconds. Add the 2 tablespoons of olive oil and heat for another 10 seconds until hot but not smoking.

2. Add the chopped onion and sauté over medium-high heat for 8–10 minutes or until the onions are soft and golden brown.

3. Add chicken to the onion mixture in the pot and sauté for 3 minutes or until lightly browned on both sides.

4. Add the chicken stock or diluted chicken soup concentrate to the pot. Add salt if needed and the pepper.

5. Cover pot and bring to a boil. Immediately turn off heat, remove chicken breasts, and cool. If using dark meat, let it remain in hot broth for three minutes.

6. Preheat oven to 325°F.

7. Remove the chicken pieces to a bowl until cool enough to handle.

8. Strain all of the soup, reserving the onions, and measure 3 cups of broth. Reserve the rest for later use.

9. Shred the chicken and return to the bowl. Combine with the onions.

10. Heat a clean 3-quart ovenproof pot or Dutch oven over high heat for 20 seconds. Add the remaining tablespoon of oil and heat for another 10 seconds. Add the rice and stir to coat well. Remove from heat, add the shredded chicken and reserved onions, and stir to combine.

11. Add all of the remaining spices to the 3 cups of broth, and pour this into the chicken and rice.

12. Bring broth to a boil. Cover pot and place in preheated oven for 20–25 minutes or until rice has absorbed all of the liquid.

13. To serve, run a knife along the inside of the pot to separate the rice from the sides. Place a plate over the top and invert so that a smooth cake-like structure comes out. Serve with lemon sauce if desired (see *agristada*, page 86).

Note: If mixture falls apart don't worry; just serve on a platter or in a bowl. It will still taste as good.

Yield: 4–6 servings

TINA'S TIDBITS

- *If you have the time, poach chicken parts, with skin and bone attached, for 40 minutes or until meat is tender. This will yield much more flavorful chicken.*
- *Basmati rice is an ancient, cultivated, long-grain rice originally from the Himalayan mountain region. It gets its nutty, aromatic quality from an aging process that reduces its natural moisture content.*

IRAQI CHICKEN WITH RICE, CHICKPEAS, AND RAISINS

According to Rivka Goldman, the author of Mama Nazima's Jewish-Iraqi Cuisine, *Iraqi cooks typically combine garbanzo beans and raisins with meat or chicken for a sweet-savory flavor component. The following recipe is adapted from one of her family recipes.*

½ teaspoon kosher salt
10 grindings of black pepper
½ teaspoon *pimentón de la Vera* (Spanish smoked paprika) or sweet paprika
½ teaspoon garlic powder
1 teaspoon ground ginger
½ teaspoon ground coriander
½ teaspoon ground cumin
2 chicken breasts
2 chicken thighs

2 chicken legs
1 tablespoon extra virgin olive oil
1 medium onion, chopped (about 1¼ cups)
1 cup basmati rice
One 8-ounce can tomato sauce
1⅓ cups water
2 tablespoons fresh lemon juice
¾ cup dark raisins
One 15-ounce can chick peas, rinsed and drained

1. Combine the first 7 ingredients in a small glass bowl; you should have about 4 teaspoons of mixture.

2. Place 2 teaspoons of the spice mixture in a gallon ziplock plastic bag.

3. Wash the chicken pieces, pull off and discard the skin, and pat dry. Cut chicken breasts and thighs in half horizontally. You may use all breasts or thighs or legs if you wish, but cut large pieces in half.

4. Place chicken pieces in the bag with the spices. Seal bag and shake to coat the chicken. Set aside for at least 30 minutes. If longer, place bag in the refrigerator.

5. Preheat oven to 350°F.

6. Heat a large, ovenproof sauté pan (or decorative casserole that can be used on a cooktop) for 20 seconds. Add the oil and heat for another 15 seconds.

7. Add 4 or 5 pieces of chicken to the hot pan, skin side down, and cook for 4–5 minutes or until lightly gold. Remove cooked chicken to a plate and repeat with the remaining chicken pieces. Remove from pan and set aside.

8. Add chopped onions to the used sauté pan and fry for 3 minutes or until lightly golden brown.

9. Add the rice and stir to completely coat with oil. Deglaze the pan by adding the tomato sauce, water, and lemon juice and scraping any particles of the chicken from the bottom. Add the remaining ingredients plus the reserved spice mixture and mix.

10. Place the chicken pieces meat side up in the rice mixture. Cover and bake for 30–45 minutes or until the chicken is tender and the rice has absorbed all of the liquid.

Yield: 4–6 servings

TINA'S TIDBITS

- *In this recipe I use garlic powder instead of fresh garlic. Combining dry powders requires the use of garlic powder for even distribution. Never use garlic salt, since the salt settles to the bottom of the jar, rendering the last few teaspoons very salty with little garlic taste.*
- *Sautéing rice in oil before adding liquid produces rice that is firm and distinct but has more starch to adhere to each other when molded.*

SESAME HALVAH

Halvah or halwa means "sweet" and refers to any firm, sweet confection in the Middle East and India made with nut butter or starchlike rice flour or semolina. In America the most recognized halvah is the one made from sesame seed paste. You could always find the big chunks of halvah at Jewish delis, and a recurrent joke in the 1950s and '60s was that bar mitzvah boys' profiles would be carved out of halvah for their receptions!

2 cups granulated sugar	1 teaspoon fresh lemon juice
3/4 cup cold water	1 teaspoon vanilla
1/4 cup egg whites at room temperature (about 2 large egg whites)	1/4 teaspoon cinnamon
1 pound tahini (unflavored sesame paste)	Pinch of ground cloves (optional)

1. Combine the sugar and water in a 2-quart saucepan. Bring to a boil over medium-high heat, stirring only once or twice until sugar is dissolved. Reduce the heat to medium, and cook for 10–15 minutes or until mixture forms a firm ball when dropped into a small bowl of ice water (approximately 240°F on candy thermometer). Remove from heat when done.

2. Meanwhile, using a handheld mixer, beat the egg whites until firm but no dry peaks form. Set aside.

3. Using the same beaters on the mixer (no need to clean first), combine the sesame paste, lemon juice, vanilla, and cinnamon in a medium bowl.

4. Fold the egg whites into the sesame seed paste until thoroughly combined.

5. Place the bowl on a damp towel. Turn the mixer to medium speed, and slowly pour some of the hot sugar syrup into the sesame mixture, rapidly combining the two. Continue to add the syrup slowly while beating until all the syrup has been used.

6. Pour the mixture into a glass loaf pan or 8-inch square pan, and smooth the top. Cover with plastic wrap, and refrigerate until firm, preferably overnight.

7. To serve, unmold the halvah from the pan and cut into small bars or squares, or just serve with a knife and let guests cut off pieces as they wish.

Yield: 15–20 servings

TINA'S TIDBITS

- *It is important that you always start with fresh, not overly roasted sesame seed paste or the finished halvah will have a burnt or rancid flavor.*
- *Placing a bowl on a damp towel will prevent the bowl from spinning when using a handheld mixer or a whisk. This leaves your other hand free to add ingredients while mixing.*
- *If halvah does not appear firm enough, then freeze or keep refrigerated until ready to serve. It will be easier to slice and pick up.*

Syrian Apricot Compote in Rose Water Syrup

Apricots originally grew in China thousands of years ago. Today most of our fresh apricots come from California, and the large, prized, dried apricots come from Turkey and Syria. Because apricots bruise easily, their farm to market popularity peaks in June and July. Good-quality dried apricots, however, can be purchased year-round, so I have adapted a classic Middle Eastern recipe to use the dried variety.

6 ounces dried apricots
2 cups water
1 cup sugar

1/2 teaspoon rose water
1/4 cup slivered almonds
1/2 cup pistachios

1. Combine apricots with water in a microwavable bowl. Microwave on high for 2 minutes, and let the apricots sit in the water, covered, for 2 hours or until soft.

2. When apricots are soft, drain them, separate in half (if desired), and reserve the soaking water.

3. Measure ½ cup of soaking water and place in a clean glass bowl. Add the sugar, and microwave on high for 1 minute or until sugar is dissolved. Set aside to cool. Add rose water.

4. Toast slivered almonds in a 325°F oven for 4 minutes or until lightly golden and fragrant.

5. Place the apricots in a serving bowl. Add the pistachios, toasted almonds, and enough rose water syrup to partially cover the bowl. Stir to combine and chill until ready to serve.

Note: This mixture is traditionally eaten alone in shallow dishes but may be served, with additional syrup, over vanilla ice cream, yogurt, or sponge cake for a more Western dessert.

Yield: 4 or more servings

TINA'S TIDBITS

- *Microwaving dried foods submerged in water for 2 or 3 minutes allows them to hydrate significantly faster than letting them soak at room temperature for 5 hours or overnight.*
- *Although the kernel of the apricot pit is used, after roasting, for flavoring sweets and liqueurs, in its raw state the pit is poisonous and should not be used.*

JEWS AND THE ORANGE TRADE

*T*he sweet orange of the twenty-first century has roots that go back thousands of years, and those roots were literally tilled by our Jewish ancestors. The world owes the widespread popularity of this juicy fruit to the farmers and merchants throughout the Mediterranean region; most of these professions were manned by Jews and Arabs.

Oranges trace their roots to the wild variety grown in China and the Cochin region of India and Burma. This orange was very bitter, but it was still popular with the Romans, who were always in search of the new and exotic. They shipped young saplings to the port of Ostia, which was the hub of all Roman commerce. Trees were planted along the Mediterranean coast and on the island of Sicily. Citrus and citron production was very important at the beginning of the first millennium, and because Jews were involved in their cultivation, the citron became the symbol of the Jews on Roman coins, synagogue motifs, and even gravestones. After the fall of the Roman Empire in the fifth century, orange cultivation died out until the Arabs began to conquer the lands throughout the region. Citrus growing began to flourish again in the eighth century due to Arab technology and expertise in irrigation techniques. By the twelfth century Jews were developing groves of citrus fruits in mainland Italy, Sicily, Corfu, southern Spain, and Northern Africa under the Moors' educated eyes.

The Jews were involved in orange agriculture because they had been involved, since ancient times, with the cultivation of another citrus fruit, the *etrog*, or citron. The *etrog* looks like a large (five or more inches), knobby lemon. It is very fragrant but contains little or no juice. It is prized for its fragrance and for its thick rind, which can be candied and is widely popular in baked goods to this day. The Jews cultivated the *etrog* to fulfill the commandment, on Sukkot, in Leviticus 23:40, "On the first day you shall take the product of *hadar* trees, branches of palm trees, boughs of leafy trees, and willows of the brook, and you shall rejoice before the Eternal your God seven days." These are the four species that form the *lulav* and *etrog*.

The *etrog* is not allowed to be used for this ceremony during Sukkot unless it is "perfect." It needs to have a beautiful yellow color, it has to be symmetrical, and most important, it must have a *pitam*, a piece of the stem protruding from the end of the *etrog*. If the *pitam* has fallen off or if the *etrog* has spots or nicks, then the *etrog* is rendered unsuitable for fulfilling the mitzvah of shaking the four species in the sukkah.

Because the *etrog* was so delicate, Jewish merchants needed to personally travel to the lands where they were grown to transport them back to the Jewish community. When they arrived in southern Italy and other coastal Mediterranean regions, they saw the other citrus fruits that the Jews were growing, and they brought some of those new citrus products back to Central, Eastern, and Northern Europe. In fact, Jewish peddlers in London, Amsterdam, and other large cities in Northern Europe continued to sell oranges and other citrus produce from their pushcarts as recently as the early 1900s.

Jewish communities that thrived in mostly Arab lands incorporated oranges into their cooking, and orange blossom water was a common flavoring agent in syrups and sweets.

When I was in Spain, I saw groves of orange trees throughout Cordoba. These trees carried the tart Seville oranges. My guide showed me that you can always distinguish a tart orange from a sweet one because the former has a scalloped leaf that consists of a small leaf near the stem that branches out into a larger leaf. These tart oranges form the basis of the classic English orange marmalade. According to legend, the sweet oranges were later introduced to England by Richard the Lion-Hearted after eating the Jaffa orange during the Crusades in the Holy Land.

Before the cultivation of sweet oranges, Seville varieties were rarely used for cooking. With the addition of sugar, oranges were commonly used in recipes. Perhaps the centuries of involvement with the citrus trade, stemming from a biblical tradition, accounts for the myriad of recipes for orange confections in the cooking of the Jewish Diaspora.

MOROCCAN ORANGE AND OLIVE SALAD

Jews were the cultivators of the orange groves throughout the Mediterranean region. The Moors brought the bitter oranges (similar in taste to a blood orange) to Córdoba and the south of Spain. From there the taste for oranges migrated south to Morocco.

4–5 large blood or navel oranges
2 tablespoons fresh lemon juice
3 tablespoons walnut oil
2 cloves garlic, finely minced

Salt to taste
1/4 cup Arabian olives (see recipe below)
Chopped fresh mint or paprika for garnish (optional)

1. Slice off the tops and bottoms of the oranges.

2. Using a sharp knife, slice off the peel and the pith from the oranges following the natural curve of the fruit.

3. Cut each orange horizontally into 1/4-inch thick slices. Cut each slice into quarters and place in a bowl.

4. Combine the lemon juice, walnut oil, garlic, and salt in a screw-top jar and shake to combine. Add more lemon juice or salt if needed.

5. Toss some of the vinaigrette with the oranges, and then add the olives and toss.

6. Place salad on a plate, and garnish with some mint or a sprinkling of paprika if desired.

Yield: 4–6 servings

ARABIAN OLIVES

I call these olives "Arabian" because the spices represent the Moors' influence on the Spanish palate through the introduction of Middle Eastern spices to Iberian cuisine.

4 ounces pitted green olives, drained
1/4 teaspoon ground cumin
1/4 teaspoon dried oregano
1/4 teaspoon lightly crushed dried rosemary leaves
1/4 teaspoon dried thyme
1 bay leaf
1/4 teaspoon fennel seed
2 cloves garlic, lightly crushed
2 tablespoons sherry vinegar
1 teaspoon grated lemon zest

1. Place the drained olives in a clean glass jar that is just large enough to hold the olives and the remaining ingredients with 1 inch of headroom.

2. Add the remaining ingredients to the jar, and fill the jar with water just to cover all of the olives. Shake well and marinate at room temperature for 2 days.

3. Store indefinitely in refrigerator.

Yield: About 1 cup of olives

TINA'S TIDBITS

- *The best way to tell if a citrus fruit has a good flavor is to scratch the peel with your fingernail. Even if the fruit is tart, the scent should be sweet and full-bodied; a lemon will smell like a lemon lollipop if good.*
- *It is better to add dressing to citrus fruit at the last minute; otherwise the dressing will macerate the fruit or pull the juices out of the fruit.*
- *Use a jar just slightly larger than the one the olives came in so that the olives can be covered with a minimum amount of liquid and lessen the amount of air in the jar.*

ASPARAGUS WITH MALTAISE SAUCE

Maltaise always refers to orange, and here you have a hollandaise sauce made with orange juice and zest. For a quick and pareve (nondairy) version, you can whisk orange zest and some juice into a top-grade commercial mayonnaise.

1 pound asparagus
Zest of ½ orange
½ stick unsalted butter
1 large egg yolk

2 teaspoons fresh lemon juice
Pinch of salt
Freshly ground pepper to taste
1 or more teaspoons of orange juice

1. Break the asparagus stalks at the tender point or cut 6 inches in length.

2. Rinse thoroughly and place in a flat baking pan. Cover with plastic wrap and microwave on high for 4 – 4½ minutes or until bright green and crisp tender. Keep warm while making the sauce.

3. Julienne the zest of the orange. Place in a shallow bowl with water to cover, and microwave for 45 seconds. Drain and set aside. Reserve 3 or 4 strands to use as garnish.

4. Melt the butter in a microwavable measuring cup. Set aside.

5. Put the egg yolk, lemon juice, pinch of salt, and pepper to taste in a food processor work bowl, and pulse on and off to combine.

6. With the food processor motor on, add the melted butter in a slow, steady stream. Add the zest and the juice, and process until incorporated.

7. Serve sauce over the warm asparagus, and garnish with the reserved orange zest.

Yield: 6–8 servings

TINA'S TIDBITS

- *If you hold asparagus spears in the middle and at the end and bend them slightly, they will always break where they start to be tender. However, for formal presentation it is better to cut your spears all the same length.*
- *Combine egg yolk and lemon juice at the last minute; otherwise the acidic lemon juice will "cook" the yolk and make it grainy and curdled while waiting to be combined with the other ingredients.*
- *To julienne means to cut into long thin strips. The easiest way to create a julienne of orange zest is with a 5-hole zester. The zest is the colored part of the rind of a citrus fruit with no bitter pith attached.*

SALMON WITH PINK PEPPERCORN CITRUS SAUCE

Lots of ingredients, easy to make, and a perfect example of the positive attributes of citrus fruit! I love serving this sauce with a side of salmon, poached or grilled, as part of my post-Yom Kippur break fast meal. Everything can be made in advance. Just mix the fruits with the sauce at the last minute, and you will wow your guests.

2 teaspoons sherry vinegar
2 teaspoons soy sauce
2 teaspoons pink peppercorns
2 teaspoons finely julienned ginger
1/4 teaspoon ground ginger
1/4 teaspoon salt
1/8 teaspoon celery seed
1/8 teaspoon hot red pepper sauce
1/4 cup extra virgin olive oil

4 salmon fillets, 5–6 ounces each
Salt and freshly ground black pepper
2 tablespoons chiffonade of cilantro
1/2 medium lemon, sectioned and cut into medium dice
1/2 medium lime, sectioned and cut into medium dice
1 medium orange, sectioned and cut into medium dice
1 medium Texas ruby red grapefruit, sectioned and cut into medium dice

1. To make the vinaigrette, mix the first 8 ingredients in a glass bowl. Whisk in 1/4 cup oil in a slow, steady stream. Set aside, reserving 2 tablespoons.

2. Sprinkle the salmon fillets with salt and pepper, and brush with the reserved vinaigrette. Grill over hot coals until done (10 minutes per inch thickness).

3. Stir the remaining 5 ingredients into the vinaigrette, and spoon over each fillet. Serve immediately.

Yield: 4 servings as an entrée, 10 servings as a side dish

TINA'S TIDBITS

- *To chiffonade an herb, lay the leaves on top of each other, roll them up tight like a cigarette, and slice very thin slices through the roll crosswise. The result will be thin wisps of herbs that float through the air like chiffon.*
- *To section a citrus fruit, cut off the top and bottom peel so you can see the fruit inside. Cut one section of the peel completely off from top to bottom. There should be no white pith adhering to the fruit. Using that first cut as a guide, continue to remove the remaining peel in five or six more vertical cuts down the side of the fruit. Next, place your knife parallel to the section membrane and cut to the center. Do the same thing on the other side of that section. It will remove easily. Repeat on the left and right side of each section until all the fruit is removed.*

  This technique works perfectly with all citrus fruit, although it is somewhat easier with oranges and grapefruit because of their larger size.

ORANGE CHICKEN

No orange juice in here, just zest, but since there were Jews in China on and off for over a thousand years, and since this dish is so popular in restaurants, I am including this authentic recipe that just so happens to be kosher!

½ pound chicken, thinly sliced into 1 × 2 × ⅛-inch pieces
1 tablespoon soy sauce
1½ teaspoons cream sherry
1 egg white
Pinch of pepper
1 tablespoon cornstarch
1 teaspoon fresh minced ginger
2 cloves garlic, minced
6 pieces of hot dried red pepper

8 pieces of fresh or dried orange peel (1 × 1 inch)
1 tablespoon cream sherry
1 tablespoon soy sauce
1 teaspoon chili paste (available in Asian food section of store)
2 tablespoons sugar
2 cups oil
1 tablespoon oil
1 teaspoon dark sesame seed oil

1. Marinate the chicken in the first five ingredients. Set aside.

2. Combine the ginger, garlic, dried peppers, and orange peel. Set aside.

3. Combine the remaining sherry, soy sauce, chili paste, and sugar.

4. Heat the 2 cups of oil in a wok until oil begins to shimmer, just before it begins to smoke. Add the chicken in one or two batches, and cook for 2 minutes or until tender. Remove to a platter.

5. Heat a clean wok for 20 seconds, and add 1 tablespoon oil. Swirl the oil about in the pan and heat for 15 seconds. Add the garlic-orange peel mixture and stir-fry for 30 seconds.

6. Return the meat to the wok and then add the sherry-chili paste mixture. Stir-fry until all the moisture is evaporated, and add the sesame seed oil. Serve immediately.

Yield: 2–3 servings or 4–5 servings if part of a full Chinese meal with multiple entrées

TINA'S TIDBITS

- *Coating meat with egg white and cornstarch gives the texture of a subtly breaded food without the breading.*
- *I prefer to use cream sherry for cooking because the flavor doesn't dissipate when food is cooked over high heat.*
- *Use an inexpensive steel wok for many types of cooking. It does not require major scouring, and the shape of the wok promotes faster cooking because all sides as well as the bottom are your cooking surface.*
- *Chinese sesame seed oil is not tahini. This is dark clear oil from black sesame seeds.*
- *Almost all authentic Chinese recipes are adaptable to a kosher kitchen because they don't use milk products and rarely use smoked pork. Veal is a perfect substitute for pork, mimicking the color and texture perfectly.*

BAKED APRICOTS IN ORANGE BLOSSOM SYRUP

Orange blossom water is ubiquitous in Jewish cooking from the Levant to the Maghreb.

6–8 ripe apricots
2 tablespoons sugar
2 tablespoons orange juice
2 tablespoons orange liqueur, Grand Marnier, triple sec, or Cointreau
$\frac{1}{4}$–$\frac{1}{2}$ teaspoon orange blossom water

TOPPING:
2 tablespoons sugar
2 tablespoons finely chopped almonds
Fine zest from $\frac{1}{4}$ large orange
1 tablespoon softened butter or pareve margarine

1. Preheat oven to 325°F.

2. Wash the apricots and cut in half along the crease of the fruit. Remove pits. Place apricots cut side up in a buttered dish just large enough to hold the fruit without crowding.

3. Combine the 2 tablespoons of sugar with the orange juice, liqueur, and orange blossom water. Microwave for 20 seconds to partially dissolve the sugar. Pour over the fruit.

4. Combine the topping ingredients with your fingertips, and sprinkle evenly over the center of each fruit half.

5. Bake for 10–15 minutes (depending on the size and ripeness of the fruit).

6. Broil for 3 minutes or until tops are slightly golden.

Yield: 6–8 servings

TINA'S TIDBITS

- *Any stone fruit (fruit with a pit) can be used for this recipe—plums, nectarines, pluots (cross between a plum and an apricot), or cherries.*
- *When a recipe that is baked calls for nuts, the nuts should not be roasted beforehand or they will get overcooked and bitter.*
- *Serve the hot fruit as is or with ice cream or thick yogurt.*

Jaffa Cakes

While researching citrus fruits for this book, I came across the story of McVitie's Jaffa Cakes. In England, cakes and biscuits (cookies) are not taxed, but chocolate-covered biscuits are charged a 15% tax as a luxury item. McVitie's was sued by the government in 1991 because the "cakes" were thought to really be biscuits. McVitie's won its case when it proved that its product became dry and hard when stale, like a cake, unlike a biscuit, which softens when old. The company was able to avoid taxation on its chocolate-covered confection. I was actually more interested in the connection of the name to the port of Jaffa in Israel, known for its orange shipments, so I created this recipe in tribute to the little cookie that isn't a cookie but is!

1 stick unsalted butter
½ cup castor or superfine sugar
1 egg
½ teaspoon vanilla extract
Finely grated zest of ¼ large orange
½ cup flour
¾ cup cake flour
¼ teaspoon salt

½ teaspoon baking soda
¼ cup milk (skim is fine)
1 tablespoon orange juice
6 ounces semisweet or bittersweet chocolate, cut into pieces
1 teaspoon solid shortening (pareve) or oil
6 ounces orange marmalade

1. Preheat oven to 350°F. Line 2 cookie sheets with parchment paper or lightly grease and set aside.

2. Cream the butter and the sugar with an electric mixer on high speed until the 2 ingredients are well combined and light and feathery. Scrape down sides of bowl.

3. Add the egg and beat on medium high until mixture is lemon colored and very creamy. Add the vanilla and orange zest and mix.

4. Combine the flour, cake flour, salt, and baking soda together in a small bowl and set aside.

5. In a small glass measuring cup, measure the milk, and add the orange juice.

6. Add half the milk mixture to the bowl with the butter, sugar, and eggs, and mix on low until mostly combined.

7. Add all of the dry ingredients and the remainder of the milk mixture to the mixing bowl. Mix on low only until ingredients are combined. Do not overmix or finished cookies will be rubbery.

8. Use a 1-ounce ice-cream scoop or a tablespoon to scoop batter onto parchment-lined or greased cookie sheets, leaving 1½ inches between each cookie.

9. Bake for 6–8 minutes or until cookies are lightly golden on the sides and the tops spring back when touched. Remove parchment paper from the hot pans, and let the cookies cool on the paper on the counter or a wire cooling rack until no longer warm.

10. Meanwhile, place the chocolate and shortening in a small saucepan that is placed in a larger saucepan filled with 1 inch of water. Melt chocolate over medium heat. Stir to make sure all chocolate is melted. Remove from heat.

11. To assemble the cookies, spread about ½ teaspoon of orange marmalade on the flat side of each cookie. Let them air-dry for 5 minutes. Spread about 1 heaping teaspoon of the chocolate on top of the marmalade.

12. Let cookies dry at room temperature, or refrigerate until chocolate topping is firm. Cookies may be frozen.

Yield: Approximately 2 dozen cookies

THE MAGHREB AND AFRICA

The Maghreb, which in Arabic means "coming from the land where the sun sets," encompasses three countries that previously had large Jewish populations: Tunisia, Algeria, and Morocco. More than one million Jews lived in this region until the middle of the twentieth century. Today the Jewish population numbers less than two thousand, with most—about fifteen hundred—living in Morocco.

The Jewish presence in North Africa dates back over twenty-five hundred years to the destruction of the First Temple. Folklore tells of fleeing priests who carried one of the Temple doors to the island of Djerba in Tunisia to be used in a synagogue. Hebrews settled in the region with the Phoenicians and lived peacefully alongside the Berbers until the Arab invasion in the seventh century C.E. More Jews settled the region after the Spanish and Portuguese expulsion in the late fifteenth century, and they were joined in the seventeenth century by a number of Italian Jews.

Typical of many of the other countries in this part of the world, after World War II many of the Arab nationalist forces fought for independence, and the countries of the Maghreb were no longer under French control. With the establishment of the State of Israel, these Arab-led countries escalated hostilities toward the Jews. Restrictions were placed on the Jewish inhabitants, and militant factions were allowed to wreak havoc in the Jewish communities. As a result, most Jews left this region for France, North America, South America, and Israel.

⤳ TUNISIA ⤳

According to the Web site www.harissa.com, a site devoted to all things Tunisian Jewish, "Tunis Jews have literally adored eating, drinking, and swallowing our culinary patrimony. Very few anorexics in our ranks, but a lot of fat men and women. . . ." A study was conducted at the University of Stockholm where a Jewish Tunis mother was hired to feed all of her ethnic dishes to three gorillas for three months. After only one week of three meals a day, the gorillas were observed to be attached to the woman, and their demeanor was complacent and relaxed!

These comments give some insight into the wonderfully elaborate and fulfilling food that is part of the culinary heritage of Jews in Tunisia. Tunis Jews make all holidays and life-cycle events into a major celebration centered on copious quantities of many different dishes. Fried foods and other dishes doused with oil are particularly attractive to these Jewish cooks.

Although there have been many attacks on the few remaining Jewish communities, and al-Qaida terrorists ran a bus into the wall of the oldest synagogue in Africa on the Tunisia island of Djerba in 2002, the government has mandated protection for the Jews, and they are granted complete religious freedom.

ALGERIA

Although Algeria is the largest of the three countries in the Maghreb, its Jewish population wasn't as great as that of Morocco. After World War II over one hundred and forty thousand Jews lived in the country. Today fewer than one hundred Jews reside in the cities of Algiers and Oran. Most Algerian Jews immigrated to France in the mid-1960s. Over twenty-five thousand immigrated to Israel.

Algerian Jews historically immersed themselves in the culture of the peoples who governed them while maintaining their own religious identity and customs. When the Arabs governed, Algerian Jews learned their grammar, read their literature, studied their science, and spoke Judeo-Arabic, but they never forsook their religious traditions. They were welcoming to European Jews coming to settle there and their community became one of the most sophisticated and Westernized Jewish communities in North Africa. After the immigration of Italians to Tunisia in the seventeenth and eighteenth centuries, the Jews added Italian to their language repertoire, along with Berber, Arabic, Spanish, Ladino, and Hebrew. In the early 1800s, Algerians were given French citizenship, and French schools were established throughout the country. This foundation made it much easier to immigrate to France and assimilate into the French culture when most Algerian Jews left in the two decades after World War II.

MOROCCO

The history of Moroccan Jews is not dissimilar to that of their brethren elsewhere in the Maghreb. Inhabitants of the land since ancient times, the rise and fall of the Jewish population followed the ebb and flow of living conditions at home and abroad. During World War II the Jews were subjected to the harassment of the Vichy government of France, which controlled Morocco.

Shortly after the establishment of the State of Israel, there were riots in Oujda and Djerada in which forty-four Jews were killed, and an official economic boycott was prompted against Moroccan Jews.

When Morocco gained its independence in 1956, Jewish immigration to Israel was suspended. In 1963 the immigration prohibition was lifted. Though the undertones of anti-Semitism are still present, Morocco has one of the most tolerant environments for Jews in the Arab world today.

Although the Jewish population is aging and many young Moroccan Jews don't return after studying abroad, the Moroccan community has established a ritual of making pilgrimage to some of the tombs of ancient sages. This brings back the Moroccan Jewish émigré to the land and helps keep the community's roots alive while the newer generations are growing up in relatively peaceful surroundings.

↬ THE FOOD OF THE MAGHREB ↫

Although you will find couscous in all three countries of the Maghreb, the flavors and ingredients used in each cuisine are not the same. According to Simone Gozlan, a French émigré from Morocco, the food of her youth is not the same as that of her husband, who grew up in Tunisia. Moroccans use a lot of dried fruits in their cooking, and their couscous contains chickpeas as well as raisins. Prunes stuffed with almonds and other fruits are often cooked with meats for a rich and complex flavor, and cumin and cinnamon are often the spices of choice in these preparations. Olives and preserved lemons are used in many recipes for a tart flavor addition. The famous dish *bestilla*, made with chicken in a flaky crust or phyllo dough, is flavored with sugar, cinnamon, and almonds as well as cilantro, onions, and parsley.

Tunisians do not use sugar at all in their cooking; coriander seed and caraway seed are more common, and chickpeas are never used. Other spices used to enhance the flavor of their dishes are aniseed, cumin, saffron, cinnamon, and harissa, a fiery mixture of spices made into a paste with olive oil. Olive oil is used for frying *briks*, a Tunisian specialty of deep-fried, flaky dough filled with meats or vegetables.

Algerian cooking bears some resemblance to Moroccan cooking, but the French influence is more readily seen in many of its dishes. Ginger, cumin, cinnamon, and pepper reflect the influence of the spice trade on this region. Olives are incorporated into many of its dishes. Salads are dressed with olive oil, although mayonnaise is used in some dishes, showing the French influence. Almonds are prevalent, and one of the best-known desserts in Algeria is the gazelle's horn, the crescent-shaped almond paste cookie found in most bakeries throughout the world today.

↬ ETHIOPIA ↫

The Beta Israel of Ethiopia trace their ancestry back thousands of years. Theories abound as to their origins, including that they are the lost tribe of Dan, descendants of Jews who fled Israel for Egypt after the destruction of the First Temple in 586 B.C.E., or descendants of King Solomon and the Queen of Sheba.

The Beta Israel Jews lived peacefully in the hills of Ethiopia until 1973, when regime changes in Ethiopia, the Yom Kippur War, and a threat of an Arab oil embargo if relations were maintained with Israel caused great hardships for this segregated group of Jews. Thousands of Betas were killed or injured during riots, and many fled to squalid refugee camps in the Sudan. Beginning in 1984 with Operation Moses and in 1991 with Operation Solomon, over twenty-five thousand Jews (nearly 85 percent of the Ethiopian Jewish community) were successfully, albeit clandestinely, airlifted out of Ethiopia via Sudan to Israel. In the years since, Ethiopians have slowly integrated into fully industrialized Israel from their rural, tribal existence. With over 60 percent of the Ethiopian Jewish population under the age of eighteen, educating the next generation is their hope for successful assimilation.

ᕔ Uganda, Ghana, and Zimbabwe ᕔ

*I*n the 1880s, British missionaries converted the powerful Bagandan warrior Semei Kakungulu to Christianity. By the turn of the century, his Old Testament Bible reading had drawn him to Judaism. By 1919 he had converted himself, his family, and his community to Judaism. Difficult times befell the "People of Judah" during the reign of Idi Amin, but over five hundred members of the community kept their faith and continue to reach out to the world to let them know they exist. The Abayudaya community originally relied solely on subsistence farming of mangoes, cassava, pineapples, and bananas. They are now developing coffee cooperatives to bring in additional revenue to modernize their community.

In Western Ghana, the Jewish community is called "the House of Israel." They believe they are descendants of Jews who migrated south through the Ivory Coast. This community was founded in the latter part of the twentieth century.

The Lemba are a group of a few thousand black Jews in the region of Zimbabwe whose genetics link them to the *kohanim* (priests) of Palestine. Although their religious practices date back millennia, they have only been actively practicing their belief in one God since the early 1900s.

The white South African Jewish community is the most Westernized group in all of Africa. The history of this community follows similar migratory patterns of Europeans to the New World. Beginning with the pogroms in the 1800s all the way to World War II, the Jews who immigrated to Cape Town and Johannesburg did so to escape religious persecution and to make a new life for themselves. Ashkenazi Jews make up the overwhelming majority of the Jewish community. Food traditions follow Eastern European culinary tastes with the addition of local produce and meats.

East African Groundnut (Peanut) Soup

The peanut was originally cultivated in South America. When Columbus came over, he was introduced to the peanut and brought it back to Spain. The trade routes set up throughout the Near and Far East, with the help of many Jewish traders, spread the use of the peanut, and the African slaves brought peanuts back to the New World and particularly the southern states of the U.S. Considered to be the food of the poor, the peanut was not widely consumed in this country until the Civil War and was not in full production as a major industry until the beginning of the twentieth century when new methods of cultivation and production were introduced in the South, the area with the most former African citizens, the original importers.

2 chicken breasts, preferably boneless and skinless
One 10.5-ounce can chicken broth concentrate
2 chicken broth cans of water
1 onion, peeled and cut into eighths
1 large leek
2 carrots, peeled and coarsely chopped

¼ cup long-grain rice
1 small dried hot red chili pepper
½ teaspoon salt
½ cup peanut butter, preferably smooth (although chunky is okay)
3 tablespoons chopped roasted peanuts

1. Rinse the chicken breasts in cold water. Place them in a 3-quart saucepan with the chicken stock concentrate and the 2 cans of water.

2. Trim off all but 2 inches of the green part of the leek. Slit the leek in half lengthwise and rinse thoroughly under cold running water. Coarsely chop the leek and add to the chicken in the pot.

3. Add chopped onion and carrots to the other ingredients in the pot. Bring to a boil, simmer, covered, over moderately low heat for 20–25 minutes or until chicken meat is cooked.

4. Remove the chicken from the soup. Shred the meat and set aside.

5. Place the soup and the vegetables in a blender, and blend until very smooth. Return the soup to the saucepan, and bring to a boil.

6. Add the rice, chili pepper, and salt. Cover and reduce the heat to low. Cook for 20 minutes until rice is cooked through.

7. Slowly pour ½ cup of the soup into the peanut butter and whisk to make a smooth mixture.

8. Add the peanut butter mixture to the soup, cover, and simmer for 5 minutes.

9. Top each bowl of soup with some shredded chicken meat and a sprinkling of chopped peanuts.

Yield: 4 servings

TINA'S TIDBITS

- *In order to hasten the production of the soup, boneless chicken breasts are used. However, real canned chicken broth must be used to compensate for the lack of extra flavor from whole pieces of chicken with skin and bones.*
- *The green parts of leeks are never used in cooking other than to wrap around edible foods. They are too tough to eat. Always cut the leek at the point where the green starts to show and discard the green parts.*
- *Leeks grow in very sandy soil, so slit the leek down the middle and open out the leaves as if you were shuffling a deck of cards in order to let rinsing water remove any sand trapped on the inside.*
- *Always add liquid slowly to peanut butter so that it will be free of lumps and not look curdled in your soup.*

ARTICHAUD AU CITRON
(ARTICHOKES WITH LIME)

Rachel Gomel Israel's family escaped the Spanish Inquisition and made their home in Egypt. In 1956 Rachel's father, who manufactured Nasser's uniforms, was abducted with other prominent members of the Jewish community. After two months of incarceration, he was released, and in 1958 the family was forced to leave Egypt and moved to Brazil. Her family founded the Sao Paolo synagogue, Major Haim, named after the last great rabbi of Egypt, Haim Nahum, who was a family member. Rachel and her husband moved to the United States in the 1970s. She is a vibrant, intelligent woman whose culinary skills equal her love of life. Here is a recipe that has been in her family for decades. The French name is due to the French influence on cooking and language in Egypt when she was growing up.

2 packages of frozen artichoke hearts (preferably Egyptian or French)
1–2 tablespoons extra virgin olive oil
4 large cloves of garlic, finely minced

Juice of 3 limes
$\frac{1}{2}$–$\frac{3}{4}$ cup chicken broth (or water with 2 teaspoons chicken bouillon)

1. Defrost artichoke hearts and pat dry. Set aside.

2. Heat a large (10- to 12-inch) frying pan over high heat for 15 seconds. Add enough olive oil to lightly coat the entire bottom of the pan. Heat oil for another 10 seconds. Reduce the heat to medium, and add the garlic. Sauté garlic until oil is fragrant and just beginning to turn lightly golden.

3. Halve the limes horizontally, and remove the juice using a reamer or a fork to press out the liquid while squeezing the halves. Add the juice to the frying pan along with the broth or water and bouillon. There should be about $\frac{1}{4}$ inch of liquid in the bottom of the pan.

4. Carefully place each artichoke heart into the frying pan, making sure that they are placed in one layer.

5. Simmer the artichoke hearts for 10 minutes, basting occasionally with the liquid. If liquid runs low, add additional broth or seasoned water. If after 10 minutes there is an abundance of liquid, remove the artichokes to a serving dish and boil the liquid down until syrupy before pouring over artichokes. Check to see if salt is needed (most bouillon and canned broth provide enough).

6. Serve immediately as a side dish with rice and an entrée.

Yield: 4–6 servings

TINA'S TIDBITS

- *Frozen artichokes are flash frozen and taste most like fresh without all of the extra work. Canned are soft and preserved with citric acid, which alters the flavor of this dish immensely.*
- *The acid in this dish preserves the color of the artichokes as well as giving the dish a wonderful flavor.*
- *Do not waste the zest of the limes because they are not used in the recipe; instead, use a zester to remove thin strips of zest from the limes before you cut them in half. The zest may then be frozen in plastic wrap for future use.*
- *If you scratch a lime with your fingernail, the scent will tell you how sweet and full-flavored the lime juice will taste. The sweeter the smell, the sweeter the taste.*

TUNISIAN SPICED CARROTS

Harissa is to Tunisia what ketchup is to America, the traditional accompaniment to many foods. Harissa can be very hot, as it is a spicy mixture of chilies, garlic, cumin, coriander, caraway seeds, and olive oil. Different foods absorb this condiment differently, so always adjust to your own preference.

1 pound carrots, thinly sliced
1 teaspoon whole caraway seeds
½ tablespoon of harissa, or to taste
2 large cloves of garlic, minced
2 tablespoons extra virgin olive oil

1 or more teaspoons red wine vinegar
Kosher salt to taste
Freshly ground black pepper to taste
Fresh mint, finely chopped for garnish (optional)

1. Add ½ inch of water to a 3-quart saucepan. Lightly salt the water.

2. Add carrots and cook over moderate heat until tender when pierced with a fork (10–15 minutes).

3. Drain the carrots and place in a serving bowl.

4. Add the caraway seeds and harissa to the carrots, and gently stir with a rubber spatula or wooden spoon. Set aside or refrigerate for later use.

5. Place the remaining ingredients in a small screw-top jar, and shake to thoroughly combine. Let the dressing rest for 30 minutes, if possible, to allow the garlic to infuse the oil.

6. Pour dressing over carrots and toss well. Sprinkle with mint, if using, and serve.

Yield: 4–6 servings

TINA'S TIDBITS

- *Never use large amounts of water when cooking vegetables or you will lose some of the nutrients if the vitamins are soluble in water. Vitamin A, found in carrots, is actually fat soluble, but the color of the cooked carrot will be diminished if cooked in too much water.*
- *If you do not like biting into bits of raw garlic, just crack the garlic open with the side of a broad knife and add it to the olive oil mixture. After half an hour or so, the flavor will be imparted to the oil, and you can discard the whole garlic.*

BESTILLA
(MOROCCAN PIGEON PIE)

This classic Moroccan dish is often served on Shabbat by the Jews of the region, but this could also be the wow dish you prepare for company, as we do in our house at my husband's request (this recipe is one of his absolute favorites). The chicken mixture may be frozen after step 2. When ready to complete the bestilla, reheat the chicken and onion mixture in the microwave to facilitate removing the skin. Proceed with step 3 to continue to complete the dish.

1 pound onions, grated
3/4 cup minced parsley
5 tablespoons sugar
2 tablespoons snipped coriander
1 cinnamon stick
1 teaspoon ground cinnamon
1 teaspoon freshly ground black pepper
1/2 teaspoon salt
1/2 teaspoon saffron threads
3 pounds chicken pieces

2 tablespoons margarine
7–12 eggs well beaten
Vegetable oil
1 cup slivered almonds
1/4 cup granulated sugar
1 1/2 teaspoons cinnamon
1 cup melted pareve margarine
1 pound phyllo dough
Confectioners' sugar & cinnamon (for garnish)

1. Combine the first 9 ingredients in a large Dutch oven.

2. Add the chicken pieces and coat with the onion mixture. Add the 2 tablespoons of margarine, and heat the mixture to boiling. Reduce the heat and simmer for 1 hour, turning meat frequently.

3. Remove the chicken, and save all of the onion mixture. Scrape off as much of the onion mixture from the chicken as possible. Skin and bone the chicken and tear meat into shreds. Set aside.

4. Stirring often, cook the onion mixture over medium-high heat until mixture is quite thick, about 20 minutes. Discard the cinnamon stick.

5. Beat 7 eggs in a bowl. Add to the onion mixture and stir as you would when making scrambled eggs. Add more eggs, if necessary, to get a firm egg mixture. Set aside.

6. Heat 1/2 inch oil in a small frying pan, and cook the almonds for 1 minute or until golden. Drain and coarsely chop. Combine the almonds with the sugar and cinnamon and set aside.

7. Brush some melted margarine on a 12- to 14-inch pizza pan, and place a sheet of phyllo dough with the edge of the dough at 12 o'clock and the extra hanging off the pan at 6 o'clock. Add 7 more layers, making sure that you brush each layer thoroughly with the margarine and that the overhang of the dough looks like a pinwheel. *Note*: I place the dough hanging off the pan like the hands of a clock: 6, 9, 12, and 3; then 7, 10, 1, and 4 o'clock.

8. Spread the egg mixture evenly over the dough but not up the rim of the pan. Spread the chicken mixture over this. Sprinkle with the almond mixture. Gently fold each layer of dough over the filling, brushing with additional margarine if layers become dry.

9. Layer 4 sheets of dough (12, 3, 6, and 9 o'clock), with margarine brushed in between, over the enclosed filling. Fold all of these layers under, using the sides of your pinkies to tuck the dough under so you don't tear it.

10. Flip the pie onto another greased pizza tin, and brush all loose leaves of dough with margarine. Repeat the procedure in step 9 to this side of the pie. Tuck the ends under. Invert the pie back into the original pan, and cover with the last 2 phyllo leaves, which have been brushed with melted margarine and placed centered and at right angles to each other.

11. Place in a **cold** oven and set the temperature at 350°F. Bake until top is golden. Carefully invert the pie into the second pizza pan, and bake for 20 more minutes.

12. Sprinkle with confectioners' sugar and cinnamon to make a nice design, and serve immediately.

Yield: 1 12-inch pie, 8–12 servings

TINA'S TIDBITS

- *Never have a moist towel come in direct contact with phyllo dough or it will get soft and stuck together irreparably.*
- *When filling phyllo pastries, the drier the ingredients the more likely your dough will crisp evenly.*
- *The chicken can be cooked in advance and frozen with all of its onion mixture. When ready to assemble, defrost the chicken and reheat so that the onions and sauce can be easily scraped off the meat and the skin can be easily removed.*
- *Shaped bestilla can be prepared and kept tightly covered for 2–4 hours before baking. If it is very cold from the refrigerator, then bring to room temperature before placing in cold oven.*

SANBAT WAT
(ETHIOPIAN SHABBAT STEW)

Often declared the national dish of Ethiopia, a wat *is a stew, and* doro wat *is a spicy chicken stew eaten with one's fingers using injera bread to scoop up the morsels of food and gravy and to temper the heat of the seasonings. Sanbat means "Sabbath," and Ethiopian Jews, no matter how poor, would find a way to add a little bit of chicken to their daily stew to elevate their food for their Sabbath table.*

Although my assistant, Avvennett, is from Ethiopian lineage, I took my direction from Joan Nathan and adapted her recipe from The Foods of Israel Today *to create this wonderful dish. More pepper flakes, hot harissa, or Berber seasoning may be added to spice this dish to your palate.*

3 large onions, finely chopped
Salt and freshly ground black pepper
3 tablespoons corn or peanut oil
4 large cloves of garlic, finely minced
2 teaspoons freshly grated peeled ginger
1 tablespoon cumin
1 tablespoon nutmeg
1 tablespoon ground coriander

$\frac{1}{2}$ teaspoon red pepper flakes
$\frac{3}{4}$ cup water
1 teaspoon cinnamon
1 teaspoon turmeric
One 8-ounce can of tomato sauce
1 chicken, cut into 8–12 pieces (if large, cut thighs and breasts in half)

1. Heat a large skillet or casserole for 20 seconds over medium-high heat. Add the onions, sprinkle with salt and pepper, and sauté in the dry pan for 2 minutes.

2. Add the 3 tablespoons of oil and stir to evenly coat the onions. Add the garlic and ginger and continue to sauté until the onions are soft. Do not let the garlic brown or it will become bitter.

3. Add the cumin, nutmeg, coriander, pepper flakes, and $\frac{1}{2}$ cup of the water. Combine well and simmer for 4 minutes.

4. Add the remaining spices, the remaining $\frac{1}{4}$ cup water, and the tomato sauce, and cook at a boil for 5 minutes.

5. Add the chicken pieces, turning to coat thoroughly with the sauce. Cover. Reduce temperature to medium or a gentle simmer, and cook for 30–40 minutes until the chicken is tender. Serve with rice and injera (Ethiopian flatbread).

Yield: 4–6 servings

TINA'S TIDBITS
• *Part of the Ethiopian cooking technique for* wat *is to sauté the onion in a dry pan first. This helps break down the onion so that it will thicken the sauce.* • *Spices, especially brown ones, should be stored in the freezer to retain their flavor.* • *Fresh ginger is easily peeled using the edge of an ordinary spoon*

MOROCCAN CHICKEN KEBABS

Whether served as part of an assortment of mezes, or small plates, or laid on a bed of couscous as part of a Moroccan meal, kebabs can be found throughout the Middle East and North Africa. This method of cooking and the use of spice demonstrate the recipe's migration westward with the Moors.

½ medium onion, diced
2 tablespoons lightly packed chopped fresh mint
⅓ cup extra virgin olive oil
¼ teaspoon crushed red pepper
1 large clove garlic, minced

1 teaspoon ground coriander
½ teaspoon ground cumin
1 tablespoon lemon juice
1 pound boneless chicken breasts

1. Combine the first 8 ingredients in a 1-quart nonreactive bowl.

2. Remove the fillet from the chicken breasts, and cut all parts of the chicken into ½-inch cubes.

3. Combine the chicken with the marinade in the bowl and allow it to sit for at least ½ hour, but longer is better.

4. Skewer the chicken on metal skewers or on bamboo sticks, and grill for about 6 minutes, basting occasionally with the remaining marinade. Serve as a first course to a Moroccan meal.

Yield: 6–8 servings

TINA'S TIDBITS

- *To identify the fillet of the breast for removal, look for the pearlized white membrane running lengthwise through the triangular piece of meat. Pull gently on that piece and it will slide out of its thin membrane pocket. If you don't see the membrane, it might have already been removed before sale.*
- *Although the membrane can be eaten, it is best to remove it before grilling so that the meat won't curl up when the membrane becomes tight and pulls on the delicate chicken breast.*

Moroccan Lamb Tagine with Prunes

The following recipe is very easy to make and is incredibly delicious. Make this recipe a day or two in advance to let the flavors meld, or you can make it far in advance and freeze it. Don't add the nuts until just before serving.

¼ cup extra virgin olive oil
1 large or 2 medium onions, grated
3 cloves of garlic, minced
2 pounds boneless lamb shoulder or 4 lamb shanks
¼ teaspoon saffron threads
½ teaspoon ground ginger
½ teaspoon coriander

2 teaspoons cinnamon
2 cups pitted prunes
3 cups water
½ cup almond slivers
1 teaspoon sesame seeds
1 tablespoon honey
1 or more teaspoons lemon juice or to taste

1. Heat the oil in a large Dutch oven or tagine, and sauté the onion and garlic for a minute until soft. Add the lamb and cook for 2 more minutes until the meat and bones (if meat isn't boneless) begin to lightly brown.

2. Add the spices, prunes, and water to the meat and onion mixture, and simmer covered for 1 hour.

3. While the meat is cooking, lightly toast the almonds in a 350°F oven for 5 minutes and the sesame seeds on a different baking pan for 2 minutes. Do not let them burn! Set aside until needed.

4. After the hour, if the meat is tender, add the honey and adjust the tagine's sweetness with the lemon juice. Sprinkle the top of the tagine with the almonds and sesame seeds just before serving.

Yield: 6–8 servings

TINA'S TIDBITS

- *Lamb shoulder is often not one solid piece of meat. Be sure to remove obvious chunks of fat and gristle before using.*
- *Smaller pieces of meat allow the flavors of the sauce to permeate better. Don't cut the meat smaller than 1-inch cubes, however, as they might disintegrate upon cooking and won't be visually appealing.*
- *Foods cooked with fruit and/or spices actually benefit from sitting a day or so before serving.*
- *If you are feeding only one or two people, you can freeze smaller portions in 1-quart freezer bags that lie flat and require little freezer space.*

Moroccan Meatball Tagine with Couscous

This dish is terrific for company in the sukkah. Incorporating the fall vegetables, pumpkin or butternut squash, with the sweetness of the raisins and prunes makes this a delicious addition to your holiday meal. In addition, the tagine tastes even better the next day and is easily portable outside to the sukkah in its casserole dish.

1½ pounds ground beef
½ medium onion, grated
2 tablespoons finely chopped parsley
1 egg
½ cup unseasoned bread crumbs
½ cup tomato sauce
Salt and freshly ground black pepper to taste
3 tablespoons extra virgin olive oil, divided use
5 medium onions, thinly sliced

1 quart water
½ cup dark raisins
8–12 soft pitted prunes
½ cup slivered almonds, lightly toasted
2 pounds pumpkin or butternut squash, peeled and cut into 1-inch chunks (about 4 cups)
½ cup brown sugar
1 teaspoon cinnamon

1. Place the meat in a 2-quart mixing bowl and add the grated onion, parsley, egg, bread crumbs, tomato sauce, salt, pepper, and 1 tablespoon of the olive oil. Mix the mixture well and set aside until ready to make the meatballs.

2. Heat a large Dutch oven and add the remaining 2 tablespoons of olive oil. Sauté the sliced onions in the oil until golden brown.

3. Add the water to the onions and bring to a boil.

4. Shape the meat into walnut-sized balls, and drop into the simmering liquid. Cook the balls until firm, about 10–15 minutes.

5. Combine the raisins and the prunes in a small glass dish and cover with water. Microwave on high for 3 minutes, and let sit while the meatballs cook.

6. When the meat is firm, transfer the meat, onions, and all liquid to a 13 × 9-inch casserole.

7. Drain the fruits and add them to the casserole along with the almonds and pumpkin.

8. Sprinkle the brown sugar and cinnamon over the food, and bake in a preheated 350°F oven until the squash is tender and almost all of the liquid has been absorbed. Serve with couscous.

Yield: 6–8 servings

Couscous

1½ cups water or chicken broth
1 tablespoon butter or margarine
1 cup couscous

1. Bring liquid and margarine to a boil in a 1-quart saucepan.

2. Add the couscous and stir to combine. Immediately cover and turn off the heat.

3. Allow the couscous to sit for 5 minutes. Fluff with a fork. Place in the middle of a large serving platter with the meat and vegetables around it, or serve separately from a bowl.

Yield: 6–8 servings

TINA'S TIDBITS

- *Caramelizing the onions means cooking the onions until the natural sugars in the onions start to turn brown. In this recipe, if the onions aren't a distinctive brown, the gravy will not be well balanced in flavor and will have little color. The onions will not caramelize if cooked with water or another vegetable high in water content.*
- *When making meatballs, do not squeeze the meat together heavily or the meatballs will be very tough.*
- *Microwaving dried fruit or beans in water for 3 minutes is the equivalent of soaking for 1 hour in warm water.*

Tabikha
(Algerian Festive Stew)

This tabikha *is an Algerian Jewish beef stew. Its name comes from the Arabic, meaning "a cooked dish." The implication is that it was slow cooked in an ovenlike setting. Although one might associate the cooking time with a Shabbat meal cooked overnight, Clifford Wright, the food historian, says that this dish was more often served to brides following their wedding eve bath and for bar mitzvah celebrations, thus giving it a prestigious stature.*

4 tablespoons extra virgin olive oil, divided use
2–2½ pounds beef stew meat, cut into 1-inch chunks
2 medium onions, finely chopped (about 2 cups)
2 tablespoons finely minced garlic (about 4 large cloves)

2 tablespoons prepared harissa, or to taste
1 14.5-ounce can diced tomatoes with their liquid
1 8-ounce can tomato sauce
1 cup water
Cilantro or mint leaves for garnish (optional)

1. Heat a 3- or 4-quart saucepan for 15 seconds over high heat. Add 2 tablespoons of the olive oil to the pan and heat for another 10 seconds. Reduce heat to medium high and add half of the meat. Brown on all sides, and remove to a bowl. Add the rest of the meat to the pan and cook until brown. Remove to the bowl with the meat and set aside.

2. Return the pan to the stove and heat on high for 5 seconds. Add the remaining 2 tablespoons of olive oil to the pan, and add the finely chopped onions. Sauté onions over medium-high heat until lightly caramelized and golden brown.

3. Add the garlic and the harissa to the onions, and stir over low heat for 2 minutes to thoroughly combine the ingredients.

4. Return the meat to the pan and stir to coat well. Add the diced tomatoes, tomato sauce, and water, and bring to a boil.

5. Reduce the heat, cover, and cook until the meat is tender (1–3 hours, depending on how tough and lean the meat is).

6. Serve with couscous or rice garnished with the optional chopped cilantro or mint.

Yield: 6–8 servings

TINA'S TIDBITS

- *Cooking oil should never be added to a cold pan because it will adhere to the pan and cause the food to stick more readily. Always heat the pan first for 15-20 seconds; then add the oil and heat for 10 seconds before adding any food. Cooking and cleaning the pan will be much easier using this technique.*
- *Browning meat first, rather than just combining all of the ingredients, will add significant flavor to this dish. It will also add a rich color to the finished stew.*
- *Always pat your meat dry first or it will not brown.*

UGANDAN FALL HARVEST FRUIT SALAD

I created this recipe for Reform Judaism *magazine to honor the Abayudaya Jews and their leader J. J. Keki, whom I met when he came to Dallas for a fundraiser. This salad contains the three most eaten fruits in Uganda: bananas, mango, and jackfruit. Bananas are actually a staple of the Ugandan's diet. Per capita consumption is 500 pounds a year! Many of the spices in this recipe are now grown in Uganda, a legacy of the spice trade route through Africa centuries ago.*

3 ripe mangoes, peeled and cubed, divided use
1 20-ounce can of jackfruit in syrup
1 cup coarsely chopped mixed dried fruits (apples, peaches, pears, apricots)
2 bananas, peeled and sliced into ½-inch slices
1 small can mandarin oranges, drained

Pinch of kosher salt
1 cup sweetened shredded coconut
1 teaspoon prepared garam masala or to taste
1 teaspoon tamarind liquid concentrate or lemon juice
Honey (optional)

1. Use a mango cutter to remove the fruit from the pit, or slice from the stem to the bottom of the mango, running your knife along the edge of the pit on both sides. Cut the flesh away from the skin of the mango, and cut into ½-inch dice.

2. Puree about ⅓ to ½ of the mango cubes to make 1 cup of mango puree. Place puree in a serving bowl with the remaining cubed mango.

3. Remove and drain the jackfruit, and cut the translucent white ovals into strips lengthwise. Add to mango mixture.

4. Add the dried chopped fruits, sliced bananas, mandarin oranges, and salt to the bowl, and gently stir with a rubber spatula. Set aside.

5. In a small processor work bowl, combine the coconut, garam masala, and tamarind concentrate (or lemon juice). Turn the machine on, and pulse the mixture until it forms a paste.

6. Stir the spice paste into the mixed fruit carefully, using a rubber spatula. Taste to see if any honey is needed.

7. Refrigerate until ready to serve. May be served for dessert or as an accompaniment to grilled meats.

8. Just before serving, you can sprinkle a little extra coconut on top as a garnish.

Yield: 8–10 servings

TINA'S TIDBITS

- *To ripen mangoes, place them in a brown paper bag. Adding a banana to the bag will hasten the process.*
- *To dice a mango easily, cut it in half along the seed and remove the seed. Score the meat just to the skin by slicing lengthwise and then crosswise about 1/2-inch apart. Bend the skin back and the meat stands up like a porcupine's back. Run a knife along the skin to dislodge the fruit and you will have a perfect 1/2-inch dice!*

TUNISIAN GUIZADA

The shipping port of Livorno in Italy did much trading with Tunisia in the sixteenth century. As a result, many Livornese Jews settled in Tunisia and brought their culinary customs with them. Here the almond paste cookies of Italy are transformed with the local ingredients of North Africa with its Arab ingredients, pistachio nuts, and orange blossom water.

$1\frac{1}{4}$ cups shelled pistachio nuts
$\frac{1}{2}$ cup extra fine or bar sugar
1 tablespoon imported orange blossom water

1 large egg
1 large egg yolk
$\frac{1}{8}$ teaspoon almond extract

1. To chop the nuts, use a large French chef's knife and rock it back and forth over the pistachios until very small pieces are formed. If you have a processor, place pistachios in the processor's work bowl and pulse the machine on and off 50 times to chop the nuts into small pieces but not so finely chopped that they look like meal.

2. Preheat the oven to 350°F.

3. Add the remaining ingredients to the nuts, and stir well to thoroughly combine.

4. Line mini muffin pans with paper liners, and drop 1 tablespoon of nut mixture into each cup (about 18–20 cups).

5. Bake for 14–18 minutes (depending on whether you have a standard or convection oven), until tops are slightly golden and a toothpick inserted into the center of a *guizada* comes out clean but moist. You don't want them to be too hard when cool.

6. Remove from oven and immediately turn the filled papers on their side. When cool, store in an airtight container or heavy plastic storage bag.

Yield: 2 dozen pastries

TINA'S TIDBITS

- *Imported orange blossom water is more concentrated and therefore doesn't burn out during baking and adds a better flavor to the finished product. I use a brand from Lebanon or other parts of the Middle East.*
- *When using a processor to chop nuts, it is very important to pulse the machine rather than just turning it on. Pulsing throws the nuts up and chops them evenly rather than having them circulate on the bottom of the bowl, creating nut butter.*
- *Always turn your muffins on their sides immediately after baking to avoid the bottoms "sweating" from the steam. This prevents gummy bottoms.*
- *When mixtures contain fruit or strong flavoring, their flavors will be enhanced if they are made a day in advance of eating.*

MOROCCAN MINT TEA

This recipe is simple to make and a refreshing, authentic addition to your Moroccan meal, whether served hot or cold. Moroccans like their tea sweet, so add sugar to your taste.

1 tablespoon green tea
$\frac{1}{3}$ cup packed fresh mint leaves
$\frac{1}{4}$ cup sugar or more to taste

2 drops orange blossom water
1 quart boiling water

1. Pour some additional boiling water into the teapot you will be using, and swirl it about to warm the pot. Discard the water.

2. Add all of the ingredients to the prepared teapot and stir. Let steep for 6 minutes, and strain into decorative glasses or tea cups.

Yield: 1 quart mint tea

TINA'S TIDBIT

- *Dried mint should never be used to make mint tea. Always use fresh mint to avoid a musty, bitter taste.*

SPAIN

After the destruction of the First Temple in 586 B.C.E., when all Jews were expelled from Judea, and before the Arab conquest of Spain in 711 C.E., Jews dispersed along the coastline of the Mediterranean in North Africa and southern Spain. For more than a thousand years they lived in communities where they were

sometimes treated very well and sometimes persecuted, but they thrived. They were established traders, craftsmen, and agrarians who added to the economic growth of the communities where they lived. Nowhere was this success more evidenced than in Spain.

For three hundred years after the Arab conquest of Spain in 711 C.E., the Jews lived successful, influential, and peaceful lives under Muslim rule. Toledo, Granada, and Córdoba were centers of Jewish learning and commerce. However, following the capture of Córdoba in 1148 by the Almohads, who imposed Islam on Christians and Jews alike, life became very difficult, and many Jews immigrated to Egypt and the Middle East. Probably the most famous émigré from Spain was Moses Maimonides, who left Córdoba and settled in Egypt.

In 1492, the seven-hundred-year Arab reign in Spain came to an end simultaneously with the termination of two thousand years of rich Jewish history in that country. However, because of the Jewish expulsion, 1492 also marked the beginning of the spread of a distinct culinary heritage throughout the entire Mediterranean that affected all the cuisines from Italy to Turkey to Greece and the Balkans. The established Arab trade routes had introduced spices, melons, oranges, eggplant, olives, wheat, grapes, and rice into Spanish kitchens.

The culinary practices using these ingredients were subsequently dispersed throughout the world to wherever the Spanish Jews emigrated.

The laws of kashrut required Jews to cook differently than their Christian counterparts in Spain. Jews fried foods in olive oil rather than lard, since pork products were forbidden. They grew their own grapes and became vintners to ensure the wine would be kosher. They raised their own cattle to provide the milk and the properly slaughtered meat for their diets.

The prohibition of cooking on Shabbat inspired the creation of many dishes that could either be made in advance and preserved with vinegar or slow cooked from Friday until the dish could be eaten on Saturday afternoon. These culinary practices helped the "secret Jews" (crypto-Jews) who remained in Spain adapt in a world where many had converted to Christianity to escape the Inquisition. The Conversos, or Marrano Jews (the word *marrano* is likely derived from the Spanish word for "pig"), went to church and outwardly lived the lives of Christians. However, it was the basic precepts of kashrut observance that were used during the Inquisition to convict the crypto-Jews. Maids and neighbors turned in people who they saw setting the table in a decorative way on Friday nights or whose chimneys were smokeless because they ate only cold foods on Saturdays. Eating flat "crackers" in the spring or not eating at all for twenty-four hours in the early fall was associated with Passover or Yom Kippur and rendered an indictment against the crypto-Jews.

Many holidays fell into oblivion in this world of the Converso, but Passover, the High Holy Days, and Shabbat were observed as best as the secretive Jew could follow.

In 1492 over two hundred thousand Jews were expelled from Spain. Today, only fifteen thousand Jews live in that country, most of whom arrived in the twentieth century and have no connection to the once-great community of the Golden Age of Spain.

Marinated Olives

Olives and oranges are often combined in foods of the Mediterranean. Here the ingredients almost call out their location as foods of Morocco and Spain are joined to create a great nibble at cocktail parties, as a part of a meze or tapas assortment.

8 ounces garlic-stuffed green olives, drained
1 medium orange
1 teaspoon dried pepper flakes
1 tablespoon finely snipped cilantro leaves
½ teaspoon kosher salt

1 teaspoon Spanish smoked paprika (*pimentón de la Vera*) or sweet paprika
1–2 tablespoons extra virgin olive oil, preferably Spanish or Italian
1 tablespoon fresh orange juice (optional)

1. Place drained olives in a 1-quart glass bowl.

2. Remove the zest, or peel, from the oranges with a zester, creating long thin strands. Add to the olives.

3. Add the remaining ingredients and stir to coat olives well. If olives appear too dry, add 1 tablespoon of fresh orange juice to the mixture.

4. Return olives to their original container and chill, preferably overnight.

5. Serve as part of a mixed platter of mezes with wine and cheese.

Yield: 2 cups olives

TINA'S TIDBITS

- *In general, I prefer the fine, featherlight shards of orange peel (or zest) that you get from using a rasplike grater. However, in this recipe the zest is used for color and variety of shape in addition to being a flavor enhancement.*
- *A zester is a 5-inch tool with a slightly curved metal head that has five or six holes at the top that create strands of citrus peel when scraped along the fruit.*
- *If garlic-stuffed olives are not available, pitted olives may be substituted, with 2 large, finely diced cloves of garlic added to the mix.*

Tortilla Española (Spanish Tortilla)

In Spain this dish is called tortilla de patata; *in the rest of the world it is called Spanish tortilla. It resembles a potato frittata with egg binding the ingredients together, but this is potatoes with a little egg rather than the other way around. This is a wonderful tapas to serve because it can be cut into wedges or little squares for individual bite-sized portions. It can be served at room temperature and so can be made in advance. The fact that it is always made with olive oil instead of lard raises the question of whether or not it was originally a Jewish dish.*

3–4 large white baking potatoes, peeled
1 large onion
1 cup olive oil

Coarse salt
4 large eggs

1. Thinly slice the potatoes by hand or with the 3-mm cutting blade on your processor.

2. Thinly slice the onion.

3. Heat the oil in a 10-inch frying pan.

4. Layer the potatoes and the onion in the hot oil, alternating potatoes and then onions, and sprinkling each layer with a little coarse salt.

5. Every few minutes turn the mixture over in the pan to cook the potatoes and onions lightly. The mixture should not brown, and care should be taken not to break up the slices of potato.

6. When the potatoes are tender, drain the mixture in a colander, reserving 3 tablespoons of oil.

7. Beat the eggs in a large bowl, and add the potato mixture. Gently press down on the mixture to allow the eggs to cover. Let sit for 15 minutes.

8. Heat 2 tablespoons of the reserved olive oil in a large skillet until very hot. Quickly add the potato mixture and spread it out evenly. Reduce heat to medium.

9. When the mixture begins to brown on the bottom, invert a large round plate over the pan, and flip the pancake over onto the plate.

10. Slide the pancake from the plate into the frying pan, raw side down, and cook until light brown on the bottom. Repeat the process 2 more times so that each side has been cooked twice. If the mixture sticks the first 2 times, don't worry, just patch it up. The egg mixture will hold it together.

12. Serve the tortilla at room temperature, cutting it either into wedges or into bite-sized squares for appetizers.

Yield: 8–10 servings

TINA'S TIDBITS

- *Use a rubber spatula or turner when turning the potatoes and onions so that you can maintain some of the layering. A metal turner will cut into the potato and create too many little pieces.*
- *Always use a plate that is larger than your frying pan when flipping your tortilla over, and wear a protective mitt on the hand holding the plate over the pan.*
- *For larger parties I cut the circle into 1-inch squares and put a toothpick in each so guests can help themselves. They then become* banderillas, *or skewered pieces of meat or food. The name comes from the barbed dart used in bullfighting.*

CROSTINI WITH TAPENADE

Tapenade is the quintessential Mediterranean spread. Create your own unique version with the addition of garlic in the mix, or more sun-dried tomatoes and less roasted peppers. Freshly roasted peppers are always the best to use, but I have never had a complaint when I used the jarred peppers instead.

12 or more thin slices of French bread
1 large clove of garlic, cut in half
¼ cup extra virgin olive oil
20 large Calamata or other cured olives

One-half 7-ounce jar roasted peppers or 1½ freshly roasted red bell peppers
2 pieces of sun-dried tomatoes (about 1 tablespoon)

1. Preheat the oven to 400°F.

2. Rub one side of each slice of bread with the cut sides of the garlic.

3. Brush the olive oil over the garlic-seasoned sides.

4. Place the bread on a cookie sheet and bake for 5 minutes or until golden.

5. Meanwhile, make the tapenade. With the flat side of a heavy knife, crack the olives and remove the pits.

6. Place the olives in a processor work bowl and process until fairly smooth. Scrape down the sides of the work bowl.

7. Drain the roasted peppers and pat dry. Add the peppers and the sun-dried tomatoes to the olive mixture and process until smooth.

8. To serve, spread tapenade over the bread crostini, and serve at room temperature.

Note: The tapenade mixture can be stuffed into mushrooms, covered with a little mozzarella, and baked until the mushrooms are hot and the cheese has melted.

Yield: ¾ cup

TINA'S TIDBITS

- *If garlic starts to get dry, either cut a sliver off the edge to expose a new layer or make hatch marks on the cut side to release its juices.*
- *The best way to remove the smell of garlic from your hands is to rub them on a stainless steel sink or a pot in your kitchen. The metal neutralizes the smell.*
- *Most supermarkets are happy to take your baguette or ficelle (thin baguette) and put it through the bread-slicing machine. This will save you time and from having to clean up all the crumbs from slicing the bread.*

MANCHEGO CHEESE WITH QUINCE PRESERVES

The nuttiness of the manchego *coupled with the sweet-tart taste of the* membrillo *is a great combination. Jews were instrumental in growing quince and were cheese makers five hundred years ago.*

Two ¼-pound wedges well-cured *manchego* cheese

½ pound quince paste (*membrillo*) or quince marmalade

1. Trim the rind from each cheese wedge. Place the wedge on its side, and slice into ¼-inch-thick triangles.

2. Slice the *membrillo* paste into the same size triangles as the cheese, and place a slice of the *membrillo* on top of a slice of the cheese. If you are using the marmalade, gently spread some of the marmalade on top of each cheese slice.

3. Serve at room temperature.

Yield: 2 dozen or more portions

TINA'S TIDBIT

- *I like to cut little flowers out of a strip of* membrillo *and put that on top of the cheese for a more decorative presentation.*

Tostada con Salsa Tomaquet
(Catalan Bread with Tomato Spread)

A standard offering at a tapas bar, this is perfect peasant food to make when tomato season is at its height. This recipe is probably the forerunner of crostini with tapenade.

1 loaf dense country bread or 2-inch wide country
    baguette
1 large clove garlic, cut in half lengthwise
3 medium red tomatoes (about 1 pound)
Coarse salt and freshly ground black pepper
¼ teaspoon sugar
½ teaspoon red wine or sherry vinegar
¼ cup extra virgin olive oil
¼ cup lightly packed whole basil leaves

1. Preheat the oven to 400°F.

2. Slice the bread or baguette into ½-inch slices. Rub the cut side of the garlic over the bread slices, and place them on a large cookie sheet. Bake the bread slices until golden and crisp (6–7 minutes). Remove from the oven and set aside.

3. Cut tomatoes in half crosswise. Remove the seeds by slightly squeezing the tomato, cut side down, over a sink.

4. Using a coarse hand grater, grate the tomatoes over a 1-quart bowl. Discard the skins.

5. Add the salt and pepper, sugar, and vinegar to the tomato pulp. Stir in the olive oil.

6. Stack the basil leaves, and roll them into a tight cigar. Finely slice the roll crosswise. Add the basil strips to the tomato mixture and stir well to combine. Refrigerate until ready to use.

7. When ready to serve, spread some of the tomato mixture over the bread slices and serve sprinkled with a little coarse sea salt on top.

Note: A small piece of cheese can be placed on top, or drizzle a little bit of oil on top of the mixture before sprinkling with salt.

Yield: 8–10 servings

TINA'S TIDBITS

- *Similar to a bruschetta, another way Spaniards make this tapas is to literally rub the cut side of the tomato on the hard crisp baguette slices and let the bread do the grating!*
- *Although this mixture can be made in advance, it is generally not a good idea to mix sugar and vinegar with a fruit for a long time, as it will pull moisture out of the food.*

PECHUGA DE POLLO CON PORTO
(BONELESS CHICKEN BREAST WITH PORT)

So much has been said about the expulsion of Jews from Spain that one must also remember that a short seven years later they were expelled from Portugal, and the Inquisition followed the Jews all the way to Brazil! This dish is a modern creation, using two ingredients that best typify their countries of origin: port wine from Oporto, Portugal, and orange juice from Valencia, Spain.

6–8 boneless, skinless chicken breasts	2 teaspoons lemon juice
½ cup flour	1 tablespoon brandy
Salt, freshly ground black pepper, and pinch of allspice	1 teaspoon Kitchen Bouquet
3 tablespoons olive oil	2 teaspoons cornstarch
1 cup port wine (preferably Tawny Port), divided use	½ teaspoon salt
¾ cup fresh orange juice, divided use	Freshly ground black pepper to taste
	4 drops Tabasco sauce

1. To prepare the chicken breast for this recipe, first remove the fillet. The fillet is the separate, tender piece of chicken breast that is located in a clear membrane sack on the underside of each breast half. The chicken fillet or "tender" can be recognized by a thin, white pearlized tendon that runs through it.

2. Once the fillet is located, gently pull it away from the chicken breast and out of its sack. Note that the sack may have been cut when filleting the breast, so do not worry if it is not visible on inspection.

3. To remove the tendon from the fillet, hold onto the thick end of the white tendon and gently scrape a knife blade along it to slightly separate it from the fillet meat. Hold the meat back with the knife while the blade rests against the tendon. Slowly jiggle the tendon as you pull it away from the knife. The blade will scrape the meat away from the tendon as it is pulled out of the fillet.

4. Place the breast meat on a cutting board with the smooth side down. Cover with a plastic storage bag and gently pound with the heel of your hand or a smooth mallet until the chicken is ½ inch thick. If pieces are very large, they may be cut in half crosswise.

TINA'S TIDBITS

- *Chicken doesn't need to be pounded for tenderizing, just for uniformity of thickness.*
- *It is better to pound meat under a plastic bag instead of waxed paper, because shards of wax can get embedded in the meat.*
- *Port is a sweet fortified wine that is named after the city Oporto, from where it is shipped. A very acceptable flavored port from New York State can be purchased for under $10 a bottle and used for cooking. Because it is fortified, port does not need to be refrigerated after opening.*
- *Kitchen Bouquet is a vegetable-based brown-colored sauce used solely to darken a sauce and make it look richer. It can be eliminated in most cases if needed.*

5. Lightly dust the chicken in flour that has been seasoned with salt, pepper, and a pinch of allspice.

6. Heat a large frying pan for 20 seconds. Add the oil and heat for an additional 15 seconds. Sauté the chicken breasts 1 minute on each side, until lightly browned. Add half the port and ¼ cup orange juice, and simmer over low heat for 5–7 minutes or until the chicken is tender. Transfer the chicken to a warm platter and keep hot.

7. Blend the remaining ingredients. Add to the frying pan and cook until the sauce thickens. Return the chicken to the pan and turn the meat in the sauce until all pieces are coated and reheated. Serve.

Note: May be made in advance and frozen or refrigerated until ready to reheat.

Yield: 6–8 Servings

FLAN

Flan can be thick and heavy or thin and light. But a good flan should be smooth as silk and firm, but not hard, with a golden caramel that has a strong flavor but is not burnt tasting. Here is my all-time favorite. For a taste from the Maghreb, use orange blossom water, as my friends at Café Marrakesh in Dallas taught me, in place of all or some of the vanilla for a wonderfully subtle floral essence.

1 cup sugar
$\frac{1}{2}$ cup water
3 cups milk, preferably whole or 2%
$\frac{3}{4}$ cup sugar

4 large eggs
2 egg yolks
2 teaspoons vanilla or orange blossom water

1. Preheat the oven to 350°F.

2. To make the caramel, place the sugar and water in a $1\frac{1}{2}$-quart saucepan, and cook over moderate heat for 10 minutes or until the sugar becomes an amber color.

3. Using 6–8 individual ramekins, pour the caramel immediately into the cups, turning the cups around to coat the bottom and sides thoroughly. Set aside while you make the custard.

4. Heat the milk and sugar in a 2-quart saucepan.

5. In a mixing bowl, whisk the eggs and the yolks until smooth.

6. Pour about $\frac{1}{4}$ cup of the hot milk **slowly** into the eggs, stirring constantly. Add the remainder of the milk into the eggs, and whisk to thoroughly combine. Flavor with the vanilla, and strain the mixture through a sieve into a large liquid measuring cup or pitcher.

7. Pour the mixture into the caramel-coated molds.

8. Line a 13 × 9-inch baking dish with paper towel. Place the ramekins in the pan, and pour hot water around them halfway up the sides of the mold. Bake for 25–30 minutes until the custard is firm (but still jiggles a little) and has shrunk slightly away from the sides.

9. Remove from the water bath, cool to room temperature, and then refrigerate.

10. To unmold, slightly turn the mold to see if the flan is loose. If necessary, run a small, sharp knife around the inside edge of the cup. Place a plate over the ramekin and invert rapidly. Let the caramel pour out onto the flan and serve.

Yield: 8 servings

TINA'S TIDBITS

- *Egg whites are responsible for the firm edge to a flan; yolks give the flan its richness and weight.*
- *Never stir a sugar mixture after it has dissolved, or you will set up a crystalline structure in the sugar that might yield a pot of sugary sand.*
- *As water evaporates from a sugar solution, the bubbles get bigger and slower. This is a clue that the mixture will soon begin to caramelize.*
- *To see if the custard is done, slightly poke a small, sharp knife into the center of the dish. If the knife comes out clear, then the custard is done. The flan will firm up when it is cold.*
- *Cooked flans can be refrigerated for a day or two and then unmolded just before serving. Make sure the dishes are tightly covered with plastic wrap to prevent drying.*
- *Sugar syrup is **very** hot. Always use a pot holder or glove on the hand that will be holding the ramekin when you add the syrup.*

ITALY

*I*taly is home to the oldest, continuously inhabited Jewish community in Europe. The first Jews arrived in southern Italy and Rome after the destruction of the First Temple. By the time of the destruction of the Second Temple, Jews made up almost 9 percent of the Roman Empire's population. Their living conditions were

tolerable until the beginning of the fourth century when Constantine I established Christianity as the official religion of the Roman Empire. After this decree, the Jews were consistently subjected to higher taxes, exclusion from owning property, and exclusion from most professions.

Life became even worse in the twelfth century when Pope Innocent III ordered every Jew to be singled out in the community by wearing an identifying badge proclaiming his religion. In the thirteenth century Pope Gregory IX promoted the process of the Inquisition in Central and Western Europe and began to focus on the Jewish community as well as Christian heretics. The only places where Jews were not greatly harassed were in major commercial centers like Venice, Florence, Genoa, and Pisa as well as southern French cities like Avignon, Marseilles, and Arles, where the important contribution of Jews to the financial success of the papacy afforded some limited protection.

The first Jewish ghetto was established on an island in Venice in 1516. The island was referred to as the ghetto because of the foundry (*geto* in Italian) on the island. Subsequent ghettos were set up in other major cities, especially after the southern Italian Jews were expelled and crowded the northern cities. Immigrants from the Spanish expulsion in 1492 moved to the north of Italy—almost forty

thousand Jews lived on the islands of Sicily and Sardinia, then Spanish territories, and they were expelled as well.

As with all Jewish cuisine in the Diaspora, the movement of the Jews meant the migration of their regional dishes. Sicilian and Spanish cooking highlighted the seven hundred years of Arab influence. When the Jews moved east and north, they brought with them the custom of using oil instead of pork fat for frying. Eggplant, artichokes, spinach (often with raisins), and rice were the cornerstones of Italian Jewish cuisine.

Holidays influenced the foods prepared. According to Claudia Roden, using saffron to color rice or adding spinach and raisins was a way to elevate simple foods for the celebration of Shabbat. Risotto alla Milanese and other risotto dishes incorporating vegetables were the creations of observant Jews. The prohibition of cooking on the Sabbath created dishes that either slow cooked overnight or were served cold. Again, according to Roden, only the Jews ate cold pasta and rice dishes, and foods preserved with vinegar and sugar like caponata were served on Shabbat because they could be prepared in advance.

Relatives, dispersed throughout the world by the Inquisition, exchanged new foods with each other. Because of their connections in the New World and because Jews were traders, tomatoes, pumpkins, corn, and green beans were associated with the Jews in Italy. The Spanish brought these foods to Italy, but the Jews distributed their use throughout the north.

When the names of dishes include adjectives like *alla giudia, all' ebraica,* and *alla mosaica* (such as *carciofi* *alla guidia,* "artichokes Jewish style") or the names of cities that had large Jewish populations like Ancona, Livorno, Ferrara, and Venice, they quietly announce their Jewish roots.

SALMONE AFFUMICATO CON MELONE (SMOKED SALMON WITH MELON)

Here I have taken a little license and "tweaked" an icon of Italian cuisine to conform to our dietary laws. Prosciutto e melone is traditionally made in Italy by rolling a slice of the Parma ham around a wedge of rock melon. In this recipe, cubes of juicy, sweet honeydew or cantaloupe melon are wrapped with glistening, pink strands of smoked salmon to re-create the salty-sweet taste contrast of the original.

½ small, ripe honeydew or cantaloupe
4 ounces of thinly sliced smoked salmon (lox)

1 lemon
Italian flat leaf parsley for garnish (optional)

1. Cut the melon in half. Remove the seeds, and cut the flesh into 1-inch cubes.

2. Cut each slice of smoked salmon lengthwise into ½-inch strips.

3. Wrap one strip of salmon around a cube of melon, and secure it with a toothpick. Repeat with remaining ingredients.

4. If using, finely mince some Italian parsley and set aside, covered with plastic wrap.

5. Just before serving, squeeze a little lemon juice over each cube and sprinkle with a little parsley.

Yield: Approximately 3 dozen pieces, or 9–12 servings

TINA'S TIDBITS

- *Melon can be cut into 1 1/2-inch wedges and the salmon wrapped around crosswise for individual appetizer portions.*
- *Finely grated lemon zest sprinkled on the top also makes a delicious garnish.*
- *Do not expose fish to acidic liquids for long periods of time or they will "cook" the fish that comes in contact with the juice and toughen the delicate meat.*

Fiori de Zucca Ripieni (Stuffed Zucchini Blossoms)

Zucchini blossoms are found in frittatas, in salads, or stuffed and/or fried throughout Rome in summer and early fall. Although one can find recipes calling for all types of cheese or even rice fillings, the combination of mozzarella and anchovy is most strongly associated with the cooking of the Roman Jewish ghetto.

One summer I grew zucchini plants not for the vegetable but just for the blossom! It is now easier to find blossoms in high-end supermarkets in late summer. Thin slices of zucchini or eggplant can be used as a delicious but somewhat messier alternative.

12 zucchini blossoms, with stems preferably
6 ounces soft, fresh mozzarella
$\frac{1}{2}$ tablespoon anchovy paste or 6 canned anchovy fillets
$\frac{3}{4}$ cup all-purpose flour
$\frac{3}{4}$ cup water or club soda

$\frac{1}{4}$ teaspoon salt
Additional flour for dredging
Olive oil for frying
Marinara sauce, store-bought or freshly made (optional)

1. Remove stamen from inside of the flower. Rinse flower thoroughly in case any insect pollinator is present. Shake off excess water. Set aside.

2. Combine mozzarella with anchovy paste or fillets in a small processor work bowl, and using the metal blade, pulse the machine on and off until the cheese and anchovies are coarsely combined. Place mixture in a 1-quart plastic bag.

3. Place $\frac{3}{4}$ cup flour in a 1-quart bowl. Gradually add water or club soda to the flour, whisking constantly until a thick, creamy consistency is achieved. Add the salt and mix well. Set aside.

4. Place about $\frac{1}{2}$ cup flour in a shallow soup bowl.

5. Cut a $\frac{1}{4}$-inch hole in the corner of the bag and squeeze gently at the top of the bag until the cheese mixture starts to extrude from the hole.

6. Hold the tip of the bag just inside the blossom, and squeeze about 1 tablespoon of cheese mixture inside the blossom. Gently twist the open end of the blossom to keep it closed. Set aside and proceed with the remaining blossoms.

7. Heat about 1 inch of olive oil in a 2-quart saucepan or 10-inch frying pan.

8. Lightly coat each blossom with the flour in the shallow soup bowl, and then dip into the flour-water batter to completely cover.

9. Fry the blossoms in 3 or 4 small batches until golden brown and crisp (about 3 minutes).

10. Drain on paper towel and serve as is or with warm marinara sauce.

Yield: 6–12 servings

TINA'S TIDBITS

- *Long-stemmed flowers that do not have baby zucchinis attached to them are male and need to have the interior stamen removed before stuffing.*
- *To make the coating adhere better to food, always dip the moist food in flour before coating with batter. The flour adheres to the food and the batter adheres to the flour so it doesn't slide off when put into the hot oil.*
- *Two canned anchovy fillets equal 1/2 teaspoon anchovy paste.*

PUMPKIN RAVIOLI FROM MANTUA

During the Renaissance the Jews lived very well in Mantua under the Gonzaga duchy. They were very familiar with pumpkin because of New World exploration and the Portuguese and Converso connections throughout the world. Although this dish is very popular in restaurants throughout the world right now, the recipe is five hundred years old. This recipe was adapted from Joyce Goldstein's cookbook, Cucina Ebraica.

2 pounds fresh pie pumpkin or butternut squash, or 1 pound canned pumpkin puree
¼ cup freshly grated Parmesan cheese
1 cup Italian amaretti cookies (about 2 ounces)
¼ teaspoon nutmeg
½ cup finely chopped raisins (soaked in hot water for 15 minutes if too dry and hard)
Sugar to taste
1 egg
2 tablespoons dried plain bread crumbs
1 egg yolk mixed with 2 tablespoons water for sealing dough
1 stick butter melted, until light brown
¼ cup chiffonade of fresh mint

1. To prepare the pumpkin or squash, roast in a 400°F oven for 50 minutes or until soft. Cool, cut in half, and remove all seeds and stringy fibers. Scoop the meat of the squash into a bowl and mash with a fork until smooth.

2. If puree is watery, spread the puree on a rimmed baking sheet, and bake at 300°F for 10 minutes or until it appears dry. Let cool before using, or use 1 pound of canned pumpkin.

3. In a large bowl, combine the pumpkin with the next 7 ingredients and set aside while you make the dough.

Dough

2 large eggs
1 tablespoon extra virgin olive oil
2 tablespoons ice water
2 cups bread flour

1. Place the eggs, oil, and water in the food processor work bowl, and mix by turning the processor on and off twice.

2. Add 1 cup of the bread flour, and turn the processor on for 5 seconds. Scrape the sides of the bowl. Add the other cup of flour and process for 10 seconds longer. The dough will be crumbly. Pinch a little bit of dough; if it holds together, it is ready to be rolled.

3. Remove the dough and divide in half. Place on a lightly floured surface, cover, and allow to rest for 10 minutes or longer if you are rolling the dough by hand.

4. Make pasta according to machine directions. If rolling pasta by hand, divide dough into fourths and then roll out each portion as thin as possible. Cut dough into 3-inch rounds, or use a ravioli form.

5. Place 1 tablespoon of filling in the center of each circle or each template on the ravioli form. Brush a little of the egg yolk mixture on the edges of the dough, and cover with another circle of dough (or sheet if using the ravioli plate). Press dough firmly from the filling outward to remove any air trapped in the middle and seal the dough.

6. Bring a large pot of salted water to a boil and add 1 tablespoon of oil. Cook pasta until al dente. Drain and place in a large serving bowl.

7. Drizzle brown butter on top of ravioli, and sprinkle with the fresh mint chiffonade.

Yield: 4 servings

TINA'S TIDBITS

- *Although fresh pie pumpkin has a more distinct flavor, canned pumpkin will work if you are short on time.*
- *Never use salt in the pasta dough. It will make the dough tough and hard to roll.*

WINTER SQUASH GNOCCHI WITH WILTED SPINACH AND PINE NUTS

I don't remember the first time I made this wonderful version of gnocchi, but I do remember mispronouncing the name in the little South Jersey Italian restaurant thirty-five years ago. I pronounced the dish "gunochee," but its proper pronunciation is "nyoki." However you say it, these firm but not hard cylinders of cooked pasta are absolutely wonderful, especially when made with the pumpkin or butternut squash.

1½ pounds butternut squash or pie pumpkin
¾ pound russet or Yukon Gold potatoes
1 large egg, lightly beaten
½ cup grated Romano cheese
½ teaspoon minced fresh thyme or 1 pinch dried thyme
½ teaspoon finely chopped pineapple sage or pinch of dried sage
salt and freshly ground white pepper to taste

Good-sized pinch of nutmeg
¾ cup flour
6 tablespoons unsalted butter
0.5 ounce dried porcini mushrooms
¼ cup pine nuts
9 ounces fresh baby spinach leaves
½ teaspoon kosher salt
Additional Romano cheese for garnish
Freshly ground black pepper, as needed

1. Preheat the oven to 425°F. Place the butternut squash or pumpkin and the potato on the middle rack of the oven, and roast the vegetables until soft, about 40 minutes. Remove from oven and cool until easy to handle.

2. Cut the squash or pumpkin in half lengthwise and remove seeds. Scoop out the flesh, and place in a medium bowl. Mash until smooth, and measure ¾ cup of the puree. Reserve the remainder for another use.

3. Place the squash or pumpkin puree on a jellyroll pan.

4. Cut the potato in half, and scoop out the flesh into a small bowl. Mash with a fork or potato masher until smooth, and add to the pan with the squash or pumpkin puree. Place in the freezer to cool completely, but do not freeze.

5. Return the cooled puree mixture to a medium bowl, and stir in the egg, cheese, thyme, sage, salt, pepper, and nutmeg.

6. Add the flour, and stir to combine. Knead the dough on a lightly floured board for about a minute until dough holds together and is soft and still slightly moist.

7. Divide dough into thirds. Shape each portion into a rope that is about ½-inch thick. Cut rope into ½-inch pieces. If knife gets sticky, dust it with some extra flour.

8. Lightly flour a kitchen towel, a dinner-size fork, and your thumb. Holding the front of the fork facing you, pushing with your thumb, roll a piece of dough from the bottom of the fork tines, against the curve, up to the tip of the fork and then flick the dough off the fork onto the prepared towel. Repeat with the remaining dough.

9. Melt 3 tablespoons of unsalted butter in a 10-inch skillet. Keep warm while you make the gnocchi.

10. Bring a large pot of salted water to a boil, and cook ⅓ of the gnocchi for about 3 minutes or

until the centers are no longer raw. Stir once after the gnocchi rise to the top of the pot. When the gnocchi are done, remove with a slotted spoon to the heated butter in the frying pan. Lightly toss to coat with the butter. Repeat with the remaining gnocchi until all are warmed in the butter. Keep warm while you prepare the spinach and mushrooms.

11. Cover the dried mushrooms with water, and microwave on high for 3 minutes. Allow to sit for 10 minutes or until soft.

12. Carefully remove the mushrooms from the liquid, and cut into julienne strips. Melt 1 tablespoon of butter in a small frying pan, and sauté the mushrooms until they have given up their juices. Sprinkle with a little kosher salt and set aside.

13. Melt the remaining butter in a large nonstick frying pan, and add the pine nuts. Toss the nuts over medium heat until lightly golden. Immediately add all of the spinach and the salt, and toss lightly. Reduce the heat, cover, and wilt the spinach for 2 minutes.

14. To serve, divide the spinach among 6–8 plates. Place gnocchi equally on top of spinach on each plate, and spoon some of the mushrooms over all. Top with some additional grated Romano cheese and a few grindings of pepper. Serve as a first course.

Yield: 6–8 servings

TINA'S TIDBITS

- *Butternut squash is easy to find in most supermarkets. However, in early fall look for small, round, sweet, firm-fleshed pie pumpkins to enhance the flavor of the dish.*
- *When a recipe requires cooked squash, it is much easier to bake the vegetable whole and then scoop out its flesh than to try to peel the hard, slippery rind off before boiling.*
- *Do not overhandle the dough or you will activate the gluten in the flour, and the gnocchi will be dense and heavy instead of light.*

PASTA WITH SALSA CRUDA

This pasta dish is a variation of the famous insalata Caprese *made up of the season's freshest tomatoes and basil and fresh mozzarella found on the island of Capri in the very fertile region of the Campania surrounding Naples. The essence of summer, this dish must be made with the freshest and sweetest produce and soft mozzarella. The original Caprese salad is a staple at every Roman Jewish restaurant I visited. The addition of pasta makes a hearty main dish or side for fish.*

3/4 pound (2–3 large) tomatoes
1/2 pound, fresh soft mozzarella
1/2 cup lightly packed basil leaves
2 cloves garlic, finely minced
1/2 cup extra virgin olive oil

1/4 teaspoon kosher salt
Freshly ground black pepper to taste
8 ounces dried rotelle (spirals) or penne rigati
Freshly grated Parmesan cheese

1. Cut the tomatoes into 1/2-inch cubes, and place them in a 3-quart glass or ceramic serving bowl.

2. Cut the mozzarella into 1/2-inch cubes, and add to the tomatoes.

3. Layer the basil leaves, and roll them up lengthwise like a cigarette. Slice thinly crosswise through the roll to make a chiffonade—thin strands of basil that "float" like chiffon—and add to the tomato mixture.

4. Add the garlic, olive oil, salt, and pepper to the bowl, and stir to combine. Cover the bowl, and set aside at room temperature for at least 1 hour.

5. When ready to serve, cook the pasta in boiling salted water until al dente. Drain and immediately toss with the raw tomato mixture.

6. Serve at once with freshly grated Parmesan cheese and more black pepper if desired.

Yield: 6–8 servings

TINA'S TIDBITS

- *Pasta in shapes like macaroni, shells, or twists will hold onto small particles of food in chunky sauces better than long, smooth pasta.*
- *The heat of the drained pasta will wilt the basil and slightly soften the cheese to bring out their full flavor. Therefore, do not rinse pasta, as it will cool it.*
- *Eliminate the cheese for a meat meal or if you need to make the dish in advance, since the melted cheese will clump when cold.*

PASTA RIMINATA

This is an incredible dish, with a creamy sauce made with pine nuts and raisins and no cream. This recipe can be prepared in advance and is so delicious. Don't tell anyone that the base of the sauce is cauliflower. Leave out the Parmesan and you have a wonderful side dish for a meat meal. The pine nuts and raisins imply the Spanish origins, and the olive oil the Jewish connection.

1 head cauliflower, cut into florets, or one 1-pound bag frozen cauliflower
1½ cups water
½ teaspoon salt, divided use
4 tablespoons extra virgin olive oil
1 large onion, cut into ½-inch dice

2 tablespoons pine nuts
2 tablespoons dark raisins
Freshly ground black pepper to taste
1 pound rigatoni
½ cup freshly grated Parmesan cheese or to taste

1. Combine the cauliflower, water, and ¼ teaspoon salt in a 3-quart saucepan, and bring to a boil. Cover, reduce heat, and simmer until very tender, about 10 minutes.

2. Drain the cauliflower, and reserve the cooking liquid. Mash the cauliflower with a fork until relatively smooth and set aside.

3. Heat a large frying pan for 20 seconds, add 3 tablespoons of olive oil, and heat another 10 seconds. Sauté the onion in the olive oil for 5 minutes or until soft and very slightly golden.

4. Add the pine nuts, raisins, remaining salt, and pepper to taste to the onion mixture, and stir for 2 minutes or until nuts begin to turn golden.

5. Add the mashed cauliflower and ¼ cup of the reserved cooking liquid to the onion mixture, and simmer for 15 minutes or until thick, stirring often. If the mixture is getting too dry, add more of the reserved liquid to prevent sticking. When mixture is done, set aside until ready to serve.

6. Cook the pasta in boiling salted water and add 1 tablespoon of olive oil. Cook until pasta is al dente. Drain and place in a large serving bowl.

7. Pour ⅓ of the sauce over the pasta and toss. Place remaining sauce over the pasta, garnish with the Parmesan cheese, and serve.

Yield: 6 servings

TINA'S TIDBITS

- *The amount of time it takes to cook cauliflower varies. Therefore, cook the vegetable until it is really very tender. Your finished sauce will be much smoother and creamier.*
- *Add some chopped anchovies or brined olives instead of cheese to create a pareve (nondairy) dish, another inventive way to utilize the foods and flavors of a country without compromising the Jewish dietary laws.*

SPINACI CON PINOLI E PASSERINI (SPINACH WITH PINE NUTS AND RAISINS)

At Walter's Ristorante d'Italia in Providence, Rhode Island, you can experience the two-thousand-year-old cuisine of Italian Jews. I had the good fortune to eat an authentic historically accurate Jewish meal when I was there, and Walter put this dish on my radar screen. It seems that whenever you see pine nuts and raisins together and especially with spinach, the dish is screaming that it has Jewish roots from the Moorish influence in Spain. This dish is made easier by using tender baby spinach leaves. No sand, no removal of stem, and no chopping!

4 cups baby spinach (about ⅓ pound)
2 tablespoons extra virgin olive oil
½ medium onion, finely chopped

3 tablespoons pine nuts
3 tablespoons dark raisins, soaked in water if hard
Kosher salt and freshly ground pepper to taste

1. Rinse the spinach in water if gritty and drain well. Set aside.

2. Heat the olive oil in a large nonstick frying pan for 20 seconds. Add the onion and sauté for 5 minutes or until onions are lightly golden and soft.

3. Add the pine nuts and sauté until the nuts are light golden in color.

4. If the raisins have been soaking, drain. Add the raisins to the pine nuts and onions, and stir to combine.

5. Add all of the drained spinach and lightly stir the mixture just a little. Place a lid on the pan and cook over low heat for 2 minutes or until the leaves are wilted.

6. Sprinkle mixture with salt and pepper, and stir until all of the spinach is soft but still a bright green. Serve hot or at room temperature.

Yield: 4–6 servings

TINA'S TIDBITS

- *One easy way to wash spinach is placing all the leaves in a large bowl of water. The leaves will float, and the gritty sand will sink.*
- *Always dry spinach leaves well so that they don't soak up the water when cooking.*
- *If you must use frozen spinach, make sure the spinach is thoroughly defrosted and squeezed dry before sautéing with the onions. The dish will be acceptable but will not have the bright color or taste of the fresh.*
- *Use baby spinach and you will never have to devein or cut up a leaf again. In addition to its ease in use, there is no waste in volume with the small, tender leaves.*

PESCE EN SAOR
(FISH IN SWEET AND SOUR SAUCE)

This recipe was originally prepared for sailors at sea because the sauce preserved the fish over long journeys. However, the presence of pine nuts and raisins signals the Moorish influence and draws a distinct link between the Spanish Jewish émigrés and their culinary traditions. Frying foods, specifically in oil, and then preserving them in a vinegar sauce originated on the Iberian peninsula by Jews and was a necessity to fulfill the laws of Shabbat, since the food could be prepared in advance, eliminating the need to work on the day of rest. This dish is traditionally made with sardines (sarde en saor), but small, firm fillets of fish may be used as well.

2 pounds whole sardines or red mullets, or 1 pound
   sole fillets
Salt and freshly ground black pepper to taste
½ cup flour
¼ cup extra virgin olive oil

MARINADE:
2 tablespoons extra virgin olive oil
1 pound yellow onions, cut in half and thinly sliced
1¼ cups balsamic vinegar
1 tablespoon honey
Pinch of saffron (optional)
½ cup raisins
¼ cup pine nuts

1. If using whole fish, make sure that the fish is thoroughly gutted and scaled. The head of larger fish may be removed; sardines may be left whole.

2. Rinse fish or fish fillets and pat dry. Season lightly with salt and pepper.

3. Place the flour in a gallon plastic bag and season with a small amount of salt and pepper. Add a few pieces of fish to the bag and toss until completely coated. Remove fish from the bag and repeat with the remaining fish.

4. Heat a 10-inch skillet over high heat for 20 seconds. Add the olive oil and heat for 10 seconds more. Add the fish to the hot oil and fry until lightly golden brown on both sides. This should take no more than a total of 3 minutes per fillet or sardines and no more than a total of 4–5 minutes if using other small, whole fish. Drain on paper towel. Place in a nonreactive glass or porcelain casserole that just fits the fish; fish may overlap slightly. Set aside to cool completely.

5. Meanwhile, heat a clean sauté pan over high heat for 20 seconds. Add the 2 tablespoons of olive oil to the pan, and heat for an additional 10 seconds. Reduce heat slightly if oil begins to smoke.

6. Add the thinly sliced onions to the pan and sauté until the onions are soft and lightly golden. Add the vinegar, honey, saffron (if using), and raisins to the pan, and cook over moderate heat for 5 minutes or until mixture has reduced slightly.

7. Lightly roast the pine nuts in a 350°F oven for 4 minutes. Add the pine nuts to the onion mixture and remove from the heat. Adjust amount of vinegar or honey if needed.

8. When the onion mixture is warm to the touch of your finger, spoon the mixture over the fish.

9. Although the fish may be served immediately, historically the fish is allowed to marinate in the refrigerator for 1–2 days to absorb all the flavors.

10. Serve at room temperature.

Yield: 4–6 servings as an appetizer, 3–4 as a main dish

TINA'S TIDBITS

- *Traditionally, vinegar, wine, and a wine concentrate are used in this dish. However, balsamic vinegar has a richer and thicker consistency and is a perfect substitute for the concentrated wine-vinegar mixture.*
- *If the raisins are particularly sweet, honey is not needed.*
- *Another word for this type of preparation—frying and then marinating in a vinegar sauce—is escabeche.*

Zucca Gialla in Agrodolce
(Squash in Sweet and Sour Sauce)

I first saw this dish in Joyce Goldstein's Cucina Ebraica. *I was intrigued by the flavor combinations. The sweet-and-sour flavoring is so much a part of the Jewish culinary culture, and the use of vinegar implies that this dish was made in advance for the Sabbath day meal. The following is an adaptation of Joyce's recipe.*

2 pounds butternut squash
2–3 tablespoons olive oil, or as needed
Kosher salt as needed
½ cup chiffonade of fresh mint
2 large cloves of garlic, sliced lengthwise into thin slivers

½ cup balsamic vinegar or red wine vinegar
½ cup sugar (less if using balsamic vinegar)
⅛ teaspoon cinnamon
Kosher salt and freshly ground black pepper to taste

1. Cut the squash in half lengthwise, peel it, and remove all seeds and fibers from the inside. Cut each half lengthwise again and slice crosswise into ¼-inch slices.

2. Toss the squash slices with 2 tablespoons of olive oil to coat, and place the squash slices on a nonstick cookie sheet or roasting pan. Sprinkle very lightly with some kosher salt.

3. Bake for 15 to 20 minutes at 400° F or until squash is tender but firm—if the tip of a sharp knife is easily inserted and removed from the squash, it is done.

4. Layer the cooked squash with the mint and garlic slivers in a serving dish.

5. Pour any pan drippings from the squash into an 8-inch nonstick sauté pan. If there is very little oil, add 1 tablespoon of olive oil to the pan. Heat on medium for 10 seconds.

6. Add the balsamic vinegar and sugar first to dissolve, and then add the cinnamon to the pan. Cook, stirring constantly, until the mixture bubbles and thickens slightly, about 4 minutes.

7. Pour the hot syrup over the squash, and gently move and lift the squash with a rubber spatula or large plastic serving spoon (these utensils won't cut into the pieces of squash) to distribute the sauce evenly.

8. Serve at once or at room temperature, which is perfect for a buffet.

Yield: 6–8 servings

TINA'S TIDBITS

- *To chiffonade a leafy herb, layer 5-10 leaves on top of each other, and roll the leaves tightly together into a long log like a cigarette. Cutting across the log, make thin slices. When you are done, there will be thin strands of herb that almost float when you toss them in the air—hence the reference to chiffon!*
- *Balsamic vinegar is made from white trebbiano grapes. The juice is allowed to age in different types and sizes of wood barrels that impart the special sweet-tart flavor to the vinegar.*

Zabaglione

This light custard is a perfect way to end a meat meal. The egg yolks are flavored and cooked gently over simmering water to allow the yolks to expand and thicken. If the egg yolk gets too hot, it will cook and you will have very delicious scrambled eggs! The classic version of this sauce is made with Marsala wine. The French use champagne and call it sabayon. Either way, this is delicious over fruit and/or a simple pound cake.

4 egg yolks
¼ cup sugar
3 tablespoons Marsala wine

1 tablespoon water
1 tablespoon apricot brandy
2 pints fresh berries or fruit

1. Place the egg yolks and the sugar in the top of a double boiler or in a 1-quart saucepan, and whisk together until a thick ribbon of mixture pours off the whisk.

2. Place the pan with the sugar-egg mixture over another pan containing hot, but not boiling water. The mixture shouldn't be so hot that it will cook the eggs.

3. Add the Marsala, water, and brandy to the sugar-egg mixture. Whisk constantly over the warm water for 4 minutes until a nice thick custard is formed.

4. When the custard has thickened, **immediately** remove from the heat or you will have fancy scrambled eggs!

5. Have your fresh berries divided into 5 or 6 serving dishes or glasses. Pour the zabaglione over the fruit and serve.

Yield: 6 servings

TINA'S TIDBITS

- *Egg yolks are used for flavor and as a coloring and thickening agent in sauces and baked goods.*
- *Using a whisk while the sauce is cooking incorporates air into the yolks, and the yolks cook in their volumized state, creating the light, airy consistency.*

TURKEY AND THE OTTOMAN EMPIRE

For almost three thousand years there has been a Jewish presence in the region of the world now associated with Turkey. At one time the Ottoman Empire encompassed lands from the Persian Gulf in the east to Hungary, Bulgaria, and Greece in the northwest, and from Egypt and Palestine in the south to the Caucasus mountains in the north, with Istanbul designated its capital. According to the famous Jewish historian Josephus, the great Greek philosopher Aristotle met with Jews on a trip throughout western Asia.

During the Byzantine period Jews experienced great persecution in a heightened Christian environment. In 1453, however, the Ottomans conquered the region and bestowed many privileges on the Jews. Life was so good that a letter was sent from Rabbi Yitzchak Sarfati to Jewish communities in Europe encouraging them to leave the persecutions they were experiencing in Christian Europe and come to Turkey (Anatolia, as it was called then). The Jews were encouraged to live in Constantinople and set up their own governing communities.

When the Jews were expelled in 1492 from Spain, Sultan Bayazid II actively encouraged the immigration of the Spanish refugees to his shores. He is quoted as commenting that Ferdinand was not very wise, since he stripped Spain of all its assets when he expelled the Jews. Turkey prospered, and so did the people in the Jewish communities of Constantinople, Izmir, Safed, and Salonika. In 1856 the Ottoman Empire established equality for all citizens of its country. This meant that the Jews no longer governed themselves but were part of the greater civic community.

The twentieth century brought some difficult times to this region. The Ottoman Empire declined after siding with the Germans during World War I, and the rise of anti-Semitic activities led many Jews to move to Western Europe, the Americas, and Palestine, which became a British mandate after World War I. However, those Jews left behind during World War II were protected due to Turkey's hard-won neutrality. Although Turkey's diplomats fought to save their Jewish citizens from camp deportation while they were in Nazi-occupied territories, a shipload of Romanian Jewish émigrés on their way to Palestine were denied asylum when their ship broke down, and the ship sank into the Black Sea, killing all but one of the 769 passengers.

Today the rich heritage of the Sephardic Jews is still felt in Turkey, though only twenty-six thousand remain to carry on their rich, ancient traditions.

Rachel Amado Bortnick, a Sephardic historian, Ladino instructor, and the founder of the online group Ladinokomunita (a virtual community made up of over nine hundred Ladino-speaking members worldwide, found at www.sephardicstudies.org/komunita), sat with me in her kitchen and related stories from her childhood in Izmir, Turkey. A descendant of Spanish Jews on both sides of her family, her history mirrored countless textbooks on post-expulsion migration. The Amado family migrated from Spain, probably to Portugal and then to Bayonne, where they lived for at least two centuries before moving to Izmir in the eighteenth century. Her mother's side of the family was named Algranti, which means "from Granada."

Growing up in Izmir meant picking a young, green almond fruit off the tree in the yard, sprinkling it with a little salt and biting into its slightly tart fruit. In the center was a viscous sweet gel where the almond nut had not yet begun to form. Figs were so large that they were peeled to reveal their purple fruit. Izmir apricots tasted like no other in the world, and that's why most of the large dried apricots produced in Turkey come from there. All varieties of melons abounded and were there for the choosing. Is it any wonder that the only definition of dessert on an Izmir table was fruit?

The meal consisted of three courses, with a variety of small vegetables or salads always served on the side. This is very typical of this region of the world. Shabbat meals always started with fish in lemon sauce.

The first course would be the vegetable course, which was the vehicle for any protein on the menu. *Irviya kon gayina*, for example, is peas with chicken. The chicken is listed second, implying that you will find small pieces of chicken supplementing the peas and other vegetables rather than the other way around. Chicken was rarely served except on Shabbat and special occasions. Lamb was the more common meat used in the mostly vegetarian community.

The second course consisted of a rice or noodle dish. Sometimes a little of the first course was added to the rice, but generally this was eaten unadulterated with the salads on the side.

The third course was always fruit. Apples were served peeled, as were oranges and tangerines. Rachel demonstrated how to present an orange. The finished product looked like an orange on a decorative stand. See instructions on page 95. Fruits were always served without sauce.

Sweets, many of which Turkey is famous for, are never served at meals. They are for entertaining and snacking.

LIPTAUER CHEESE

Liptauer cheese is actually a sheep's milk cheese from the Liptauer province in Hungary. However, in most German-speaking regions of Europe, Liptauer refers to a cheese highly flavored with herbs and seasoned and colored with the indigenous sweet paprika that Hungary is known for producing.

¼ pound cottage cheese
4 ounces cream cheese
½ stick unsalted butter
1 tablespoon gin
1 teaspoon anchovy paste
½ teaspoon dry mustard

1 tablespoon caraway seeds
1 tablespoon *fresh* Hungarian sweet paprika
Salt and pepper to taste
1 tablespoon capers
2 tablespoons chopped chives

1. Place the cottage cheese in a processor work bowl, and pulse on and off until relatively smooth.

2. Add the cream cheese and butter to the work bowl, and process until the butter-cheese mixture is thoroughly combined. You might need to stop and scrape down the sides of the bowl a few times until the mixture is smooth.

3. Add the gin, anchovy paste, dry mustard, caraway seeds, paprika, and salt and pepper, and process until well combined.

4. Add the capers and pulse on and off 10 times to distribute them evenly.

5. Spoon into a serving bowl and refrigerate for at least a few days to "ripen."

6. Just before serving, fold in the chopped chives and mound on a plate or shape into a ball. Chill until firm.

Yield: 1 cheese ball, 8–10 servings

TINA'S TIDBITS

- *The major flavor component in gin is juniper berries.*
- *One teaspoon of anchovy paste is equal to 4 canned anchovies.*
- *Unless you can buy paprika in very small quantities, it is best to store your paprika in the freezer to retain its flavor and color.*

Ottoman Watermelon and Olive Salad

I first tasted this wonderful combination of flavors on the island of Santorini in the Adriatic Sea. As bright as the iconic sun-drenched, white stucco walls and blue domed rooftops are on this island, this dish is vibrant with color and flavor to match its surroundings. Enjoy this dish any time of year but especially when watermelon is at its sweetest!

3 cups watermelon, cut into ½-inch cubes
1 very small red onion, cut into thin rings (or ½-cup sliced half rings)
½ cup pitted Calamata olives
½ cup crumbled feta cheese
¼ cup extra virgin olive oil

2 tablespoons lemon juice
Salt and freshly ground pepper to taste
Pinch of sugar
2 tablespoons chiffonade of fresh mint
1 teaspoon sumac (optional)

1. Arrange the watermelon, onion rings, and olives on a platter. Sprinkle with the crumbled feta cheese.

2. Combine the olive oil, lemon juice, salt, pepper, and sugar together in a small, screw-top jar.

3. Sprinkle the mint over the platter, and drizzle the vinaigrette over the salad.

4. Dust the salad with the sumac and serve.

Yield: 4–6 servings

TINA'S TIDBITS

- *If preparing the salad in advance, keep ingredients in separate bowls so that the flavor of the onions doesn't overpower the other ingredients.*
- *It is important to dress the salad (pour dressing on it) at the last minute so that the watermelon won't absorb the liquid and become mushy.*
- *Sumac is a red berry grown on bushes throughout the Middle East whose flavor is tart like a lemon. Paprika may be substituted for color, but the flavor will be different.*

ORZO WITH DRIED CHERRIES

Orzo is more closely associated with Greece and the Ottoman Empire, but it is actually a form of pasta that in Italian means "barley," because of its shape. All the flavorful ingredients in this recipe belie the delicate taste of the finished product.

1 cup orzo
¼ teaspoon crumbled saffron threads
4 teaspoons grated orange zest
4 tablespoons orange juice
Salt to taste

1 tablespoon hazelnut oil
¼ cup dried cherries or raisins
2 tablespoons lightly toasted, coarsely chopped
   hazelnuts or slivered almonds
1 scallion, thinly sliced

1. Bring 2 quarts salted water to a boil. Add the saffron and the orzo, and cook for 7–10 minutes or until orzo is al dente. Drain, rinse under cold water, and drain well. Place orzo in a serving bowl.

2. In a small bowl, combine the orange zest, juice, and salt to taste. Whisk the hazelnut oil into the juice mixture until it is incorporated.

3. Toss the dressing with the orzo, and add the cherries, almonds, and scallion. Serve at room temperature.

Yield: 6 servings

TINA'S TIDBITS

- *Dijon mustard (1/4 teaspoon) can be added to the zest and juice before the oil is added. The mustard will help bind the oil to the juice, creating an emulsion. This will make a more uniform sauce for the orzo.*
- *Pasta will break down and become mushy if mixed with a high-acid food for a prolonged period of time, so don't make this dish more than a few hours in advance of serving.*

Ottoman Tsatsiki
(Cucumber Yogurt Dip)

All tsatsikis are not created equal. Eaten as a side salad on a tray of mezes or as a dip with pita chips, this authentic recipe bears no resemblance to the packaged variety in the supermarket.

1 large cucumber
1 cup Greek yogurt or ½ cup unflavored yogurt and
  ½ cup sour cream
2 cloves garlic, coarsely chopped
1 tablespoon olive oil

Lemon juice to taste (2–3 teaspoons)
Salt (very little) and freshly ground black pepper to
  taste
2 tablespoons chopped fresh dill or mint

1. Peel the cucumber and cut it in half lengthwise. Remove the seeds from both halves.

2. Coarsely cut half of the cucumber and place in a processor work bowl. Cut the other half into ¼-inch dice. Set aside.

3. Add the yogurt and the garlic to the work bowl with the cucumber, and pulse on and off until the mixture is coarsely smooth and there are no large pieces of garlic floating around.

4. Pour the mixture into a bowl and add the olive oil, lemon juice, salt, pepper, and dill or mint.

5. Add the diced cucumber, reserving 1 tablespoon for garnish. Stir to combine well. Pour into a serving bowl. Garnish with the remaining diced cucumber and possibly a sprig of dill. Serve with lavash crackers or toasted pita.

Yield: 4 or more servings

TINA'S TIDBITS

- *In most recipes using cucumber, the seeds should always be removed to prevent a very watery finished product.*
- *The easiest way to remove cucumber seeds is to cut the cucumber in half lengthwise and run the tip of a spoon down the middle, scraping the seeds away.*
- *Commercially prepared American yogurt does not have the same consistency as Greek or Middle Eastern yogurt. Greek yogurt must be used so that the final mixture won't be thin and watery. If necessary, sour cream may be substituted as per recipe.*

MAMALIGA
(ROMANIAN POLENTA)

When corn was introduced to Europe after the discovery of the New World, it was widely received. However, growing conditions were not favorable in many regions, and colloquial biases to certain grains such as oats or rye diminished interest in corn. The Romanians loved the corn and the porridge made from its grain, mamaliga. *The Jewish community subsisted on the cornmeal porridge morning, noon, and night, adding slightly different ingredients to each meal to vary the taste. The love for* mamaliga *was so great that Romanian Jews were referred to as "Mamaligas" long after they crossed the Atlantic.*

2 cups milk, preferably whole or 2%
2 cups water, divided use
1 cup polenta or coarse corn meal
$\frac{1}{2}$ teaspoon salt, or to taste (depends on saltiness of feta)
10 grindings of fresh white pepper

2 tablespoons butter (salted butter is okay if desired)
2 ounces feta cheese, drained and crumbled
$\frac{1}{2}$ cup small-curd 4% fat cottage cheese
2 tablespoons finely grated Parmesan cheese
Sour cream (optional)

1. Heat 2 cups of milk and 1 cup of water in a microwave oven for $1\frac{1}{2}$ minutes. Set aside.

2. Combine 1 cup polenta with 1 cup of water, salt, and pepper in a 2-quart saucepan.

3. Add the hot liquid to the polenta mixture and place over medium heat, stirring constantly with a whisk for about 7 minutes, until the milk has been absorbed by the meal. The mixture will feel thick but still runny. Remove from the heat.

TINA'S TIDBITS

Variations on this recipe include:
- *Use all water and pareve margarine and serve with stews or pot roast.*
- *Add cream cheese instead of feta and 2 tablespoons of sugar and even add some raisins for a sweet, but not traditional, alternative.*
- *At Walter Potenza's restaurant I first tried the following polenta fritters stuffed with anchovy paste. Joyce Goldstein, in her book* Cucina Ebraica, *calls them* Rebecchine de Gerusalemme. *Using this recipe for* mamaliga, *the fritters are even more rich and delicious.*
  1. *Place one tin of anchovy fillets with the oil in the can in a small frying pan, and cook over low heat, mashing the anchovies into a paste.*
  2. *Cut slices from the* mamaliga *that are 1/2-inch thick and as wide as they are tall.*
  3. *Carefully slice each square in half so that each side is 1/4-inch thick.*
  4. *Spread a little anchovy paste over one half, and sandwich both sides together.*
  5. *Beat 1 egg with 1 teaspoon of water in a shallow bowl, and cover a plate with 1/2 cup of flour.*
  6. *Heat a frying pan for 20 seconds. Add 1/4 inch of oil in the pan, and heat for another 10 seconds.*
  7. *Dip the polenta squares in the egg to moisten, and coat thoroughly with the flour.*
  8. *Add coated squares to the frying pan 3 or 4 at a time, and fry over moderately high heat until the squares are crisp and lightly golden. Remove from oil, drain on paper towel, and serve immediately or when still warm.*
  9. *Serves 4–6 if you don't use all of the* mamaliga *and don't double the anchovies.*

4. Stir in the butter, crumbled feta, and cottage cheese. Mix until butter has melted and cheeses are evenly distributed throughout the mixture.

5. Preheat an oven to 350°F.

6. Grease an 8-inch square baking dish. Stir the cornmeal to break up any lumps, and pour mixture into pan. Smooth top and sprinkle with the Parmesan cheese.

7. Bake for 30 minutes or until top is golden brown. Serve immediately or at room temperature, or chill and cut into slices and brown in butter in a frying pan. Serve as is or topped with a little sour cream.

Yield: 16 2-inch X 2-inch pieces

TURKISH STUFFED GRAPE LEAVES

At the end of the grape harvest, the leaves are washed and brined to preserve them for later use. Ottoman and Middle Eastern Jewish cooks made use of everything that was available to feed their families regardless of their wealth. Since most meals consisted of little meat and copious amounts of vegetables and fruit along with starch, stuffed grape leaves were an important addition to any meal or party. This recipe is vegetarian, and the addition of the cinnamon and allspice along with the raisins and pine nuts hints strongly of its Sephardic roots in Spain, with its Moorish influence.

2 tablespoons olive oil
2 medium onions, chopped
1 clove garlic, minced
One 8-ounce jar grape leaves in brine
1 cup uncooked long grain rice plus 2 cups water
3 tablespoons toasted pignoli nuts (pine nuts)
4 scallions, finely chopped
2 tablespoons minced fresh dill
2 tablespoons finely chopped Italian parsley
2 tablespoons minced fresh mint
½ teaspoon cinnamon

½ teaspoon allspice
3 tablespoons raisins
1 teaspoon kosher salt
¼ teaspoon freshly ground pepper or to taste
⅔ cup olive oil
 cup lemon juice
⅔ cup water, plus additional as needed during cooking
1 teaspoon sugar
Broken grape leaves or lettuce leaves for the bottom of the pot

1. Heat 2 tablespoons olive oil in a large skillet, and sauté the onion for 5 minutes. Add the garlic and sauté until onions are lightly golden. Place mixture in a 2-quart mixing bowl.

2. Soak the separated grape leaves in a bowl of warm water for 5 minutes while you make the filling.

3. Combine the rice with the 2 cups water, and microwave on high for 5 minutes. Drain.

4. Toast pine nuts in a 350°F oven for 3–4 minutes until lightly golden.

5. Add the rice, scallions, dill, parsley, mint, cinnamon, allspice, pine nuts, and raisins to the onion mixture. Season with the salt and pepper.

6. Remove the leaves from the bowl of water and rinse under cold running water. Separate the leaves and place shiny side down on a board. If the leaves are small, place two together.

7. Remove any stems from the leaves.

8. Place 2 teaspoons of the rice mixture near the stem end of the leaves. Fold leaf over filling once. Fold in sides and then proceed to tightly roll up leaf until the end to make a neat roll.

9. Place some broken vine leaves or lettuce leaves in the bottom of a 4-quart Dutch oven so the rolls won't stick to the bottom of the pot. Arrange the rolls in the pot seam side down.

10. Combine the remaining ⅔ cup oil, lemon juice, ⅔ cup of the water, and sugar, and pour over the rolls in the Dutch oven.

11. Place a heavy plate or a plate and some weights on top of the rolls, and simmer 40 minutes.

12. Add the remaining water as needed, and cook for a total of 50 minutes or until the rice is tender.

13. Cool and serve at room temperature. May be refrigerated until later use, but bring to room temperature before serving, as olive oil will solidify in the refrigerator and the rolls will be hard to separate.

Yield: 3–4 dozen rolls

TINA'S TIDBITS

- *I find it helpful to partially cook the rice beforehand, thus preventing the possibility of crunchy, undercooked rice in the finished product.*
- *Toasting the pine nuts before adding to the filling significantly enhances the flavor of the filling.*
- *Do not substitute another nut for the pine nuts. Most nuts will be too hard and destroy the mouth feel of the finished product.*

TOMAT REYNADO
(TURKISH STUFFED TOMATOES)

When meat was expensive and difficult to come by, stuffing vegetables was a perfect way to extend the small amount of protein in a meal. Vegetables were plentiful and perfect vehicles for the meat. Here is a recipe that Rachel Bortnick described to me in her home; it was a family favorite.

1 pound ground beef
1 medium onion, grated
2 tablespoons fine semolina (quick cream of wheat is okay)
2 eggs, divided use
2 tablespoons chopped parsley
1 tablespoon finely chopped fresh basil (optional)

$\frac{1}{2}$ teaspoon salt
$\frac{1}{2}$ cup flour
Salt and freshly ground black pepper to taste
10 medium tomatoes
Pinch of salt and sugar
Extra virgin olive oil, as needed

1. Combine beef, onion, semolina, 1 slightly beaten egg, parsley, and basil in a 2-quart bowl. Mix first with a fork and then with your hands, but do not overhandle the mixture. Set aside.

2. Cut tomatoes in half. Remove and discard seeds. Hollow out tomato halves and reserve pulp. Salt interiors, turn upside down on paper towels, and pat dry.

3. Fill tomato halves with meat mixture.

4. Season flour with salt and pepper, and place in a small, shallow bowl.

5. Beat the remaining egg in another small, shallow bowl.

6. Heat a 10-inch frying pan over high heat for 15 seconds. Add enough oil to cover the bottom of the pan to a depth of $\frac{1}{4}$ inch. Reduce heat to medium high.

7. Dip the tops of the meat-filled tomato into the flour and then into the beaten egg.

8. Place the stuffed tomatoes floured side down into the hot oil, and fry for 1 minute until tops are golden brown.

9. Turn over tomatoes and arrange tomatoes with browned filling side up in an ovenproof dish.

10. Finely chop reserved tomato pulp Add pinch of salt and sugar to taste. Place some tomato mixture on top of each tomato.

11. Bake stuffed tomatoes in a 350° F oven for 10–15 minutes or until meat is firm and tomatoes still hold their shape.

Yield: 8–10 servings

TINA'S TIDBITS

- *Semolina is coarse grains of wheat. If there are no sources of finely ground grain in your area, use the quick, but not instant variety of cream of wheat cereal.*
- *Handle ground meat lightly to prevent the mixture from getting too dense.*
- *Use a less lean form of ground meat for this recipe so that the semolina can absorb the juices and swell, creating a moist, light filling.*

BULGARIAN BAKED CHICKEN WITH BARLEY

Delicious, comforting, and very easy to make, this is a classic Shabbat dish in Bulgaria and is transformed into a festive dish when served with agristada *(see page 86).*

1 chicken cut into eighths or 4 large breasts or
  thighs with skin and bone
1 onion, peeled but left whole
2 tablespoons extra virgin olive oil

1 cup pearled barley
Salt and pepper to taste
Lemon slices for garnish (optional)
Chopped parsley (optional)

1. Rinse chicken pieces under cold running water and place in a 4-quart saucepan.

2. Pierce the onion 6 times with the point of a sharp knife, and add it to the chicken. Cover ingredients with water, and add the oil.

3. Bring the chicken to a boil, and then partially cover and reduce heat so that the water just simmers. Cook until the chicken is tender, about 30–45 minutes.

4. Remove the chicken from the liquid, and keep warm and covered while you make the barley.

5. Pour the broth from the saucepan into a measuring cup and measure out $3\frac{1}{2}$ cups. If necessary, add some water. Place in a 2-quart saucepan.

6. Add the barley and cook, partially covered, over low heat for 25 minutes or until barley starts to swell but is still tough.

7. Lightly oil a baking dish large enough to hold the chicken in one layer but not larger than you need or the barley will dry out too much.

8. Place the barley and remaining cooking liquid in the baking dish, and top with the chicken, skin side up. Sprinkle chicken with salt and pepper, and bake in a preheated 350°F oven for 20 minutes or until the liquid has been absorbed and chicken skin has browned.

9. Garnish with the lemon slices or chopped parsley and serve.

Note: Delicious eaten as is, or serve with *agristada* (see page 86).

Yield: 4 servings

TINA'S TIDBITS

- *Chicken skin should not be removed before stewing, as it imparts a rich flavor to the broth. The fat can always be removed after chilling the broth, and the skin can later be removed from the meat.*
- *Pearled barley has had the bran removed and is steamed and polished.*

AGRISTADA
(EGG LEMON SAUCE)

Agristada is definitely an offshoot of the well-known avgolemeno sauce from Greece, to the south of Bulgaria. In this recipe whole eggs are used to lighten the intensity of the egg yolk flavor. I prefer this delicate flavor to the more metallic taste that can result when using solely egg yolks.

2 eggs
2 tablespoons extra virgin olive oil
2 tablespoons all-purpose flour
2 cups chicken broth (may be made from bouillon cube or canned)

2 tablespoons fresh lemon juice
Kosher salt and freshly ground pepper to taste
Zest of 1 lemon in long strips
1 tablespoon minced fresh parsley

1. Beat the eggs in a 1-quart bowl with the oil until combined.

2. In a small dish, combine the flour with enough chicken broth (about 3 tablespoons) to make a smooth paste, and slowly add to the eggs as you whisk the mixture.

3. Gradually add the remaining chicken broth and lemon juice, stirring constantly to combine.

4. Pour mixture into a 2-quart saucepan and stir constantly over medium heat until mixture thickens and coats the back of a spoon. Season to taste with salt and pepper.

5. Strain the mixture directly into a serving dish and serve warm, not hot, garnished with the lemon zest and parsley.

6. Serve over chicken or vegetables.

Yield: Approximately 2¼ cups, enough to sauce two cooked chickens.

TINA'S TIDBITS

- *There is no substitute for fresh lemon juice, so throw away the green bottle!*
- *Lemons should be stored at room temperature to yield the most juice. If refrigerated, microwave lemons for 25 seconds before juicing.*
- *Strain any type of custard mixture before pouring into serving containers or baking to remove thick egg-white strands that might have formed when adding liquid.*
- *To serve this sauce over fish, substitute fish or vegetable broth for the chicken broth.*
- *To produce a lighter, more ethereal sauce, separate the eggs and then whip the whites to a soft peak before folding them into the sauce.*

GREEK LAMB STEW

This is a dish representative of all the culinary influences of the region—spices from the Middle East, olives and oranges from the Mediterranean, and lamb from the hills. The only ingredient that makes this recipe more contemporary and less Jewish is the wine. In ancient times Jews didn't cook with wine.

½ cup golden raisins
½ cup plus 3 tablespoons cream sherry
2 pounds boneless lamb, cut in 1-inch cubes
1 cup fresh orange juice
4 cloves minced garlic
2–4 tablespoons extra virgin olive oil, as needed
1½ cups frozen pearl onions, defrosted
1 teaspoon saffron threads or ⅛ teaspoon powdered saffron
2 teaspoons ground coriander

2 teaspoons dried thyme
1½ teaspoons ground cumin
½ cup slivered almonds
1 tablespoon flour
½ cup dry red wine
Salt and freshly ground pepper to taste
3 medium tomatoes, seeded and cubed
½ cup halved, pitted Calamata olives
2 tablespoons fresh lemon juice

1. Soak the raisins in the ½ cup cream sherry for 1 hour or longer.

2. Marinate the lamb in the orange juice and garlic at least 2 hours at room temperature. Drain and reserve the marinade.

3. Heat 2 tablespoons of the olive oil in a Dutch oven and brown the lamb. Do not crowd the meat. Brown in two batches if necessary. Remove the lamb to a bowl with a slotted spoon.

4. Add the remaining 2 tablespoons of oil to the pan if pan is dry. Heat for 10 seconds. Add onions and sauté until a light golden brown. Add the spices and the almonds, and sauté for another 5 minutes.

5. Stir in the flour with a whisk and cook for 1 minute. Add the raisins with the sherry, the reserved marinade, and the red wine. Stir to mix, and season to taste with the salt and pepper.

6. Return the lamb to the pot, add the tomatoes and the olives, and cook until the meat is tender, about 1½ hours. If the sauce is too watery, remove meat from pot, boil sauce until preferred thickness, and then return meat to sauce.

7. Add the 3 remaining tablespoons of cream sherry and the lemon juice. Reheat all of the ingredients and serve.

Note: The stew can be made with dark chicken thigh meat instead of lamb.

Yield: 6–8 servings

TINA'S TIDBITS

- *I use cream sherry in recipes because the fortified liquor does not lose its flavor during cooking and it adds a richer flavor to the dish than does dry sherry.*
- *An acid food must always be present in a marinade, because it is the agent that tenderizes the meat.*
- *Be aware of the form of your saffron. If you are using the powdered form, 1/16 teaspoon is equivalent to a pinch of saffron strands!*

Greek Psari Saganaki

In Greece this dish is most often made with shrimp. To conform to the Jewish dietary laws that prohibit eating shellfish, I took the bright colors and flavors of this dish and incorporated fish indigenous to the waters around Greece in order to be able to serve it in my own home. Basically, that is how Jewish cooks throughout time have adapted local recipes for their kosher kitchens.

1 pound branzino fillets (about 2 fish) or tuna steaks
Juice of ½ lemon
4 tablespoons extra virgin Greek olive oil, divided use
1 medium onion, diced
2 large cloves garlic, peeled and cut in half
One 28-ounce can crushed tomatoes
½ teaspoon sugar

1 tablespoon fresh oregano, chopped
Salt and pepper to taste
1–2 tablespoons ouzo or other licorice liqueur (amount depends on your taste)
2 tablespoons Metaxa or other brandy
1 cup feta cheese, cubed

1. Place the fish fillets in a 7 × 11-inch glass dish. Add the lemon juice and coat the fish well. Set aside.

2. Heat 2 tablespoons of the olive oil in a 3-quart saucepan. Add the onion and halved garlic, and cook until lightly golden.

3. Add the crushed tomatoes, sugar, oregano, and salt and pepper to taste, and cook uncovered over moderate heat for 20 minutes or until thickened. Remove the pieces of garlic.

4. Heat a cast-iron skillet or heavy, uncoated sauté pan for 15 seconds. Add the remaining 2 tablespoons of olive oil and heat for another 15 seconds. Drain the fish. Season lightly with salt and pepper, and place in the hot skillet. Cook over moderately high heat for 2 minutes or until the fish is lightly golden on one side.

5. Turn the fish over, and add the ouzo and the brandy to the frying pan. Heat for 10 seconds and then ignite the liquids. When the flames die out, place the fish in a 2-quart ovenproof serving dish.

6. Cover the fish with the warm tomato sauce, and top with the cheese.

7. Place the dish in a preheated 400°F oven and bake until the cheese is melted but not browned. Serve with pasta or rice as desired.

Yield: 4 servings

TINA'S TIDBITS

- *Soaking fish in lemon juice imparts a subtle flavor to the meat, which will remain even after baking with a strongly flavored sauce. However, do not let the fish sit in the juice more than 15-30 minutes or the acid will start to "cook" the fish and make it tough.*
- *Brandy and liqueurs must be warm in order for them to ignite. However, if the liquid is heated too long, the alcohol content will burn off and no flame will be produced.*
- *If finishing a sautéed fish dish in the oven, make sure the initial cooking of the fish isn't too long or your completed dish will be tough and dry.*

KATAIFI WITH CREAM FILLING (KONOFA)

This is a multinational dish; kataifi dough is associated with Greece, while the dish is a popular dessert for special occasions in Egypt and Syria, according to the food historian and writer Claudia Roden. A few years ago I made this for a large Rosh Hashanah gathering at my home, and it has been one of the most requested desserts ever since. The Muslim community prefers to use a mild white cheese in the filling, but Jewish cooks prefer the rice flour–milk filling.

SYRUP:
2½ cups granulated sugar
1¼ cups water
Juice of ½ small lemon
2 tablespoons orange blossom water

FILLING:
¾ cup rice flour
5 cups milk
½ cup sugar
1 teaspoon vanilla extract
½ cup heavy cream

DOUGH:
1 pound *kataifi* dough, defrosted
½ pound unsalted butter, melted
½ cup chopped pistachios or walnuts for garnish (optional)

1. To make the syrup, boil the first 3 ingredients for 10 minutes. Add orange blossom water and cool completely in a shallow bowl in the refrigerator or freezer if you are in a hurry. Syrup **must** be cold but not frozen.

2. Mix the rice flour with enough milk to make a thin paste. Heat milk in a 2-quart saucepan until boiling. Add rice flour paste and mix with a whisk until smooth. Simmer over low heat for 15 minutes. Stir constantly at first, using a rubber spatula, until mixture thickens. Be careful not to let it burn on the bottom. Stir in sugar and vanilla when it is thick.

3. Place mixture in a bowl and cool for ½ hour. Add heavy cream when cool.

4. Place *kataifi* dough in a 4-quart bowl and carefully pull the strands apart. Pour the melted butter over the dough and lightly toss with fingers until all the strands are coated.

TINA'S TIDBITS

- *Do not attempt to substitute another starch for the rice flour. The flour not only thickens the mixture, but it imparts a taste reminiscent of rice pudding.*
- *In place of the orange blossom water, 1 1/2 teaspoons vanilla may be used to flavor the syrup. However, nothing compares in flavor to the orange blossom water, and a bottle will last for a very long time on your pantry shelf. Treat yourself—this ingredient is worth seeking out in the stores.*
- *Kataifi looks like shredded wheat and is actually phyllo dough that has been extruded into thin threads.*
- *If you can't find kataifi, use phyllo dough and assemble the mixture using layers of phyllo brushed with butter as for baklava (see pages 92-93).*

5. Spread half the dough in the bottom of a 13 × 9-inch baking dish. Spread the filling over the dough, and spread the remaining dough over the filling. Press down lightly with your palms.

6. Preheat oven to 350°F. Bake pastry for 1 hour. With pastry still in the oven, raise the temperature to 425°F and continue baking for 15 minutes or until lightly golden.

7. Remove from oven and immediately pour syrup over pastry. Run a knife along the sides of the pan to allow syrup to seep to the bottom.

8. Cut into squares, and serve warm or at room temperature.

Yield: 20–25 servings

Baklava

Baklava can be traced back to Assyria in the eighth century B.C.E., when it was originally made with a bread dough layered with some nuts and honey. Although it became popular throughout the Ottoman Empire and Syria, it is most associated with Greece. This may be because the Greeks invented phyllo dough, the dough used for construction of the baklava layers. Phyllo actually means "leaf," and the dough is, in fact, as thin as a leaf.

4 cups walnut pieces, almonds, pistachios, or a mix—depending on country of origin
1 cup sugar
$3/4$ teaspoon ground cinnamon
$1/8$ teaspoon ground cloves
1 pound phyllo dough
2–3 sticks melted unsalted butter

SYRUP:
1 cup water
$1\frac{1}{2}$ cups sugar
$1/2$ cup honey
1 cinnamon stick
2 strips of lemon zest, $1/2$ inch wide and length of lemon
1 tablespoon lemon juice

1. Place half of the nuts in a processor work bowl and pulse on and off until a fine texture. Place them in a medium bowl. Add the remaining nuts to the work bowl and repeat the procedure. Add the sugar, cinnamon, and cloves to the nuts. Mix well and set aside.

2. Butter a 13 × 9-inch baking pan.

3. The phyllo dough is folded in the box lengthwise before it is rolled. Unroll the dough. Take one of the sheets of dough and place it folded in the pan so that it fits perfectly. Open up the fold of the sheet of dough and brush the inside with butter. Refold the other half over the dough. You have just created two layers of dough. Brush the top of the dough with the melted butter, and place another sheet of folded dough on top. Open dough, brush with butter, and then close the "page." Do this 4 more times with 4 more full sheets of dough so that you have used a total of 6 sheets of dough.

4. Spread $1/3$ of the nut mixture on top. Layer 6 more folded sheets of dough using the previous method. Spread with $1/2$ of the remaining nut mixture.

5. Spread 6 more folded sheets of dough on top of this, making sure to brush the butter in between each layer. Top with the remaining nut mixture, and layer the remaining dough on the top. Brush the top with melted butter.

6. Score the top of dough with a sharp knife, making parallel lines $1\frac{1}{2}$ inches apart. Score on a diagonal again $1\frac{1}{2}$ inches apart. Make the cuts about $1/4$ inch deep.

7. Bake in a 325°F oven for 45–50 minutes or until golden. Meanwhile, make the syrup while the baklava is baking.

8. Combine all of the ingredients for the syrup in a saucepan, and heat for 30 minutes over a low heat to barely simmer. Remove from the heat and discard the cinnamon stick and lemon peel.

9. Allow the baklava to cool for 10 minutes, and then evenly pour the syrup over all of the pastry. Wait at least 30 minutes or until thoroughly cool, and cut completely through the dough to make the individual pieces. Place pieces on cupcake papers and serve.

Yield: 4–5 dozen pieces

TINA'S TIDBITS

- *Baklava is actually easy to make; just make sure you keep unused sheets of phyllo covered with plastic wrap and then with a damp towel. Don't let the damp towel come in contact with the dough, or it will get soggy and stick together.*
- *Most packages of phyllo have sheets that are about 13 inches wide and 18 inches long. If you place the edge of the short end of dough inside up against the long end of the pan, you can brush butter on that half sheet and then fold the rest of the phyllo over it to fit into the pan perfectly. This creates even layers of dough without having to fold the excess dough under and creating thick edges.*

SERVING FRESH ORANGES IN THE TURKISH STYLE

According to Rachel Bortnick, fresh fruit was the dessert of choice in Turkish homes. Sweets were relegated to snacks and entertaining. The following instructions for cutting and presenting an orange at a meal are from her hometown of Izmir.

1. Cut a small slice of rind off the bottom of the orange so that the orange will sit flat on a plate. Do not cut so deeply as to cut into the fruit.

2. Make 6–8 cuts from the top of the orange, through the peel to within ½ inch of the bottom of the orange.

3. Carefully separate each section of the peel away from the fruit. Do not remove it from the fruit or break the rind.

4. Gently roll each section of peel inwards toward the fruit to create a tight roll of peel at the base.

5. Repeat this technique with the remaining sections of peel. The finished product will look like the orange is nestled in a decorative base.

6. For added flair, gently separate each section so the orange looks like it is in bloom.

Yield: 1 serving

Borekitas kon Kalavasa (Bulgarian Squash-Filled Cookies)

The migration of the Sephardi culture is reflected in this recipe. Since the Moors brought squash from the Middle East, and Columbus introduced pumpkin from the New World, one can find squash recipes (mostly used in sweetened fillings for ravioli, borekas, and pastries) in communities that were established following the same routes that the Jews traveled when escaping the Inquisition.

Typical of most European pastries, these little filled cookies are not very sweet. They could be sprinkled with sugar before baking, but that is not the traditional method of preparation.

1¾ cups all-purpose flour
2 tablespoons granulated sugar
¼ teaspoon salt
1 stick unsalted butter
½ cup water
10 ounces frozen cubed butternut squash or 1 cup canned pumpkin

⅓ cup granulated sugar
½ cup finely ground (1⁄16-inch pieces) walnuts
½ teaspoon ground cinnamon
2 tablespoons unflavored dry bread crumbs
1 egg mixed with 1 tablespoon water
Sugar for topping (optional)

1. To prepare the dough, place flour, sugar, and salt in a 2-quart bowl and stir to combine.

2. Place the stick of butter in a 1-cup glass measuring cup and microwave on high for 45 seconds or until butter is melted. Add the water to the cup until the foam line comes to the 1-cup line.

3. Stir the butter-water mixture as you pour it into the bowl of flour.

4. Using a wooden spoon or spatula, quickly combine the flour-butter mixture until a smooth, slippery soft dough is formed.

5. Refrigerate dough for 15 minutes or longer while you prepare the filling.

6. Cook squash in the microwave for 4 minutes with no additional water.

7. Blot the squash dry with a towel, and mash with a fork until no lumps remain. You should have 1 cup cooked squash.

8. Combine the squash with the sugar, walnuts, cinnamon, and bread crumbs.

9. Remove dough from the refrigerator and roll out on a floured surface to about ⅛ inch thick. Cut 2- to 3-inch circles from the dough.

10. Place 1 teaspoon of filling in the center of each circle and fold dough over filling, matching edges and pressing down to seal with the side of your pinkie. Place on a parchment-lined cookie sheet.

11. Using the tines of a fork, crimp the pinched edges together to seal and make a decorative design. Bend the cookie slightly to form crescents.

12. Brush the tops of the cookies with the egg-water mixture, and if desired (but not traditional), sprinkle some additional sugar on top.

13. Bake in a preheated 375°F oven for 18–20 minutes or until golden. Makes about 2 dozen cookies.

Note: There will be some filling left over, which can be frozen for future use or used to stuff ravioli.

Yield: 2–3 dozen pastries

TINA'S TIDBITS

- *Squash can be very watery, so use only butternut squash or pie pumpkin to make this filling.*
- *Bread crumbs are often used in European baking to absorb excess liquid, whether it is in a filling or in between phyllo layers in a strudel.*
- *This dough is like the classic* pâte à choux, *or cream puff dough, except there are no eggs in this batter.*
- *Pressing edges of pastry with the tines of a fork is effective in creating a seal so the filling will not ooze out during baking.*

INDIA

India's Jews come from four distinct groups: the Bene Israel, the Cochin Jews, the Sephardic Jews from Europe, and the "Baghdadis" from Iraq. The Bene Israel and the Cochin Jews claim to be the longest Jewish inhabitants of India.

The "black" Cochin Jews (Cochin is a city in southwest India) are dark-skinned Jews who trace their ancestry to the lost ten tribes who came with King Solomon in search of spices. The "white" Cochin Jews were in India as early as the thirteenth century, coming from Spain and later from Portugal and Holland in search of spices and, judging from the time frame, probably to establish themselves far from the Inquisition. However, this group of Jews had to move from their original home in Cranganore to Cochin in the late fifteenth century to escape the wrath of Portuguese invaders. The maharajah welcomed the Jews to Cochin, and they settled in an area of the city that was called Jew Town. The name of the city remains the same to this day. The Cochin Jews were always involved in the spice trade. The Malabar Coast was certainly known for its pepper, but cinnamon, ginger, cloves, nutmeg, cardamom, and other spices also grew in the region. The division of labor saw the white Cochins directly involved with the trading of the spices and the black Cochin Jews more involved with the handling, curing, and manufacturing of the ground spice. Under the Dutch in the seventeenth and eighteenth centuries, the Cochin community flourished. When trade in the region of Cochin declined, its importance and its Jewish population diminished. Some Jews migrated north, but mostly they left for Israel.

The Bene Israel also claim that they are descendants of the ten tribes of Israel. Their ancestors were shipwrecked off the west coast of India on the Konkan Coast in the second century B.C.E. after escaping persecution in the Galilee region. According to legend, only seven couples survived, and their offspring were cut off from other Jewish communities until they were discovered in the eighteenth century by traders from Baghdad. Although they had assimilated into local communities, they maintained the practices of Jewish dietary laws, circumcision, and observance of Shabbat as a day of rest. In the early 1990s, Tudor Parfitt, a Jewish studies professor at London's School of Oriental and African Studies, initiated a research study examining the DNA of four thousand Bene Israel to see if information could corroborate the link to the ancient tribes of Israel. The study indicates they are probable descendants of Israelite *kohanim*.

The last group of Jews to arrive in India are the Baghdadi Jews. They established a trading network stretching from Syria and Baghdad to Bombay and Calcutta, all the way to Hong Kong and Japan. By the late eighteenth century, Bombay was home to the largest Jewish community in India, which included Bene Israel Jews as well as Iraqi and Persian Jews.

Although this is the last of the three major sects of Jews in India, the last migration to this country took place during and after World War II, with the

Eastern European Jews escaping the Holocaust. By the end of the 1940s, the Jewish population in India numbered some twenty-six thousand. After the war, the rise of Indian nationalism made it uncomfortable for the Jewish communities, which were closely associated with the British. Almost all Jews migrated to Israel, England, or the United States, leaving a handful of elderly Jews behind.

As in all Jewish communities around the world, Indian Jews translated their culinary tastes and the laws of kashrut to embrace the foods of the region. Living along the spice route meant that pepper, cinnamon, allspice, nutmeg, and cloves were readily used in their dishes. Hot peppers, especially green ones, figured prominently in Indian cuisine, as did coconut milk. The latter was utilized often in the Indian kosher kitchen, since there was no dairy in the coconut liquid and it could be used to enhance many meat dishes.

MANGO SALAD DRESSING

Indians are very fond of mangoes, which are in season only from March to May. They are so beloved that they preserve many of their mangoes in chutneys and pickles to enjoy long after the season is over. Here is a delicious dressing to use over any salad.

½ cup finely chopped mangoes
¼ cup rice wine vinegar
3 tablespoons oil

2 tablespoons honey
1 teaspoon chopped mint
1 teaspoon chives

1. Combine all ingredients in a screw-top jar and shake until combined.

2. Serve with mixed greens tossed with some nuts or dried fruit bits, like cherries or cranberries.

Yield: 1 cup dressing

TINA'S TIDBITS

- *Rice wine vinegar is not as tangy as other vinegars and makes a perfect base for a fruit-flavored dressing*
- *If you would like a smooth, slightly thick dressing, place the mangoes, vinegar, and honey in a food processor work bowl and pulse on and off 5 times or until the fruit is pureed. Slowly pour in the oil while the machine is running until an emulsion is formed. Add the mint and chives and pulse on and off 8 times, just until the herbs are chopped but not pureed.*

BENE ISRAEL SHABBAT CHICKEN CURRY

June Penkar lives in Dallas and was my personal guide to the cooking of the Bene Israel Jews from the west coast of India. Her great-grandfather was a justice in the maharajah's court, and her grandfather went to school with the princes. The Jews were never discriminated against and were allowed to prosper in India.

The different regions where her grandparents grew up influenced her culinary style; different regions emphasize different flavors and ingredients. The hallmark of Bene Israel cooking is the use of coconut milk, which is pareve, to thicken sauces and a good amount of garlic, ginger, onions, and tomatoes. Although garam masala is used throughout India, its use in Indian Jewish cooking is prominent. Chicken was the most common dish for Shabbat. The following recipes are all from my friend June, a wonderful woman, Hadassah president, and fantastic cook!

3 jalapeño peppers
2-inch piece of fresh ginger, peeled and cut into 6 pieces
5 large cloves of fresh garlic
1 bunch cilantro leaves and top stems
2 tablespoons oil
3 whole cardamom pods
3 whole cloves
2-inch stick of cinnamon, broken into two pieces
2 large onions, finely chopped (about 4 cups)
4 Roma tomatoes, seeded and chopped
2 tablespoons ground coriander

$\frac{1}{2}$ teaspoon turmeric
1 teaspoon ground cumin
3 pounds assorted chicken pieces, no wings
1 russet potato, peeled and cut into 12 chunks
Salt and freshly ground black pepper to taste
$\frac{1}{2}$ cup water or chicken bouillon
One 5.5-ounce can of coconut milk (about $\frac{1}{2}$–$\frac{3}{4}$ cup)
1–2 teaspoons prepared garam masala (Caution: All garam masala are not created equal. Some are so hot that $\frac{1}{2}$ teaspoon is more than enough. Taste a little first to decide what amount to use.)

1. Place the peppers, ginger, and garlic in a processor work bowl and pulse on and off until the contents are coarsely chopped. Add the cilantro and pulse on and off to create a coarse paste. Set aside.

2. Heat a large, deep frying pan for 20 seconds over high heat. Add the oil and heat for 15 more seconds. Do not allow the oil to smoke. Reduce the heat to medium high and add the whole cardamom, cloves, and cinnamon. Sauté for 1 minute or until the spices become fragrant.

3. Add the onion to the pan and sauté until golden brown.

4. Add $\frac{1}{4}$ cup (or more depending on how hot you like your curry) of the fresh jalapeño-cilantro paste to the pan and sauté for another 2 minutes.

5. Add the chopped tomatoes and the dried spices to the mixture and cook until the mixture looks fairly dry.

6. Remove all of the skin from the chicken parts, and add the chicken to the frying pan, making sure that you turn the chicken pieces around to coat with the onion-spice mixture. Add the potato pieces and do likewise.

7. Add salt and pepper to taste and $\frac{1}{2}$ cup water or bouillon, and stir gently to combine.

8. Cover the pan and cook over low heat for 30–45 minutes or until the chicken pieces are tender.

9. Remove chicken pieces to a platter. Add the coconut milk and garam masala to the pan and stir to thoroughly combine.

10. Return the chicken to the pan and cook for another 5–10 minutes to combine flavors.

11. Place chicken on a serving platter, pour sauce over, and serve with rice—preferably fragrant basmati rice.

Yield: 4–5 servings

TINA'S TIDBITS

- *When processing a mixture that contains a large quantity of green herbs, always process the herbs last. Overchopping in the processor brings out the chlorophyll taste in the herbs and makes your mixture taste "grassy."*
- *Always sauté your onions alone before adding other vegetables. The golden brown is the natural caramelizing of the sugars in the onion, which gives the onion its sweet taste. Sautéing with other vegetables initially will stew the onions and not bring out the sweetness.*
- *Nowadays chicken has more fat under the skin; therefore it is advisable to remove the skin before cooking.*
- *To seed a tomato, cut it open horizontally, hold it over the sink cut side down, and give a squeeze and a shake and it's seeded!*
- *The easiest way to cook rice: Combine water, salt (if using), and rice in covered glass casserole. Microwave on high for 5 minutes, on medium for 15 minutes, and then let sit for 5 minutes. That's it!*

Nirvana Chicken Wings

I call these wings "nirvana" because they could transport you to paradise. They are easy to make, messy to eat, and loads of fun—a modern interpretation of Indian cuisine that's far from "Shabbat chicken."

4 tablespoons pareve margarine
2 tablespoons curry powder
¼ cup dry white wine
2–3 pounds chicken drummettes

1 cup mango chutney
¼ cup shredded coconut
1 tablespoon finely chopped scallion
2 tablespoons finely chopped peanuts

1. Melt the margarine in a saucepan, and stir in the curry powder. Cook for 2–3 minutes, and add the wine. Remove from heat.

2. Remove any excess fat from the chicken parts. Wash and pat dry. If using whole wings, discard the tip and cut the two-bone section and drummette apart.

3. Place the chicken parts in a roasting pan, and baste with the curry sauce. Bake for 20 minutes in a 350°F oven.

4. Chop up any large pieces of mango in the chutney, and spread the chutney over the chicken parts. Bake for 30 minutes or until chicken is tender.

5. Place the chicken on a serving platter, and pour sauce into a 1-quart saucepan. Reduce the sauce by one-third over moderate heat.

6. Pour the sauce over the chicken, and sprinkle with the coconut, scallions, and peanuts. Serve.

Note: May be made in advance and reheated in the microwave or oven. Garnish with the coconut, scallion, and peanuts only after reheating and before serving.

Yield: 8–10 servings as an appetizer

TINA'S TIDBITS

- *Classic Indian cooking technique calls for cooking the spice for a brief period to bring out the flavor. However, when working with powder, be very careful not to brown the spices or they will taste bitter.*
- *It is not necessary to remove the tip or third portion of the chicken wing if you are serving the wings in a casual setting with lots of napkins. Cut them into drummettes and wing sections for a more formal cocktail party as instructed above.*

Curried Turkey and Rice (with Vegetarian Option)

This recipe incorporates all the components of an Indian curry dish, including the accompaniments. However, this is a creation from my own kitchen at a time when I had leftover turkey and all cookbooks called for milk or cream as the base of the sauce. As our ancestors did, I tweaked an established recipe to conform to the dictates of kashrut, and a new recipe was born.

4 tablespoons pareve margarine (or butter if vegetarian)
1 onion, diced
1/3 cup flour
1 tablespoon curry powder or to taste
3/4 teaspoon salt
2 cups chicken broth or vegetable substitute
2 cups diced cooked turkey, extra firm tofu, or assorted cooked vegetables

1 cup frozen peas, defrosted (optional)
Raisins
Peanuts
Coconut
Chutney
1 cup basmati, jasmine, or long-grain rice
2 cups water
1 teaspoon salt

1. Melt the margarine or butter in a 2-quart saucepan.

2. Add the diced onion and sauté until the onion is golden.

3. Whisk in the flour, curry powder, and salt until well combined (about 20 seconds).

4. Add the broth slowly but steadily while you whisk the mixture. Keep whisking until the mixture begins to bubble and thickens. Add the turkey, tofu, or vegetables.

5. Reduce the heat and add the peas, if using.

6. Serve the mixture with rice (see recipes below), and top with the other ingredients if desired.

Yield: 4 servings

Basic Method for Cooking Rice

1. Combine 1 cup rice with 2 cups water and 1 teaspoon salt in a 3-quart saucepan.

2. Bring the rice mixture to a boil. Cover the pot, reduce the heat to low, and cook for 20 minutes or until all the water has been absorbed. Serve.

Microwave Method for Cooking Rice

1. Combine 1 cup of rice with 2 cups of water and 1 teaspoon of salt in a 2-quart covered glass casserole. Place in microwave oven and heat for 5 minutes on high.

2. Gently swirl mixture in casserole, return to microwave, and cook on medium power for 15 minutes. Let casserole sit for 5 minutes before removing cover and tossing rice with a fork to fluff. Serve.

TINA'S TIDBITS

- *Curry is actually a combination of many spices. Use a good-quality curry powder from a reputable source if you are not going to make your own mixture.*
- *A velouté sauce is a white sauce that uses chicken, beef, or vegetable stock in place of milk or cream.*
- *Unflavored liquid soy creamer may also be used as a milk substitute for a pareve sauce.*

CURRIED LENTILS AND VEGETABLES

The British, Dutch, and Portuguese traders sailed the spice trade route starting in the South China Sea, with major stops in the Moluccas (Spice Islands) for nutmeg, mace, and cloves, to Sri Lanka and the Malabar Coast on the southwestern tip of India, where cinnamon and black pepper were exclusively grown. These spices plus the chilies and cardamom from inland routes were the basis of many curry spice blends of the region.

1 cup red lentils
2 tablespoons olive oil
2 medium onions, chopped
1 tablespoon minced garlic
1 teaspoon ground coriander
1 teaspoon ground cumin
1 teaspoon turmeric
½ teaspoon chili powder
¼ teaspoon ground cardamom
2 good pinches of ground cloves
¼ teaspoon cinnamon
4 ounces sliced mushrooms

3 yellow crookneck squash, sliced
2 carrots sliced
1 cup vegetable broth
One-half 6-ounce can tomato paste
Salt and freshly ground black pepper to taste
One 8-ounce can chickpeas, drained
½ cup roasted peanuts (optional)
3 cups cooked basmati or jasmine rice (1 cup raw rice + 2 cups water)
½ cup unflavored yogurt (thick Greek yogurt is best) (optional)

1. Boil lentils in enough water to cover for 15 minutes or until they are soft but not mushy. Set aside.

2. Heat the oil in a 3-quart saucepan and sauté the onion and garlic over medium heat until the onions are soft but the garlic does **not** brown.

3. Add the spices and the vegetables and sauté for 3 minutes.

4. Add the broth, tomato paste, and salt and pepper to taste. Add the chickpeas. Cover and simmer for 8 minutes or until vegetables are tender.

5. Drain the lentils and add to the vegetables. Add the nuts and serve over the rice with the yogurt if desired.

Yield: 4–6 servings

TINA'S TIDBITS

- *Different varieties of lentils vary little in flavor, but the color choice enhances this recipe.*
- *Curry is not a single spice but a mixture of many. This recipe includes the individual spices and creates a wonderful flavor not equaled by store-bought mixtures. In an emergency, 1 1/2 to 2 tablespoons of Madras curry powder may be substituted.*
- *Basmati and jasmine rice add a subtle nutty flavor to your dish. White or brown rice may be substituted, but "converted" or polished rice should never be used as it will not absorb the flavors appropriately.*

INDIAN COCONUT RICE PUDDING

Here's another recipe I adapted from June Penkar. This is a perfect dessert for a meat meal or for anyone who is lactose intolerant. There is no butter or milk in this recipe, but this dish is still creamy and delicious, especially if you like a subtle hint of coconut flavor.

½ cup basmati rice
½ cup water
One 13.5-ounce can coconut milk
2 cans of water
¾–1 cup sugar

Large pinch of kosher salt
½ cup raisins, optional
Powdered cardamom
Toasted sliced almonds for garnish (optional)

1. Combine the rice and ½ cup water in a small glass bowl, and microwave on high for 2 minutes.

2. Pulse the partially swelled rice and any remaining water in a processor 10 times until grainy.

3. Place the rice in a 3-quart saucepan, add the coconut milk, and stir. Fill the empty can twice with water and add it to the rice.

4. Cook over medium-high heat until mixture begins to boil. Add the sugar, salt, and raisins to the pot, and reduce heat to a simmer. Stir every 5 minutes to prevent scorching the rice. Cook the mixture for 30–40 minutes or until the liquid is reduced enough to see the grains of rice on the surface of the pudding.

5. Transfer pudding to a serving casserole or individual dishes. Sprinkle surface of the rice pudding with cardamom, and add the toasted sliced almonds if using. Serve warm or at room temperature.

Yield: 6–8 servings

TINA'S TIDBITS

- *For a more American version, add 1 teaspoon vanilla extract to the finished pudding and sprinkle cinnamon on top.*
- *Brown basmati rice may be used for this recipe. Cover rice with 1 cup of water before microwaving on high for 5 minutes, and then proceed with the remaining directions.*
- *According to June, this pudding gets more liquid if refrigerated and does best if allowed to remain at room temperature. I suggest that you refrigerate after a day.*
- *Rice pudding will always appear more liquid when hot, so don't overcook unless you want to re-create your grandmother's version that gets cut with a knife into squares!*

JEWISH TRADERS ON THE SPICE ROUTE

"Worth your weight in gold" might be a compliment today, but in ancient times "worth your weight in salt" would mean a financial windfall for the recipient. Spices of all sorts were in such demand that they were often used as currency. The word "salary" derives from the salt payment that was given to Roman soldiers, and

the Visigoths demanded three thousand pounds of pepper as partial payment for sparing Rome in the fifth century. Salt was the only method of food preservation in ancient times. Spices such as pepper, cinnamon, and cloves were necessary to make the food palatable and counteract the saltiness.

Jews played a significant role in the spice trade as early as biblical times (tenth century B.C.E.). Chapters 5 and 10 of I Kings recount Solomon's inheritance from King David of vast lands that gave him control of the major trade routes between Egypt, Mesopotamia, and Anatolia (often referred to as the Kings Highway) and routes to the southern Arabian peninsula, where the vast majority of spices were traded. His three-year trade expedition with Hiram, as told in I Kings, referred to a long sea voyage from Ezion-Geber (near Eilat) to the island of Chryse, somewhere in the Indian Ocean east of the Ganges River, to seek out spices. The hardships and dangers encountered on long expeditions over sea and land made the transport very costly and the price of spices very expensive, but it only fueled the desire for the exotics more. This desire ushered in the age of exploration. Christopher Columbus—often thought to be a Converso—set sail on the last days of the Jewish expulsion from Spain in 1492.

The Portuguese explorer Vasco da Gama sailed east for a quick route to the Spice Islands in 1497, and Magellan sailed across the Pacific for similar reasons in 1521. During the fourteenth and fifteenth centuries, Jews were restricted from oversees trade. However, the Italians soon replaced Christian intermediary traders with Jews, which moved the Jewish traders back into the spice trade with the Orient.

The Inquisition sent many Jews and "New Christians" to Amsterdam, South America, and the West Indies. From the mid-sixteenth century to the late eighteenth century, Jews who settled in Amsterdam built a trading empire on a scale that was unimaginable in the past. Their business acumen made a significant contribution to the colonial expansion of the Dutch Empire in the seventeenth century. In the mid-1600s the Jewish Mendes family (former Conversos from Spain and Portugal) built a commercial fortune controlling the major portion of the pepper and spice trade in Northern Europe. During this period Jews were actively trading in spices from Yemen, India, and the Dutch East Indies to Europe and the New World. The Mendes family was one of the first Sephardic families to grow and prosper in New

York, Philadelphia, and Newport, based on its trading skills with Jews in Holland.

The flavors of cinnamon, cloves, pepper, and ginger can be found in many recipes prepared in Jewish homes throughout the Diaspora and especially in major trading centers such as Aleppo in Syria, Cochin in India, the Moluccas Islands in Dutch East India (Indonesia), Cape Town in South Africa, and Amsterdam.

SPICE ROUTE NASI GORENG

The first time I ate nasi goreng *(Indonesian fried rice) was at the Bali Restaurant in Amsterdam, and it was one of many dishes on a* rijsttafel *or "rice table." The Dutch adopted the style of offering many dishes on a table that resembled a Ferris wheel during their occupation of Indonesia at the height of their involvement in the spice trade from the late seventeenth century.*

I have combined the basic concept of nasi goreng *with the spices from Indonesia and the west coast of Africa near Elmina, the major Dutch trading port in west Africa that sent spices, gold, palm oil, and timber to Europe and the New World.*

2 cups basmati or medium-grain rice
3½ cups chicken broth
¼ cup oil
2 medium onions, cut into ½-inch dice
3 cloves garlic, minced

2 cups cooked chicken or leftover turkey, julienned
2 tablespoons *tsire* (see recipe below)
4 tablespoons peanut butter, chunky or smooth
¼ pound *merguez* (lamb sausage), Italian sausage, or smoked turkey, cubed

1. Combine the rice and the broth in a large saucepan and bring to a boil. Reduce the heat, cover, and simmer for 20 minutes.

2. Spread the cooked rice on a rimmed cookie sheet to cool and dry for 1 hour. May be placed, uncovered, in the refrigerator to cool faster.

3. Make the *tsire* peanut and spice mix (see recipe below). Set aside.

4. Heat a wok or 4-quart pot over medium-high heat for 20 seconds. Add the oil and heat for another 15 seconds. Sauté the onion over medium heat for 5 minutes, and add the garlic and sauté 5 minutes more or until the onions are lightly golden. Do not burn the garlic.

5. Add the rice, and stirring constantly, cook the rice for 5 minutes or until it is lightly browned.

6. Add the prepared *tsire*, peanut butter, and meats to the pot, and cook over low heat for 10 minutes or until heated through. Stir occasionally.

TSIRE PEANUT AND SPICE MIX

10 cloves
½ teaspoon whole allspice (about 30)
2-inch piece of cinnamon stick
½ teaspoon red chili flakes
½ teaspoon ginger
½ teaspoon ground nutmeg
½ teaspoon salt
½ cup dry roasted or cocktail peanuts

1. Heat a small frying pan or saucepan for 15 seconds. Add the cloves, allspice, and cinnamon and stir until the spices become fragrant. Remove from heat, cool, and grind the spices to a powder in a spice grinder or mortar and pestle. Place in a small processor work bowl.

2. Add the remaining spices and the peanuts to the work bowl and process until finely chopped.

Yield: 6–8 servings

TINA'S TIDBITS

- *Fully cooked deli chicken or turkey can be sliced 1/2-inch thick at the market counter, and then you can easily cut it into 1/2-inch cubes at home.*
- *Six cups of leftover rice (save the containers of Chinese takeout rice!) can be substituted, but you will not have the added flavor of the chicken broth.*
- *Store dark spices in your freezer to preserve their flavor, especially if you don't use certain varieties very often.*

SYRIAN SPICED MEAT WITH EGGPLANT AND PRUNES

The English traders would sail the spices across the Arabian Sea up the Gulf of Suez to the Mediterranean to Syria and Turkey. The major center of trade connecting the spice trade route of the sea with the Silk Road over land was in Syria and Turkey. Aleppo, in northern Syria, had a large Jewish population involved with trade, and the Jewish women of that city were renowned for their culinary abilities.

2 pounds ground chuck meat
2 teaspoons ground allspice
2 teaspoons ground cinnamon
1 teaspoon kosher salt
Pepper to taste
3 tablespoons corn or canola oil
6 medium onions, halved lengthwise and cut into fourths crosswise
4 large red potatoes, halved lengthwise and cut into 1-inch slices
12 ounces pitted prunes

1 large eggplant, quartered lengthwise and cut into 1-inch slices
Two 6-ounce cans of regular tomato paste (not flavored)
¼ cup light brown sugar
¾ cup fresh lemon juice
1 tablespoon Worcestershire sauce
½ tablespoon tamarind concentrate (optional), available in Asian markets
Salt and pepper to taste

1. In a 2-quart bowl, combine the ground meat with the allspice, cinnamon, salt, and pepper. Distribute the spices evenly by first mixing with a fork and then with your hands.

2. Place the oil in the bottom of a 6-quart Dutch oven or metal casserole.

3. Place half of the onion slices in the bottom of the pot, and cover with half of the meat, making sure that you press the meat evenly and firmly into the onions.

4. Scatter half of the potatoes, prunes, and eggplant over the meat.

5. Repeat with the remaining onions, seasoned meat, potatoes, prunes, and eggplant.

6. In a 3-quart bowl, combine the tomato paste with the remaining ingredients along with salt and pepper to taste into a smooth sauce. Pour the sauce evenly over the meat and vegetables and gently swirl the pan to allow the sauce to evenly permeate the dish. I sometimes poke holes in the mixture to allow the sauce to initially penetrate the interior.

7. Cover the pot and bring to a boil over medium-high heat. Keeping the liquid at a medium simmer, cook the mixture for 2 hours or until the potatoes are tender and the sauce is thickened. If you prefer, the mixture can be cooked in a preheated oven at 300–350°F for about the same amount of time. Just make sure that the sauce is simmering so that it will thicken properly in a reasonable amount of time.

8. Serve with rice flavored with some pine nuts and sautéed onions if you like.

Yield: 10–12 servings

TINA'S TIDBITS

- *Ground meat used in a casserole should not be too lean or it will become very hard after prolonged cooking. Eighty to ninety percent lean is acceptable for these purposes.*
- *Ground meat will become tough and rubbery if it is squeezed tightly when combined with other ingredients. Using a fork or your fingertips is a better technique for mixing.*
- *Like all stews that contain many ingredients, this recipe tastes even better the next day.*

GRILLED FISH WITH SPICE RUB

This simple recipe for fish duplicates the itinerary of a ship sailing the spice route! The honey, lemon juice, and olive oil bring it right to the port in Alexandria or Istanbul. Any firm fish can be used as long as it holds together when grilling.

1 tablespoon cumin seed
1 tablespoon coriander seed
1 tablespoon whole black peppercorns
$\frac{1}{3}$ cup salted pistachio nuts
3 large cloves of garlic, finely chopped
1 tablespoon finely chopped candied ginger
1 tablespoon sweet paprika
$1\frac{1}{2}$ teaspoons ground cinnamon

$\frac{1}{2}$ teaspoon salt
1 teaspoon wildflower honey
3 tablespoons extra virgin olive oil
1 tablespoon fresh lemon juice
2 tablespoons chopped fresh parsley
$1\frac{1}{2}$ pounds fillet of fish such as halibut, tuna, or
    salmon, $\frac{3}{4}$ inch thick

1. Combine all of the ingredients for the rub in a small processor work bowl. Process until a coarse paste is formed. Set aside. Alternatively, place the first 5 ingredients in a bowl or plastic bag and press with the back of a spoon or rolling pin until coarsely crushed. Add remaining ingredients to the bowl and set aside.

2. Rinse the fish and pat dry.

3. Rub the fish with some of the spice rub to coat well. Allow to sit for 20 minutes at room temperature. If marinating for several hours, keep food in the refrigerator but bring to room temperature before grilling.

4. Grill the fish for 3 minutes per side or until firm but springy to the touch.

Yield: 3–4 servings

TINA'S TIDBITS

- *Always choose a firm fish for grilling so it won't fall apart.*
- *Never place your brush or hand into the bowl of spice rub, then onto the meat, and back to the marinade. You will contaminate the mixture, and any leftovers could be dangerous to your future health.*
- *Never let fish sit in a marinade or rub containing a lot of acid for longer than 30 minutes; otherwise the acid in the mixture will "cook" the fish, and grilling will cook the same fish twice, making it tough.*
- *To avoid the smell of fish in your kitchen, remove the paper wrapped around the fish and discard immediately. Most of the time it's the paper that's the culprit in causing bad odors.*

GRILLED CHICKEN WITH SPICE RUB

Here is a similar recipe (for chicken instead of fish) but one could say the ship went north, since all sweetness is eliminated in this recipe and there are more garlic and herbs.

1 tablespoon cumin powder
1 tablespoon curry powder
1 tablespoon paprika
1 tablespoon coriander seed, crushed
1 tablespoon black peppercorn, crushed
1½ teaspoons cinnamon

½ teaspoon salt
3 tablespoons extra virgin olive oil
1 large clove of garlic, chopped
1 tablespoon minced fresh oregano
2 tablespoons minced fresh cilantro
2 pounds boneless, skinless chicken breasts

1. Combine all of the ingredients for the rub in a small bowl. Mix well and set aside.

2. Separate the fillet from the chicken breast, and remove the pearlized white tendon from the fillet (for detailed instructions see page 52). Cut the chicken pieces in half crosswise. Rinse and pat dry.

3. Rub the chicken with some of the spice rub to coat well. Allow to sit for 20 minutes at room temperature. If marinating for several hours, keep food in the refrigerator but bring to room temperature before grilling.

4. Grill the chicken for 3 minutes per side or until firm but springy to the touch.

Yield: 6–8 servings

TINA'S TIDBITS

- *Using crushed seeds not only gives the chicken texture, but it absorbs and retains the oil on the surface better.*
- *If your grilled chicken has ever come out raw on the inside, the only explanation is that you didn't remove the fillet or "tender" from the breast and heat couldn't penetrate to the interior. Look for a white, pearlized string running through the meat and pull the piece of meat containing it away from the breast.*

SPICED ANGEL PECANS

I call these angel pecans because they truly are heavenly! A perfect treat to make in the fall when pecans are freshly harvested, you can serve them to guests in your sukkah.

1 egg white
1 tablespoon unsalted butter, melted
1 teaspoon vanilla
1 pound pecan halves
$\frac{1}{2}$ cup sugar

$1\frac{1}{2}$ teaspoons cinnamon
$\frac{1}{4}$ teaspoon ground allspice
$\frac{1}{2}$ teaspoon nutmeg
$\frac{1}{2}$ teaspoon salt

1. Preheat oven to 250°F.

2. Place egg white in a 2-quart bowl and beat with a whisk until light and foamy.

3. Fold melted butter and vanilla into the whites. Add the nuts and gently stir to coat all the nuts with the egg white mixture.

4. In a small bowl, combine the sugar, cinnamon, allspice, and salt, and gently fold into the nuts to coat evenly.

5. Spread the nuts onto a jelly roll pan lined with parchment paper, and bake for 45 minutes, stirring the nuts after the first 25 minutes. Nuts should be very crisp and dry.

6. When completely cool, store in an airtight container or freeze in ziplock freezer bags until ready to use.

Yield: 4 cups

VARIATIONS

For Savory Nuts: Substitute 1 teaspoon Worcestershire sauce for vanilla, and use $1\frac{1}{2}$ teaspoons Lawry's seasoned salt, $\frac{1}{4}$–$\frac{1}{2}$ teaspoon garlic powder, and $\frac{1}{4}$ teaspoon curry powder instead of the spices. Prepare as directed above.

For Orange-Spice Nuts: Substitute 1 teaspoon orange extract for the vanilla, and use $\frac{1}{2}$ teaspoon cardamom instead of the nutmeg. Prepare as directed above.

TINA'S TIDBITS

- *Beating the egg white for coating provides more surface area for the sugar to adhere to and makes the pecans more crunchy and "heavenly"!*
- *Pareve margarine or oil may be substituted for butter to make it suitable to serve at meat meals.*

EAST AND SOUTHEAST ASIA

There have always been two major factors in the spread of the Jewish Diaspora: commerce and persecution. The arrival of Jewish émigrés in East Asia and their subsequent egress from that region were no exception.

One hundred years ago a letter was found in Western China that was written by a sheep merchant in 718 petitioning for the right to sell his animals. It was written in Persian-Hebrew. Evidence of traders coming from the Near East—Persia, Mesopotamia—has been found all along the Silk Road. Around the year 960, a group of Persian Jews arrived in the city of Kaifeng, which at that time was the capital of the Sung Dynasty and the center of trade on the Silk Road. The Kaifeng museum has a stone tablet dated in 1489 that commemorates an old synagogue that the Jews were given permission to build at the time of the first millennium. There is also a street in the old Jewish quarter whose name is "The Lane of the Sect That Teaches the Scriptures."

There is no documentation of the survival of Jewish practices in that region until the new waves of Jewish immigrants started to arrive in the mid-nineteenth century. The first groups to arrive in Shanghai were Sephardic Jews from Iraq and Bombay. Two families, the Sassoons and Hardoons, were instrumental in establishing very successful Jewish business and religious communities in that city.

Thousands of Russian Jews came to China in the early twentieth century to escape pogroms. They migrated to northern China through Siberia and remained in that part of the country until 1931, when the Japanese invaded Manchuria. Many

Russian Jews then moved to Shanghai, where they joined the already thriving Ashkenazi and Baghdadi communities. In 1937 mainland China was invaded by the Japanese, who later occupied the Shanghai region. From December 1941 to 1945 the Japanese created a ghetto in Hong Kou where they interned those Shanghai Jews who were associated with Allied countries and the "stateless" Jewish refugees who had escaped from Germany, Austria, and Poland—over twenty-one thousand Jews. Deemed from neutral countries, Shanghai's Iraqi and Russian Jews were left alone. At the end of the war, many Jews were found living in all areas of the Far East after having escaped from Nazi tyranny. There were estimates of over twenty-four thousand Jews in Shanghai alone. With the rise of Communism, most of the community migrated to the United States, Australia, Israel, and Hong Kong. At one point there were seven synagogues in Shanghai. Today, there are two, and the seven-hundred-seat Ohel Rachel Synagogue, the first built in that city, has only been allowed to be open since 1999, one day at a time, for Rosh HaShanah, Chanukah, and Passover.

With commerce opening up between China and the rest of the world, the Jewish community in the city of Shanghai now numbers a few hundred. They hold services and even have a kosher restaurant. This restaurant reflects the food heritage of the Chinese Jewish community. Like many other

Jewish communities in the Diaspora, the common denominator for food preparations is to have the local cuisine conform to the laws of kashrut; no pork or shellfish is consumed, and food is not prepared with any milk products. The Jews of old Kaifeng were actually referred to as the "people who removed the sinew," a tradition whose origins stem from Jacob wrestling with the angel in Genesis 32.

Asian cuisine is probably the easiest to adapt to a kosher kitchen. The substitution of veal (not chicken) for pork renders a dish identical in taste and texture to a recipe that calls for pork. The sauces are almost always vegetable-based. Oyster sauce is not allowed, but thick "dark soy" can be substituted without a problem. Thai fish sauce is usually made with anchovies, and although traditional red curry paste is made with 5 percent dried shrimp paste, there are many high-quality brands available in North America that are vegetarian, do not contain anything t'reif (nonkosher), and have excellent flavor. If ingredients are added in the proper order, a homemade Chinese dish will taste just as good, if not better, than one served in any restaurant you can imagine.

ASIAN SPINACH SALAD WITH CANDIED WALNUTS AND FRIED TOFU CROUTONS

This is not an ancient recipe, but it is a good example of how observant Jews in far-reaching areas of the world used the ingredients readily available to build upon the foundation of Jewish dietary laws.

⅓ cup corn oil
2 tablespoons dark sesame seed oil
3 tablespoons rice wine vinegar
1 tablespoon cream sherry
2 × ½-inch strip of lemon zest
1 teaspoon soy sauce
1 scallion, white part and 2 inches of green, sliced ½ inch thick
1 teaspoon minced ginger
1 clove garlic, minced
Pinch of crushed red pepper
Salt and freshly ground pepper to taste
1 teaspoon brown sugar
1 tablespoon minced fresh basil
10 ounces fresh baby spinach or spinach-mesclun mix

1 cup fresh bean sprouts
⅓ cup julienne-sliced bamboo shoots
½ cup blanched snow peas, finely sliced lengthwise
3 ounces extra firm tofu, cut into ½-inch cubes (about 25 cubes)
1 tablespoon honey
1 teaspoon soy sauce
Oil for deep-frying
1 egg white (about 3 tablespoons)
½ cup dried panko bread crumbs
¼ cup water
¼ cup sugar
2 teaspoons five-spice powder
1 teaspoon salt
1½ cups walnut pieces

1. Combine the first thirteen ingredients in a blender and blend until relatively smooth. Set aside in a screw-top jar until ready to use.

2. Rinse and dry the spinach and bean sprouts. Place in a large salad bowl with bamboo shoots and snow peas.

3. Marinate the tofu squares in honey and soy sauce for 10 minutes. Heat oil in a 1-quart saucepan to a depth of 1 inch. Roll the tofu in the egg white, and coat thoroughly with the bread crumbs. Fry the tofu until golden, and drain on paper towel.

4. Preheat the oven to 375°F. Bring the water, sugar, five-spice powder, and salt to a boil in a 1-quart saucepan.

5. Add the walnuts and stir for 1 minute. Spread the nuts onto a nonstick jellyroll pan or a pan lined with parchment paper. Bake walnuts for 7 minutes or until they are dark golden and most of the liquid has evaporated.

6. Remove the nuts from the baking pan and cool on an oiled counter or cookie sheet. When cool, break the pieces up and store in freezer until ready to use.

7. To assemble the salad, toss the greens with some of the vinaigrette until lightly moistened. Top salad with some of the walnuts and the tofu croutons and serve with remaining vinaigrette on the side.

Yield: 4–6 servings

TINA'S TIDBITS

- *"Blanching" literally means "to whiten," but with reference to vegetables it means cooking in boiling salted water for 30 seconds to 1 minute and then plunging the vegetables into ice water to stop the cooking process. This is done to set the bright color and heighten the flavor of the food by bringing out the natural sugars in the food. This technique should always be used on green vegetables that are to be served cold in a salad or as crudités with dip.*
- *Panko is a type of bread crumb from Japan that is large and irregular in shape and gives food an excellent crunchy coating.*

Szechuan Cold Spicy Noodles

This is the real McCoy—an original that I have been making for over thirty years before bottled dressings were the norm. Made with jarred sesame paste (not tahini!), it has a wonderful musty flavor. However, peanut butter is a great substitute. Thinking like a Jew in ancient China, I would prepare this cold dish in advance and serve it for Shabbat lunch. Remember, it was the Chinese who gave the world noodles!

1 chicken breast, cooked, boned, and shredded
1 pound fresh or frozen Chinese egg noodles (lo mein) or ½ pound dried
2 tablespoons corn, canola, or peanut oil
1 tablespoon sesame oil

SAUCE:
3 tablespoons Chinese sesame seed paste or peanut butter
6 tablespoons soy sauce
1 tablespoon red wine vinegar
1 tablespoon chili pepper oil
1 teaspoon sugar
2 tablespoons chopped scallion
½ tablespoon chopped ginger
½ tablespoon chopped garlic
½ teaspoon ground pepper
1 tablespoon Chinese black sesame seed oil
1 tablespoon chopped roasted peanuts
1 tablespoon chopped fresh scallions

1. Put the noodles into boiling water and cook until water returns to a boil. Immediately add ½ cup **cold** water to the pot and return to a boil. Noodles should be tender shortly after the water has come to the boil for the second time. Drain the noodles, but **do not rinse.**

2. Place 2 tablespoons vegetable oil on a large rimmed platter. Add noodles and top with the 1 tablespoon sesame oil. Toss the noodles until well coated with the oils.

TINA'S TIDBITS

- *The Chinese method for cooking noodles is easy and always produces a product that is not too soft. Stopping the cooking action by adding the cold water is the secret to perfect noodles.*
- *When buying jarred Asian sesame seed paste, make sure the paste isn't too dark, which could be a sign of over-roasting and bitterness.*
- *Chili pepper oil is clear and bright orange. Any liquid hot sauce can be substituted, but add a little more vegetable oil to the sauce to keep the proper consistency.*
- *Coating the noodles with the two oils first is imperative so that they don't stick together and to prevent the noodles from absorbing all the sauce and clumping.*
- *To prepare in advance, toss the noodles with the oils and shred the chicken on top. Store the sauce and chopped vegetables separately, and combine everything just before serving.*
- *I like to serve this in a shallow rimmed platter so I can present it and then toss at the table without the noodles falling out of the serving dish.*

3. Shred the chicken by hand or with a coarse grater directly onto the center of the noodles. Cover with plastic wrap and refrigerate until ready to serve.

4. Combine the sesame seed paste (or peanut butter) and the soy sauce in a processor work bowl. Process until mixture is smooth. Add the remaining sauce ingredients and pulse on and off until combined. If too thick, add a little more oil, water, or soy sauce to get the desired consistency and flavor you want.

5. When ready to serve, pour the sauce over the chicken and noodles, and sprinkle the chopped peanuts and scallions on top. Toss to combine and serve. For a pretty presentation, toss the noodles at the table just before serving.

Note: Half a cucumber, finely shredded, may be added to this dish along with the chicken or instead of the chicken for a vegetarian variety.

Yield: 6–8 servings if part of a Chinese meal with several courses

Soba Noodles with Shitake Mushrooms and Tofu

Here's another noodle dish, but this one is Japanese. The meaty mushrooms and the tofu provide a substantial meat alternative for a vegetarian dish. These noodles are made from the same grain as kasha, which is really not a grain but a seed, so one could argue that these noodles (if 100% buckwheat flour) are kosher for Passover. Check the package to make sure wheat flour wasn't used as well.

8 large dried shitake mushrooms
$\frac{1}{4}$ cup cream sherry
$\frac{1}{4}$ cup soy sauce
$1\frac{1}{2}$ × $\frac{1}{4}$-inch piece of fresh ginger, peeled
2 teaspoons brown sugar or honey
8 ounces dried soba (buckwheat) noodles

1 tablespoon peanut oil
6 ounces firm tofu, cut into $\frac{1}{2}$-inch cubes
2 scallions, finely cut in $\frac{1}{8}$-inch rounds
$\frac{1}{4}$ cup carrot strips made with a zester or very finely julienned
Wasabi for extra flavoring (optional)

1. Place the mushrooms in a 1-quart bowl and cover with at least 1 cup of water. Microwave uncovered for $3\frac{1}{2}$ minutes, and soak for 15 minutes or until very soft.

2. Squeeze the mushrooms over the bowl (reserving the liquid), and slice the mushrooms into $\frac{1}{8}$-inch strips, discarding the stems. Set aside.

3. Strain the mushroom liquid into a measuring cup using a paper coffee filter or double mesh strainer, or very carefully pour out the liquid so the sandy sediment stays in the bowl. You need to have $\frac{3}{4}$–1 cup mushroom liquid. Set aside.

4. In a 1-quart saucepan, bring the sherry to a boil and ignite with a flame. Swirl the pan until the flame disappears. Add the soy sauce, mushroom liquid, fresh ginger, and brown sugar, and boil over medium heat for 10–15 minutes or until liquid is reduced to $\frac{3}{4}$ cup (about half).

5. Meanwhile bring 2 quarts of water to a boil in a 4-quart pot. Add the soba noodles, and when the water returns to a full boil, pour $\frac{1}{2}$ cup of cold water into the pot. Bring to a boil again and cook for 5 minutes more or until the noodles are cooked but still al dente. Drain. Rinse noodles with cold water and place in a serving bowl.

6. Heat 1 tablespoon of peanut oil in a nonstick pan,. Lightly sauté the tofu for 2 minutes. Add the shitake mushroom slices and sauté until heated.

7. Remove the ginger slice from the hot sauce, and pour half of the sauce into the mushroom-tofu mixture. Heat this mixture, stirring, until tofu and mushrooms are coated with the sauce. Add the remaining sauce to the soba noodles and toss well. Pour the mushroom mixture over the soba, and garnish with the sliced scallion and carrot slivers. Serve warm or at room temperature, with wasabi on the side.

Yield: 4 servings

TINA'S TIDBITS

- *I am probably the only cooking instructor who would recommend using cream sherry in Asian cooking. However, most recipes call for a small amount of sugar, and using this sherry, which is sweeter, eliminates the necessity for added sweetner. Cream sherry retains its flavor when exposed to high heat, so it is a very good choice for hot stir-frying.*
- **Never** *buy cooking sherry! By law it has a certain percentage of salt added to it. This goes back to Victorian times, when the cook couldn't be monitored in the downstairs kitchen! Buy a decent bottle of domestic cream sherry for about $7 that is palatable and useful for many purposes.*

Tamarind Marinated Grilled Salmon with Thai Curry Sauce on Rice Flake Noodles

With or without the noodles, this dish is terrific. My only regret is that I can't just eat the sauce with a spoon! Actually, this sauce could be thinned down to be a soup with pieces of chicken and canned straw mushrooms as a garnish.

2 large cloves garlic, finely minced
2 tablespoons tamarind or Thai fruit concentrate
1/3 cup water
1/2 teaspoon salt
2 teaspoons ground coriander

1 1/2 teaspoons brown sugar
1/4 teaspoon freshly ground black pepper
1 tablespoon vegetable oil
1 1/2 pounds skinless salmon fillet, cut crosswise into 1 1/2-inch strips

1. Combine all of the ingredients except the salmon in an 11 × 7-inch rectangular dish. Add the salmon to the marinade and coat well. Let the mixture marinate for at least 15 minutes but no more than 1/2 hour.

2. When ready to grill, heat a grill on high and cook the salmon for 3 minutes per side or until the fish is firm but still springy to the touch. Estimate 10 minutes per inch of thickness for the cooking time of the salmon.

3. Serve as is or with the following Thai curry sauce over wide rice flake noodles.

Thai Curry Sauce

One or two 5-ounce bags rice flake or *Chantaboon* noodles
2 tablespoons vegetable oil
2 large cloves of garlic
1 1/2 tablespoons finely minced fresh peeled ginger
3/4 teaspoon ground coriander
1/2 tablespoon curry powder

2 teaspoons Thai red curry paste
1/2 tablespoon sweet paprika
3/4 teaspoon ground cumin
1 1/4 cups unsweetened coconut milk
1 tablespoon tomato paste
1 tablespoon soy sauce
1 1/2 tablespoons light brown sugar

1. Bring a 3-quart pot of water to a boil, and just before making the following sauce, cook the noodles. Drop noodles into the boiling water and add a cup of cold water to the pot. Bring the water to a boil again, and check noodles after 2 minutes to see how soft they are. Meanwhile, make the curry sauce.

2. Heat a 1-quart saucepan for 20 seconds. Add the oil and heat for 15 seconds. Add the garlic and ginger and sauté for 20 seconds over moderately high heat but **do not burn** the garlic.

3. Combine the coriander, curry powder, curry paste, paprika, and cumin. Whisk the spices into

the garlic mixture and stir over low heat for 20 seconds. Whisking constantly, add the remaining ingredients and heat thoroughly. Do not boil.

4. When the noodles are done, drain them, place on a platter, and toss with some of the sauce. Top with the grilled salmon fillets and enough remaining sauce to coat well. Reserve any remaining sauce to pass. Serve.

Yield: Serves 4–6 people

TINA'S TIDBITS

- *Premeasured ingredients can be combined in a small bowl if they are to be added to the recipe at the same time and if they are either all dry or all liquid. Mixing the two in advance can often result in loss of flavor or texture.*
- *Coconut milk is not made from milk. It is the pulverized meat of the coconut and water, and the Jews of India and Thailand utilized its pareve properties to the fullest.*

STEAK WITH CELLOPHANE NOODLES

The technique and the ingredients in this recipe are the cornerstone for all beef and lamb stir-fry dishes; lamb with scallions, beef with bok choy or snow peas, and so on all use the same marinade and technique. This recipe, with the substitution of green bell peppers instead of the broccoli, is the iconic dish known as pepper steak that was found in all Cantonese restaurants in the 1950s. The cellophane noodles are the fried "Styrofoam" noodles that are used for a garnish. They are fun and wow your guests but are not necessary for the success of this dish.

1 ounce cellophane noodles (optional)
½ pound steak, preferably partially frozen
3 tablespoons soy sauce
1½ tablespoons cream sherry
1½ teaspoons cornstarch
1 teaspoon sugar

1 small bunch broccoli, stems sliced and florettes, separated
2 teaspoons finely chopped ginger root
⅛ teaspoon cayenne pepper or to taste (optional)
2 cups corn or peanut oil (if making noodles)
3 tablespoons corn or peanut oil

1. Over a deep bowl, use a pair of sharp scissors to cut the cellophane noodles into 4-inch lengths. Separate the noodles. Set aside.

2. Using a sharp chef's knife or cleaver, trim off and discard any fat on the meat, and thinly slice the meat on a diagonal against the grain. This can be done more easily if the meat is almost frozen. Sliced meat should be about 2 inches long and ½ inch wide and as thin as can be.

3. In a small bowl, combine the soy sauce, cornstarch, sugar, and sherry. Add the sliced meat and toss it until it is well coated. Set aside.

4. Have the noodles, steak, broccoli, ginger, cayenne, and oil ready and within easy reach. If not making noodles, proceed to step 6.

5. Heat the 2 cups oil in a deep pot or wok until it is almost smoking. A noodle dropped into oil will cook in **1 second**. If oil is ready, drop in a handful of noodles at a time. Cook for 3 seconds and immediately remove to paper towels. Fry the remainder in the same way.

6. Heat a wok for 30 seconds. Add 1 tablespoon oil and heat for 30 seconds. Turn the heat down if the oil begins to smoke. Add the broccoli stems and stir-fry for 1 minute. Add the florets and cook until a bright emerald green. Remove both to a bowl.

7. Add another 2 tablespoons of oil to the wok and heat. Add ginger root and stir-fry for 5 seconds. Add the meat and cayenne and stir-fry for 1 or 2 minutes.

8. Add the broccoli to the pan and stir-fry to combine thoroughly and reheat.

9. Serve immediately by placing the meat mixture in the center of a large heated platter. Arrange the noodles around the perimeter.

Note: As a main course this will serve 4. This recipe can be doubled, but never use more than 1 pound of meat in a stir-fry dish or the flavor of the dish will change unfavorably.

Yield: 4–6 servings

TINA'S TIDBITS

- *Remember, if you are not making the cellophane noodles, then this recipe needs only 3 tablespoons oil!*
- *The entire area of a wok is your cooking surface so it is imperative to keep the food moving in order to cook it in 2–3 minutes.*
- *Because stir-frying is very fast, all of your ingredients must be premeasured and ready to go. However, premeasuring small quantities of oil in a little bowl will result in inaccurate quantities, since much of the oil will adhere to the bowl.*

PUMPKIN WITH SPICED COCONUT CUSTARD

Although this recipe is Thai in origin, it mimics the preparation that the Puritan settlers first used when introduced to this native plant. A rabbi at the Chabad house in Bangkok told me that pumpkin, which is readily available in Thailand, is often used for Jewish holidays in the Sephardi manner to represent all-encompassing prosperity.

One 4- to 5-pound pie pumpkin
3 eggs
½ cup dark brown sugar
Pinch of salt

1 teaspoon cornstarch (optional)
⅛ teaspoon cinnamon
⅛ teaspoon ground cloves
One 14-ounce can coconut milk

1. With your knife angled 45 degrees toward the center, cut a large hole in the top of the pumpkin.

2. Remove and discard all of the stringy fiber from the interior of the pumpkin (discard seeeds if you don't want them for roasting), but save the lid.

3. Lightly scrape the inside of the pumpkin with the tines of a fork. Set aside.

4. Preheat the oven to 350°F. Line a low-sided jelly roll pan with foil.

5. Whisk the eggs until well beaten, and add the remaining ingredients. Whisk until well combined.

6. Pour the mixture into the prepared pumpkin, and replace the top of the pumpkin.

7. Bake for 1½–2 hours until pumpkin is soft and custard is set. Serve hot or warm, scooping out some of the cooked pumpkin with the custard.

Yield: Serves 4–6

TINA'S TIDBITS

- *Use a round pie pumpkin (stores will state this), not a jack-o-lantern variety, for this dish. Kabocha or white pumpkin can be used as well.*
- *The acidity of the pumpkin will determine if custard looks curdled. It isn't really curdled and will taste just as good, without having to use starch to bind the custard together and change the custard's texture.*

RUSSIA AND CENTRAL AND EASTERN EUROPE

The Jews of this continuously altered political region are the Jews with whom most North American Jews are most familiar. In the thirteenth and fourteenth centuries, the Polish monarchs encouraged Jews to come to Poland to help develop the trade and market economy of the region. At this time Jews were being persecuted

throughout Europe. If they weren't responsible for the death of Christ, they were responsible for the plague. If they were not beaten or executed, they were required to live in dark, overcrowded ghettos or small villages where they could barely survive. Of course, another way to deal with the Jewish scourge was to expel them altogether.

Poland looked good in those days, so thousands of Jews from the beginning of the Crusades to the end of the fifteenth century resettled from Germany, Austria, Hungary, and Lithuania into the land then known as Poland. The French and Northern Italian Jewish immigrants who immigrated to Germany in the tenth century created a language within their newly assimilated Jewish communities that combined elements of their Laaz (Jewish/French dialect), medieval German, biblical and mishnaic Hebrew, and Aramaic. This came to be the primary language of Western European Jews. When these Jews migrated to Poland, they introduced this language to the Polish Jewish community. Using Hebrew as the common denominator and introducing the Slavic language into the mix, Yiddish as we know it today was born. This language helped to define a community and protect them, because non-Jews didn't understand this language. On the other hand,

Yiddish defined who was a Jew to the outside world and made them targets for persecution.

In the middle of the seventeenth century, there was a Cossack revolt, and the Polish army was overthrown. The Cossacks, under the leadership of Bogdan Chmielnicki, joined with the Polish peasants in attacking the Jews. The Chmielnicki massacres, as they were called, were carried out over a period of eight years. One hundred thousand Jews were killed, tortured, or poorly treated. As a result, many Jews fled back to Germany, Holland, Central Europe, and the Balkans. The Yiddish language went with them as well.

Beginning in 1790, and into the early twentieth century, Western European Jews were slowly emancipated and allowed to interact with all members of the community, secure jobs in these communities, and pursue their own religious beliefs without restrictions. Eastern European Jews were also thriving, although their community was still insular, with little contact with the outside world. At this same time Russia was expanding her borders westward, and more than 1.2 million Jews in Poland and Lithuania came under her rule. By 1835 the Pale of Settlement, stretching from the Baltic Sea to the Black, was established. Jews were forced to

Left: *Prune Tzimmes, page 134*

leave their homes east and west of this territory and were evacuated from their homes in the big cities of this region to move into shtetls, or little villages, throughout this area.

As a result of the success of the Jews within the non-Jewish communities of Germany and parts of Eastern Europe and the need for a scapegoat for Russian economic and political decline, Jews became targets of fear and jealousy, and by the 1880s anti-Semitism was on the rise. Pogroms (Russian for "violent mass attacks") began in 1871 in Odessa and continued for the next thirty-five years. In Romania, the government's support of anti-Semitism in the late 1800s was responsible for the migration of over seventy thousand Jews to the United States.

Russia tried to diminish its Jewish population by conscription into the army. Boys were taken away at twelve, before bar mitzvah, forced to eat pork, and required to serve for twenty-five years. The government hoped that after this long time the soldiers would forget that they were ever Jewish. This was the major impetus for the migration, often illegally, to the United States, Palestine, and South Africa. By 1900 New York City had the largest

Jewish population of any city in the world. By 1904 over sixty-four thousand Jewish families lived in six thousand tenements on the Lower East Side.

Many recipes you expect to find in this section are dispersed throughout the book and most likely in the Icons section—and with good reason. Because of the mass migration of over two million Jews from Eastern Europe, the Pale of Russia, and Romania at the end of the nineteenth century and the beginning of the twentieth, generations of Jews in America viewed only the foods coming out of this area as Jewish. The recipes have been tweaked to adapt to foods readily available—people in the South use red snapper in their gefilte fish because it is plentiful in the Gulf—but the roots are still in the Ashkenazic kitchen of the past. Most Americans don't know that bagels are a peasant snack from the shtetls in the Pale, but all know they are found throughout America and well loved.

Although we no longer subsist on herring, black bread, and an onion as our midday meal, we can see the connection in foods that were "dressed up" for Shabbat or holidays in the poverty-stricken homes of this region.

"HOMEMADE" PICKLED HERRING IN CREAM SAUCE

Today most of the traditional Ashkenazic dishes are available already prepared in delis and supermarkets. We no longer brine our own fish to preserve it. However, we can add fresh ingredients to the prepared product to elevate the taste and heighten the memory. This recipe is one such example. Auntie Yetta taught it to me when I was in my teens, and I have made her recipe every year since.

2-pound jar of pickled herring snack bits (no sour cream sauce)

1 medium Bermuda or Spanish onion
1–2 cups heavy sour cream

1. Drain herring and jarred onions, reserving the liquid. Place herring pieces and pickled onions in a medium mixing bowl.

2. Thinly slice the onion into rings and add to the herring, along with enough sour cream to be thick but still slightly runny. Refrigerate for a day or longer, and add additional sour cream or reserved juice if needed.

3. Store and serve in a glass bowl.

Yield: 2 quarts

TINA'S TIDBITS

- *Although I have given you the traditional preparation above, I generally cut the onion in half to create half moons. This prevents a ring from hanging by the spoon's handle and dripping sour cream all over your tablecloth or rug!*
- *Always keep herring in a glass container; plastic will absorb the odor, and metal will change the flavor or color of this highly acidic preparation.*

RUSSIAN CABBAGE BORSCHT

My mother was a first-generation American. She learned to speak Yiddish when her cousins escaped Poland in the early 1930s to come and live near her. She was poor growing up, and her cooking as an adult reflected the reverence she had for the simplest of ingredients. I still feel guilty when I throw a salad together for dinner. When I was growing up, we started dinner every evening with our own individual salad bowls garnished with four tomato wedges, a green pepper ring, and a radish rose centered on top. She didn't make elaborate or ethnic foods, but her sound, basic Ashkenazic cooking was always perfectly cooked and presented.

This soup is a perfect representation of less is more and the love affair the Eastern European cooks had with all things sweet and sour. The original recipe was shown to me with a shiterein (a handful or a pinch—a nondescript amount of ingredient—of this and that). Here is my recipe for another generation.

3 strips of flanken meat (short ribs), about 1½ pounds
2½ quarts water
1 large onion
One 15.5-ounce can peeled tomatoes in liquid
One 8-ounce can tomato sauce

1 medium or ½ large head of cabbage, finely sliced into shreds
Salt and freshly ground pepper to taste
1 cup dark raisins
¼ cup dark brown sugar or to taste
Lemon juice (optional)

1. Rinse off meat and place in a 4-quart pot. Add the water, bring to a boil, and simmer for 30 minutes, skimming the top of the soup occasionally to remove the brown foam.

2. Add the onion, after piercing it 4 or 5 times with a sharp knife. This technique allows the flavor of the onion to permeate the soup without the onion disintegrating.

3. Squeeze the canned tomatoes through your fingers so that you get uneven strings of crushed tomato. Add this and any liquid from the can to the pot. Add the tomato sauce.

4. Add the shredded cabbage, salt and pepper to taste, and the raisins to the soup pot, and cook for 1½ hours partially covered.

5. After 1½ hours, add the brown sugar and adjust the seasonings to your taste, using some lemon juice, if needed, to balance the sweet-and-sour taste.

6. Cook for ½ hour more. Remove the onion, break up the meat into pieces, remove the bones, and serve.

Yield: 6–8 servings

TINA'S TIDBITS

- *This soup, like most soups, tastes even better the second day and freezes very well.*
- *If the soup is too thin for you, either add additional tomato sauce or thicken with an* einbrenne, *which is a mixture of equal parts pareve margarine and flour that is added in small amounts to the hot soup to create the desired thickness.*
- *Flour can never be added directly to a hot liquid without creating little floating lumps. Mixing it into a fat first will allow the flour to dissolve slowly and evenly.*
- *When preparing soup, it is always a good idea to cook meat alone in water for the first 30 minutes. The coagulated blood and any other impurities from the bone rise to the surface as a foam that is easily removed, which helps clarify the soup.*

LENTIL SOUP

Although lentils are more often associated with India and the Near East, Jewish traders helped bring these staples of Middle Eastern regions to Eastern Europe. Easy and delicious—all you need is some hot bread and maybe a salad, and that's dinner.

2 cups lentils
1½ pounds flanken or short ribs
2 quarts water
2 tablespoons oil
1 large onion, diced

3 carrots, diced
2 stalks celery diced
Salt and pepper to taste
2–3 Polish sausages or frankfurters

1. Place lentils in a glass bowl and cover with 2 inches of water. Microwave for 3 minutes and then set aside for 1 hour or until slightly softened. Drain and set aside.

2. In a 3-quart pot, bring the 2 quarts of water to a boil with the meat. Simmer for 30 minutes, skimming off the foam that rises.

3. Heat an 8-inch frying pan for 15 seconds. Add the oil and heat for another 15 seconds. Add the diced onion and sauté in the oil until it is golden. Add to the pot with the meat.

4. Add the lentils and the remaining ingredients, except the sausage, to the pot, and simmer for 1 hour or until the meat and lentils are tender.

5. Remove the flanken to a plate. Remove bones and cartilage, and cut the meat into small pieces if not eating the meat separate from the soup.

6. Place the soup in a food mill or blender and process until smooth.

7. Return the soup to a clean pot, and add the sliced Polish sausage and cubed meat, if desired. Simmer for another 10 minutes or until the sausage has imparted its flavor to the soup and is completely heated through. Serve.

Yield: 4–6 servings

TINA'S TIDBITS

- *This soup is pureed; however, if you want to leave the soup chunky, take extra care to cut your vegetables in uniform shape.*
- *A blender does a much better job of pureeing soups than a processor because all the ingredients are pulled down to the blade by the whirlpool effect. If you are using a processor, you must add only the solids to the work bowl first or the soup will have a coarse texture.*
- *An alternative method of serving this recipe is to keep the flanken whole after the soup is cooked. Serve the soup first and the meat as an entrée accompanied by a starch and a vegetable.*

PRUNE TZIMMES

Tzimmes has its origin in medieval Germany, where it was the custom to have meat stews that contained fruit and vegetables. Perhaps the Persian and western Asian culinary habit of using fruits with meat made it up the Rhine. The sugar-beet-growing region of southwestern Poland surely influenced the addition of sugar to the recipe, and the use of sweet potatoes is only a few centuries old, since the sweet potato wasn't introduced to Eastern Europe from America until the sixteenth century.

1 pound pitted prunes
1 tablespoon peanut oil
1 small onion (about 3 inches in diameter), finely diced
1 large clove garlic, minced
4–5 pounds brisket or boneless chuck roast

Salt and freshly ground black pepper to taste
4 carrots, pared and sliced into 1½-inch chunks
2 sweet potatoes, pared and cut into eighths
¼ cup sugar
1 tablespoon lemon juice (or to taste)

1. Cover prunes with cold water. Microwave on high for 3 minutes, and let soak for 30 minutes or longer, until soft.

2. Heat a large Dutch oven for 20 seconds. Add the oil and heat for another 10 seconds. Add the onion and garlic and sauté for a few minutes until the onion is golden. Do not let the garlic brown or it will become bitter. Add the meat and sear on all sides. The meat probably won't lie flat; don't worry, just sear all sides.

3. Transfer the meat to a large roasting pan, preferably one with a lid (if not, use heavy-duty foil to cover). Add prunes and soaking water to the meat and bring to a boil on your cooktop. Add salt and pepper.

4. Cover roasting pan tightly and transfer to a preheated 300°F oven. Cook the meat for 3–4 hours, depending on the size and thickness of your brisket.

5. Remove the meat and prunes from the pan. Put the potato and carrot chunks in the bottom of the pan, and place meat and prunes on top.

6. Sprinkle sugar and lemon juice into the gravy. Stir to combine, and cover tightly with lid or heavy-duty foil.

7. Place the roasting pan in a 350°F oven for 45–60 minutes or until the meat and potatoes are tender. Adjust the seasonings if necessary.

8. Remove the meat and cool, preferably overnight in the refrigerator.

9. Slice the meat when it is firm, and return to the vegetables and gravy to reheat.

Note: If your meat is small enough to fit into a large Dutch oven or pot, you may cook it on the top of the stove for 2 hours and then proceed to step 5.

Yield: 8–10 servings

TINA'S TIDBITS

- *A Dutch oven is a large, squat, 4- to 6-quart pot with two small handles.*
- *The dull side of the foil should always be facing up when roasting in the oven because the dull side absorbs the heat and helps the roasting process. However, **never** use the dull side up on a turkey, because it will dry out the white meat—use shiny side up for that.*
- *To freeze the vegetables and fruits, remove from the gravy, cool completely and then place in a freezer bag, place a straw in the bag, and close the bag up to the straw. Suck out all the air in the bag and then seal. This will prevent ice crystals in the air from piercing the vegetables and making them soggy. Freeze the gravy in a jar or bag in the same way*

Kasha Varnishkas

Kasha is probably the grain most identified with Eastern European Jews, but the grain (actually a seed) least eaten by contemporary American Jews. This earthy, chewy grain could easily replace rice or potatoes on the modern Jewish table, but it doesn't. What a pity! There is nothing like pot roast gravy on a pile of little brown granules mixed with golden fried onions and mushrooms to transport one back to the "good ol' days" that weren't so good but are long, long gone.

"Try it, you'll like it" . . . and it's good for you too!

1 cup kasha	2 cups boiling water
1 egg, slightly beaten	2 beef or vegetable bouillon cubes
¼ cup oil	½ teaspoon salt
1 medium onion, finely diced	Freshly ground black pepper to taste
4 ounces sliced mushrooms	8 ounces pasta bow ties

1. Heat a 2-quart saucepan over medium-high heat and add the kasha. Pour the beaten egg over all of the kasha and stir constantly until egg evenly coats the grains and each grain separates from the rest of the kasha. This should be done over a medium heat so that the egg does not cook before it coats the kasha grains. Put kasha in a bowl.

2. Reheat pan for 10 seconds then place the oil in the used pan and sauté the onions for 3 minutes. Add the sliced mushrooms and sauté another 3–5 minutes or until the mixture is golden.

3. Return the kasha to the pan with the onions and mushrooms. Add the boiling water, bouillon cubes, salt, and pepper, and stir to dissolve the bouillon. Cover and cook over a low flame for 15 minutes or until the kasha is tender.

4. Meanwhile cook the pasta bow ties according to package directions.

5. Combine the kasha and bowties and serve as is or with some gravy from your meat entrée on top.

Yield: 4–6 servings

> ### TINA'S TIDBITS
>
> - *Coating the uncooked granules with the raw egg prevents the kasha from swelling up. If you eliminate this step, you will feel like you are eating a bowl of Wheatena.*
> - *Always sauté onions alone initially before adding other vegetables with a high water content. This allows the sugars in the onion to caramelize and makes the onion sweeter.*
> - *Although any pasta shape can be used, bow tie pasta is to kasha what grape jelly is to peanut butter!*

POTATO KUGEL

There's a famous Yiddish song that says, "Monday a potato, Tuesday a potato . . . and for Shabbat a potato kugel!" Whole books with variations have been written about kugel as well—as they should, since a kugel, or pudding, was an inexpensive way to bulk up an ingredient like potatoes or carrots to fill up a family. If your grandmother fried her onions first, do so. If mushrooms and carrots were added in your family's kugel, go ahead. This is a delicious, proportionately correct potato kugel for you to enhance to your liking and memory.

6–8 large white or Yukon Gold potatoes, raw
1 medium onion
3 eggs, beaten well
1 tablespoon salt
½ teaspoon freshly ground pepper

½ cup matzah or cracker meal
¼ cup oil or rendered chicken fat
Additional oil or chicken fat for greasing pan and
   coating top of kugel

1. Wash and grate the raw potatoes by hand or in a processor fitted with the grating disc; there is no need to peel potatoes. Put grated potatoes in a colander, rinse with cold water, and drain well. Place in a large bowl.

2. Grate the onion as you did the potatoes. If you are using a processor, change to the cutting blade, and add ¹/₄ of the grated potatoes to the grated onion and pulse on and off to make a coarse paste. Add this mixture to the grated raw potatoes in the bowl.

3. Add the eggs and the remaining ingredients, including the ¹/₄ cup oil or chicken fat and mix well. (Use your hands if you need to.)

4. Oil a 2-quart casserole or 13 x 9 pan, and pour potato mixture into the prepared pan. Drizzle an additional tablespoon of oil or room temperature chicken fat over the top of the mixture, and lightly spread with your hand to coat evenly.

5. Bake in a preheated 350°F oven for 45 minutes or until top is crisp and golden. If need be, kugel may be placed under broiler for 3 minutes or until top is golden.

Yield: 12–15 servings

TINA'S TIDBITS

- *Potatoes absorb a great deal of salt, so more salt than you would normally need must be added to make your kugel taste right.*
- *The reason potatoes discolor is the oxidation of the potato starch in the tuber. If the potato is rinsed well and drained, your kugel will not be gray on the inside.*
- *Never grate the onion with the potato, because when you drain the mixture, a great deal of the onion flavor will be lost.*

COULIBIAC

Not everyone in Russia was poor. Some advisors to the czar, or "court Jews," lived well, if only for a short time.

This recipe is long, but not difficult. It can be prepared in advance and even frozen, since the salmon has already been poached (you can buy it that way if you like). Each step can be made separately and then put together when you want.

1 recipe for rice-cheese filling (see page 138)
1 recipe for mushroom duxelles (see page 138)
1 recipe for herbed crepe (see page 139)
½ pound salmon, cut into 1½-inch strips
1 cup water

½ cup dry white wine
1 package frozen puff pastry
1 egg white combined with ½ tablespoon water for egg wash
Port wine cream sauce (optional; see page 139)

1. Prepare recipes for mushroom duxelles, rice and cheese filling, and herbed crepe. Set aside until you are ready to prepare salmon and assemble coulibiac.

2. Combine water and wine in a 10-inch sauté pan with lid. Bring to a simmer and add the salmon. Lower heat, cover, and cook for 4 minutes or until salmon is springy to the touch and just cooked through. Immediately remove from liquid and place on a cloth towel to drain.

3. Roll one sheet of the puff pastry into an 18 × 16-inch rectangle. Place the herbed crepe centered over the dough.

4. Spread half the rice and cheese filling down the middle third of the crepe.

5. Spread half the mushroom duxelles over the rice, and lay the poached salmon strips down the center.

6. Cover the salmon strips with the remaining duxelles, and cover with the remaining rice and cheese filling.

7. Draw the long edges of the dough together over the filling, and pinch to seal. Draw up the sides, cutting off any excess dough, and pinch decoratively to seal. Place the rolled dough seam side down on a parchment-lined cookie sheet that has low sides.

8. Brush the coulibiac with egg white wash, and cut 2 ¼-inch steam holes on top. Decorate the top with any rolled dough scraps, and brush decorations with the egg wash as well. Refrigerate for at least 30 minutes.

9. When ready to bake, remove coulibiac from the refrigerator, and preheat the oven to 425°F.

10. Bake the coulibiac for 10 minutes at 425°F, then reduce the oven to 350°F, and continue to bake for 10–15 minutes longer or until golden. Insert a metal tester in the center of the roll to make sure the interior is hot. Cover with foil (shiny side facing up) if the dough is golden and the mixture needs more time to heat through.

11. Serve sliced with port wine cream sauce if desired (see page 139).

Yield: 8–12 servings

Mushroom Duxelles

½ ounce dried porcini mushrooms
¼ cup cream sherry
1½ pounds fresh mushrooms
½ stick unsalted butter
1 shallot, finely chopped

½ cup finely chopped onion
½ teaspoon thyme
½–¾ teaspoon salt
Nutmeg to taste (should be subtle)
Pepper to taste

1. Rinse the dried porcini mushrooms with cold water and drain well. Place in a glass bowl and add the sherry. Microwave for 20 seconds and allow the mushrooms to soften in the liquid while you prepare the rest of the ingredients for the duxelles.

2. Wash and drain the fresh mushrooms, and mince in a processor until finely chopped.

3. Melt the butter in a 2-quart saucepan. Add the shallot and onion, and sauté for 5 minutes or until golden.

4. Add the minced mushrooms and the seasonings, and stir to combine.

5. Place the soaked mushrooms (reserve the liquid) in a processor work bowl (be careful not to get any sand from the liquid in the work bowl). Pulse the machine on and off until a fine paste is formed. Add the soaking liquid and process to puree. Add this mixture to the saucepan.

6. Sauté over low to medium heat until the duxelles is reduced and thickened. Be careful that the mixture doesn't stick. Adjust seasonings. Set aside until ready to use. May be refrigerated for a day or two or frozen for later use.

Rice and Cheese Filling

2 tablespoons butter
¼ cup finely minced scallions
2 tablespoons flour
1 cup milk

2¼ cups leftover cooked rice (or ¾ cup raw rice cooked in 2¼ cups water for 20 minutes)
2 tablespoons minced dill
¼ cup parmesan cheese
Nutmeg to taste
Salt and pepper to taste

1. Melt the butter in a saucepan and sauté the scallions until wilted. Whisk in the flour and cook for 1 minute over low heat.

2. Add the milk all at once and rapidly mix the sauce until thickened.

3. Add the remaining ingredients and adjust seasonings if necessary. Set aside until ready to assemble coulibiac.

Herbed Crepe

2 teaspoons vegetable oil
2 eggs
1/2 cup flour
1 cup milk (preferably 2% or whole)

Pinch of salt
1 tablespoon chopped fresh chives
1 tablespoon chopped fresh parsley
1 tablespoon chopped fresh dill

1. Brush a nonstick jelly roll pan with the oil. Set aside.

2. Beat eggs with a handheld electric mixer for 30 seconds or until pale yellow.

3. With mixer on medium, add the milk in a steady stream, and then add the flour until a smooth batter is formed.

4. Add the remaining ingredients and mix just to combine. Let mixture rest at room temperature for 20–30 minutes.

5. Preheat oven to 425°F.

6. Spread the mixture in the prepared jelly roll pan and bake for 12 minutes. Let cool in pan until ready to assemble.

Note: This mixture will get a little rubbery if made far in advance of assembly.

> ### TINA'S TIDBITS
>
> - *Although the puff pastry readily available in your supermarket freezer is quite good, it is pareve. It would be worth a little time to find butter-based puff pastry for this dish. It is superb.*
> - *Nutmeg should always be added to recipes containing cheese or mushrooms. The flavor enhances the natural taste of those ingredients. Make sure, however, that your cheese sauce doesn't smell like egg nog!*
> - *The base of the sauce for the rice and cheese filling is a classic medium white sauce that is also the base for a macaroni and cheese sauce: 2 tablespoons of butter to 2 tablespoons of flour, with 1 cup of milk. Substitute margarine and chicken broth to that proportion and you have a velouté sauce, which is often used to create a non-dairy sauce for a meat dish that will conform to the laws of kashrut.*

Port Wine Cream Sauce

5 tablespoons unsalted butter, divided use
1/4 cup minced shallots
1/2 cup port wine

1/2 cup heavy cream
1/2 teaspoon fresh lime juice
Salt and pepper to taste

1. Melt 2 tablespoons butter in a heavy saucepan and add the shallots. Sauté for 3 minutes or until soft.

2. Add the port wine, and over high heat, reduce the liquid by half.

3. Add the lime juice and cream. Heat just to the boiling point and then reduce to a low simmer.

4. Whisk in the remaining butter 1 tablespoon at a time. Remove from the heat. Adjust seasonings, and serve with coulibiac.

RUGELACH

Thirty-five years ago I sat in Mrs. Goodman's kitchen and she gave me this recipe. It was the first time I had ever made them and they were great. Over the years I realized that although everyone seems to have the same recipe with the same proportions, mine always came out lighter and flakier. I pass on my three "secrets" to you in my Tidbits. At one time I used to make a thousand of these at a time for the largest kosher caterer in Philadelphia. Nowadays, I am content to make a double batch of 150 for my friends and family.

8 ounces cream cheese
8 ounces salted butter
2 cups all purpose flour
1½ cups sugar

2–3 teaspoons ground cinnamon
1 cup raisins
¾ cup chopped walnuts
Confectioners' sugar

1. Cream the cheese and butter together on high speed with an electric mixer until well combined and light and fluffy (the mixture should feather out from the edge of the bowl). Scrape down the sides of the bowl. Add flour and turn your mixer on and off **only** until dough looks like the flour has been incorporated. Remove the dough from the bowl and lightly drop it on a smooth surface a few times until it forms a compact mass. (Pressing with your hands could soften the butter and change the consistency of your finished product.)

2. Divide mixture into 8 cylinders, and refrigerate 1 hour or until dough is firm.

3. Roll each portion of dough onto a board that is heavily "floured" with confectioners' sugar. Roll out into a 6 × 9-inch rectangle.

4. Combine the sugar, cinnamon, raisins, and walnuts in a bowl.

5. After the dough is rolled out, sprinkle with some of the sugar-nut mixture. Roll dough into a log from the long side. Pinch the seam together on the bottom and the ends slightly under.

6. Cut filled logs into 8 or 9 pieces, and place on an ungreased or parchment-lined cookie sheet. Repeat with remaining dough logs.

7. Bake in a 350°F oven for 12–15 minutes or until golden. Cool completely before freezing.

Yield: 5–6 dozen cookies

TINA'S TIDBITS

- *Using salted butter in a pastry is the exception. Here it is necessary to evenly distribute salt in non-liquid dough.*
- *Handling this dough as little as possible keeps the fat content from dissolving into the flour, with the result more like puff pastry instead of cookie dough.*
- *Always roll this dough on a board covered with confectioners' sugar. This sugar helps balance the richness of the dough with the sweet filling.*
- *Confectioners' sugar contains 2-3 percent cornstarch, which helps absorb moisture and prevent the dough from sticking to the counter or rolling pin.*
- *The raw dough or the baked rugelach can be frozen for later use.*

WESTERN EUROPE

✒ GERMANY ✒

Jews first traversed the Alps to the land of modern-day Germany and eastern France during the Roman period. They settled by rivers because they were primarily traders. The Radenites (from Persian for "knowing the way") were Jewish traders in the ninth century who journeyed between China and the Frankish kingdoms, bringing furs, beaver pelts, swords, slaves, and eunuchs to China and bringing spices, silks, and metal to Arabia, Persia, North Africa, Germany, and France. Jews were primarily involved in this profession because of the basic distrust between Muslims and Christians. They also were fluent in many languages so they acted as interpreters during transactions.

The Jews were never accepted by the Christian communities, nor were they allowed to live near them or associate with them. They lived in fenced-off villages. However, for a time they were tolerated and were permitted to enter into business transactions with the Christians. The Crusades ended this era. Although the Crusades officially began in 1096, a crazed Monk named Peter started his own drive to the Holy Land a year earlier. On his way he pillaged and massacred any "enemy of God" on his path. The church didn't condone this but was unable to prevent the mass slaughter of Jews in Worms.

In medieval times, Jews who traveled could not reliably expect a kosher meal in the villages where they traded. They were known for taking large loaves of bread on their journeys and subsisting on preserved fish and vegetables. Some inns on their trade routes kept a pan aside that was retained solely for kosher sauces, but this practice was not common.

At home, each village had a kosher communal oven and even a few cauldrons set aside for large festivities like weddings. These ovens were used to bake challah and slow-cooked stews for Shabbat and matzah for Pesach. German Jews preferred to eat goose and duck over chicken, liked sweet-and-sour flavors in foods from meat to cabbage to fish, and baked goods encasing cheese or fruit or both, such as *fludens* or *chremslach*, and sweet crackers were their desserts of choice.

The great German migration to America peaked in the mid- to late 1800s. German Jewish merchants, financiers, and manufacturers quickly rose to prominence in the economic landscape, and German Jews were the major force behind the growth of Reform Judaism in America. The next major wave of German-Jewish immigration was in the early 1930s as Hitler was coming to power. In 1933 there were almost 600,000 Jews living in Germany; 240,000 German Jews managed to escape to the United States, and another 130,000 made it to South America.

Jews have lived in France since the Roman period. Initially they were scattered and isolated from their coreligionists. However, after the Roman conquest of Jerusalem in 70 C.E., many Jews sought asylum in Bordeaux, Arles, and Lyon in southern France. By the ninth century, good-sized Jewish communities with communal ovens, *mikvaot*, and venues for religious practice (if not actual synagogues) existed in Paris, Rouen, Alsace-Lorraine, Blois, and Lyon in addition to the already established region in Provence. Jews were active in medicine and commerce. They were so successful that they were accredited vendors to the royal court. They were also significant in the viniculture community, supplying not only the kosher wines needed by the Jews but also wines for general consumption and for church mass. In the tenth century, one of the most famous commentators of the Talmud, Rashi, established his school in Troyes, southeast of Paris, while he tended his extensive vineyard.

The First Crusade had no impact on the Jewish communities in France; however, by the Second Crusade in the mid-twelfth century, the long reign of persecution, ascribed attire, looting, taxation, and mass murders had begun. In 1240 whole communities of Jews were expelled from France. The kingdom confiscated all personal goods and property. Two years later the Talmud was put on trial and burned.

In the middle of the fourteenth century, the plague struck, and Jews were blamed for it, because they seemed to have escaped most of its effect— most likely because the Jews were not allowed to associate with the Christian community and had higher standards of personal hygiene. Nevertheless, retaliatory massacres of Jewish communities in the east and southeast of France occurred. The Jews in the south were protected from most persecution because the papal seat had moved to Avignon and the pope needed the business acumen and trade contacts of the Jews to finance the Roman Catholic Church. Jews in this region lived well in comparison to their brethren in other regions.

In the next two centuries, Marrano Jews escaped from Portugal and settled in the area of Bayonne just over the Pyrenees. Jews escaping the Chmielnicki massacres in the Ukraine and Poland came to Alsace and Lorraine.

The French Revolution granted full citizenship to its Jewish inhabitants, but that didn't stop the establishment of anti-Jewish measures to restrict where Jews could live and how they could assimilate into French society. Despite some restrictions, Jews became prominent in many social circles. The Rothschild and Pereire families were prominent financiers. Baron Edmond de Rothschild helped establish what was to become Israel's thriving wine industry by setting up vineyards in Rishon LeZion with cuttings from his own famous vineyards. The renowned novelist Emile Zola used his writing skills to protest the mishandling of the Dreyfus case, which prompted Theodor Herzl to write his treatise on the establishment of a Jewish state.

The pogroms in Eastern Europe and North Africa increased Jewish immigration to France, but World War II and the establishment of the Vichy government depleted over 25 percent of the three hundred thousand French Jewish population. In February 1941 there were forty thousand Jews interned in southern French camps. By April 1942 only eleven thousand Jews remained. It is not known whether or not the Jews were released or deported.

After the establishment of the State of Israel, anti-Semitism rose in the Middle East. Algeria and Morocco were agitating for their own independence from France (which they won in 1962 and 1956, respectively). The Jews identified with the French influence in that region, which angered the Arab inhabitants even more, leading many of the region's Jews to move to France. The Jewish community in France has thrived since the latter half of the twentieth century, though increasing anti-Semitism in recent years has led many French Jews to immigrate to Israel and North America. Still, France has the largest Jewish population in Europe and the largest Jewish population outside Israel and the United States.

ᴇ~ ENGLAND ~ᴇ

The first Jews came to England from Rouen, France, in 1066 with William the Conqueror. They were mostly moneylenders, dealing with the barons and advancing money to the Crown to support the monarchy. Jews were allowed this occupation because it was not a lucrative business for Christians, who were not permitted to charge interest to their fellow parishioners. Because they were an asset to the Treasury, the Jews were afforded protection by the Crown.

When the Crusades began, being Jewish in England was a major liability. Many Crusaders felt they needn't wait to get to Jerusalem to fight the "infidel" when so many Jews were in their midst at home. The Jews were forced to wear identifying large swatches of cloth on their clothes representing a Torah or Jewish star, their property was taken away, loans to Christians were declared null and void, and in the worst cases, Jews were tortured or killed after being accused of the infamous blood libel.

On July 18, 1290, all the Jews in England were expelled. This date coincided with Tishah B'Av, the day on the Jewish calendar marking the day the First and Second Temples in Jerusalem were destroyed. Estimates of the number of people expelled varies between five thousand and sixteen thousand, but all those who survived crossing the English Channel settled in France.

Jews did not receive permission to resettle in England for over 350 years. The level of anti-Semitism in England was so great that two of her most famous playwrights, Marlowe and Shakespeare, used stereotypic Jewish protagonists in their plays of 1589 and 1597. The irony is that no one in England had ever seen a Jew in 300 years!

In 1655 Oliver Cromwell was petitioned to authorize the return of Jews to England. No official authorization was granted, but the first synagogue was erected in 1657 by Sephardic Jews from Holland. The next immigrants were German Jews, beginning in 1690. In 1698 a decree legalized practicing Judaism in England.

Bevis Marks, a Sephardic synagogue still functioning today, was founded in 1701. By 1734 six thousand Sephardic and Ashkenazic Jews lived in England. Jews were knighted and held public office, and in 1858 the Christian oath of Parliament was changed to allow Jews to take their oath on the Hebrew Bible. Since that time there has never been an English Parliament without Jewish members.

Today almost two-thirds of England's Jewish population reside in London, the neighborhoods of Golders Green and Edgware being the biggest Jewish hubs. Both sections of London house a branch of Bloom's Deli. Often referred to as London's Second Avenue Deli, this establishment was founded in 1920 in the heart of Jewish London by a Lithuanian immigrant, Morris Bloom. But Morris wasn't the only famous Jewish culinary impresario in England.

Back in the sixteenth century when Portuguese Jews came to England as crypto-Jews fleeing the Inquisition, they introduced their special style of fish preparation to the country. Batter-dipped, deep-fried fish fillets served cold became popular. Even Lady Judith Montefiore in her 1846 cookbook, *The Jewish Manual: Practical Information in Jewish and Modern Cookery with a Collection of Valuable Recipes and Hints Relating to the Toilette*, offered a recipe for "Fried Fish in the Jewish Style." In 1860 Joseph Malin, a Jewish immigrant from Eastern Europe, left his fish shop, Malin's of Bow in the East End, to go to an Irish potato shop. There he took some of their fried potatoes, added them to some of his fried fish, wrapped it up in newspaper, and sold it. His new combination was a great hit, and he is credited with being the first in England to sell fish and chips. Here was a true amalgam of cultures: Ashkenazic, Sephardic, and Irish immigrants all lent their culinary heritage to create a new dish for their new homeland.

DILL PUFFS WITH CAVIAR

I created this recipe by combining the flavors of dill, smoked salmon (lox), and cream cheese in a vehicle that was more appropriate for entertaining than bagels, lox, and cream cheese. Here again is the classic technique for making pâte à choux, *but dill and nutmeg are added to complement the filling's flavor.*

1 cup water
½ teaspoon salt
Pinch of nutmeg
Pinch of pepper

¾ stick unsalted butter
1 tablespoon minced fresh dill
1 cup flour
4 eggs

1. In a medium saucepan, combine the first six ingredients and bring just to a boil.

2. **Immediately** remove the pan from the heat and add the flour all at once. Stir rapidly with a firm wooden spoon or spatula until a ball is formed.

3. Return the pan to the stove. Over medium heat, beat the flour ball for a minute or two, until a film forms on the pan. Remove the pan from the heat and cool for a minute.

4. Beat in 1 egg at a time, making sure that the previous egg has been totally incorporated before you add the next egg. Beat vigorously!

5. Bake for 20 minutes at 425°F. Remove and turn off the oven. Cut a little slit in the sides of the puffs to let out the steam, and return to the turned-off oven for another 5–10 minutes. Let cool completely and then fill with caviar filling (see recipe on the following page). The puffs may be frozen **unfilled** for later use.

TINA'S TIDBITS

- *I strongly advise using fresh dill in the puffs rather than dried dill weed, which can be bitter.*
- *It is important that the puffs have a dry interior so that they will hold their shape and not get too soft when filled.*
- *To successfully freeze puff shells that won't be used on the day they were made, make sure puffs are completely cooled, place on a cookie sheet in the freezer until frozen, and then remove from the sheet and place in a plastic freezer storage bag. Using a common straw, suck all the air out of the freezer bag to prevent ice crystals from forming.*
- *If you don't have fresh chives for the filling, you can always substitute the green section of scallions for an equivalent volume.*
- *If you are making the filling a day in advance, don't add the caviar to the cream cheese until the filling is at room temperature. This prevents the eggs from breaking open when mixed into the cream cheese.*

Caviar Filling

8 ounces cream cheese
¼ cup heavy cream
6 chives, about 8 inches long, ripped into 1-inch pieces
1 teaspoon fresh lemon juice

Finely grated zest from ½ medium lemon
4 ounces smoked salmon, cut into 1-inch pieces
2 tablespoons red lumpfish caviar

1. Cut the cream cheese into 8 pieces and place in a processor work bowl. Pulse the processor on and off to make the cream cheese smooth. Scrape down the sides of the bowl.

2. Add the cream and pulse on and off until combined. Add the chives, lemon juice, and zest and process for 5 seconds.

3. Add the smoked salmon pieces and pulse until the fish is small and distributed evenly. Pour the cheese mixture into a bowl, and fold in the caviar. Chill until ready to fill the puffs.

Yield: 2–3 dozen

GOUGERE

Take the classic French recipe for pâte à choux *(cream puff paste), add cheese and herbs to the mixture, and bake long enough to have the outside crisp and the inside creamy and you have a perfect appetizer for entertaining.*

1 cup water
3/4 teaspoon salt
Pinch of freshly ground pepper
1/2 teaspoon dried marjoram or thyme
Pinch of nutmeg
3/4 stick unsalted butter

1 cup flour
4 eggs
1 cup grated Swiss or Parmesan cheese
1 teaspoon dry mustard
Pinch of cayenne pepper

1. In a medium saucepan, bring the water, salt, pepper, marjoram, nutmeg, and butter just to a boil. Immediately remove from the heat and **rapidly** add the flour all at once. Beat the flour mixture until a ball is formed.

2. Return the pan to medium heat, and over medium heat beat the flour ball for another minute or two, until a film forms on the pan.

3. Remove the pan from the heat and cool for 1 minute. Using a wooden spoon or handheld electric mixer beat in 1 egg at a time, making sure that the previous egg has been totally incorporated into the dough before you add the next egg. Beat vigorously!

4. After the dough is made, beat the cheese, dry mustard, and cayenne into the dough.

5. Drop dough by tablespoon, or pipe a 1-inch circle using a pastry bag and #6 tip, onto a greased or parchment-lined cookie sheet.

6. Bake at 375°F for 25–30 minutes or until puff is golden and easily removed from the paper. Puffs will have a moist, cheese-filled center.

Yield: 3–4 dozen

TINA'S TIDBITS

- *Have all of your ingredients measured out so that the water won't boil for long and lose some of its volume.*
- *Always remove the dough from the heat before you add the eggs or you will get a thick sauce rather than a dough that will puff up in the oven.*
- *If piping your dough onto the cookie sheet, press the little points of dough down with a fingertip moistened with water. This will prevent the top of the dough from burning.*

THREE-POTATO CHEESE GRATIN

An elegant variation of potatoes dauphinois, this gratin is colorful and rich with the addition of the Montrachet goat cheese. Serve with grilled fish and a salad and you have an impressive but easy meal.

2 tablespoons unsalted butter
2 leeks, white part only, thinly sliced
8 purple potatoes, thinly sliced
8 small Yukon Gold or fingerling potatoes, thinly sliced
1 long large yam, peeled and thinly sliced
6 tablespoons all-purpose flour

1½ teaspoons salt
Freshly ground black pepper
1½ cups whole milk
½ cup heavy cream
10 ounces herbed Montrachet goat cheese
8 chives, thinly sliced
½ cup freshly grated Parmesan cheese

1. Preheat the oven to 350°F.

2. Melt the butter in a large skillet over high heat until it starts to brown. Reduce the heat to medium. Add the sliced leeks and sauté until tender.

3. Toss the potatoes in a bowl with the flour, salt, and pepper. Add to the leek mixture. Stir gently with a rubber spatula to combine.

4. Combine the milk, heavy cream, goat cheese, and chives, and add to the pan. Cook until cheese is melted and the mixture is bubbly.

5. Butter a 2-quart gratin pan or casserole. Pour the potato-cheese mixture into the prepared pan and sprinkle with the Parmesan cheese.

6. Bake for 35 minutes or until top is golden and potatoes are tender when pierced with the tip of a knife.

Yield: 6–8 servings

TINA'S TIDBITS

- *Leeks grow in very sandy soil. To remove the sand, cut off the white portion of the leek and then cut in half lengthwise up to, but not including, the root. Under running water, fan the leaves of the leek as you would shuffle a deck of cards so that the water can rinse away the sand.*
- *Eight ounces of cream cheese may be substituted for the goat cheese.*
- *A gratin may be made in advance and reheated in a microwave until hot, about 2–3 minutes depending on the depth of the mixture.*
- *When reheating in a microwave, it is most desirable to bring the gratin to room temperature first so that reheating takes the minimal amount of time and preserves the dish's proper consistency.*

CHEESE FONDUE

The word fondue *is derived from the French word for* melt. *This recipe, however, is from Switzerland. Jews have been documented as living in Switzerland since the thirteenth century. The first immigrants were from the southeast region of France, thus influencing the culinary heritage of the Swiss inhabitants and possibly the creation of this dish.*

1 clove garlic
1¼ cups dry white wine
1 pound aged Gruyère or Emmenthaler cheese, grated

1½ tablespoons cornstarch
3 tablespoons Kirschwasser
Pinch of nutmeg and pepper

1. Cut the clove of garlic in half, and rub the inside of the fondue pot with garlic. Discard the garlic clove.

2. Heat the white wine in the fondue pot on the stove until the wine is just simmering.

3. Add the cheese by thirds and stir constantly with a wooden spoon until melted and barely simmering.

4. Combine the cornstarch with the Kirschwasser and add to the cheese mixture. Stir until bubbly and add the seasonings.

5. Transfer the fondue pot to a Sterno or candle warmer. Keep warm but do not allow to boil.

6. Serve with wedges of French bread or pieces of apple if you like.

Note: If mixture gets too thick, add a little extra wine or water. If mixture starts to separate, combine 1 teaspoon cornstarch with 1 tablespoon wine and add to cheese mixture.

Yield: 6 servings

TINA'S TIDBITS

- *Alcohol will burn off somewhat during cooking, but this mixture is still strong. Substitute unsweetened grape or apple juice for all or part of the wine if you prefer.*
- *Cornstarch is used in this mixture to bind the cheese and wine together without imparting a flavor. Cornstarch thickens clear and shiny, as opposed to flour, which makes a mixture opaque.*
- *Kirschwasser is a German clear cherry brandy that enhances the flavor of the cheese. It is distilled from cherries and cherry pits.*
- *Nutmeg should always be used subtly in cheese mixtures, as it complements the flavor of the cheese beautifully.*

Five-Onion French Onion Soup

The biggest problem with creating classic French onion soup in a traditional Jewish home is that the base for the soup is beef and the appeal of the soup is the copious amounts of melted cheese on the top. My sister, Sherry, came up with this delicious broth for the base, and a trip to Crested Butte, Colorado, gave me the idea of using many different textures and colors of onion in the soup. Jewish culinary ingenuity at work again!

Broth

5 quarts water
1/3 cup pareve beef-flavored bouillon
2 packets or cubes vegetarian or mushroom bouillon (for color as well as flavor)
1 large onion, coarsely chopped
1 1/2 cups coarsely chopped celery, leaves and tops included

1 1/2 cups carrots, cut into 2-inch lengths
1 cup turnips, cut into 1-inch cubes
12 peppercorns
2 sprigs parsley
1 bay leaf
1 teaspoon dried thyme
2 cloves garlic, coarsely chopped

1. Place all of the ingredients into a large Dutch oven. Bring to a boil and simmer for 3 hours.

2. Strain the stock through a fine sieve or cheesecloth, and refrigerate until needed.

Onion Soup

3 tablespoons unsalted butter
1 leek, white part only, sliced lengthwise in half and into 1/4-inch crosswise strips
1 large red onion, thinly sliced
1 large Bermuda onion, thinly sliced
10 ounces pearl onions, peeled but kept whole
5 scallions, white part only, thinly sliced
Salt to taste

Freshly ground black pepper to taste
4 tablespoons flour
2 cups dry white wine
2 or more cups of prepared broth (see recipe above)
8 slices French bread
1 clove garlic, split in half
8 ounces Gruyère cheese, grated

1. To make the soup, melt the butter in a 3-quart saucepan, add the onions and salt and pepper to taste, and slowly sauté the onions until they are very soft and lightly golden. Scrape the pot well to incorporate any of the brown residue.

2. Sprinkle the onions with the flour and stir for 2 minutes.

3. Add the wine and stir frequently until mixture comes to a boil. Add 2 cups of reserved broth and heat for 15 minutes. Add more broth if you want a different consistency. There is no right or wrong amount.

4. Meanwhile, rub both sides of the slices of bread with the cut edge of the garlic, and toast the bread on a cookie sheet in a 475°F oven until golden.

5. Pour the hot soup into a large tureen or 8 individual ramekins, making sure that you evenly distribute the onions.

6. Cover each serving with a piece of toast and sprinkle generously with the cheese.

7. Place in the hot oven for 20 minutes or until the soup is hot and the cheese is melted, or heat the soup in a microwave before placing in ramekins and topping with bread and cheese. This will prevent the bread from getting tough in the microwave.

Note: The ramekins may be placed under the broiler for a minute or two if you like the cheese browned more.

Yield: 8 servings

TINA'S TIDBITS

- *A Dutch oven is a 4- or 6-quart lidded pot with two short handles that can be used on the top of the stove, instead of the oven, to make "pot" roast and thus conserve a great deal of energy. It can also be used in the oven when you don't want direct heat cooking your food.*
- *Adding flour to the onions is a way of creating a roux for thickening the soup without the chance of burning the flour before the vegetables are cooked.*
- *Rubbing garlic on the bread before toasting imparts a distinct but mild flavor of garlic to the bread without the need for oil to carry the garlic flavor.*

CLASSIC POT ROAST

Although pot roast is classic to American Jewish kitchens, none of our ancestors, regardless of location, used this quantity of meat in one recipe. Most meat dishes around the world were vegetables enhanced with bits of meat. The affluence of the modern Jewish community was more often displayed on the dining room table than on material possessions.

2 large onions
1/4 cup vegetable oil
One 3- to 4-pound piece of brisket or chuck roast
1 teaspoon of salt or to taste

Freshly ground black pepper to taste (about 1/4–1/2 teaspoon)
1 teaspoon or more garlic powder (or 2 teaspoons finally chopped fresh garlic)
4 or more cups water (to almost cover meat)

1. Slice the onions in half lengthwise, and slice each half into thin strips.

2. Heat a large pot or Dutch oven for 20 seconds, add oil, and heat for another 10 seconds. Add the sliced onion and sauté over moderately hot heat until the onions are very dark but not yet burnt.

3. Wash off the meat and pat dry. Add to the large pot and sear on all sides. (Searing adds flavor to the gravy and helps prevent the meat from drying out.)

4. Sprinkle the meat with the salt, pepper, and garlic powder, and add enough water to almost cover the meat.

5. Cover the pot and bring the liquid to a simmer. Reduce the heat to low and cook the meat until the gravy has reduced to make thin but strong gravy and the meat is tender, about 2 hours. Check for seasonings. Remove the meat and cool the meat and the gravy separately.

6. If you desire thicker gravy, prepare an *einbrenne* by melting 2 tablespoons of margarine and adding 2 tablespoons of flour to it, stirring until mixture is brown. Add this to the gravy and heat until gravy is desired thickness. Adjust seasonings if necessary.

7. Slice the meat when it is cool. If there is time, refrigerate meat until firm, then slice. (Refrigerated meat is even easier to cut). Return the meat slices to the gravy. Reheat in the microwave and serve.

Yield: 6–8 servings

TINA'S TIDBITS

- *The rich color and taste of the gravy are directly proportional to the length of time the onions are cooked. If you make a pot roast and you deem it "tasteless," there's a good chance that you were in a rush that day and didn't take the time to brown the onions sufficiently and the final product was bland.*
- *This dish, like most meat dishes, tastes much better the next day. In addition, the meat is much easier to slice cold.*
- *Potatoes and carrots could be added to the meat during the last hour of cooking if desired.*

Soupe de Poissons
(Bouillabaisse)

There has been a strong Jewish presence in southern France since the fall of the Second Temple, when Jewish captives were brought by Roman legions to that region. In the fifteenth and sixteenth centuries, many Jews arrived in Provence from Spain and Portugal to escape the Inquisition. The following recipe illustrates the culinary influence of these Jews, with the inclusion of fennel, orange, and saffron from the Iberian Peninsula.

⅓ cup extra virgin olive oil
1 onion, thinly sliced
1 leek, white part only, thinly sliced
One 8-ounce package of prepared fish stock concentrate or 1 pound fish head and bones plus 1 cup of water
2½ cups water
1 cup dry white wine
1½ pounds ripe Roma tomatoes, cut into eighths
¼ teaspoon fennel seeds, lightly crushed
1 clove garlic, chopped
One 1 × 3-inch strip of orange zest

1 sprig of parsley
1 bay leaf
1 pinch of saffron threads or one tiny pinch of saffron powder
Salt and freshly ground pepper to taste
1 clove garlic, sliced in half lengthwise
4 large, thick slices of country French bread
1 pound sea bass or halibut
1 pound snapper or sole
Rouille (optional; see recipe on the following page)
Freshly grated Parmesan cheese (optional)

1. Heat a 4-quart Dutch oven over high for 20 seconds. Add the olive oil and heat for 10 seconds. Add the sliced onion and the sliced leeks, and sauté over medium heat for about 5 minutes until the onion is soft but not turning brown.

2. Add all of the ingredients through the salt and pepper to the Dutch oven, cover, reduce the heat to low, and simmer for 45 minutes.

3. When the soup is done, strain the mixture through a fine strainer into a clean 3-quart saucepan. Press down gently on the vegetables to extract their juices. Discard the vegetables and bones (if using).

4. Adjust the salt and pepper to taste.

5. Rub the cut edge of the garlic over the surfaces of the bread slices.

6. Toast the bread in a preheated 350°F oven for 5 minutes or until firm and lightly golden.

7. Bring the soup to a simmer and add 2-inch pieces of two or more varieties of fish. If one fish is thicker than the other, add the thicker fish to the stock first and cook for 3 minutes before adding the remaining fish. Cook the fish for a total of no more than 5 minutes. Fish will continue to cook in the hot broth even after removing from heat.

8. To serve, ladle some soup in a soup bowl and place a slice of bread on top. Spoon some rouille on top of the bread and sprinkle with freshly grated Parmesan cheese if you like.

Easy Rouille

2 large cloves of garlic
6 fresh basil leaves
2 ounces drained, roasted red bell peppers
¼ cup fresh bread crumbs

1–2 tablespoons hot soup
1 cup good-quality mayonnaise
Cayenne, salt, and freshly ground black pepper to
taste

1. Combine the garlic, basil, and roasted red peppers in a processor work bowl and process until pureed.

2. Add the remaining ingredients and process until smooth. Refrigerate until ready to use.

Yield: 6 or more servings

TINA'S TIDBITS

- *If you are only using one or two very mild fish, then you could add some of the rouille to the soup (by first adding some soup to the rouille in a small glass bowl until a smooth paste is formed and then adding to the soup). This would give you a slightly thicker and more flavorful soup.*
- *There are three ways to remove zest, depending on the final result desired:*
  1. *Use a vegetable peeler to get one long strip of zest for flavoring.*
  2. *Use a zester to get thin strands for flavoring and garnish.*
  3. *Use a rasp grater to get fine shreds for flavoring that will blend into food.*

EASY SAUERBRATEN (GERMAN BRISKET)

Sauerbraten normally takes time to make, since the meat has to marinate in the vinegar mixture for days. Here is a faster version that comes close to its German roots.

2 tablespoons extra virgin olive oil
1 large onion, chopped into ½-inch dice (about 2 cups)
2- to 3-pound cut of brisket or other cut suitable for slow cooking
1 large clove of garlic, minced
1 tablespoon flour
5 grindings of black pepper

⅓ cup apple cider vinegar
1½ cups water
4 teaspoons pickling spice
1 inch piece fresh ginger, peeled
2 or more tablespoons light brown sugar to taste
1 pound baby carrots
6–8 ginger snap cookies

1. Heat a 4-quart Dutch oven over high heat for 20 seconds. Add oil and heat for another 10 seconds. Reduce the heat to medium high.

2. Add the chopped onion to the pan and sauté for 3 minutes or until lightly golden.

3. Rinse the meat and pat dry with a paper towel. Add meat to the onion and brown on both sides—about 3 minutes per side.

4. Add the garlic, flour, and pepper and stir to combine with the onions and meat.

5. Combine the vinegar, water, pickling spice, fresh ginger, and 2 tablespoons brown sugar in a liquid measuring cup. Pour over the meat and stir to deglaze the pan.

6. Preheat the oven to 300°F while you bring the liquid to a boil.

7. Cover the meat with a lid and place the pot in the preheated oven. Bake for 2 hours and then add the baby carrots. Return the meat to the oven and bake for another hour or until the meat is fork tender.

8. Remove the meat from the liquid.

9. Add 6–8 ginger snaps to the pan and stir until they are completely dissolved and the mixture has thickened. Boil for a few more minutes if the gravy is too thin. Adjust seasonings if necessary. Skim off excess fat from the gravy, or refrigerate and remove the fat from the gravy when the mixture is cold.

10. Chill the meat before slicing. Place sliced meat in a casserole dish and add the gravy to the meat. Reheat in a low oven or microwave. Serve with potato pancakes or noodles.

Yield: 6 servings

TINA'S TIDBITS

- *The German origins of this are evident by the use of ginger (in the pickling spice) and ginger snaps to create the piquant, spicy flavor.*
- *For this recipe, it is important to use a cut of meat marbled with some fat to keep the meat from drying out during cooking.*
- *If you do not have pickling spice, use 1 bay leaf, 1 cinnamon stick, 1 teaspoon coriander seeds, 1 teaspoon allspice, and 1 teaspoon mustard seeds to approximate some of the flavors in the commercially prepared mixture.*
- *Using 1/4 cup rice wine vinegar and 1/4 cup apple juice for the apple cider vinegar will cut some of the "bite" in the sauerbraten sauce, especially if your ginger snaps have a real peppery taste.*

Sweet and Sour Red Cabbage with Apples

Although the last two ingredients in this recipe indicate their modern influence, this was a typical recipe among Jewish peasants throughout Eastern Europe. Everyday cabbage and onions were slightly elevated by the precious apple, and the vinegar helped preserve it for Shabbat or later use.

1 small red cabbage (about 1½ pounds)
¾ cup red wine vinegar
¼ cup sugar
½ tablespoon salt
2 Braeburn or Gala apples
2 tablespoons cooking oil

1 small onion, cut in half lengthwise and thinly sliced
1 whole onion, peeled and pierced with 6 whole cloves
4 cups boiling water
¼ cup dry red wine
3 tablespoons red currant jelly or raspberry jam

1. Wash and core the cabbage, and cut into quarters lengthwise. Cut each quarter crosswise into ¼-inch strips. Place in a large bowl with the vinegar, sugar, and salt.

2. Peel, core, and thinly slice the apples.

3. In a 5-quart Dutch oven, heat the oil and sauté the sliced onion for 4 minutes until it is lightly golden. Add the apple and sauté for 5 minutes longer.

4. Put the cabbage and the whole onion in the Dutch oven with the apples.

5. Pour the boiling water over all the cabbage and bring to a boil.

6. Reduce the heat to moderate and cook for 1 hour, stirring occasionally to prevent sticking.

7. When cabbage is ready, remove from heat, stir in the wine and jelly, and season to taste with salt, pepper, and more sugar if necessary.

Yield: 4–6 servings

TINA'S TIDBITS

- *Although this dish can be served freshly made, it tastes better refrigerated overnight and then served warm.*
- *The secret to preserving the beautiful purple color in cooked red cabbage is to cook it with apples and/or vinegar.*

SUMMER FRUIT SOUP

There are no cherries in here to epitomize a Hungarian fruit soup, but the fresh flavors of summer are represented deliciously. Jewish homes rarely served sweets for dessert. Meals often ended with fresh fruit or fruit compotes. Here is a wonderful way to bridge the divide between European custom and American palates.

2 pounds of frozen peaches or 2 ½ pounds of fresh peaches
1 cup orange juice
1 cup water
½ teaspoon cinnamon

⅔ cup honey
Juice of ½ lemon
1 large (3–4 pounds) cantaloupe
¼ cup apricot brandy
Blueberries (for garnish)

1. If using fresh peaches, peel and pit the fruit. Cut the peaches into chunks and place in a 2-quart saucepan with the orange juice, water, cinnamon, honey, and lemon juice. Simmer for 15 minutes or until peaches are tender.

2. Using a slotted spoon, transfer the peach chunks to a processor work bowl and puree. Pour into a large bowl and add the liquid from the saucepan.

3. Peel, cut into chunks, and puree the cantaloupe. Combine with the peach mixture and the apricot brandy, and chill.

4. Serve garnished with blueberries in individual bowls.

Yield: 8–10 servings

TINA'S TIDBITS

- *If fresh fruit is not available or at its flavor peak, substituting frozen fruit is an excellent alternative. Growers often process their fruit on location, and the blanching process locks in the color and sweetness of the produce.*
- *For a delicious alternative, try freezing this mixture according to ice-cream maker directions. Make sure the puree is cold before adding to the machine.*
- *The apricot brandy not only adds flavor to the soup, but it will prevent the mixture from freezing rock hard, so it will make a perfect sorbet.*

CHOCOLATE CHIP MERINGUES

The first documented example of meringue was in an English cookbook written by Lady Elynor Fettiplace in the early 1600s for her family. She called them "white biskit bread." Since the first sugar refinery in England wasn't established until the 1540s this commodity wasn't readily available to home cooks and might have only been used in the royal houses of Europe at that time. However, in 1692 Francois Massialot published a cookbook with the recipe for meringues and since then these light-as-air confections have been considered French in origin. This treat is very popular at Passover because no flour or matzah meal needs to be used.

½ cup egg whites (about 4–5 large egg whites), at room temperature
Scant ¼ teaspoon salt
¼ teaspoon cream of tartar (optional for Passover)

1 cup sugar
1 teaspoon vanilla extract
8 ounces semisweet chocolate chips or chopped chocolate pieces

1. Preheat the oven to 275°F. Cover 2 cookie sheets with parchment paper or aluminum foil. Set aside.

2. In a medium, clean, grease-free bowl, with an electric mixer on high speed, whip egg whites until foamy.

3. Add the salt and cream of tartar, and whip until soft peaks form.

4. Add half the sugar gradually, whipping until stiff but not dry peaks form.

5. Add the vanilla and continue to beat in the remaining sugar until the mixture no longer feels gritty when rubbed between two fingers.

6. Fold in the chocolate chips.

7. Drop by rounded teaspoon 2 inches apart on covered cookie sheets.

8. Bake until completely firm and dry, but still white, about 25 minutes; you should be able to lift cookies easily from the paper or foil.

9. Remove paper or foil from the cookie sheet with the meringues still attached to cool cookies completely. Store in an airtight container when thoroughly cooled.

Yield: 3–4 dozen

TINA'S TIDBITS

- *Never grease a cookie sheet to be used for baking meringues; they need to anchor to their base in order to puff up properly.*
- *When covering a cookie sheet with foil, **always** put the foil on dull side up. The dull side absorbs the heat and helps brown the underside of the baked product.*
- *Although cream of tartar acts as a leavening and stabilizing agent in meringues, these pastries can be made without it and would be suitable for Passover. Just make sure that you add the sugar slowly and beat the whites until formed into stiff but shiny peaks.*
- *Stiff peaks are defined by how firmly the egg white mixture stands up on its own when the beaters are pulled up out of the mixing bowl.*

TAHITIAN CROISSANT BREAD PUDDING

Many Portuguese Jews escaping the Inquisition settled in Bayonne, France, and earned a reputation as excellent bakers and chocolatiers. The following are some classic recipes with a little modern help in honor of those creative Jews who put French pastry on the map.

8–10 croissants, about 27 ounces
12 ounces bittersweet, semisweet, or milk chocolate, cut into ½-inch chunks (Lindt or Dove bars are very good)
1 cup heavy cream

1 Tahitian vanilla bean or 2 teaspoons vanilla extract
1 cup sugar
3 large eggs
3 egg yolks
3 cups milk

1. Butter a 13 × 9-inch glass baking dish. Preheat the oven to 350°F.

2. Break or slice the croissants into 1-inch pieces, and place half in the prepared pan. Evenly distribute the chocolate chunks over the bread, and cover the chocolate with the remaining croissant pieces.

3. If using a vanilla bean, heat the cream in a measuring cup in the microwave for 2 minutes. Cut the vanilla bean in half lengthwise, and place it in the cup, completely covered by the cream. Allow the bean to steep for at least 5 minutes or longer if the bean is fairly dry. When the bean is softer, scrape out all of the vanilla seeds from the inside of the bean into the warm cream. Discard the hull of the bean. If using vanilla extract there is no need to heat the cream. Just add extract to cream and then proceed to step 4.

4. In a medium bowl, combine the sugar with the eggs and egg yolks, whisking well. Add the milk and the flavored cream, and stir to incorporate thoroughly.

5. Pour the egg mixture through a sieve directly over the croissants. Lightly press down on the bread to make sure it is covered with the custard.

6. Place the pan in a larger pan, and pour hot water in the larger pan to a depth of 1 inch.

7. Bake in the preheated oven for 45 minutes or until a sharp, thin knife inserted into the center of the pudding comes out wet but clear. Serve warm, with rum sauce if desired (see recipe on the following page).

TINA'S TIDBITS

- *It is not necessary to heat the cream if you are using vanilla extract. Heating the extract will cause some of the flavor to dissipate with the heat.*
- *I recommend that you **always** strain a custard mixture before you bake it. Straining removes any bit of invisible solid egg white or partially cooked yolk that would make the finished custard lumpy.*
- *Placing a custard-based mixture in a pan over a pan of water is referred to as using a bain-marie or "Mary's bath." This is the equivalent of a double boiler in the oven and protects the custard from getting tough and rubbery.*

Rum Sauce

1 stick unsalted butter
1 cup sugar

1 egg
⅓ cup rum

1. Melt the butter in the top of a double boiler over simmering water.

2. Whisk the sugar and the egg together in a small bowl and add to the butter. Stir until the sugar is dissolved and the egg is cooked. The sauce will appear thick.

3. Allow the sauce to cool for 10 minutes. Stir in the rum and serve alongside the bread pudding.

Note: This sauce can be refrigerated until later use and warmed slightly in the microwave or over simmering water.

Yield: 10–12 servings

CROQUEMBUCHE

This confection was invented by the famous French pastry chef Antoine Careme in the late 1700s. The cake is served at festive occasions and weddings. Although Careme lived in Paris, the creative center for French patissiere was actually in Bayonne, just over the Pyrenees from Portugal. The pastry industry was heavily influenced by the Converso confectioners who came from Portugal after the Inquisition and established themselves in this region. Their access to the finest ingredients was due in large part to their relatives' involvement in the trade industry throughout the world.

2 containers of frozen miniature cream puffs (about 60 total)
1 cup sugar

⅓ cup water
3 tablespoons white corn syrup

1. Defrost cream puffs in their container in the refrigerator or use frozen.

2. To make the caramel, combine the remaining ingredients in a heavy 2-quart saucepan and bring to a boil over medium-high heat.

3. When the sugar is dissolved (mixture will be clear), cover saucepan and allow syrup to boil until bubbles thicken, about 5 minutes (this allows the steam to wash the sides of the pan, dissolving all of the sugar crystals).

4. Remove the lid and boil the mixture until it begins to caramelize (mixture will boil slower and the bubbles will get bigger before the color turns from beige to amber). The mixture will continue to get dark after heat is turned off, so do not let it get too dark or it will taste burnt. Remove from heat.

5. Place a round of 10 cream puffs on your serving plate.

6. Dip the remaining cream puffs lightly in the syrup to coat the bottom, and immediately stack the puffs to form a pyramid or "tree."

7. Take a fork and dip it into the sugar mixture. Pour this mixture off the fork, holding the fork high above the cream puffs so that the sugar forms strands. Moving the fork through the air, drape the "tree" with sugar "tinsel."

8. To serve, use forks or spoons to pull some of the puffs off the mound and place on plates, or pull off with your fingers and pop in your mouth!

Yield: One tower, 20 servings

TINA'S TIDBITS

- Croquembouche *means to "crack in your mouth."*
- *Originally shaped like a fez hat (with a flat top) it is now often served in a conical shape.*
- *For a more decorative presentation, candied fruit or nuts can be attached to the cream puffs after stacking but before coating with the spun sugar.*
- *This preparation is similar in concept to teiglach and would make an interesting addition to a Rosh HaShanah lunch.*

DACQUOISE

Do not panic! Dacquoise can be made in little mounds and served as cookies with or without the chocolate ganache in the middle. However, if you really want to wow your guests and live up to culinary heritage, this cake is worth making.

4 ounces toasted whole almonds
4 ounces toasted hazelnuts
1½ tablespoons cornstarch
1¼ cups sugar, divided use
6 large egg whites
½ teaspoon cream of tartar
¼ teaspoon salt
½ teaspoon almond extract
1½ teaspoons vanilla extract

¾ cup half-and-half cream
6 egg yolks
1 cup sugar
2 squares unsweetened chocolate
1 pound unsalted butter, softened at room temperature
3 tablespoons Kirschwasser, clear framboise, Grand Marnier, or rum
1 teaspoon vanilla extract
1 cup toasted sliced almonds

1. Make an outline of a 9-inch heart, 8-inch round, or 16 × 5-inch rectangle pan, 3 times on 2 sheets of parchment paper to fit 2 cookie sheets. Set aside.

2. Preheat the oven to 400°F.

3. Place the toasted nuts in a processor work bowl, and pulse until the nuts are fairly fine. Add the cornstarch and **1 cup** of the sugar, and pulse to combine into a fine mixture. Set aside.

4. Beat the egg whites with an electric mixer until foamy. Add the cream of tartar and the salt, and begin to beat at high speed, adding 2 tablespoons of the remaining sugar. Add the almond and vanilla extracts and the remaining sugar, and continue beating until stiff but not dry peaks are formed.

5. Sprinkle the nut-sugar mixture over the egg whites, and gently but rapidly fold it in until the mixture is evenly distributed but still very light.

6. Fill a 14-inch pastry bag fitted with a #6 plain tip with some of the meringue, and pipe along the edges and in the center of the shapes. Refill bag as needed to make three heart, round, or rectangular shapes. Gently smooth over the meringue with a small spatula and place in the oven. **Immediately** reduce oven to 275°F and bake for 1½ hours or until dry.

7. Cool on pans for 15 minutes and then carefully peel the paper away.

8. To prepare the butter cream, scald the half-and-half in a 2-quart saucepan. While the cream is heating, whisk the egg yolks and the sugar in a small bowl. Add the scalded cream to the egg mixture, whisking constantly until combined. Return the cream-egg mixture back to the saucepan and stir constantly as you heat the mixture over medium-low heat until it thickens. **Don't boil the mixture.**

9. Pour the custard into the bowl of an electric mixer and place the bowl either in the refrigerator

or over another bowl of ice to bring the mixture to near room temperature. Meanwhile, melt the chocolate in a dish over hot water. Set aside.

10. When the mixture has cooled down, return the bowl to the mixer, and beat the butter into the custard piece by piece until all of the butter has been incorporated. If the mixture curdles, return it to the saucepan and whisk rapidly over low heat until the mixture smoothes out.

11. Add the liqueur and the vanilla to the mixture, and divide the mixture $2/3$ and $1/3$ into clean bowls. Add the chocolate to the $1/3$ mixture and stir well to combine. Chill the buttercreams for a little while if they are too soft. Do not let them harden.

12. To assemble the cake, place one of the meringues on a plate. Spread $1/3$ of the natural buttercream over the meringue. Cover with another meringue, and spread half of the remaining natural buttercream over that. Top with the last meringue. Spread the top of the cake with the chocolate buttercream, reserving some of the frosting to pipe rosettes or designs on top of the cake when it is completed.

13. To finish the cake, spread the remaining natural buttercream around the sides of the cake, and using your hand, gently press the toasted sliced almonds into the buttercream. Using a medium star tip, pipe the remaining chocolate buttercream along the top edge in whatever design you want. Refrigerate until ready to serve.

Yield: One cake, 16 servings

TINA'S TIDBITS

- *Before grinding roasted hazelnuts, remove their skins by covering the hot nuts in a dish towel for 5 minutes. Rub the nuts in the towel to loosen most of the skins and then proceed with the recipe.*
- *Separate the yolk from the white over a small bowl in case the yolk breaks. The yolk is high in fat and any presence of fat in egg white will prevent the white from expanding.*
- *Egg whites that are at room temperature will yield a larger volume when whipped than cold egg whites.*
- *Meringues may be sealed airtight and frozen until ready to assemble the cake.*

THE NEW WORLD
AND LATIN AMERICA

A few years ago, before Castro became ill, I had the opportunity to visit Cuba as part of a Jewish humanitarian medical mission. I was very anxious to meet with the remaining Cuban Jews and learn about their surviving culinary traditions on an island that had been sequestered from the Western world and Jewish practice for almost fifty years.

Today's Cuban Jewish food bears little resemblance to the flavorful recipes of prerevolutionary kitchens. Traditionally, the tastes of Spain, Africa, and the Caribbean were blended with exotic spices brought from the Middle East and China. Cookbooks by expatriate chefs show, for example, that the ubiquitous sofrito (a combination of onion, green pepper, and tomatoes with other optional ingredients) added color and flavor to many entrées and side dishes. Today, those ingredients are luxuries that seldom enhance the food of the average Cuban meal.

South American cuisine has always represented an amalgam of regional foods and spices coupled with the food habits of the Spanish, Portuguese, French, and Dutch settlers who arrived in that region over the last five hundred years. Although the first Jew to set foot on Latin American soil was Christopher Columbus's translator, Luis de Torres (although he was converted to Christianity just before he got on the ship!), the real history of the Jews in Latin America can be traced to the first Jews who came to Recife, Brazil, in 1500 from Portugal to escape the Inquisition. When the Inquisition was officially enforced for Portugal by the pope in 1531, the lives of Jews or Conversos in Portuguese Brazil were made difficult. As Jews were persecuted and their lands confiscated, they moved to other parts of South America and the Caribbean, wherever the Inquisition couldn't hurt them.

After World War II, there was also a substantial influx of Eastern European Jews to Argentina, Columbia, Venezuela, and Brazil. Today, Argentina has the largest population of Jews in Latin America.

The following recipes represent both the old and new cooking in Latin America.

LEFT: *Grilled Steak with Chimichurri Sauce and Orange Slices, page 177*

169

Sopa de Elote (Mexican Corn Soup)

When I was Chef Field at Marshall Field in Dallas, I ran a weekly program with guest chefs from local restaurants. This recipe is one I have taught in my classes based on a recipe given to me by a private chef in one of our local Mexican restaurants. This soup is a perfect beginning to an otherwise light dairy meal and is representative of the Mexican palate.

6 cups milk
⅔ cup masa harina
1 pound frozen kernels of corn
2 tablespoons cornstarch dissolved in ¼ cup milk
4 tablespoons unsalted butter
½ medium onion, diced

1 teaspoon chili powder
1 teaspoon cumin powder
1 teaspoon garlic powder
1 teaspoon freshly ground black pepper
1 teaspoon salt
1 ounce canned diced green chilies (optional)

1. Combine the first 4 ingredients in a large bowl and set aside while you sauté the onion.

2. Heat a 4-quart pot for 20 seconds. Add butter and sauté the onion in the butter until lightly golden. Add the spices and seasonings, and cook over low heat for 3 minutes.

3. Combine all of the ingredients and puree in a blender.

4. Place pureed mixture in a clean 4-quart pan and heat over low heat, stirring often until mixture is very hot and thick. If necessary, add more milk to get the desired consistency.

5. Stir in chilies, if using, just before serving.

Yield: 8–10 servings

TINA'S TIDBITS

- Masa harina *means "dough flour," and it is actually made from the lime-treated corn that is made into masa for tortillas. It is a variety of fine corn flour.*
- *This soup will freeze well and can be reheated, but it will probably need to be thinned out with additional milk or water.*
- *Because the soup is so thick, garlic powder is better than fresh garlic for uniform flavoring.*

Chilean Pastel de Choclo

A very popular casserole all over South America, this particular recipe is a favorite in Chile. The spices, olives, corn, and hard-boiled eggs show the Iberian influence in this dish.

1 pound boneless chicken breast
1 carrot, peeled and cut into 8 pieces
½ onion, peeled and cut in half
1 small stalk of celery, cut in half
Salt and pepper to taste
3 cups water
¼ cup raisins
½ cup water
2 tablespoons extra virgin olive oil
2 pounds ground beef
4 medium onions, coarsely chopped
1 clove garlic, minced
¼–½ teaspoon red chili flakes

2 teaspoons ground cumin
1 teaspoon sweet paprika
Salt and freshly ground black pepper to taste
4 hard-boiled eggs, cut into quarters lengthwise (optional)
½ cup pitted black olives
2 cups frozen corn kernels, thoroughly defrosted and drained
2 tablespoons soy creamer
6 large leaves of basil, finely minced
1 tablespoon extra virgin olive oil
1–2 tablespoons sugar

1. Place the chicken breasts, carrot, onion, celery, and a little salt and pepper to taste in a 3-quart saucepan with the water. Bring to a boil and reduce the heat to a low simmer. Cover the pan and cook for 10 minutes or until the chicken is tender and just cooked through. Discard the vegetables; reserve the stock, if desired, for another use; and when cool enough to handle, shred the chicken. Set aside, covered, until ready to use.

2. Microwave the raisins and a ½ cup water for 3 minutes on high. Set aside until needed.

3. Heat a large frying pan for 20 seconds. Add the 2 tablespoons of olive oil and heat for another 10 seconds. Add the ground beef and stir well, breaking up any clumps of meat that form.

4. Reduce the heat to low-moderate, and add the onions, garlic, drained raisins, red chili flakes, cumin, paprika, salt, and pepper. Cook uncovered for 15 minutes, and transfer the meat mixture to a deep 3- to 4-quart casserole. Lay the quartered eggs over the meat, if using. Sprinkle the olives evenly over the eggs.

5. Arrange the shredded chicken evenly over the olives.

6. Preheat the oven to 350°F.

7. Place the defrosted and drained corn kernels and the soy creamer in a blender container. Cover and blend on high for 30 seconds or until puree is relatively smooth. Add basil and blend for 10 seconds to disperse the chopped herb.

8. Heat the 1 tablespoon of olive oil in a medium nonstick skillet and cook the corn mixture for approximately 5 minutes over moderate heat until the mixture looks like thick cream of wheat cereal. Stir occasionally to prevent clumping.

9. Pour the corn mixture over the chicken and smooth out the surface of the puree. Sprinkle with the sugar and bake for 20 minutes.

10. Raise the oven heat to 450°F but do not remove the casserole from the oven. Bake for an additional 5–10 minutes or until the corn puree is golden brown. Serve.

Yield: 6–8 servings

TINA'S TIDBITS

- *To save time, leftover roasted chicken, skinned and boned, may be used instead of the cooked chicken breasts.*
- *If you put the beef and chicken in a 13 × 9-inch casserole, you might need to make a double recipe of the corn topping to adequately cover the casserole. Cook for the same amount of time as above.*
- *Since corn is processed right after it is picked, frozen corn is sweeter than fresh corn sold in the supermarket a week after it was pickd.*

GRILLED CHICKEN BREASTS WITH SOFRITO

About fifteen years ago, the Jewish community in Cuba petitioned Castro to provide them with chicken for Shabbat in order to fulfill their religious obligation! The government conceded to provide chicken for communal dinners, and every Friday night the Jews of Havana congregate at the Patronato for dinner and services. Smaller gatherings occur in a few smaller Jewish communities in Cuba as well.

The cooks told me that they either bake chicken with a simple marinade or make chicken fricassee with a basic sofrito. I have adapted the marinade to use with boneless chicken breasts, which are then grilled or sautéed. The sauce can be spooned on top of the grilled breasts or added to the frying pan after the chicken is cooked.

1–1½ pounds boneless chicken breast
¼ cup lime juice
2 tablespoons extra virgin olive oil

1½ teaspoons ground cumin
1 tablespoon soy sauce

1. Separate the fillet from the underside of the chicken breasts.

2. Combine all of the remaining ingredients in a glass bowl or casserole.

3. Add the chicken breasts and fillets and marinate for 2 or more hours in the refrigerator.

4. Grill on both sides until chicken is done but still moist and tender, about 7 minutes total; **or** heat 1 tablespoon of oil in a frying pan and sauté the chicken until golden on both sides and done in the center, about 7–8 minutes. Reserve the marinade. Set chicken aside and keep warm until ready to serve with the sofrito sauce (see recipe below).

SOFRITO

3 tablespoons olive oil
1 large onion, cut into ½-inch dice
1 green pepper, cut into ½-inch dice
3 Roma tomatoes, seeded and chopped
4 large cloves of garlic, minced
1 bay leaf
¼ teaspoon ground cumin

¼ teaspoon crushed dried oregano
⅓ cup cream sherry
3.5 ounces pimento-stuffed green olives, coarsely sliced
½ cup dark raisins
Salt to taste

1. Heat a 10-inch frying pan over high heat for 20 seconds. Add the olive oil and heat for another 10 seconds. Add the onion and sauté for 4 minutes or until lightly golden.

2. Add the diced green pepper and the chopped tomatoes to the pan and continue to cook for another 4–5 minutes, until the vegetables are soft.

3. Add the remaining ingredients, except the olives and raisins, and let it cook over low heat for 3 more minutes. Set aside. May be made in advance and refrigerated until needed.

4. After chicken is cooked, reheat the sofrito and add the marinade.

5. Bring sofrito and marinade to a boil over medium heat, and add the olives and raisins. Simmer for 3 minutes.

6. Return sautéed chicken to the pan with the sauce to warm and serve. Alternatively, serve grilled chicken on a platter topped with sauce. This dish is traditionally served with rice.

Yield: 4–6 servings

TINA'S TIDBITS

- *The fillet of the chicken breast has a white pearlized tendon running through it. The fillet needs to be removed to ensure even cooking of the breast.*
- *To seed a tomato, cut the tomato in half crosswise and hold the tomato over the sink, cut side down. Gently squeeze and shake once, and all the seeds should fall out.*
- *The sofrito may be used with other meats and fish, with or without the olives, raisins, and marinade. It is also a great filling for empanadas (Cuban knishes!).*
- *Leftover chicken can be diced and added to the sofrito for a great meal alternative.*

Fao de Queijo (Brazilian Cheese Puffs)

A São Paulo restaurant chain opened its first restaurant in the United States in Dallas, of all places. On each table was a basket filled with these puffs. One of my dear friends, Debby Luskey, is a phenomenal cook who happens to be from Brazil, and she gave me the following recipe for the Brazilian equivalent of miniature Yorkshire puddings.

½ cup milk
½ cup vegetable oil or melted butter
2 eggs
1½ cups *polvilho doce* (yucca flour)—found in Hispanic markets

½ teaspoon salt
½ cup Parmesan cheese
½ teaspoon garlic powder
⅛–¼ teaspoon cayenne pepper
Butter or nonstick spray for the pans

1. Preheat oven to 350°F.

2. Combine the milk, oil or butter, and eggs in a blender container and blend.

3. Add the *polvilho doce*, salt, cheese, and spices, and blend thoroughly.

4. Spray or grease 24 mini muffin pans.

5. Fill the muffin cups ¾ full. Bake for 12–15 minutes or until large golden puffs are formed.

6. Serve immediately, although they are still good at room temperature.

Yield: 2 dozen puffs

TINA'S TIDBITS

- *Unused batter may be stored, covered, in the refrigerator for days and then poured into prepared pans and baked.*
- *Unused batter does not need to be reblended if it was made with oil. Just stir and use the batter.*
- *Refrigerated batter that contains butter needs to be brought to room temperature to avoid uneven distribution of fat in the finished product.*

GRILLED STEAK WITH CHIMICHURRI SAUCE AND ORANGE SLICES

The use of sherry vinegar, cumin, and oranges speaks volumes about the Iberian influence on the cooking of South America.

½ cup tightly packed parsley
¼ cup chopped onion
4 cloves of garlic, chopped
1 teaspoon ground cumin
¼ teaspoon dried oregano
¼ teaspoon cayenne pepper
½ teaspoon coarse salt

1 teaspoon black peppercorns
2½ tablespoons sherry vinegar
⅓ cup extra virgin olive oil
1½ pounds steak (rib eye, skirt, or club)
4 navel or Valencia oranges
Flour tortillas (optional)

1. Combine the first 8 ingredients in a processor work bowl. Pulse on and off until the garlic and parsley appear to be minced and make a coarse paste.

2. Add the vinegar and olive oil, and pulse until well blended. Let the mixture sit for a few hours to allow the flavors to meld.

3. Brush steaks with 2 tablespoons of the sauce and let sit for ½ hour. Marinate skirt steak in half of the sauce for 3–4 hours to tenderize.

4. Cut the tops and bottoms off the oranges and cut away all of the rind, leaving a ball of orange. Slice the oranges horizontally into ¼-inch slices. Set aside.

5. Grill the steak over medium-hot coals until medium rare (about 10 minutes per inch of meat.)

6. Slice the steak across the grain and place on the center of a platter. Place the orange slices around the meat and drizzle with some of the remaining chimichurri sauce.

Note: If you like, you may place some of the meat, sauce, and oranges in a tortilla and wrap it up, like eating fajitas. This is not traditional but fun!

Yield: 4 servings

TINA'S TIDBITS

- *The acid in a marinade will help tenderize tougher cuts of meat. Tender cuts use the marinade for its flavor alone.*
- *Regardless of the tenderness of your meat, always slice meat on a diagonal to avoid cutting directly on the grain of the muscle, which would create long strings of chewy meat. This is most true with beef.*

HUACHINANGO VERACRUZ (VERACRUZ-STYLE SNAPPER)

Fresh ingredients, bright sunny colors, and tender juicy fish—this is a classic recipe equally at home on the Costa del Sol of Spain or the Gulf Coast of Mexico.

1½ pounds fish fillets (preferably snapper, redfish, or trout)
1 large or 2 medium limes
3 tablespoons olive oil
1 large onion, sliced thin
2 medium green peppers, sliced in strips
2 cloves garlic, finely minced

2 medium tomatoes, seeded and diced
One 6-ounce can tomato juice
2 jalapeño peppers, sliced, or 2 teaspoons jarred peppers
¼ cup sliced pimento-stuffed green olives
1 bay leaf
¼ cup dry vermouth

1. Preheat oven to 350°F.

2. Place the fish in a 13 × 9-inch glass baking dish, and squeeze the lime juice over the fish. Shake the dish to make sure that all of the juice comes in contact with the fish. Set aside.

3. In a large sauté pan, heat the olive oil and sauté the onions for 5 minutes or until golden.

4. Add the green pepper and sauté for 3 more minutes.

5. Add the garlic and tomatoes and sauté until the tomatoes start to give up their juices.

6. Add the tomato juice, jalapeño peppers, olives, and bay leaf, and bring to a boil.

7. Remove from the heat and add the vermouth.

8. Drain the fish, spoon tomato-pepper mixture on top.

9. Bake for 18–22 minutes or until fish is firm but springy. Serve.

Yield: 4–6 servings

TINA'S TIDBITS

- *Fish should not be exposed to highy acidic foods for more than 1/2 hour or the fish will begin to "cook." Exposure to citrus-juice marinades for a few hours can make the fish very tough when it is ultimately cooked over heat.*
- Huachinango *means "snapper" in Spanish.*

Pecan-Crusted Fish Tacos with Pineapple Salsa

Here is a perfect example of the migration of Jewish cooking. I created this taco to incorporate all the flavors of the Southwest United States while adhering to the tenets of kashrut.

1 pound fish fillets, skin removed (salmon, sea bass, halibut, or black cod), cut into 1-inch strips
¼ cup soy sauce
1 tablespoon light brown sugar
6 ounces regular (not lite) beer
2 large cloves garlic, finely minced
1 cup pecans, coarsely chopped

2 tablespoons flour
¼ teaspoon salt
Freshly ground black pepper to taste
2 tablespoons extra virgin olive oil
1 tablespoon unsalted butter
4–6 flour tortillas

1. Combine the soy sauce, brown sugar, beer, and minced garlic in a glass loaf pan or small casserole. Add the fish and marinate for no more than 1 hour.

2. Combine the chopped pecans, flour, salt, and pepper on a plate. Firmly press all sides of the fish into the pecan mixture to coat well.

3. Preheat the oven to 400°F.

4. Heat a cast-iron skillet over high heat for 20 seconds. Add the olive oil and butter and heat until the butter is melted and bubbling.

5. Reduce the heat to medium high, and add the fish fillets to the pan. Cook on one side for 1–2 minutes until the nuts are golden brown.

6. Flip fish over, place the entire frying pan in the oven, and bake for 3–4 minutes more or until the fish is firm but still springy.

7. Serve on a flour tortilla with the following accompaniments.

Yield: 4 servings

Pineapple-Mint Salsa

½ ripe pineapple, peeled, cored, and finely diced
½ jalapeño pepper, seeds and inner ribs removed, finely diced
⅓ cup finely diced red onion
1 tablespoon finely minced fresh Mexican mint marigold (or tarragon)
1 tablespoon finely minced fresh mint
Juice of half a lime
Pinch of sugar (optional, if pineapple isn't sweet)

Combine all of the ingredients and refrigerate.

Ancho Chili–Margarita Mayonnaise

¼ cup mayonnaise
1 teaspoon Tequila
½ teaspoon Grand Marnier or triple sec
Fresh lime juice to taste
⅛–¼ teaspoon ancho chili powder

1. Whisk the mayonnaise in a small bowl until smooth.

2. Add the remaining ingredients and stir to combine.

TINA'S TIDBITS

- *Never fry in just butter, because it has a tendency to burn. Use half the amount of butter called for in a recipe, and substitute olive oil for the difference. This will give your food a higher smoking point so it won't burn and you will still have the flavor of butter.*
- *Never use salted butter for frying under any circumstance, as it will burn even faster and the salt will pull moisture out of the environment and cause more splattering.*
- *Mexican mint marigold grows in warmer climates but tastes very similar to tarragon, for an easy substitution. Basil could be used as well.*

Mermelada de Guayaba (Guava Marmalade)

Throughout Cuba, ice cream made from evaporated or sweetened condensed milk was served for dessert. However, the communities of Santa Clara and Sancti Spiritus served us guayaba (guava) marmalade on little plates. It is very easy to make and incredibly intense in flavor, unadulterated by any added ingredients other than fruit and sugar.

Here is my version of the marmalade, which I serve over pound cake or banana ice cream. It is also great as a dip for strawberries or other fruits.

1 pound fresh or 1-pound bag frozen guavas (look for it in Hispanic markets)

3½ cups sugar
¼ cup water

1. Cut the fruit in half crosswise, scoop out all the insides including the seeds, and place in a 2-quart heavy saucepan.

2. Add the sugar and water, and stir until the sugar is moist. Heat pan on medium high.

3. Stir **only** until sugar is dissolved, and then simmer about 10 minutes or until a teaspoon of the mixture, dropped into a dish of ice cubes and water, comes out thick and syrupy.

4. Put sauce through a food mill or fine strainer to remove all of the seeds, and place the sauce in screw-top jars. Store in the refrigerator. (If mixture is too thin, you can return the sauce to a clean pan and cook it down until it is the right consistency.)

5. Serve as a sauce over ice cream or as a dip for fresh fruit. If your final mixture is very thick, serve as a spread on bread or with crackers and cheese.

Yield: 1 pint sauce

TINA'S TIDBITS

- *Putting ice cubes in the water prevents the water temperature from rising and gives you a better idea of the consistency of the syrup at room temperature.*
- *Overstirring a mixture high in sugar can cause the sugar to crystallize and make your mixture very gritty when it is cooled.*

CUBAN RUGELACH—"GUAVALACH"

Combine a love of cooking with all things Jewish, add one Jewish Cuban expat, and you have a recipe for "guavalach," courtesy of Libby Zucker, which I have adapted for the modern kitchen. This is how Jewish recipes are born!

In Cuba, guava paste is eaten with cream cheese. In Hispanic bakeries one can find guava pies often having a layer of cheese. It is one of those perfect food combinations transformed into an Ashkenazic classic pastry beloved by all.

1 cup all-purpose flour
Pinch of salt
4 ounces of cream cheese
1 stick unsalted butter
11 vanilla wafers

2/3 cup finely chopped walnuts
4 tablespoons of brown sugar
Guava paste—found in the Hispanic food aisle in a round metal tin, round plastic tin, or long box
Confectioners' sugar for rolling out dough

1. Place flour and salt in a processor work bowl. Pulse on and off 3 times to combine.

2. Cut cream cheese and butter in small chunks, and sprinkle as evenly as possible over the flour in the food processor. Pulse the processor on and off until all the ingredients come together and almost form a ball.

3. Divide dough in half and shape into 2 logs. Cover dough with plastic wrap and refrigerate for 1 hour or overnight.

4. Preheat the oven to 350°F degrees.

5. Put vanilla wafers into the food processor and process into crumbs. Combine with the chopped walnuts and set aside until needed.

6. Remove the dough balls from the refrigerator. Sprinkle confectioners' sugar over your rolling board and pin. Roll out one log of dough into a 6 × 12-inch rectangle. Sprinkle half of the wafer mixture over the dough, and sprinkle 2 tablespoons of the brown sugar over that.

7. Cut strips of guava paste into $1/4$-inch-wide lengths. The length of the strip will vary depending on the package of the guava paste. Place a line of guava paste 1 inch from the long side of the bottom of the dough. Place another line of guava paste 1 inch from the long side of the top of the rectangle of dough. Place a third line in the middle of the dough equidistant from the other strips. Sprinkle half ($1/3$ cup) of the vanilla wafer/chopped walnut mixture evenly over the dough.

8. Tightly roll up the dough from the bottom over the filling, and pinch the edges together to seal. Turn the sides under, and place seam side down, pressing the roll together to make it compact and slightly longer.

9. Cut the log into $1 1/2$-inch pieces and place on a parchment-lined cookie sheet.

10. Repeat with the other log of dough, and bake for 15–20 minutes or until the cookies are light brown.

Yield: 6–8 servings

TINA'S TIDBITS

- *Vanilla wafers are an inexpensive alternative to walnuts to create a crunch in the center of the cookies.*
- *Because the guava paste is not spreadable, the spacing of the lines of the guava will help distribute the fruit paste evenly throughout the pastry.*
- *Rolling dough on a board "floured" with confectioners' sugar not only prevents the dough from sticking, but also creates a light sugar glaze on the surface of the pastry.*

JEWS AND THE VANILLA AND CACAO TRADE

Vanilla is a baking staple in everyone's kitchen. Attempt to make a chocolate chip cookie without it and your taste buds will immediately notice its absence. Usually, the only topic of discussion concerning vanilla is whether to use vanilla bean, vanilla extract, or vanillin in your recipe.

A much more interesting topic centered on this member of the orchid family would be how we are indebted to seventeenth-century Jewish settlers in South America for its popularity.

The first Jews to settle in South America were predominantly Portuguese. The native Indians liked these new, gentle immigrants and trusted them more than the French or Spanish conquistadores, who came to the New World to plunder their peaceful villages and take over their lands.

In 1660 a grant was given to David Nassy to create a settlement in Cayenne (an island city now part of French Guyana) for a group of Jewish colonists from Brazil and Amsterdam. However the Dutch governor, Jan Classen Lagedijk, did not want the Jews in his territory. It was the local Indians who convinced the governor to let the Jews stay, and they settled in Remire, establishing a close bond with the native Arawaks. This bond would prove to be very important to the Jews.

Jewish inhabitants of Guyana and the Caribbean mainly concentrated on sugar production. However, as they became successful, local colonists became resentful and implored the governing countries to put restrictions on the Jews so they wouldn't monopolize the sugar industry. The English tried to inhibit the Jewish involvement in this industry by establishing very restrictive laws. Jews were not allowed to hire Christians (most of the slaves or indentured servants were converted to Christianity when they arrived in the New World). They were also restricted to owning only one or two slaves (depending on the island). They had to look for other agricultural industry that was less labor intensive.

Because the Indians trusted the Jews more than any other people in the region, they taught them the secrets of vanilla cultivation and the process of extracting the flavor from the bean without it spoiling. No one else was entrusted with this secret. This is documented in a letter sent to the Dutch West India Company in 1684 from the Dutch commander of Pomeroon, lamenting the death of Salomon de la Roche, who took the secret of vanilla extract production to his grave and depleted the regional vanilla supply as a result.

At this time, cacao was being exported to Amsterdam and promoted only as a medicinal preparation. The introduction of sugar and then vanilla from South America and the Caribbean elevated the interest in cacao significantly. No longer were cacao beans used only as a medicinal elixir.

Benjamin d'Acosta de Andrade, a Portuguese Converso, is credited with establishing, in the mid-1600s, the first cacao processing plant in French territory on the island of Martinique. As Jews became more successful in this endeavor and powerful in the shipping community, they were perceived as threats to society. In 1685 the "Black Code" stipulated that all commerce had to be transferred to French hands and all Jews were to be expelled from the islands of Martinique and Guadeloupe. Many Jewish families relocated to the island of Curaçao. Curaçao, situated off the coast of Venezuela, is a great source for cacao beans. The Jews began to process cacao for export and ship it to the thriving Dutch merchants in Holland. This trade depended on the network of Jewish traders in Amsterdam. Because Jews are not allowed to charge interest to each other (Exodus 22:24), it was easier for trading to exist among Jews on "futures" of cacao for the necessities that were needed to reestablish their businesses on Curaçao.

Jewish growers of sugar and vanilla sent their products, along with the cocoa they were processing and refining, to their Portuguese relatives in Amsterdam and Bayonne, France. (Bayonne is considered the birthplace of French pastry because the Portuguese Jewish bakers used these ingredients in their dessert creations.) From there, chocolate as we know it spread through the Jewish network of traders throughout Europe.

BUDINO CIOCCOLATO
(ITALIAN CHOCOLATE PUDDING)

This Italian recipe shows the strong influence of its Spanish/South American roots. Essentially a chocolate flan, the subtle cinnamon flavor is reminiscent of Mexican chocolate.

1 cup sugar
½ cup water
1½ cups milk
3-inch piece of stick cinnamon
3 ounces dark sweet chocolate

3 large eggs
3 egg yolks
⅓ cup sugar
1 teaspoon vanilla

1. Preheat the oven to 350°F.

2. To make the caramel, place the sugar and the water in a saucepan and cook over moderate heat until the sugar dissolves and caramelizes to a light golden brown.

3. Using 6–8 individual ramekins, pour the caramel immediately into the cups, and turn the cups around to coat the bottom and sides. It is much easier to do this if you work with one cup at a time and keep the pan of sugar over a very low flame so it won't harden before you get all of the cups coated.

4. Heat the milk, cinnamon stick, and chocolate in a small saucepan until the chocolate dissolves. Do not let the milk boil. Keep warm over a low flame.

5. Beat the eggs, egg yolks, sugar, and vanilla in a 2-quart bowl until thickened, about 3 minutes.

6. Discard the cinnamon stick, and add the milk mixture to the egg mixture, beating constantly until thoroughly combined.

7. Strain the mixture into a large pitcher, and carefully pour the custard into the prepared ramekins.

8. Arrange the ramekins in a 13 × 9-inch pan lined with a paper towel, and pour boiling water in the pan so that the water comes halfway up the sides of the ramekins.

9. Bake for 25–30 minutes or until the custard is firm and pulls slightly away from the sides (or a thin, sharp knife inserted partially in the center of the custard comes out clean).

10. Remove from the water bath and cool. Before serving, invert each ramekin on a plate and allow the caramel sauce to coat the custard and plate. Serve.

Yield: 6–8 servings

TINA'S TIDBITS

- *When caramelizing sugar, never stir the sugar mixture once the sugar is dissolved. Stirring can cause the thickened syrup to crystallize and result in a gritty mass.*
- *Using a cinnamon stick steeped in liquid imparts the flavor of the spice without the grittiness of the powder.*
- *Straining a custard mixture before pouring into molds helps remove any particle of egg white that might have solidified when mixed with a hot liquid.*

ROULAGE LEONTINE

Dionne Lucas was on television long before Julia and Emeril, and she introduced the American cook to this classic French recipe. It is actually quite easy to make. (I baked my first roulage *when I was ten!)*

5 large eggs, separated
¾ cup sugar
6 ounces dark, sweet chocolate
3 tablespoons coffee or 3 tablespoons water with 1
  teaspoon instant espresso

Pinch of salt
1 teaspoon vanilla
1 cup heavy cream
1 tablespoon confectioners' sugar
1 teaspoon vanilla

1. Lightly oil a 15 × 10-inch jelly roll pan. Insert a piece of waxed paper or parchment paper cut exactly to fit on the bottom of the pan. Lightly oil the top of the paper. Set aside.

2. In a medium bowl, beat the sugar into the egg yolks until it is a light, creamy consistency and pale yellow in color.

3. Break the chocolate into pieces and combine it with the 3 tablespoons of liquid in a small saucepan. Place this pan into another larger pan filled with 1 inch of water. Cook over a medium flame and stir until the chocolate melts. Set aside to cool slightly.

4. Add chocolate, salt, and vanilla to the egg yolk mixture, and stir well.

5. With clean beaters, beat the egg whites until stiff. **Gently** fold the egg whites into the chocolate mixture until well combined.

6. Gently spread the mixture over the prepared pan to prevent the loss of air in the batter.

7. Bake at 400°F for 5 minutes. Reduce the temperature to 350°F and bake for an additional 15 minutes.

8. Remove from the oven, and cover the cake with a damp cloth or paper towel and allow to cool for 10 minutes.

9. Remove the cloth carefully, and loosen the roll from the sides of the pan. Cover the pan with clean waxed or parchment paper, and invert the cake. Gently peel off oiled paper and discard.

10. Place the bowl you will be using for whipping the cream in the freezer for 15 minutes.

11. Beat the cream until slightly thickened. Add the sugar and vanilla, and continue beating until the cream is stiffly beaten and spreadable.

12. Spread the roll with whipped cream. With the help of the paper on the bottom, roll the cake up from the narrow side. Sift with confectioner's sugar just before serving. This cake freezes well. Just defrost in the refrigerator 1 hour before cutting. Dust with confectioners' sugar before serving.

Yield: One cake, 10–12 servings

TINA'S TIDBITS

- *Egg whites that are at room temperature will yield a larger volume when whipped than cold egg whites.*
- *Whipping heavy cream over a bowl of ice will prevent it from turning yellow when it sits.*
- *Because a double boiler has an indented rim on the top it is not a good idea to use it when melting a small quantity of food. I prefer a one-quart saucepan over a two-quart saucepan or over an 8-inch frying pan to create the double boiler effect.*

MUSTACCHIONI

I adapted this recipe from Claudia Roden's Book of Jewish Food. *The recipe is from Trieste, which was a major port of call in northeastern Italy, once a part of the Austrian Empire. The ships from Livorno would stop there before or after embarking on trade routes throughout the Mediterranean. The prevalence of the almonds and the chocolate speaks to its Converso roots.*

7 ounces dark bittersweet chocolate
1 cup lightly roasted slivered almonds
3 eggs

½ cup sugar
2 tablespoons orange liqueur (such as Hallelujah from Israel or Grand Marnier)

1. Preheat oven to 350°F. Place paper cups in mini muffin pans. Set aside.

2. Break the chocolate into relatively small pieces and place in a processor work bowl along with the remaining ingredients.

3. Pulse the processor on and off until the mixture forms a relatively smooth paste (it will still be a little coarse).

4. Fill mini muffin papers ⅔ full, and bake for 10–12 minutes or until tops are crisp but insides are still soft. Allow muffins to cool, and store in an airtight container.

5. Alternatively, you can use cooking spray on the mini muffin pans or an 8-inch round cake pan. If using the cake pan, bake for 20–25 minutes until set.

Yield: 18 miniatures or one 8-inch cake

TINA'S TIDBITS

- *Always pulse your processor when you have nuts or chocolate in the work bowl. This will throw the food up as it is cut rather than risking some portion of the food turning into a paste while the rest is not broken down properly.*
- *When a recipe calls for eggs, always use large eggs. Large eggs are 24 ounces per dozen. If you use jumbo eggs (which are 30 ounces per dozen), you would effectively add the equivalent of an extra egg to this recipe and change the consistency of the finished product.*
- *Cacao comes from trees that have to be grown within 20 degrees of the equator.*

Mexican Dark Chocolate Bark

Thinking about Montezuma's love of chocolate and the ingredients the Aztecs used with their cacao beans to make his favorite elixir, I created the following modern incarnation of the beverage in candy form.

12 ounces semisweet Callebaut or Scharffenberger chocolate or chocolate chips
¼ teaspoon chipotle chili powder

¾ teaspoon cinnamon
2 tablespoons coarsely ground coffee

1. Break the chocolate into pieces if not using chips. Place dark chocolate in a glass bowl and microwave for 45 seconds on medium high (level 8). Stir the chocolate gently with a rubber spatula.

2. Return the bowl to the microwave for another 30 seconds on medium high (level 8). Remove the bowl from the microwave and stir chocolate gently until all pieces are melted. This time should be enough even for thick chocolate chunks.

3. Combine the remaining ingredients with the chocolate and spread on a piece of parchment paper or waxed paper. Do not make the chocolate too thin or the bark will melt too easily when handled.

4. Chill the bark at room temperature and cut or break into pieces.

Note: Raisins or nuts may be added as well or used to replace the coffee grounds if desired.

Yield: about 2 cups or 1 pound of chocolate bark

TINA'S TIDBITS

- *Chipotle chilies are jalapeños that have been dried and smoked. You can also use ancho chili powder, but it is fruitier and not so spicy. Ancho chilies are dried poblano peppers.*
- *Because you are not carefully tempering the chocolate (melting and cooling the chocolate to specific temperatures, which creates a chocolate that is more malleable and shiny), the finished chocolate will have a matte finish.*
- *An extra sprinkling of cinnamon or coffee grounds on top will adhere to the bark if sprinkled on before the chocolate hardens.*
- *Another alternative is to use Thai curry powder and coconut in place of the chilies and ground coffee.*

CHANUKAH CHOCOLATE TRUFFLES

Although the connection of coins to Chanukah celebrations is traced back to the Hasmoneans' minting their own state coin after their victory, giving children money and then subsequently chocolate coins is a decidedly European tradition whose origins are probably in the late eighteenth century and the early nineteenth. Jews figured prominently in chocolate manufacturing in Europe at that time, and creating coins of chocolate would allow even poor children to participate in the growing tradition of giving gelt to children at Chanukah. These chocolate morsels are as rich as any to be found in Europe then or now. Wrapped in malleable gold foil or aluminum foil, they can be flattened to look like a coin or just covered in foil in the shape of a ball.

6 ounces chocolate, dark, milk, or white
$\frac{1}{4}$ cup sweet unsalted butter
2 egg yolks
1 tablespoon coffee liqueur, cognac, or Grand Marnier

Dried sweetened cherries, cranberries, or raisins
Cocoa
Gold foil paper or aluminum foil

1. Place the chocolate in a 1-quart bowl. Place the bowl in a 1-quart saucepan filled with hot but not boiling water. (A small double boiler may be used if you prefer, but scrape all the chocolate out of the ridge of the pan.) Over low heat, melt the chocolate and stir to remove any lumps.

2. Remove the bowl of chocolate from the hot water bath.

3. Cut the butter into 4 pieces and gradually whisk in the butter one piece at a time until all the butter is incorporated.

4. Whisk in the yolks until thoroughly combined. The mixture may look grainy and separated, but don't worry.

5. Whisk in the cognac or other flavoring. This should smooth out the mixture.

TINA'S TIDBITS

- *Truffles get their name from the hard-to-find, irregularly shaped, wrinkled fungus that grows 3 to 12 inches below ground. After being sniffed out by pigs or dogs, the truffle is carefully dug up, with much dirt clinging to its crevices. These luxurious fungi are mimicked in equally rich chocolate morsels that are traditionally coated in unsweetened cocoa to resemble the dirt of the vegetation of the same name.*
- *White chocolate is not really chocolate at all, since it is made with only cocoa butter and not any of the chocolate solids. As a result, working with white "chocolate" is more difficult, and you will often find the finished product grainier. Since we are adding even more fat to this confection with the butter and yolks, the mixture will separate when mixing. However, the alcohol will bind the mixture together in the final mixing. These truffles must be kept cold at all times, as they melt more easily than the dark or milk truffles.*
- *The yolks in this recipe are essentially cooked by the alcohol in the liqueur, so there is no need to worry about the raw yolks.*
- *Coffee enhances the flavor of chocolate markedly, which is why Kahlua or other coffee liqueur is my first recommendation. The French often use champagne, but that is too subtle for my personal taste.*

6. Cover and refrigerate for an hour or until the mixture is firm but not rock hard.

7. Working quickly, so that your hands do not melt the truffles, place a heaping teaspoon of chocolate in your hand. Press a dried cherry (or other fruit) into the center of the chocolate and shape into a rough ball about ¾ inch in diameter, completely encasing the fruit. Handle the chocolate as little as possible to prevent melting.

8. Roll the truffle in cocoa, using only your fingertips. Place on a plate lined with plastic wrap and refrigerate until firm.

9. Wrap the truffles in gold foil or aluminum foil to resemble coins or place in little paper petit four cups and refrigerate covered until ready to serve.

Note: If truffles are stored in paper cups they might need to be redusted with cocoa before serving.

Yield: 2–3 dozen truffles

CHOCOLATE CHIP CAPPUCCINO BROWNIES

The expulsion from Spain and Portugal at the end of the fifteenth century sent many Jews fleeing to Holland, Brazil, and the Far East. Trade routes were set up from the Caribbean and the Far East to Holland, and Jewish immigrants were directly responsible for the brisk trade in cocoa and coffee from their newfound countries to their relatives trading on the Dutch market. Combined with the spice trade, these brownies are emblematic of all the routes!

Two college students in Seattle were waxing ecstatic about a brownie they had gotten from a friend, one at home in Texas and one at camp in California. After fifteen minutes of discussion, they realized that they were both talking about the same girl and the same brownie! Here's my daughter's favorite care package from home.

1½ sticks unsalted butter
1 pound light brown sugar
1–1½ teaspoons instant espresso powder
1 tablespoon water
¾ teaspoon cinnamon
2 eggs

2 tablespoons vanilla extract
2 cups all-purpose flour
2 teaspoons baking powder
½ teaspoon salt
6 ounces chocolate chips or white chocolate chips

1. Place the butter in a 3-quart saucepan and add the brown sugar. Stir over medium heat until the butter melts and the sugar dissolves. Remove from heat and add the espresso powder, water, and cinnamon, and stir to combine. Set aside to cool while you measure the other ingredients.

2. Preheat the oven to 350°F. Line the bottom of a 9 × 9-inch pan with parchment paper, and butter or spray the sides of the pan to prevent sticking.

3. Meanwhile, using a handheld mixer, beat the eggs and the vanilla into the butter mixture (still in the saucepan). Add the flour, baking powder, and salt, and mix to combine. Using a rubber spatula, add the chocolate chips and stir by hand to thoroughly incorporate without melting the chips.

4. Spread the mixture in the prepared pan and bake for 20–25 minutes or until a toothpick comes out clean when inserted in the center of the pan. The mixture should be very moist, but not liquid.

5. Cool and cut into 1½-inch squares.

Note: This recipe may be doubled and baked in a 16 × 11 × 1-inch pan for 30 minutes.

Yield: 3–4 dozen small bars

TINA'S TIDBITS

- *Do not overbake these brownies! When they're done, a toothpick inserted into the center of the pan will come out clean.*
- *Never cut brownies while they are hot or the sides will mash down.*
- *I keep a jar of instant espresso in the freezer to use whenever a recipe calls for some coffee flavoring.*

Vanilla Custard Ice Cream

Ice cream made from a custard base will be smoother and creamier than one made from an uncooked base. Here the little specks of vanilla bean add color and texture to a wonderful frozen dessert.

2 cups whole milk
2/3 cup sugar
2 teaspoons vanilla extract or 1 vanilla bean, cut open lengthwise

6 egg yolks
Pinch of salt
1 cup heavy cream

1. Combine the milk and the sugar in a 1-quart saucepan. If using the vanilla bean, add it now. Stir constantly over medium heat until the milk begins to scald and the sugar is dissolved. Scrape the inside of the vanilla bean into the milk mixture and discard the outer bean. If using vanilla extract, add it now and stir to combine.

2. In a small bowl, whisk the egg yolks with the salt until a light lemony color.

3. Whisking rapidly, slowly add some of the hot milk to the egg yolks until combined and the egg yolks are warmed. Return the milk and egg mixture to the saucepan with the rest of the milk mixture.

4. Cook over low heat, stirring constantly until the mixture forms a thick custard and coats the back of a spoon. This will take 5–7 minutes.

5. Strain the mixture through a sieve into a clean bowl, and place the bowl in a larger one filled with ice.

6. Stir in the heavy cream and allow to cool completely.

7. Place in an ice-cream maker and follow the manufacturer's instructions.

Yield: About 1 quart

TINA'S TIDBITS

- *Because the whole milk is cooked with the yolks first, the finished ice cream will not be grainy with ice crystals.*
- *Vanilla bean can be reused. Rinse it off, pat it dry, and bury it in a pint of sugar. After a week the sugar will be subtly vanilla scented.*
- *Straining a liquid containing cooked egg ensures a smooth finished product.*

CRÈME BRÛLÉE

The translation of this dish is "burnt cream." The correct method for making this vanilla-scented custard is listed below. Many restaurants now pour a custard over fruit and then glaze it with sugar melted to the hard crack stage and call it by the same name ... it's not the same.

2½ cups heavy cream
¼ cup sugar
4 egg yolks
1 teaspoon vanilla extract

1 tablespoon Kirschwasser or cognac liqueur, or ½ tablespoon orange blossom water
½ cup sugar

1. Preheat the oven to 300°F.

2. Scald the cream in a heavy saucepan. Stir in the ¼ cup sugar to dissolve and set aside.

3. Beat the yolks until smooth. Slowly add a few drops of cream to the mixture while you stir rapidly with a spatula or whisk. **Do not** whisk so rapidly that you cause the mixture to foam. Add the remainder of the cream in a slow and steady stream as you constantly stir to prevent the egg from "cooking." Add the vanilla and your choice of liqueur or orange blossom water. Stir to combine.

4. Strain the mixture into a large measuring cup and then pour into individual brûlée ramekin cups.

5. Place cups in a paper-towel-lined pan to prevent sliding, and add hot water to come halfway up the sides of the ramekins.

6. Place in the oven and bake for 25 minutes or longer (depending on size of the pan) until set and a small, sharp knife inserted in the center of the dish comes out clean. Remove the dishes from the water and refrigerate.

> ### TINA'S TIDBITS
>
> - *To scald means to bring the milk to just below boiling point. Little bubbles will appear around the edge of the liquid.*
> - *A piece of paper towel in the bottom of the pan prevents the ramekins from sliding in the boiling water and burning you when removing them from the oven.*
> - *Always add a few drops of hot liquid to eggs before adding the eggs to the bulk of the mixture. This prevents the egg from cooking and creating lumps.*
> - *Kirschwasser is a very delicate, clear cherry liqueur that is often mistaken for vanilla; cognac adds a subtle flavor; and orange blossom water transforms this custard into an exotic, nonauthentic but delicious North African–French dessert.*
> - *It is very important that the layer of sugar is not too thick or it will be gritty under the crisp, glazed topping.*

7. Place the chilled ramekins in a larger pan filled with ice cubes.

8. Sift the ½ cup sugar lightly over the crème no thicker than $\frac{1}{16}$ inch. Lightly pack the sugar down.

9. Place dishes 8 inches from the broiler and broil for 2–3 minutes or until the sugar is caramelized, or evenly pass a blowtorch flame over the sugar to caramelize. Remove from the ice-cube pan and serve or refrigerate from 1–8 hours before serving. Refrigeration longer than 8 hours could result in the caramel getting soft.

Yield: 7–8 servings

ARUGULA SALAD WITH DATES AND CHÈVRE

Vanilla is generally associated with desserts, not salads. However, the subtle sweetness this extract brings to the dressing really complements the salad ingredients.

Sephardic Jews often serve pomegranates for the New Year because they are a new fruit of the season and common myth says they contain 613 seeds, which correspond with the 613 mitzvot, or commandments, in the Torah.

4 ounces arugula, about 4 cups
8 large, pitted, soft Medjool dates
¼ cup diced red onion
4 ounces crumbled goat cheese (see note)

¼ cup dry-roasted, shelled sunflower seeds
Freshly ground black pepper
¼ cup pomegranate vanilla vinaigrette (see recipe below)

1. Rinse the arugula and pat dry with paper towels. Place in a salad bowl.

2. Lightly oil a cutting knife and cut the dates in half lengthwise. Cut each half crosswise about 2 or 3 times. Set aside.

3. Toss the arugula with ¼ cup of the dressing. Place on 4 or 5 individual plates. (Alternatively, see step 6.)

4. Evenly distribute the dates, onion, crumbled goat cheese, and sunflower seeds on each plate.

5. Grind a little black pepper on top, and drizzle with the remaining dressing.

6. You can also toss everything together in one large bowl and serve.

Note: ¼-inch-thick rounds of goat cheese whose edges are rolled in cracked pepper may be added to individual salads as an alternative to the crumbled goat cheese.

Yield: 4 servings

POMEGRANATE VANILLA VINAIGRETTE

½ cup extra virgin olive oil
¼ cup unseasoned rice wine vinegar
¼ cup pomegranate molasses (available in Middle Eastern markets)
2 teaspoons sugar or 1 teaspoon honey
1 teaspoon Adams Best vanilla or any rich vanilla extract
Salt and freshly ground pepper to taste

Combine all of the ingredients in a screw-top jar. Shake until well blended.

TINA'S TIDBITS

- *If you are presetting your salad plate on the dinner table for a party, reserve the chopped onion in a dish in the refrigerator, and sprinkle on at the last minute to avoid having the room filled with the scent of onions.*
- *Medjool dates are the large, soft date variety that are easily cut or mashed into a paste if needed. Try to avoid a package of chopped dates, as they are heavily coated with sugar to prevent sticking.*
- *Adams Best vanilla is only available in the Southwest or online. It is a blend of vanilla and vanillin and tastes somewhat like Mexican vanilla without the bad chemicals. I like it because the flavor doesn't dissipate when exposed to high heat. A good-quality vanilla extract will certainly do.*

CELEBRATION OF THE JEWISH HOLIDAYS THROUGHOUT THE WORLD

LEFT: *Kneidlach (Matzah Balls), page 311*

SHABBAT

Rabbi Abraham Joshua Heschel taught that God could have made a mountain or a spring that he created holy, but he didn't, he made time holy: "The Sabbaths are our great cathedrals; and our Holy of Holies is a shrine that neither the Romans nor the Germans were able to burn."*

For most of us today, our spirituality is enhanced by the concrete activities of observance in our lives. On Shabbat, the only holy day mentioned in the Ten Commandments, we are commanded to rest—an activity that was never afforded to our ancestors in Egypt—and, like God, reflect on all that we have created during the week. How we celebrate Shabbat gives us a spiritual connection to God, and how we look upon and assess our activities of the previous week gives us the opportunity to right the wrongs we have committed and devote our time toward spiritual learning and enlightenment. For many of our ancestors, Shabbat was a chance to emotionally escape from the world of harsh abuse and persecution. For us today, Shabbat can be the much-needed respite from material pursuit and inner pressures and a chance to find inner peace and spiritual renewal.

How does the Torah instruct us to "keep the Sabbath" with regard to food? And how have the interpretations of the laws in the Talmud affected our culinary traditions? We are instructed to eat three distinct meals on Shabbat. Since Shabbat is often referred to as "the Queen," all food prepared for Shabbat should be befitting of a queen. Even

the poorest of households would elevate their daily provisions. For members of Bene Israel living on the western coast of India, fish was plentiful, but on Shabbat they would prepare chicken, which was not readily available, to honor the Sabbath. Ethiopian Jews would serve the famous chicken stew *doro wat* for the same reason.

Poor Eastern European Jews living in shtetls in the Pale would elevate the foods of their daily diet for Shabbat. The salted herring, black bread, and onion of daily sustenance were combined with a sweet apple, a biblical fruit, to create chopped herring. This dish is still served at Shabbat *Kiddush* and festive occasions. Whole-grained dark breads were replaced with finely milled white flour, as prescribed in Leviticus 24:5, "You shall take choice flour and bake of it twelve loaves." The braided white challah is the most recognizable icon of Shabbat.

The many prohibitions related to eating and working on Shabbat created some of the most well-known foods associated with Jewish cuisine. The cholent and tzimmes of the Ashkenazic world, the Sephardic *hamins* in the Middle East, and the tagine in the Maghreb (North Africa) all derive their roots from Sabbath cuisine.

---

* Abraham Joshua Heschel, *The Sabbath* (New York: Farrar, Straus and Giroux, 1951), p. 8.

There is a midrash that says that God told Israel that if they accepted the Torah and followed it, they would have a share in the world-to-come—not heaven, but the messianic age. When Israel asked what that would be like, God said to them, "Shabbat will give you a taste of what it will be like."

SCHMALTZ
(RENDERED CHICKEN FAT)

This recipe should probably be listed under icons, but since our ancestors found every possible use for the Sabbath chicken, I thought it would be appropriate to include it here. You can find rendered chicken fat in the kosher frozen foods section of many supermarkets, but if you make your own, it will taste ten times better.

8 ounces chicken fat
1 medium onion, cut into ½-inch dice

1. Cut the raw chicken fat into ½-inch chunks.

2. Heat a 10-inch skillet over medium heat and add the chicken fat.

3. After about ¼ inch of liquid fat forms, add the diced onion and cook over medium heat until the onion is a dark golden brown and the fat is completely melted. The once invisible membrane on the fat will now be crisp and mixed in with the fried onion.

4. Remove all solids from the rendered fat and save for a later use. Pour the liquid fat into a clean jar and refrigerate for months for later use.

Yield: Approximately ¾ cup

TINA'S TIDBITS

- *Every time you cook a chicken and remove some of the raw fat, freeze the fat in a freezer bag until you have enough to render some fat.*
- *Rendered chicken fat will freeze very well and you can scoop out whatever amount you need when you need it.*
- *Chicken fat has the least amount of cholesterol of any animal fat, including butter.*
- *Rendered chicken fat will be liquid at room temperature. For over thirty years Sammy's Roumanian, on the Lower East Side of New York, has served liquefied schmaltz in IHOP-type syrup bottles on their tables so that you could pour it on your potatoes.*
- *Don't throw the onion mixture away! The griben, gribbenes, greebeners (in Texas), as it's called in Yiddish, is incredible mixed into mashed potatoes or just spread on matzah if you like.*

CHOPPED LIVER

Another by-product of the Shabbat chicken—thank goodness those Eastern European Jews didn't waste anything! Copious amounts of golden onions are added to softly cooked chicken livers and chopped to the degree of smooth that your grandma made.

Is it any wonder that the foie gras industry was run by Jews? They knew their chopped liver!

3 medium onions, finely diced
3 tablespoons chicken fat or oil
8 ounces chicken livers

3 hard-boiled eggs (see recipe below)
Salt and pepper to taste
More oil or mayonnaise (optional)

1. Sauté the onions in the fat until a dark golden brown.

2. Remove any green membrane from the livers. Broil the livers just until lightly seared. Add the livers to the onions and sauté just until the livers lose their pink, raw color.

3. Put the liver, onions, and hard-boiled eggs through a meat grinder or combine in a food processor until a desired texture is achieved. Season with salt and pepper and add more oil or mayonnaise if the mixture is too dry. Serve with crackers or on a bed of lettuce as a first course.

Yield: 1$\frac{1}{2}$–2 cups

How to Hard-Boil an Egg

1. Place eggs in a non-aluminum pot with cold water to cover and a little salt. Bring to a boil.

2. When water boils, cover the pot, turn off the heat, and allow eggs to sit for 15 minutes. Peel under cold running water, and you will have perfect hard-boiled eggs.

TINA'S TIDBITS

- *Green on the liver does not mean that the liver is spoiled. It is just some of the bile that would make the chopped liver taste bitter, which is why it should be removed.*
- *Do not overcook your eggs or they will not blend well with the liver when chopped.*
- *Modern cooks often use mayonnaise to moisten the liver mixture. I prefer oil or rendered chicken fat, and then I season the mixture with salt and pepper to taste.*

VEGETARIAN CHOPPED LIVER

I was a child when Uncle Barney had his eightieth birthday party in a Jewish vegetarian restaurant. I still remember the mound of "chopped liver" on a bed of lettuce with some tomato slices. Over the years I compared recipes for vegetarian chopped liver, and I will say that my students like the taste of this mock chopped liver even more than the real thing. I know the ingredients sound bizarre in this day and age of fresh or high-quality frozen vegetables, but try it, you will be surprised how much you like it.

3 large onions, sliced
2 tablespoons oil
1-pound can cut green beans, drained
1-pound can green peas, drained
16 Ritz crackers

6 hard-boiled eggs
½ cup chopped walnuts
Salt and pepper to taste
2 tablespoons mayonnaise

1. Sauté the onions in the oil until a dark golden brown.

2. In a food processor, combine the green beans, peas, onions, crackers, eggs, and walnuts using a pulsing action to chop the mixture fairly fine.

3. Season with salt and pepper, and moisten with a little mayonnaise if needed to have it resemble real chopped chicken livers. Serve with bread or crackers.

Yield: 6–8 servings

TINA'S TIDBITS

- *Because you cannot use chicken fat here, I would recommend the use of mayonnaise to season and bind the mixture together rather than oil.*
- *Whipped salad dressings are never a substitute for high-quality mayonnaise.*
- *Never use fat-free or low-fat mayonnaise in this mixture unless you are planning to serve it right away. The cellulose used to thicken the mayonnaise to make it appear like the original variety will absorb moisture from the vegetables and make the mixture thick and gummy.*

Bukharan Shabbat Chicken Palov

Cultures might remain the same, but in this day and age countries often change borders and names. Bukhara is now Uzbekistan and Tajikistan, but its culinary heritage can best be defined as an amalgam of Turkish and Iranian food traditions. Here is a recipe for a Shabbat chicken dish from this region that I adapted for the cook who has no time to wait for chicken to boil and then be deboned!

1½ pounds boneless chicken breasts
Salt and freshly ground pepper to taste
2 tablespoons corn or peanut oil, divided use
1 medium onion, chopped into ½-inch dice
2 cups coarsely shredded carrots (about 2)
2 apples such as Jonagold or Gala (if available,
　substitute quince for 1 apple)

½ cup raisins
1 teaspoon ground cumin
½ teaspoon cinnamon
2 cups canned chicken broth
1 cup basmati rice

1. Slice the boneless chicken breasts into ¼-inch slices. Sprinkle with salt and pepper.

2. Heat a 3-quart saucepan over high heat for 20 seconds. Add 1 tablespoon of the oil and heat for 10 seconds. Reduce heat to medium high if oil begins to smoke. Add the chicken pieces and sauté for 2 minutes until lightly golden. Remove to a plate and set aside.

3. Add the remaining tablespoon of oil and heat for 10 seconds. Add the onions and sauté until lightly golden.

4. Add the carrots and apples or apples and quince and sauté an additional 5 minutes until soft.

5. Return the chicken to the pot and stir to recombine.

6. Add the raisins and all of the seasonings to the chicken-fruit mixture.

7. Microwave the broth and the rice, covered, for 5 minutes on high.

8. Add the rice and broth to the pot with all the ingredients. Stir gently to combine.

9. Reduce the heat to medium. Cover the pot and simmer the mixture for 15 minutes or until the rice is tender.

Yield: 6 servings

TINA'S TIDBITS

- *Although sautéing boneless chicken breasts is quicker than poaching whole chicken pieces in water, you need to be very careful not to overcook the boneless white meat for fear of it drying out. If available, try boneless chicken thighs for a more foolproof alternative.*
- *Do not add salt to rice cooked in prepared chicken broth, as the broth contains enough salt.*
- *Thin julienne of carrots is available in small bags at many markets. These may be substituted for the 2 coarsely shredded carrots.*

YEMENITE FRUIT AND NUT STUFFED ROASTED CHICKEN

The following recipe utilizes the many fruits and nuts indigenous to Yemen. I combined these ingredients with the classic Yemenite hot condiment zhoug, *which adds a kick to the chicken. Not your usual Shabbat chicken dinner!*

1 tablespoon olive oil
½ cup uncooked rice
1 cup boiling water
6 moist dried figs, diced
½ cup walnut pieces
½ cup slivered almonds

½ cup raisins
2 teaspoons sumac
1 teaspoon kosher salt
1 roasting chicken
2 cups orange juice
2 teaspoons red *zhoug* or *shatta*

1. Heat the oil in a 1-quart saucepan over medium heat. Add the rice and sauté until rice is lightly golden.

2. Add the boiling water to the rice, cover, and simmer over low heat until all of the water is absorbed, about 10–15 minutes.

3. Add the figs, walnuts, almonds, raisins, sumac, and salt to the rice. Combine well.

4. Stuff the chicken with the rice mixture and place in a roasting pan. Combine the orange juice and *zhoug* or *shatta* and pour over the chicken.

5. Bake in a 350°F oven for 1½ hours. Baste often with the juices while baking. Serve.

Yield: 4 servings

TINA'S TIDBITS

- Shatta *is a condiment that is often sold as "red"* zhoug. *The use of red chilies instead of green makes it more mild, but don't be fooled; it's still quite hot and a perfect complement to the slightly sweet orange juice.*
- *If available, 1 1/2 cups of leftover cooked rice may be substituted for the 1/2 cup of raw rice and 1 cup of water in the recipe. Omit step 2 and proceed with the remainder of the recipe.*

SHABBAT ROASTED TURKEY WITH VEGETABLES

Cooking the turkey over a bed a vegetables keeps the meat very moist and gives you a fantastic side vegetable and clear gravy. Once you give up the notion of thick, opaque turkey gravy, you will fall in love with this flavorful version. My grandfather had a deli during the Depression, and this is my mother's version of her father's recipe, so I am a little biased!

1 turkey, 10–18 pounds
5 carrots, peeled and coarsely chopped
3–4 large onions, diced
3 stalks of celery, coarsely chopped
½ pound mushrooms, sliced

½ pound chicken livers, chopped (see note under Tina's Tidbits)
One 28-ounce can crushed peeled tomatoes
2–3 cloves garlic, finely chopped
Salt, pepper, paprika, and garlic powder, to taste
1 tablespoon chicken fat or margarine

1. Salt the cavity of the turkey and rinse. Set aside.

2. Place the carrots, onions, celery, mushrooms, chicken livers, and tomatoes in the bottom of a large roasting pan. Season to taste with the seasonings and the fresh garlic, being light-handed with the salt if using a kosher turkey.

3. Place the turkey on top of the vegetables, breast side up. Season the turkey all over with the salt, pepper, paprika, and garlic powder.

4. Rub the tablespoon of fat all over the turkey skin with your hand. Use a little more fat if necessary to cover the wings and legs well. Cover with a tent of aluminum foil, being sure that the **shiny side** is facing out.

5. Roast the turkey at 325°F for 15–18 minutes per pound or until the internal temperature of the breast meat is about 170°F and thigh meat 180°F. Baste often with the juices in the pan. If necessary, you can add 1 cup of boiling water to the bottom of the pan.

6. Allow turkey to rest outside of oven for 15 minutes before carving.

7. Remove vegetables with a slotted spoon and place in a serving dish. Pour remaining liquid into a gravy boat. Skim the excess fat off the top of the gravy either with a spoon or by laying paper towels gently on the surface to absorb the fat. Serve.

Yield: 8 or more servings

TINA'S TIDBITS

- *If you keep kosher, first broil the chicken livers until almost done (which removes all of the blood) before dicing and adding to the vegetable mixture.*
- *Turkey cooked this way can be made the day before. Just slice the meat and place it in a large baking dish. Store the gravy and vegetables separately in the refrigerator. When ready to serve, pour some of the clear gravy over the sliced meat and reheat in the microwave. Reheat the vegetables and remaining gravy in the same way and serve. Your turkey will be moist and flavorful, and you won't have any last-minute mess in your kitchen!*
- *Foil only protects the breast meat from drying out if the shiny side is facing out, because that side reflects the heat away from the bird. If the dull side was placed facing out, it would absorb the heat and overcook the meat, making it dry.*

BREAD STUFFING

If you think culinary migration only existed in the "Old Country" centuries ago, think again. My classic, non-bacon bread "stuffing" was met with curiosity by my Texas students, whose "dressing" always used cornbread as the base. Eighteen hundred miles and many colloquial traditions apart—not much different than our ancestors' culinary traditions between Spain and Turkey.

3 tablespoons extra virgin olive oil, plus additional
   for greasing the pan
1 onion, diced
2 ribs celery, chopped
2 cups chopped mushrooms
7 cups white bread cubes with crusts (approximately
   1-pound loaf)
1 teaspoon dried thyme

½ teaspoon crushed rosemary
½ teaspoon sage
¼ teaspoon marjoram
¼ teaspoon nutmeg
Salt and pepper to taste
2½ cups chicken broth or vegetable broth
1 egg

1. Sauté the onion in the olive oil until lightly golden. Add the celery and mushrooms and sauté until the vegetables are soft and have given up their juices. This will take an additional 10 minutes.

2. Place bread cubes in a large bowl.

3. Combine the seasonings with the chicken broth and egg. Mix well.

4. Grease a 2-quart casserole with some additional olive oil. Set aside.

5. Add the onion mixture to the bowl with the bread cubes and toss.

6. Add the broth and egg mixture, and stir until the mixture is **very moist** and almost runny. If necessary, add a little more broth.

7. Pour mixture into the prepared casserole and bake at 350°F for 30–40 minutes.

Yield: 8 servings

TINA'S TIDBITS

- *For a very soft stuffing, bake for the first 25 minutes covered with foil, and then remove foil for the remainder of cooking time.*
- *Any bread can be used, but remember that different breads absorb different amounts of liquid. If in doubt, let stuffing rest for 15 minutes before placing in the oven to bake. If the mixture looks too solid, add some more broth, **not** another egg.*
- *Baking stuffing separately means no waste left in the bird and less chance of bacteria growing in the stuffed cavity.*

NOT SO BASIC CHICKEN SALAD

There is absolutely nothing better for chicken salad than cooked soup chicken. It is soft, flavorful, and just the right consistency. Make this salad on Friday and your Saturday lunch is taken care of in advance. This is a technique I learned from my mother-in-law, Gladys Wasserman.

3 cups shredded cooked chicken (from soup chicken; see page 347, *Basic Chicken Soup*)
1¼ cups finely diced celery
3 or more carrots

1 tablespoon grated onion or to taste
Salt and pepper to taste
1 cup mayonnaise
1 can jellied cranberry sauce (optional)

1. Place the shredded chicken into a large bowl.

2. Dice the celery and add it to the chicken.

3. Clean the carrots, trim both ends, and grate them into the bowl with the chicken and the celery.

4. Add the onion, seasonings, and mayonnaise and mix until well blended and moistened. If necessary, add more mayonnaise.

5. Line a bowl with plastic wrap and spoon the chicken mixture into it. Press down firmly on the chicken so that it will mold. Refrigerate until ready to serve.

6. Slice the cranberry sauce into ½-inch slices. Using a decorative cutter or sharp knife, cut out designs in the sauce.

7. To serve, turn the bowl with the chicken salad upside down on a serving plate. Remove the bowl and plastic wrap, and coat the chicken salad with a thin layer of mayonnaise. Garnish with the cranberry sauce cutouts, and serve with crackers or rolls.

Yield: 6–8 servings

TINA'S TIDBITS

- *It is much easier to remove the chicken meat from the skin and bone when it is warm. If chicken soup was made in advance, reheat the meat in the microwave for 1 1/2 minutes or until the skin easily slides off the meat.*
- *Shredded chicken is easier to mold than cubed chicken. The added advantage is that as you shred the meat with your fingers, you can catch that stray piece of wishbone or cartilage.*
- *Grated carrot will add moisture to the chicken salad, but it will not be runny because the meat is in shreds and absorbs some of the good juices.*

GRILLED CHICKEN WITH BASIL-GARLIC TOMATO SAUCE

Shabbat chicken doesn't have to mean soup chicken or whole roasted chicken. It is better not to stress over the meal and enjoy Shabbat than to prepare an elaborate meal and not enjoy the shared experience with loved ones and friends. Here is an easy, delicious dish that can be made in the dead of winter because it does not rely on fresh tomatoes, and chicken can always be grilled outside as long as the grill is not covered in 6 feet of snowdrifts!

1–1½ pounds boneless chicken breast
2 tablespoon extra virgin olive oil
2½ tablespoons balsamic vinegar
2 cloves garlic, finely minced
One 1-pound can imported peeled plum tomatoes

1 teaspoon olive oil
1 large clove garlic, minced
1 tablespoon minced shallot
1 tablespoon chiffonade of fresh basil

1. To prepare the chicken breast for this recipe, first remove the fillet. The fillet is the separate, tender piece of chicken breast that is located in a clear membrane sack on the underside of each breast half. The chicken fillet or "tender" can be recognized by a thin, white pearlized tendon that runs through it.

2. Once the fillet is located, gently pull it away from the chicken breast and out of its sack. Note that the sack may have been cut when filleting the breast, so do not worry if it is not visible on inspection.

3. To remove the tendon from the fillet, hold onto the thick end of the white tendon and gently scrape a knife blade along it to slightly separate it from the fillet meat. Hold the meat back with the knife while the blade rests against the tendon. Slowly jiggle the tendon as you pull it away from the knife. The blade will scrape the meat away from the tendon as it is pulled out of the fillet.

4. Cover the breast meat with a plastic bag, and lightly pound the meat to a uniform thickness. Cut the breasts into 4-ounce pieces if they are unusually large.

5. Combine the olive oil, vinegar, and garlic in a nonreactive bowl and add the chicken pieces. Turn to coat well and marinate for at least ½ hour.

6. When ready to cook, start the grill and begin to make the sauce.

7. Remove the tomatoes from the can and coarsely chop them into approximately ¼-inch pieces. Place in a measuring cup. If necessary, add some of the liquid from the can to make 1 cup of tomatoes.

8. Heat the olive oil in a medium sauté pan, and add the garlic and shallots. Reduce the heat to low and sauté for 2 minutes.

9. Add the tomatoes and simmer for 5 minutes or until sauce is reduced slightly. Season with salt, if necessary, and a little pepper. Keep warm until chicken is done.

10. Meanwhile, grill the chicken over hot coals for 2–3 minutes per side, until the chicken is done but still very moist.

11. Add the chiffonade of basil to the sauce, spoon the sauce over the chicken, and serve.

Yield: 4–6 servings

TINA'S TIDBITS

- *Do not overcook grilled chicken! The rule is to estimate cooking time based on the thickness of the meat. Plan on 10 minutes per inch. Chicken breasts usually cook in 5 minutes.*
- *The easiest way to peel garlic is to lay a large knife on its side over the clove of garlic and smack it lightly to crack the garlic. This will dislodge the paper-like skin on the garlic clove and make it very easy to remove. It is also much easier to mince fresh garlic once it has been smacked flat.*
- *To chiffonade basil, layer the basil leaves and roll them up like a cigarette. Slice thin slices through all thicknesses. This will give you thin, delicate strips of the herb.*
- *Because canned tomatoes often contain seeds, and seeds can make a tomato-based sauce bitter, an old Italian cooking trick is to add a little bit of sugar to the sauce.*

MANDELBRODT

This is a classic recipe for mandelbrodt. *They are very satisfying dunked in a "glass" of hot tea. This Eastern Europe tradition was popular way before biscotti came into vogue in the twentieth century.*

2¾ cups flour
2 teaspoons baking powder
¼ teaspoon salt
1 cup sugar
6 tablespoons oil
Juice of ½ orange

3 eggs
1 tablespoon grated zest of orange
1 teaspoon vanilla
½ cup slivered almonds
Cinnamon and sugar mixture for topping

1. Combine the flour, baking powder, and salt in a small bowl and set aside.

2. Cream sugar and oil until light and well combined. Add juice, eggs, zest, and vanilla and beat well.

3. Stir in the flour mixture and almonds and mix well.

4. On a greased cookie sheet, form 2 loaves of dough about 4 inches wide and 10 inches long. Sprinkle the tops with cinnamon and sugar, and bake for 45 minutes at 350°F.

5. Remove the loaves from the oven. Cut the loaves on a diagonal into ½-inch slices. Place each slice cut side down on the cookie sheet and return to the oven for 5–7 minutes or until lightly golden. Turn each slice over and return to the oven for an additional 5 minutes. Cool and serve.

Yield: 4 dozen

TINA'S TIDBITS

- Mandelbrodt *literally means "almond bread" in Yiddish.*
- *In Hungary and some other Eastern European countries, this cookie is called* kamishbread.
- *The use of oil points directly to Jewish origins, because baking throughout Europe and the Iberian Peninsula before the twentieth century utilized either butter or lard.*

ZIMSTERNE COOKIES

Zimsterne cookies are traditionally served after the Havdalah service. Shaped like stars to represent the three stars that signify the end of Shabbat, the cookies are made with honey and spice so that some of the sweetness of Shabbat can be taken into the new week. The spices mimic those found in the b'samim box used during Havdalah.

1 stick unsalted butter
8 tablespoons (½ cup) solid white shortening
1½ cups sugar
1 egg
2 tablespoons honey
½ teaspoon vanilla
2½ cups all-purpose flour
½ cup cake flour
¼ teaspoon salt
1 teaspoon baking soda

2 teaspoons cinnamon
2 teaspoons ginger
2 teaspoons cloves
Confectioners' sugar for rolling dough

DECORATIVE ICING:
1 cup confectioners' sugar
¼ teaspoon vanilla
1–2 tablespoons milk

1. Using an electric mixer, cream the butter, shortening, and sugar together until light and fluffy. Add egg, honey, and vanilla and beat well, scraping down the sides of the bowl if necessary.

2. Add the dry ingredients and mix well. Form the dough into a ball, flatten it slightly, place it in a plastic bag, and refrigerate for 1 hour or longer.

3. Roll the dough out ⅛-inch thick on a surface that is lightly coated with confectioners' sugar (instead of flour). Cut the dough with a 2-inch star cookie cutter.

4. Bake on a parchment-lined cookie sheet at 375°F for 6–8 minutes or until cookies are lightly golden. Remove from the oven.

5. Allow cookies to cool for 5–10 minutes while you make the icing.

6. To make the icing: Place the cup of confectioners' sugar in a small bowl. Whisk in the vanilla and 1 tablespoon of the milk until smooth. If the mixture is too thick, whisk in some more milk until the mixture resembles mayonnaise in consistency.

7. Brush the icing over the tops of the warm cookies and allow them to sit at room temperature until the cookies are cool and the icing is dry and no longer sticky. Store in an airtight container at room temperature, or freeze until later use.

Yield: 5 dozen

TINA'S TIDBITS

- *Hydrogenated fat, such as solid white shortening, will make the cookie harder or crisper. Margarine may be substituted, but it will change the "spread" of the cookie.*
- *The high concentration of sugar in this recipe will make the cookie firm but also chewy. Using all honey would make it even chewier, so a combination of the two is recommended.*
- *Dark spices, such as cinnamon and cloves, should always be stored in the freezer to protect their flavor, especially if you do not use them often.*

ROSH HASHANAH
AND YOM KIPPUR

We incorporate certain foods into our celebration of the High Holy Days because of custom, not biblical dictate. The only prescription in the Talmud for this celebration is for *hidur mitzvah*, taking the extra time to exalt God by making our holiday table and ourselves more beautiful by using our best china and silver or getting our hair cut and wearing new clothes for the holiday. Through these actions, we enhance the meaning of the High Holy Days.

The choices of food to represent the holiday have depended on the region, societal customs, and socioeconomic standing of the Jews. Ashkenazic Jews express their wish for a sweet and fruitful year by dipping apples and challah in honey. Kreplach, toothsome pockets of meat-filled dough served in chicken soup, is a modern interpretation of a medieval German custom of placing a wish for the New Year into a piece of dough and then wearing it as an amulet around the neck. Sephardim conduct seders serving seven foods and reciting seven blessings. They also serve fruit in covered baskets so no one knows what's inside, just as no one knows what the New Year will bring.

Normally, two loaves of elongated challah are served for Shabbat, but for the High Holy Days a round challah, sometimes containing raisins, is customary. The round challah is fraught with meaning. It is symbolic of the crown of God, our Sovereign; it represents a year filled with never-ending good. A ladder of dough placed on top represents the question of who will ascend or descend in health or wealth in the coming year. A lesser-known custom is to bake the challah in the shape of a bird, based on Isaiah 31:5, "As hovering birds, so will the Eternal protect Jerusalem."

It is customary to eat foods that symbolize sweetness, abundance, and fertility. Sight association and sound/word plays on names of foods lend themselves to using these foods symbolically as positive reflection for the coming year.

The following are some of the foods that Jews worldwide serve for the New Year:

- **Carrots**: *Meren*, Yiddish for "carrots," also means "more." In addition, sliced carrots look like gold coins.

- **Pomegranates** are supposed to contain as many seeds as the 613 mitzvot, and they represent a new fruit of the season.

- **Apples**: The *g'matria* (number association) of *tapuach* (Hebrew for "apple") is equal to that of *seh Akeidah*, "lamb of the binding," referring to the story of Abraham and Isaac. Apples also represent fertility and the story of Sarah and Isaac.

LEFT: *Round Challah, page 219*

- **Fish**: The whole fish or head is served. This represents a wish for a year placing you at the "head" of life. Another interpretation is that a fish never closes its eyes and, like God, is ever watchful over us.

- **Beets**: In Hebrew the word relates to "removal," as removal of our sins and our enemies.

- **Leeks**: In Hebrew the word sounds like "to cut"—may our spiritual enemies be cut down.

- **Pumpkin** represents the hope that as a thick covering protects the vegetable, God will protect us.

Cooking for Yom Kippur is an oxymoron. Or is it? How does one write about food for a holiday when you aren't supposed to ingest anything for twenty-five hours?

Actually food is prominent in the traditions of Yom Kippur, starting with the *s'udah hamafseket*, the meal preceding Yom Kippur. This meal is obviously important because we need to build up reserves of energy and water to make it through the fast. Although this is pragmatic, the Talmud states that "just as it is a mitzvah to fast on the tenth of Tishrei, it is a mitzvah to eat on the ninth" (*Yoma* 81b). Much joy and preparation therefore go into the Erev Yom Kippur meal before the *Kol Nidrei* service ushers in the Day of Atonement.

Chicken is often the entrée of choice for Jewish holiday meals. However, there is also an old ritual associated with Yom Kippur called *kaparot*, which is a ceremony using a chicken as a scapegoat for one's sins. A chicken is waved around one's head while the person recites a prayer requesting that the chicken be sacrificed instead of the waver. The bird is then slaughtered and given to the poor or its value donated to charity. Because of its magical underpinnings, this ceremony hasn't survived in this format. Today, if this ritual is performed, coins are substituted for the chicken. They are placed in a handkerchief, waved over one's head, and then donated as *tzedakah* for the poor.

There are no prescribed foods for the meal preceding or following the fast of Yom Kippur; however, there are many customs based on common sense. According to Dr. Elliot Berry, a clinical nutritionist at Hebrew University Hadassah Medical School, you should drink water frequently throughout the day prior to fasting and avoid salty or highly sweetened foods that will make you thirsty. Cutting down on caffeine intake the week before Yom Kippur will help avoid withdrawal headaches while fasting. This is common sense, but did you know that you should include foods like pasta, sweet potatoes, or whole-grain breads in your *s'udah hamafseket* because stored complex carbohydrates in the liver help you retain water? So that's why I have no ankles after Pesach!

Common sense and custom prevail as well for breaking the fast. If you break the fast with a noncarbonated drink and a piece of bread or dry cake, your blood sugar won't spike, and afterwards you will be able to enjoy a full meal. This is probably why synagogues offer these items directly after the close of the *N'ilah* service before people go home.

Most customs throughout the Diaspora prescribe breaking the fast with wine or tea and a simple bread or cookie. Once these are ingested, a light meal follows, usually consisting of dairy foods and salted fish. One advantage to this type of meal is that you can prepare almost everything in advance—a necessity if you are going to spend your time in synagogue praying for forgiveness and redemption, rather than thinking about cooking times and slicing techniques!

Round Challah

Moist, cake-like challah is a big hit at my Rosh HaShanah open house. Divide the dough into two-thirds and one-third to make two loaves, but never use all the dough to make one giant crown or the center will surely be raw after the normal baking time is reached.

7–8 cups bread flour, divided use
2 packages rapid rise yeast
1½ cups water
2 sticks pareve margarine or butter, or 1 cup corn oil
¼ teaspoon yellow food coloring
¾ cup sugar

2 tablespoons poppy seeds (optional)
1 tablespoon salt
4 large eggs
1 cup raisins (optional)
Egg wash: 1 egg mixed with 1 tablespoon water

1. In a large mixer bowl combine **6** cups of the flour and the yeast. Stir to combine.

2. Heat the water, margarine, food coloring, sugar, poppy seeds, and salt in a saucepan until very warm (140°F). Water should be uncomfortably hot to your finger but not hot enough to burn you. (It will feel like hot tap water.)

3. Add the warm liquid mixture to the flour while the mixer is on low. As the liquid is being incorporated, add the eggs. Mix thoroughly.

4. Gradually add the remaining flour **only** until a fairly firm dough is formed. This process should take about 7 minutes whether you are using the dough hook on your mixer or are kneading it by hand. The mixture will be satiny smooth.

5. Create a warm, draft-free space for your dough to rise by turning on your oven to 400°F for 1 **minute**. Lightly grease a bowl with some oil, and turn the dough in the bowl to oil all sides. Cover with plastic wrap and place in the **turned off** oven until doubled in size, about 30–45 minutes.

6. Punch down the dough and divide in half or in thirds. Roll each piece into a rope about 15 inches long. Hold one end 2 inches above the work surface and wrap the rest of the dough around it to make a large coil. Pinch the ends together to prevent unraveling while baking. Place the formed breads on parchment-lined or greased cookie sheets, and let rise in the previously warmed oven until light and doubled, about 25 minutes.

7. Remove loaves from oven and preheat to 325°F. Brush the tops of the loaves with the egg wash and bake for 25–35 minutes, depending on the size of the loaves. When the bread is done, it will be golden brown and have a hollow sound when tapped.

Yield: 2–3 loaves

TINA'S TIDBITS

- *As no amount of eggs will make the challah look golden, coloring is added. You can substitute 1/8 teaspoon saffron or turmeric for color.*
- *The amount of flour you use will be directly related to the weather; on dry, wintry days you will need less flour than on a rainy spring day, because the cold dry air will make the dough drier and the moist air in spring will require more flour to absorb the extra moisture. The amount of flour is dictated by the feel of the dough.*
- *To let the dough rise overnight, spoon 1 tablespoon of oil inside a 2-gallon ziplock bag and rub to distribute. Place the dough in the bag, squeeze out any excess air, seal, and place in the refrigerator overnight. In the morning, remove the bag from the refrigerator and let it sit at room temperature for 30 minutes before proceeding with step 6.*
- *Never cut bread hot from the oven. The steam will cause the knife to drag through the loaf and mat the dough together.*

Dulce de Manzana (Apple Preserves)

Turkish Sephardic Jews serve this sweet apple preserve as they wish their family and friends a sweet New Year.

3 cups granulated sugar
1½ cups water
2 pounds apples, Jonagold, Gala, or Delicious

Juice of ½ lemon
1 tablespoon rose water or 1 teaspoon vanilla
¼ cup slivered almonds

1. Place the sugar and water in a 3-quart saucepan and bring to a boil over medium-high heat.

2. While the mixture is heating, peel the apples and grate them by hand with a coarse grater or use a coarse grating disk on your processor. Immediately add the apples and lemon juice to the hot sugar syrup.

3. Reduce the temperature to medium and cook for 30–45 minutes or until most of the liquid has evaporated and the mixture is quite thick. (Note: The amount of time depends on the variety of apple and its juice content.) Stir the mixture occasionally to prevent sticking.

4. While the mixture is cooking, toast the almonds in a 350°F oven for 4 minutes or until lightly golden. Set aside.

5. When the mixture is thickened (it will get thicker when it cools), add the rose water or vanilla and place in an open container until cool. The toasted almonds may be added to the mixture at this time or sprinkled on top as a garnish just before serving. Refrigerate until serving.

Yield: 3–4 cups

TINA'S TIDBITS

- *Do not use a soft apple like McIntosh for this recipe. Jonagold are my first choice for flavor and consistency, but any firm apple will do.*
- *When grating the apples by hand, use long strokes so that the apple shreds remain intact when cooked in the sugar syrup.*
- *Fruit mixtures become well balanced and mellow when allowed to sit for 24 hours.*
- *A teaspoon of hot apple mixture dropped into a bowl of ice and water will give a good indication of what the mixture will be like when chilled.*

LUBIYA
(SEPHARDIC BLACK-EYED PEAS)

I have a theory about this dish. For over two thousand years, Ethiopian Jews have celebrated the New Year by eating these peas. I think it is possible that the culinary custom spread to West Africa over the spice trading route and that slaves learned this recipe and brought it, and the tradition of eating them at the beginning of the New Year, with them to the southern United States.

3 tablespoons extra virgin olive oil
1 medium onion, diced into $\frac{1}{4}$-inch pieces
2 large cloves of garlic, minced
$1\frac{1}{2}$ cups water

3 tablespoons tomato paste
1 pound fresh or frozen black-eyed peas
$\frac{1}{2}$ teaspoon cumin
Salt and freshly ground black pepper to taste

1. Heat a 3-quart pot over high heat for 20 seconds. Add the olive oil and heat for another 10 seconds. Add the onion and garlic and sauté over medium heat until the onions are lightly golden.

2. Add the water and tomato paste, and bring to a boil. Reduce the heat to low. Add the peas and cumin, and cook covered for 1–2 hours or until the peas are tender. It might be necessary to add a small amount of additional water to the pot if the mixture looks too dry. Conversely, if the mixture is too soupy, continue to cook uncovered until some of the liquid has evaporated.

3. Remove from the heat, and add salt and freshly ground black pepper to taste. Serve hot or at room temperature. Serve alone or over rice.

Yield: 8 servings

TINA'S TIDBITS

- *Peas need time to absorb water and expand. Either soak the peas for a few hours before cooking, or cook them for a long time until they reach the desired consistency.*
- *Never put salt in the water prior to cooking beans, as it will harden the beans and prevent them from absorbing the water and becoming soft.*
- *Save leftover tomato paste by scooping out tablespoons of the paste onto a sheet of plastic wrap. Place them in the freezer, and when frozen, peel off the plastic and store in a freezer ziplock bag until needed.*

MAPLE-GLAZED CARROTS

Carrots symbolize prosperity for the New Year, and sliced they look like gold coins. The maple syrup adds the sweetness for a sweet year ahead.

5 pounds carrots, peeled and sliced ¼ inch thick on the diagonal
1 stick sweet, unsalted pareve margarine
8 scallions, white part only, thinly sliced

Finely grated zest from 1 large lime
¾–1 cup pure grade A medium amber maple syrup
Juice of 1 lime
Kosher salt and pepper to taste

1. Place 1 inch of water that has been lightly salted in a 3-quart pot. Add the carrots, cover, and cook over moderate heat until they are tender but not soft, about 15 minutes. Drain.

2. Heat a large frying pan (big enough to hold all the carrots) for 20 seconds. Add the margarine and melt completely.

3. Add the sliced whites of the scallions and the lime zest, and sauté until the scallions are soft and just beginning to turn golden. Do not burn or the flavor will be bitter.

4. Add the maple syrup and lime juice and bring to a boil. Boil the mixture for 5 minutes or until it is reduced by half.

5. Add the carrots and gently stir with a rubber spatula to coat thoroughly. Add salt and pepper to taste and serve.

Yield: 20 servings or more if part of a buffet

TINA'S TIDBITS

- *Cooking vegetables in a small amount of water prevents the water-soluble vitamins in the food from leaching out.*
- *When stirring tender vegetables, it is better to use a rubber spatula so you won't bruise the edges of the food.*

SALMON EN PAPILLOTE

Here is my foolproof answer to entertaining large groups of people. The fish will last for days in the refrigerator, although I prefer to make it the morning of an event or the day before if it is for a Yom Kippur break fast.

1 tablespoon unsalted butter
2- to 4-pound side of salmon fillet, skin removed
1–2 limes

Cayenne pepper
Fresh ginger, peeled

1. Tear off a piece of heavy-duty foil that is 4 inches longer than the side of salmon.

2. Rub the butter all over the shiny side of the foil. Place the fish on the foil with what would have been skin side down. Set aside.

3. Remove the zest from the limes in long strips with a zester and place the strips in a small glass dish. Cover with water and microwave for 45 seconds to soften. Set aside.

4. Cut away all of the white pith from the limes, and cut out each section of the limes. Set aside.

5. Season the fish lightly with cayenne. Grate some fresh ginger directly over the fish, using about 1 inch of ginger. Decorate the top of the fish with the lime sections and julienned zest.

6. Bring the long edges of the foil together. Fold over the foil lengthwise 2 times to seal tightly but leave a little room for steam over the fish. Fold up the sides as you would a present, on a diagonal from each side and then over twice to seal the edges.

7. Place the foil packet on a rimmed cookie sheet and bake at 450°F for 16–17 minutes. Immediately open the foil or the fish will continue to cook. Place on a platter and serve immediately or at room temperature.

8. If making in advance, refrigerate the cooked fish out of the foil and covered tightly with plastic wrap. Bring to room temperature before you serve.

SAUCE

1/2 cup mayonnaise
1 teaspoon Dijon mustard
1 tablespoon dry white wine
1 tablespoon finely minced fresh dill, basil, tarragon, or lemon thyme or 1 teaspoon dried herbs

1. Place the mayonnaise in a small bowl and stir to a smooth consistency.

2. Add the remaining ingredients, using more wine if the mixture appears too thick.

3. May be served immediately, although the flavors meld when made in advance.

Yield: 10–15 servings

TINA'S TIDBITS

- *Scrape the outside of the lime with your nail to ascertain the flavor of the fruit before buying (a sweet fruit will have a sweet smell). In this recipe the natural oils and flavor of the zest are important.*
- *The dull side of the foil will absorb heat faster, and the shiny side is less reactive to acid, so it is important to place the fish on the shiny side of the foil with the dull side facing out.*
- *It is imperative that the foil is sealed tightly so that the fish steams. That said, it is important to bake it on a rimmed cookie sheet so any juices that might escape don't wind up on the oven floor!*
- *When making a mayonnaise-based sauce, you must stir up the mayonnaise before you add any other ingredients or the sauce will appear lumpy.*

Sogliola con Pinoli e Passerine
(Sole with Pine Nuts and Raisins)

The Sephardic community often serves sweet-and-sour fish for breaking the fast. This flavor, as well as the pickling liquid used by Eastern European Jews, helps replenish some of the salt lost during fasting. The following Italian recipe illustrates the Spanish influence on Mediterranean cuisine. The use of raisins and pine nuts is a giveaway that this recipe probably was introduced into Italy by the Jews fleeing the Inquisition.

¼ cup olive oil
2 tablespoons red wine or balsamic vinegar
2 teaspoons honey
¼ cup dark raisins
3 tablespoons lightly toasted pine nuts
2 tablespoons chopped fresh parsley

½ cup dry bread crumbs or matzah meal
Salt and freshly ground black pepper to taste
1½ pounds fillet of sole or other thin fish (about 5–6 fillets)
1 cup dry white wine
2 tablespoons unsalted butter

1. Lightly oil a 2-quart casserole that will be able to accommodate all of the fish rolls. Set aside.

2. Combine the first 8 ingredients in a 1-quart bowl.

3. On a flat surface, place the fish rough side up. Spread about 1–2 tablespoons of the raisin-nut mixture over the fish and roll the fish, starting from the wider end of the fillet.

4. Place the rolled fillets in the prepared casserole, seam side down.

5. Gently pour the white wine around the fillets and sprinkle any remaining filling bread crumbs over the top of the fish. Dot each fish fillet roll with some butter.

6. Bake in a 400°F oven covered with greased foil for 10 minutes. Uncover and bake for 5–10 more minutes or until fish appears firm and crumb topping is golden.

Yield: 4–6 servings

TINA'S TIDBITS

- *Thicker pieces of fish can be used; however, do not try to roll thick fillets. They look unsightly and the filling will fall out. Instead, place the filling on top of each thicker fillet and proceed with the recipe.*
- *Toast the nuts at 325°F until lightly golden, about 3 minutes.* **Remember:** *Nuts roast in their own oils, so even though you remove the nuts from the oven—the source of heat—you are not removing them from the roasting source and they will continue to brown outside of the oven.*
- *Grease the foil on the shiny side. The dull side will face outward and will absorb the heat better and prepare the fish perfectly.*

SAUTÉED "FISH" WITH PECAN BUTTER

Since fish is symbolic of the eyes of God watching over us for the New Year, I created this fish with "scales" to represent the fish of folklore. It's a little time-consuming cutting out the "scales," but the finished dish is delicious and fun to see.

1–1½ pounds bass, snapper, or sea trout fillets, cut
  into 4 pieces
Salt and freshly ground pepper
Flour
1 egg lightly beaten
2–3 russet potatoes
6 tablespoons butter

⅔ cup pecans, chopped into ¼-inch pieces
Pinch of black pepper
Pinch of cayenne
4 tablespoons butter
1 tablespoon lemon juice
2 tablespoons minced parsley

1. Season the fish with salt and pepper and lightly coat with flour.

2. Peel the potatoes, and then using the peeler, slice thin slices of potato. Place the potato slices in a bowl of salted water.

3. Brush the tops of the pieces of fish with the beaten egg. Using a 1-inch round cutter, cut circles from the potato slices and overlap the circles on the egg side of the fish to make lines that look like scales.

4. Clarify the butter by melting the 6 tablespoons of butter very slowly in a small saucepan over low heat. Skim the foam off the top and discard. Carefully remove yellow clarified butter with a spoon or gently pour butter into a clean dish. Discard any water from the bottom of the pan. This should yield about 4 tablespoons of clarified butter.

5. Brush the potato "scales" with clarified butter, and refrigerate for at least ½ hour.

6. When ready to cook, heat the remaining clarified butter in a large sauté pan. Place the fish, potato side down, in the pan and cook for 4 minutes or until golden. Carefully turn the fish over and cook until done. Remove to a warm plate. Drain the pan.

7. To make the pecan butter, sprinkle the pecans with the two peppers, and heat the butter in the sauté pan used for cooking the fish.

8. Sauté the pecans for 3 minutes or until lightly golden. Turn off the heat and add the lemon juice and parsley.

9. To serve, place 1 fillet on each plate and top with some pecan butter.

Yield: 4 servings

TINA'S TIDBITS

- *To keep a coating adhering to your food when frying, always coat the food with flour first, then egg, and then the starch (breading or potato). Flour sticks to the moist fish, egg adheres to the flour, and the starch adheres to the egg. Refrigerating the fish for 30 minutes cements the layers together.*
- *Clarified butter is clear butter minus any milk solids in the melted butter. Removal of milk solids allows the fish to be fried at a higher temperature without the butter burning.*
- *If you have time, clarify butter and then place the entire pan in the refrigerator. Butter will solidify and solids and water can be easily discarded.*

Keftes de Prasa Con Carne (Turkish Leek and Meat Patties)

Adapted from a recipe by Rachel Bortnick, this is a favorite Sephardic recipe served as part of the Rosh HaShanah seder. Leeks are an important symbolic ingredient for the New Year, especially in Turkey.

6 medium leeks, white and light green part only
  (about 4 pounds before trimming)
2 medium russet potatoes (1½ pounds)
¾ pound lean ground beef
1 egg
1 teaspoon salt or to taste
Freshly ground black pepper to taste

¼ cup very lightly packed parsley (no big stems)
1 medium tomato, seeded and cut into eighths
1 cup flour
2 eggs, lightly beaten in a shallow bowl
Oil for frying
Prepared mild tomato or marinara sauce or lemon
  wedges

1. Cut off all the dark green leaves of the leeks and discard. Cut the white part lengthwise to the root and rinse thoroughly under running cold water. Cut the leeks crosswise into ¼-inch semicircles and place in a 2-quart saucepan with lightly salted water. Simmer 15 minutes and drain in a colander.

2. Meanwhile, peel the potatoes and cut into eighths. Place in a 1-quart saucepan with salted water and cook until tender, about 15 minutes. Drain and let sit in the pot to cool and dry off. Do not rinse the potatoes.

3. Press the leeks in batches in your hands to squeeze out excess liquid and then pat some more in a paper towel (this is **very** important to allow the *keftes* to hold together). Place the leeks in the work bowl of a processor fitted with the metal blade.

4. Add the meat and then the potatoes, and pulse the processor on and off until the mixture starts to combine. You might need to stop the processor a few times to scrape down the sides of the bowl.

5. Add the 1 egg, seasonings, parsley, and the tomato sections, and pulse until the mixture is well combined and a thick, slightly sticky mass is formed.

6. Have the flour ready on a flat plate, the remaining 2 eggs beaten with a fork in a shallow bowl, and about ¼ inch of oil in a large frying pan heating on medium high.

7. Take a rounded soup spoon of the mixture and drop it onto the flour. With floured fingers, lightly toss the meat mixture to coat well on both sides, and form into round patties about ½ inch thick.

8. Carefully coat both sides of the patty with the egg, and gently place it in the hot oil. Repeat with the remaining patties, and fry until golden brown on both sides.

9. Drain on paper towel and serve hot or at room temperature, with tomato sauce or freshly squeezed lemon juice. Makes about 3 dozen.

Yield: 6–8 servings

TINA'S TIDBITS

- *This mixture barely holds together, which is why you lightly toss it in the flour with your fingertips. Handling the mixture roughly will create heavy, pasty spheres instead of light meat pancakes.*
- *Turkish cooking often involves dipping the food in egg last to give the dish a finished "cap."*

Maple-Glazed Chicken Breasts with Apples

Quick, sweet, savory, contains apples—what more could you want from a New Year dish?

1½ pounds boneless chicken breasts
⅓ cup Dijon mustard
7 tablespoons good-quality maple syrup, divided use
1½ tablespoons chopped fresh rosemary
1 tablespoon cooking oil

¾ teaspoon salt
Freshly ground black pepper to taste (about ¼ teaspoon)
4 Southern Rose, Winesap, or Granny Smith apples

1. Remove the fillet from each of the chicken breasts. Remove the white membrane from each of the fillets.

2. Combine the Dijon mustard with 3 tablespoons of the maple syrup, the rosemary, oil, salt, and pepper in a bowl.

3. Place the chicken in the bowl and turn to coat all pieces well. Allow chicken to marinate for at least 30 minutes.

4. When ready to cook, heat a grill on high and, when hot, place the chicken smooth side down. Grill for 4 minutes. Turn the meat over and cook until the chicken is firm but has some "give," about 2–3 more minutes. Remove from heat and keep warm until the apples are ready.

5. Peel the apples and cut into 16 wedges each.

6. Pour 1 tablespoon of cooking oil into a hot frying pan. Sauté the apples until they are a light, golden brown.

7. Reduce the heat to low and add the remaining 4 tablespoons of the maple syrup. Sauté the apples until they are tender. (The sautéed apples may be made in advance and then briefly reheated before serving.)

8. To serve, place the grilled chicken on a serving platter, and spoon the apples and sauce over the chicken.

Yield: 4–6 servings

TINA'S TIDBITS

- *The tender or fillet of the chicken breast can often make the breast look thick and plumped up. If it is not removed, the breast will not cook evenly and the center will be raw. Look for the white, pearlized membrane to determine if the fillet is still intact.*
- *It is better to reheat food in the microwave than to warm it in an oven. Microwaves will agitate the water molecules in food to make them hot, but even a low oven can still dry out the food.*

Rosh HaShanah Noodle Kugel

Here's a delicious noodle kugel that incorporates all the symbols for a sweet and fruitful New Year. The kugel is moist, not too sweet, and contains no dairy products, so it can be served with a meat meal or for dessert.

12 ounces extra-wide dried egg noodles
1/3 cup vegetable oil (corn or canola)
4 large eggs
Two 3.9-ounce (snack size) containers or 1 cup unsweetened applesauce
1/3 cup wildflower or clover honey
1/4 cup frozen apple juice concentrate
1 teaspoon cinnamon
1/4 teaspoon ground ginger

1/4 teaspoon nutmeg
3 Jonagold or Gala apples, pared, cored, and sliced into thin semicircles (reserve 8 slices for garnish on top of kugel)
1/2 cup golden raisins (optional)
1/4 cup sugar mixed with 1/2 teaspoon cinnamon (for topping)
Nonstick cooking spray or pareve margarine

1. Preheat oven to 350°F. Grease a 13 × 9-inch baking dish with nonstick spray.

2. Cook noodles according to package directions. Drain but do not rinse. Place in a large mixing bowl. Add the oil and stir gently with a rubber spatula to coat and separate all the noodles.

3. In a 2-quart mixing bowl, lightly beat the eggs with a fork. Add the applesauce, honey, apple juice concentrate, cinnamon, ginger, and nutmeg and combine.

4. Using a spatula, add the apple semicircles and raisins (if using) to the egg mixture.

5. Pour the apple mixture into the noodles. Mix gently, but thoroughly, and pour into the prepared pan. Place reserved apple slices down the center of the casserole.

6. Lightly grease the shiny side of a sheet of foil with nonstick spray and cover the casserole, greased side down.

7. Bake for 45 minutes and remove from the oven. Uncover, sprinkle with the cinnamon and sugar mixture, and lightly spray with cooking spray or dot with margarine. Return the uncovered casserole to the oven for an additional 15 minutes or until lightly golden.

Yield: 12–15 servings

TINA'S TIDBITS

- *Because honey is 1–1 1/2 times sweeter than sugar, less is needed to sweeten most recipes.*
- *Covering a casserole with foil, dull side out, will help the food absorb heat from the oven without drying out.*
- *Always bake a noodle kugel immediately after adding the egg mixture or the mixture will settle and create a rubbery layer on the bottom and the noodles will be dry on top.*

Koliva
(Sweetened Wheat Berry Pudding)

This Greek pudding is called by many names in the Middle East. Sephardim serve this for Rosh HaShanah and Tu BiSh'vat. The addition of pomegranate seeds and dates makes it appropriate for the New Year.

1 cup whole soft spring wheat berries
4 cups water
½ cup sugar
¼ cup wildflower honey
Pinch of salt
1 teaspoon cinnamon

1 cup almonds, walnuts, pistachio nuts, or a mixture
1 cup raisins or mixed dried fruit bits
4 Medjool dates, cut in half lengthwise and pitted (for garnish)
Pomegranate seeds for garnish

1. Place wheat berries in a glass bowl and cover with boiling water. Soak the berries for 2 hours or until they are slightly softened. Drain the water. Place in a 3-quart saucepan.

2. Add the 4 cups of water to the pan and bring the water to a boil. Simmer for 45–60 minutes, or until the wheat berries are tender but firm. Drain.

3. Add the sugar, honey, salt, and cinnamon to the pot and cook over moderate heat until the honey and sugar are completely melted and thoroughly coating the wheat berries.

4. Toast the nuts in a 350°F oven for 5 minutes. Set aside.

5. Add the nuts and the dried fruit to the mixture, and spoon into a serving bowl.

6. Garnish with the sliced dates and pomegranate seeds if desired. Serve at room temperature or cold.

Yield: 8–10 servings

TINA'S TIDBITS

- *Never cook beans or grains with salt, as the salt will toughen the food and require a lengthy cooking time. Add salt afterwards if necessary.*
- *Nuts should always be stored in the freezer to keep them from becoming rancid.*

Teiglach

Three weeks prior to Rosh HaShanah, all the New York Jewish bakeries put up signs urging customers to place their teiglach orders. Most Texans, as well as many other American Jews outside of New York, are not familiar with this great dessert. I have fond memories of sitting around the table discussing politics and picking on this dessert, trying to dislodge a sweet morsel. This recipe is much easier than the original technique of cooking the dough in the honey syrup, and the results are perfect every time!

3 eggs
3 tablespoons oil
2 tablespoons water
1/2 teaspoon vanilla
2 1/2 cups flour
1/4 teaspoon salt
1/4 teaspoon ginger
1 teaspoon baking powder

1 pound wildflower honey (any honey is OK, but wildflower is the best)
1/2 cup sugar
1/2 teaspoon ginger
One 2-inch piece of orange zest, 1/2 inch wide
1 cup toasted hazelnuts, peeled
1/2 cup candied cherries or raisins

1. Preheat the oven to 375°F.

2. Combine the eggs, oil, water, and vanilla, and beat with a fork or whisk until light and combined.

3. In a medium bowl, combine the flour, salt, ginger, and baking powder.

4. Add the liquid ingredients to the bowl with the dry ingredients and stir with a fork until well combined. Knead with your hands for a few minutes until the dough is smooth and shiny. Cover with plastic wrap and let rest for 10 minutes.

5. Roll out small chunks of dough into long 1/2-inch-wide snakes and cut into 1/3-inch pieces. Roll the dough pieces briefly in your hands to make balls, and place them on ungreased cookie sheets. Bake for 20–22 minutes or until golden brown.

6. Meanwhile, combine the honey, sugar, ginger, and orange zest in a heavy 3-quart saucepan and bring slowly to a boil. Simmer for exactly 10 minutes.

7. Add the *teiglach* balls, the nuts, and the raisins or cherries to the honey mixture and stir with a wooden spoon to coat well. Place in a pie plate or individual tart tins mounded to form a pyramid.

Yield: 12 servings

TINA'S TIDBITS

- *The balls of dough can be made and frozen until you are ready to assemble the* teiglach.
- *Always freeze baked goods after they are thoroughly cooled. Place in a freezer bag and close almost all the way. Insert a straw and suck out all of the air and then seal. Defrost before using.*
- *Always stir a hot sugar syrup with a wooden spoon. Metal will conduct the heat and get too hot and plastic will melt.*

Hadgi Badah
(Almond Macaroons)

The following recipe is a variation of the ubiquitous Sephardic almond macaroon. This recipe is undeniably Iraqi, because of the inclusion of the cardamom, and it is traditionally served following the conclusion of the N'ilah service at the end of Yom Kippur. The cookies are very easy to make, especially if you use the food processor to combine all of the ingredients. Longer baking will make them hard but more golden.

8 ounces almond slivers
⅔ cup sugar
1 egg

2 teaspoons rose water
¼ teaspoon ground cardamom

1. Preheat the oven to 350°F, and cover 2 cookie sheets with parchment paper. Set aside.

2. Place almonds in a food processor work bowl and pulse the machine on and off to grind the nuts until they are fairly fine.

3. Add the sugar and pulse on and off 10 times to combine well and grind until very fine.

4. Add the remaining ingredients and pulse on and off until the mixture is well combined and a thick batter is formed.

5. Lightly shape into balls or drop by teaspoon onto the prepared cookie sheets. A sliver of almond is sometimes pressed into the top of the cookie before baking.

6. Bake for 14 minutes or until lightly golden. The longer you bake this cookie, the harder it becomes. This is a matter of personal taste and strong teeth!

7. Store in a plastic bag when cool. Keeps for a week or more.

Yield: 2–3 dozen

TINA'S TIDBITS

- *When buying nuts by weight, the rule is to double the weight of the nuts and convert that amount to cups to determine the volume. For example, 8 ounces of nuts will yield approximately 2 cups of nuts.*
- *When grinding nuts in a processor, always pulse the machine on and off to finely grind. Pulsing throws the nuts up and allows them to fall to get chopped, preventing a paste or "butter" from forming on the floor of the work bowl.*
- *Never seal food in a plastic bag while still warm. The steam given off by the warm baked good will make your product soggy and hastens the formation of mold in the bag.*

FRESH APPLE CAKE

Grated apples make this cake moist and delicious. It is a simple dessert when served dusted with confectioners' sugar, but the original West Texas version calls for a coconut-pecan topping as rich as the region's oil wells.

2 cups flour
1 teaspoon baking soda
½ teaspoon salt
1 teaspoon cinnamon
1¼ cups oil
2 cups sugar
3 eggs

2 teaspoons vanilla
3 cups grated apple (peel does not need to be removed if finely grated)
1¼ cups coarsely chopped pecans
Confectioners' sugar for dusting top (if not making the topping below)

1. Combine the flour, soda, salt, and cinnamon in a small bowl and set aside.

2. In a large mixing bowl, beat the oil and sugar together until well blended. Add the eggs and beat until the eggs are totally incorporated and the mixture is a light lemon color.

3. Mix in the vanilla and then add the flour mixture, the grated apple, and the pecans and mix well.

4. Pour into a 10-inch springform tube pan or a Bundt pan that has been sprayed with nonstick cooking spray. Bake at 350°F for 50–55 minutes or until a toothpick inserted in the center of the cake comes out clean. Remove from the oven and cool. When cool, remove from the pan and place on a serving tray. Dust with some confectioners' sugar **or** top with the following topping if desired.

TOPPING

6 tablespoons unsalted butter
2 tablespoons milk
¾ cup brown sugar

½ cup shredded coconut
½ cup chopped pecans

1. Combine all ingredients in a medium saucepan. Bring to a boil and boil for 1 minute.

2. Pour over top of cake and cool before serving.

Yield: 12 servings

TINA'S TIDBITS

- *It is very important to thoroughly combine the eggs, sugar, and oil in a cake batter before adding other ingredients. If the oil is not completely incorporated into the eggs, the finished product will be very greasy and heavy instead of light and moist.*
- *When a recipe calls for oil, it refers to vegetable oil like corn, canola, or soybean oil. Never use olive or peanut oil unless specified, because they have distinctive flavors.*
- *Once a sugar mixture comes to a boil, it should not be stirred. Stirring will create a grainy, coarse texture instead of a smooth mixture.*

SUKKOT

Many historians believe the Pilgrims' first celebration of giving thanks was patterned after the Jewish festival of Sukkot. Jews made pilgrimage to Jerusalem after the fall harvest to give thanks not only for the bounty of the earth they had just gathered but also for God's deliverance to the Promised Land. Likewise, the Pilgrims lived in temporary huts and gave thanks to God for their deliverance to the New World and the first harvest that would sustain them through the winter.

The Torah refers to Sukkot as *HaChag*, "The Festival." The symbols of this festival are the sukkah, the three-sided hut with its profusion of fall fruits and vegetables hanging from the open, star-illuminated roof; the *lulav*, with its palm, myrtle, and willow branches; and the *etrog*, or citron, a citrus fruit that looks like a huge bumpy lemon.

The Talmud (*Beitzah* 30b) recommends using nuts, almonds, peaches, grape branches, and jugs of freshly pressed olive oil to decorate the sukkah but does not suggest what to eat. One of the mitzvot of the holiday is to actually eat meals in the sukkah and invite guests to partake of the meals with you. The great kabbalist, Rabbi Isaac Luria, offered an invitation to the *ushpizin*—symbolic guests Abraham, Isaac, Jacob, Joseph, Moses, Aaron, and David—who were all great wanderers of our heritage who lived in huts.

The Torah does not dictate what should be eaten in the sukkah. Fruits, vegetables, and grains figure prominently in the harvest foods of Sukkot, as they did in the Mediterranean diet. Wheat, barley, and lentils were cultivated. Grapes, figs, and dates are cited often in the Bible. In Leviticus 20:24, "a land flowing with milk and honey" refers to the honey-sweet dates from the date palm tree whose fronds are the "backbone" of the *lulav*.

For Sukkot, Jewish cooks throughout the Diaspora have traditionally made foods that are rolled or stuffed, symbolic of the abundance of the holiday harvest. Rice and couscous dishes made with seasonal fruits and vegetables and cooked fruit compotes are prominent on menus for Sukkot as well. Most dishes are prepared as casseroles because they are easily transported from the kitchen to the sukkah.

The sukkah represents the transient nature of our material wealth. What our homes contain is temporary; what our hearts contain can lead to caring for others and *tikkun olam* (repair of the world).

BUTTERNUT-APPLE SOUP

Butternut squash was cultivated millennia before Columbus discovered it. The smooth texture of the squash lends itself to creating a thick, creamy soup without all the cream. Perfect for a dairy luncheon, this soup can easily be made pareve by using soy creamer and margarine in place of the cream and butter. Fall pie pumpkin may be substituted. Great for a sukkah meal.

One 2-pound butternut squash
2 McIntosh or Gala apples, peeled, cored, and cut up,
 or 1 cup unsweetened applesauce
2 tablespoons butter
1 cup apple cooking liquid or vegetable stock
½ cup half-and-half

½ tablespoon loosely packed Mexican mint marigold
 or tarragon
½ teaspoon nutmeg
Salt and freshly ground black pepper to taste
⅓ cup toasted pine nuts

1. Pierce the squash with a fork in 2 places and bake in a 350°F oven for 40 minutes or until a knife easily cuts into the flesh.

2. Place the cut apple pieces in a small saucepan and add water to a depth of ¼ inch. Cook covered for 8 minutes or until the apples are very soft.

3. Cut the squash in half lengthwise, remove the seeds, and scoop out the flesh. Remove apples from cooking liquid and reserve liquid. Place the squash flesh and the apples in a food processor work bowl and process until smooth.

4. Add the remaining ingredients **except** the pine nuts and process until well blended. Add additional cooking liquid if the soup is too thick.

5. Place the mixture in a clean saucepan and heat thoroughly over moderate heat for about 6 minutes.

6. Serve in individual soup bowls or little pumpkins, sprinkled with some toasted pine nuts.

Yield: 4–6 servings

TINA'S TIDBITS

- *It is much easier to bake a whole butternut squash than to try to peel it and cut it into cubes. However, if roasting a pierced squash, always do so on a low-rimmed cookie sheet to prevent any juices from spilling over and burning on the oven floor.*
- *Toast the pine nuts for 3–4 minutes or until lightly golden and fragrant. Do not let them get too dark or they will continue to fry in their own oils outside of the roasting oven and will burn.*
- *Nuts are not roasted in the oven; they fry in their own oils that are heated by the oven. As a result, removing nuts from the oven only removes them from the heat source, not from the frying source.*

Autumn Pâté

French Jews were often associated with the foie gras industry. Fattening the geese so that their livers were exceedingly large and riddled with fat in order to produce the best pâté is considered by many contemporary Jews to be inhumane and anathema to the Jewish dietary laws. Luckily, this pâté is made with chicken livers and the bird wasn't force-fed. This pâté is not smooth, but rather more like a country pâté, because of the fruits and sautéed onions included with the chicken livers.

2 stalks of celery, preferably with some leaves attached
6 black peppercorns
1 bay leaf
1/2 teaspoon finely ground sea salt
2 quarts water
1/4 cup sweetened dried cranberries
1/4 cup water
8 tablespoons (1 stick) pareve margarine
4 tablespoons rendered chicken fat
1/2 cup chopped onion

1 clove garlic
1 pound chicken livers
2 teaspoons dry mustard
1/4 teaspoon ground nutmeg
1/8 teaspoon ground allspice
4 tablespoons of apple brandy
Salt and freshly ground pepper
1/4 cup finely diced unsweetened canned apples or cooked fresh apple
1 teaspoon sugar

1. Combine the first 5 ingredients in a 3-quart saucepan and bring to a boil. Simmer for 10 minutes.

2. Meanwhile, combine the dried cranberries with the 1/4 cup water and microwave for 1 1/2 minutes. Set aside until ready to use.

3. Heat an 8- to 10-inch frying pan for 20 seconds. Add the margarine and chicken fat and melt. Fry the onion over medium heat until the onion is soft. Add the garlic and continue to sauté until the mixture is very lightly golden. Do not allow the garlic to burn. Set aside while you cook the livers.

4. Pick over the chicken livers to remove any yellow membrane. Check for and remove any green spots (this would be from the bile and would make the livers bitter). Broil the livers 1 minute on each side until lightly browned. (This is to prepare them according to the laws of kashrut.)

5. Place the livers in the simmering water mixture and reduce the heat to low. Cover and cook for 10 minutes. Turn off the heat and let rest for 2 minutes. The livers will be very tender and barely pink inside.

6. Drain the livers and discard the celery, peppercorns, and bay leaf. Place the livers in the container of a food processor.

7. Add the sautéed onion-garlic mixture with all the fat from the pan and all the spices to the livers and process until fairly smooth. Scrape down the sides of the work bowl and add the apple brandy. Process until the mixture is very smooth. Add salt and pepper to taste.

8. Place the liver mixture in a 2-quart bowl. Set aside.

9. Drain the soaking dried cranberries and combine with the diced apples and sugar.

10. Fold the cranberry-apple mixture into the liver mixture, and pour into a 1-quart bowl or mold that is lined with plastic wrap. Tap the mold on the counter 1 or 2 times to settle the mixture. Cover well and refrigerate until firm and ready to serve.

11. To serve, unmold the pâté onto a plate and serve with toasted pita or French bread.

Note: Orange liqueur and other dried fruits can be substituted, or try adding 1 heaping tablespoon drained green peppercorns to the mixture instead of the fruits.

Yield: 12 servings

TINA'S TIDBITS

- *Although pâté can be made with any liver (chicken, beef, or calf), chicken liver is the smoothest and mildest-tasting liver of the three to use.*
- *Golden raisins and pear can be substituted for the dried cranberries and apple. Poire William, a pear liqueur, can be used as well with this combination.*

MIXED-FRUIT CRANBERRY RELISH

Every fall I am approached after Thanksgiving and told stories about proud hostesses whose guests waxed ecstatic about the cranberry relish they were served. Here is a recipe that is easy to make, tastes delicious, and, because of the high sugar content and alcohol, lasts for a month or more in the refrigerator. Your Sukkot fruit relish becomes your Thanksgiving accompaniment. Enjoy the rave reviews!

12 ounces fresh cranberries
2 apples, pared, cored, and cut into chunks
2 pears, pared, cored and cut into chunks
1 cup dark raisins
1 cup sugar

½ cup fresh orange juice
1 tablespoon grated orange zest
1¼ teaspoons cinnamon
⅓ cup orange liqueur

1. Put all of the ingredients **except** the liqueur into a heavy saucepan. Bring to a boil and then reduce the heat to a slow simmer.

2. Cook uncovered for 25–40 minutes or until the mixture thickens slightly. Stir occasionally to prevent sticking. Remove from the heat.

3. Add the liqueur and stir until thoroughly blended.

4. Refrigerate for at least three hours. This mixture lasts for months in the refrigerator and freezes well.

5. Serve chilled as an accompaniment to a poultry dinner or on a sandwich.

Yield: 1½ quarts

TINA'S TIDBITS

- *The alcohol and sugar in this recipe act like preservatives and allow the sauce to last for months in the refrigerator.*
- *Make a double batch so the leftovers from Sukkot can be eaten for Thanksgiving or even Chanukah!*

Dolmas
(Turkish Stuffed Grape Leaves)

Stuffed grape leaves and cabbage are ubiquitous in the cuisines of the Jews. At Sukkot, every Jewish community has its specialty. The use of the sweet spices along with the pine nuts and raisins shows the strong Arab influence in this dish.

2 tablespoons olive oil
2 medium onions, chopped
1 clove garlic, minced
One 8-ounce jar grape leaves in brine (2 if leaves are small)
1 cup uncooked long-grain rice
4 scallions, finely chopped
2 tablespoons minced fresh dill
2 tablespoons finely chopped Italian parsley
2 tablespoons minced fresh mint
½ teaspoon cinnamon
½ teaspoon allspice

3 tablespoons toasted pine nuts
3 tablespoons raisins
1 teaspoon salt
¼ teaspoon freshly ground pepper or to taste
⅔ cup olive oil
⅓ cup freshly squeezed lemon juice
⅔ cup water, plus additional as needed during cooking
1 teaspoon sugar
Broken grape leaves or lettuce leaves for the bottom of the pot

1. Heat 2 tablespoons of olive oil in a large skillet and sauté the onion for 5 minutes. Add the garlic and sauté until the onions are lightly golden. Place this mixture in a 2-quart mixing bowl.

2. Soak the separated grape leaves in a bowl of warm water for 5 minutes while you make the filling.

3. Place the rice in a 1-quart glass bowl, cover with water, and microwave on high for 5 minutes. Drain.

4. Add the rice, scallions, dill, parsley, mint, cinnamon, allspice, pine nuts, and raisins to the onion mixture. Season the mixture with the salt and pepper.

5. Remove the leaves from the bowl of water and rinse under cold running water. Separate the leaves and place shiny side down on a board. If the leaves are small, place two together, overlapping at the stem end.

6. Place 2 teaspoons of the rice mixture near the stem end of each leaf, and roll up the leaf once to cover filling. Fold in both sides of the leaf to cover the filling, and proceed to tightly roll the leaf up toward the tip to make a neat roll.

TINA'S TIDBITS

- *Dolmas can be made in advance and stored in the refrigerator. Serve cool or at room temperature.*
- *Never use "real" lemon juice from a bottle! It bears no resemblance to the real thing. Two to three lemons will yield 1/3 cup juice.*
- *When buying lemons, scrape the outside with your fingernail and sniff. The fragrance will indicate the flavor of the lemon juice.*
- *Any remaining filling may be frozen in an airtight container for later use.*

7. Place some broken vine leaves or lettuce leaves in the bottom of a 4-quart pot or Dutch oven, so the rolls won't stick to the bottom of the pan. Arrange the rolls in the pot, seam side down, piling the rolls on top of each other as much as necessary.

8. Combine the remaining ⅔ cup oil, lemon juice, ⅔ cup water, and sugar and pour over the rolls in the Dutch oven.

9. Place a heavy plate or a plate with a weight (a heavy glass will do), on top of the rolls to prevent unraveling while cooking, and cover the pot. Simmer 40 minutes.

10. Add more water as needed to maintain about ½ inch of liquid on the bottom of the pot and cook for a total of 50 minutes or until the rice mixture in the rolls is tender.

11. Cool and serve at room temperature.

Yield: 3–4 dozen

STUFFED CABBAGE

Whether they were called holipkes, golishkes, goluptzi, *or* prakkes, *everyone who was summoned to dinner knew they were having stuffed cabbage. Let the Jews to the south stuff their meat and rice into teeny, tiny packets of grape leaves; the peasants in Poland and Russia were using big cabbage leaves to disguise the fact that there wasn't too much meat inside the tasty rolls. These rolls were traditionally served at Sukkot, probably because they were using the produce of the region and because it was transportable to the sukkah. No need to wait for any holiday to enjoy these.*

1/3 cup uncooked rice
2 cups boiling water
1 large onion
1–1 1/2 pounds ground beef
1 tablespoon salt
1/2 cup water

1 large or 2 small heads of cabbage
Two 8-ounce cans of unflavored tomato sauce
2 cups water
3 tablespoons brown sugar or to taste
1/2 cup raisins
Fresh lemon juice, to taste

1. Cook the rice in 2 cups boiling water for 10 minutes. Drain.

2. Cut onion into 1/2-inch dice. Combine with the meat, drained rice, salt, and 1/2 cup water in a bowl and mix well. Set aside while you prepare the cabbage for stuffing.

3. Cut the core out of the cabbage and place the cabbage, core side down, in a 4-quart pot, covering 2/3 of the cabbage with water. Cover the pot, bring the water to a boil, and cook the cabbage for as long as it takes to make the cabbage tender enough to remove some of the leaves, about 15 minutes. If some of the cabbage is still hard, return it to the water and cook while you start to stuff the soft leaves.

4. To fill the cabbage leaves, first cut a small inverted V out of the thick stem end of the cabbage leaf and discard. On a flat surface, place the leaf with the stem end toward you.

5. Place 2–3 tablespoons of the meat mixture at the stem end of the leaf and fold over once. Fold in both sides of the leaf, and continue rolling up the remaining cabbage to the end of the leaf. Fill the remaining leaves in the same way.

TINA'S TIDBITS

- *Rather than buy one very big cabbage, consider buying two smaller ones. The rolls will be a little bit smaller, but it will be easier to get the leaves soft.*
- *A modern trick to this old technique is to microwave the cabbage until its leaves are soft enough to roll. The advantage to this trick is that it will also cook the cabbage from the inside out.*
- *Placing some leftover or broken leaves on the bottom of the pan prevents any of the rolls from sticking and possibly scorching.*
- *Check the pot every once in a while to make sure that most of the rolls are covered with sauce.*
- *Traditionally the rice is added raw to the meat. However, partially cooking it results in rice that will ultimately blend in more with the other filling ingredients, and the filling won't fall apart when the cabbage roll is cut.*

6. Place any broken or small leaves in the bottom of a 4-quart Dutch oven. Layer the cabbage rolls over the small leaves, placing them seam side down so that they won't unravel when cooking.

7. Combine the tomato sauce, 2 cups of water, brown sugar, and raisins and pour over the cabbage rolls. Simmer for 2 hours, until the cabbage rolls are very tender.

8. Taste the sauce and add a tablespoon or more of lemon juice and more brown sugar, if needed, to properly adjust the sweet-and-sour taste. Cook for another 20 minutes.

9. Although stuffed cabbage can be served immediately, it will taste even better the next day or later.

Yield: 8–10 servings

PEAR SALAD WITH JICAMA AND SNOW PEAS

I originally taught this recipe as part of my spa cuisine class because it is very low in fat and high in fiber and flavor. I am including it here because it is the perfect salad to serve your ushpizin *in the sukkah.*

3 tablespoons pine nuts or pecans
2 cups snow peas
2 ripe pears
½ tablespoon lemon juice
3 cups fresh baby spinach
1 cup jicama
2 tablespoons balsamic vinegar

1 teaspoon Dijon mustard
1 clove garlic
2 tablespoons corn oil
2 tablespoons olive oil
1 scallion, thinly sliced crosswise
Freshly ground black pepper to taste
1 tablespoon chopped basil

1. Toast the nuts in a 350°F oven for 5 minutes or until lightly golden. Set aside.

2. String the snow peas. Blanch them in boiling salted water for 30 seconds and then plunge them into ice water. Cut them lengthwise into ¼-inch strips.

3. Peel and core the pears, cut them into ¼-inch strips lengthwise, and toss with the lemon juice.

4. Rinse the spinach well and remove any large stems. Pat dry and place in a serving bowl.

5. Peel the jicama and cut into 2-inch lengths, ¼ inch wide.

6. In a small bowl, whisk the vinegar, mustard, and garlic together. Slowly add the oils while you whisk rapidly to form an emulsion. Lightly whisk in the scallion, pepper, and basil. Allow to set for 15 minutes.

7. To arrange the salad, add the snow peas, pears, and jicama to the spinach and toss with the dressing. Spoon onto individual plates and sprinkle with the toasted nuts. Serve immediately.

Yield: 6–8 servings

TINA'S TIDBITS

- *To string snow peas, hold one pod by the top stem in your right hand and then place your thumb into the pod on top in the middle and pull the stem down. If pods are stringy, both stringy sides will peel away.*
- *The little bit of mustard in the vinaigrette will help the oil bind to the vinegar and create a creamy dressing rather than a clear liquid that will separate.*

VEGETARIAN COUSCOUS

This Moroccan-inspired dish, adapted from The Gourmet Jewish Cook *by the cookbook author and cooking teacher Judy Zeidler, is a perfect way to exploit the wonderful vegetables available during Sukkot. It makes a beautiful edible centerpiece for your dinner table in the sukkah. Served hot or at room temperature, it is equally enjoyable.*

2 tablespoons olive oil
2 large cloves garlic, finely chopped
1 medium onion, cut into $1/2$-inch dice
2 carrots, sliced into $1/4$-inch rounds
One 8-ounce can tomato sauce
$3/4$ cup dark raisins
$1/2$ teaspoon salt or to taste
1 teaspoon ground cumin
$2^1/2$ cups vegetable stock, divided use

2 small zucchini, sliced into $1/4$-inch rounds
1 small (1 pound) eggplant, cut into 1-inch dice
2 yellow crookneck squash, sliced into $1/4$-inch rounds
4 ounces mushrooms caps (any type—see Tidbit below), cut into quarters
One 15-ounce can chickpeas, rinsed and drained
4 tablespoons butter or margarine
1 cup couscous
1–2 tablespoons finely minced parsley for garnish (optional)

1. Heat a large frying pan for 30 seconds and add the oil. Heat the oil for 15 seconds and sauté the garlic and onion until lightly golden. Do not burn the garlic.

2. Add the carrots, tomato sauce, raisins, salt, cumin, and 1 cup of stock to the pan. Cover and simmer the mixture for 10 minutes or until the carrots are tender.

3. Add the zucchini and the eggplant and cook for 10 minutes. Add the crookneck squash, mushrooms, and chickpeas. Cook until all of the vegetables are tender.

4. In a large saucepan, heat the remaining $1^1/2$ cups stock and butter or margarine. Add the couscous. Cover, remove from the heat, and allow the pan to sit for 5 minutes.

5. To serve, spoon the couscous in the center of a large rimmed dish, and surround with the cooked vegetables. Pour the sauce evenly over all. Sprinkle with a little parsley for garnish if you like.

Yield: 4 servings as a main course or 8 as a side dish

TINA'S TIDBITS

- *Always heat the pan first before adding the oil. This prevents the oil from adhering to the pan and the food from sticking to the oil.*
- *You may vary the vegetables in the recipe, but always add first the vegetables that need more cooking time.*
- *Like all stews, this dish tastes even better the next day. Make the couscous right before serving, and reheat the vegetables in the microwave for 4 minutes or until hot.*
- *The fins of a portabella mushroom will blacken foods. Scrape the fins off with a spoon and discard them before using a portabella mushroom in this or any recipe.*

Sweet Potato–Pumpkin Cazuela (Casserole)

Here's a dish that is perfect for Sukkot and very easy—especially if you use the canned potatoes and pumpkins. Pumpkins are believed to have originated in North America between 7000 and 5500 B.C.E. Although prevalent in the Far East, pumpkins gained popularity in Europe beginning in the sixteenth century after their discovery in the New World. This recipe would be perfect for Thanksgiving as well as Sukkot. Substitute pareve margarine for the butter for a dairy-free dish. Don't be afraid of the coconut milk. It is very subtle and rounds out the flavors.

2 tablespoons unsalted butter or pareve margarine
$2/3$ cup granulated sugar
$1/3$ cup dark brown sugar
2 tablespoons all-purpose flour
$1/2$ teaspoon salt
$2/3$ cup unsweetened canned coconut milk
2 eggs
One 15-ounce can unflavored pumpkin puree or 1 small pie pumpkin (see instructions for cooking in Tina's Tidbits)

One 29-ounce can of yams in light syrup, drained and mashed, or 3 large yams
$1/4$ cup water
$1/8$ teaspoon ground ginger
2-inch piece of stick cinnamon, broken into pieces
$1/4$ teaspoon fennel seeds
3 whole cloves

1. Place the butter or margarine in a 2-quart glass bowl and microwave for 45 seconds.

2. Whisk the sugars, flour, and salt into the butter to combine.

3. Whisk the coconut milk into the mixture until thoroughly blended. Add the eggs and combine.

4. Add the pumpkin puree and the mashed yams and whisk until a smooth batter is formed.

5. Combine the water with the spices in a small glass cup and microwave on high for $1\frac{1}{2}$ minutes. Let the mixture steep for 5 minutes. Strain the spiced water through a fine-mesh strainer into the pumpkin-potato mixture and stir to incorporate.

6. Butter a 2-quart casserole and pour the mixture into the prepared dish.

7. Bake covered in a preheated 350°F oven for 1 hour. Serve.

Yield: 8–10 servings

TINA'S TIDBITS

- *Always use a small sugar pie pumpkin when cooked pumpkin is called for. Larger pumpkins are more watery and more like acorn squash.*
- *To cook a pumpkin, cut into large chunks, peel, and cook in boiling salted water until tender—about 20 minutes. Drain and mash.*
- *Coconut milk is not milk or dairy. It is the liquid formed from ground, fresh, hydrated coconut.*
- *This dish freezes beautifully! Just cool completely before freezing so no ice crystals form. Defrost and reheat in the microwave.*

PUMPKIN MOUSSE

All the good taste of pumpkin pie without the crust. It can be made with nondairy creamer for a pareve dessert that can easily be transported outside to the sukkah.

2 teaspoons unflavored kosher gelatin
2 tablespoons dark rum
1 cup canned unsweetened pumpkin
½ cup sugar
1 egg yolk
⅛ teaspoon nutmeg

Pinch of allspice
½ teaspoon cinnamon
¼ teaspoon ginger
1 teaspoon vanilla
¼ teaspoon salt
1 cup heavy cream or nondairy whipped topping mix

1. Sprinkle the gelatin over the rum in a small glass custard cup and let it soften for a few minutes.

2. Combine the remaining ingredients **except** the heavy cream in a medium bowl.

3. Place the custard cup with the rum and gelatin in a frying pan that contains ½ inch of simmering water. Stir the rum mixture until the gelatin is dissolved.

4. Whisk the hot gelatin mixture into the pumpkin mixture until thoroughly combined.

5. Whip the cream in a small bowl until it forms soft peaks and fold it carefully into the pumpkin mixture.

6. Spoon into six 4-ounce ramekins and refrigerate until set, about 3–4 hours.

Yield: 6 servings

TINA'S TIDBITS

- *Soaking the gelatin in the rum helps it swell so that when it is warm it will melt and be evenly distributed in the mousse.*
- *If a frozen, pre-whipped dairy or pareve topping is available, you may substitute 2 cups of that already whipped product for the 1 cup of whipping cream, however, the taste will be slightly different.*

CHANUKAH

*T*heme parties aren't new. One year I created a birthday cake for my son that covered an entire table with cupcakes, licorice, and cookies, transforming the table's surface into a giant Pac Man grid. I used modern media to enhance my creativity. Jewish cooks eight hundred years ago found their creative stimulus in themes from

the Bible, regional folklore, and daily life. The Chanukah story of the rededication of the Temple and the single vial of oil that lasted eight days instead of one prompted the use of large amounts of oil or rendered goose fat to make specialty dishes for Chanukah celebrations.

The original Chanukah culinary expression often served in Jewish homes over one thousand years ago was a cheese pancake commemorating Judith's heroic efforts on the part of her brethren. Dairy products were readily available in the warmer climates of the Diaspora. The Jews in Eastern Europe did not have easy access to dairy products, and Chanukah was celebrated sometime in December, when the weather was very cold. Historically, raising geese was a Jewish occupation, and in December the fattened geese were ready to provide the meat, fat, and down that would be needed during the cold months. Potatoes were cheap and readily available, so the Jews in the cold north reinterpreted the latke into a crisp, golden potato galette.

Symbolism is incorporated into culinary custom; foods that are regionally available dictate the expression of that symbolism. If you mix some goose or chicken fat with a plentiful supply of

radishes in the shtetl, you create a salad that was, according to folklore, one of the Maccabees' favorite foods. (Perhaps this story comes from the fact that the Roman word for *radish* means "root" and hiding in the mountains required the Maccabees to survive eating mostly root foods.)

Middle Eastern dishes made with bulgur always graced the Chanukah table, especially if delicate, but crisp, fried kibbeh was served too. North African Jewish communities relied on couscous to create a festive table, and the Dutch saw a parallel to the Hasmoneans' struggle in the siege of Leyden in 1574. At that time the Dutch organized a surprise attack on the invading Spanish camps at dinnertime, and the Spanish soldiers were forced to flee, leaving their simmering pots of stewed vegetables with meat behind. Many Dutch Jews serve a mashed stew of vegetables with garlic sausage called *hutspot* on Chanukah to commemorate this battle.

An entire chapter could be devoted to the myriad variations of fried doughnuts served around the world to commemorate this holiday, and latkes take on an entirely different meaning in Italy when made with arborio rice, raisins, and pine nuts. The common denominator of all these choices is the story of Chanukah and the survival of the Jewish way of life.

Chanukah Radish Salad Canapés

The Torah states that radishes were one of the mainstays of the Jewish slave's diet in Egypt. Both the Jerusalem and Babylonian Talmud refer to eating radishes. The red radish first became widely available in the sixteenth century, and a poor peasant's meal in Eastern Europe and Russia often consisted of black bread and radish. The addition of a little goose fat to this combo often elevated this simple food to a holiday treat. Geese were fattened in the fall and killed in the winter to save their fat for future use. A goose was often served for Chanukah, and its rendered fat was used in holiday preparations such as this.

1 pound large fresh red radishes (about 2 dozen)
2 large scallions
2 tablespoons rendered chicken fat
1½ tablespoons apple cider vinegar
½ teaspoon kosher salt or sea salt
½ teaspoon freshly ground black pepper (about 10 grinds)

1 teaspoon sugar or honey
Westphalian pumpernickel bread or whole-wheat pita
Extra chicken fat for spreading on bread (optional)
Coarse sea salt for garnish (optional)

1. Thinly slice the radishes crosswise by hand or using a thin slicing blade on a food processor.

2. Trim off the very ends of the scallions. Slice the scallions lengthwise in half through the white part. Cut the scallions crosswise into thin slices, using all of the green part as well. You should have about ⅔ cup.

3. Combine the radishes, scallions, chicken fat, vinegar, salt, pepper, and sugar or honey in a medium bowl and toss gently. Refrigerate for ½ hour to meld flavors.

4. Meanwhile cut thin pumpernickel slices in half on the diagonal or cut wedges from the pitas. Lightly toast the breads so that they are slightly crisp.

5. When ready to serve, spread a little bit of additional chicken fat on the tops of the bread triangles, and place a small mound of radish salad on the tops of the toasts. Sprinkle the tops of each radish mound with a pinch of coarse sea salt, if desired.

   Alternatively, place a few lettuce leaves on a salad plate, and mound some of the radish salad on the lettuce. Place a few triangles of bread on the side and serve.

Note: If you prefer, fragrant extra virgin olive oil may be substituted for the chicken fat.

Yield: 24 canapés or 6–8 servings

TINA'S TIDBITS

- *Red radishes tend to bleed their color when exposed to acidic foods for long periods of time. Either add vinegar an hour before serving or serve the same day as preparation.*
- *Spreading a thin layer of oil or fat on a bread base prevents the bread from getting soggy, especially when covered with a moist filling.*

Frituras de Malanga
(Taro Root Fritters)

A few years ago I went on a humanitarian medical mission to Cuba. We made a trip to the central synagogue of Havana, the Patronato, where I met some of the staff. It was here and on our mission to other cities where the small Jewish populations live that I learned some of their simple ways of cooking for Shabbat and some of the holidays.

Malanga, or taro root, has very little flavor and is very light and crisp when fried. This is how Tanya at the Patronato taught me to make them.

2 medium malanga, about 1 pound
1 small onion
1 teaspoon white or apple cider vinegar
1½ teaspoons salt
1 egg

1 tablespoon finely chopped parsley (optional in Cuba, but a nice addition)
Freshly ground black pepper (optional in Cuba, but a nice addition)
Vegetable oil for frying

1. Peel the malanga. Grate the malanga using the finest grating disk on your processor. Grate the onion in the same way. Replace the grating disk with the steel blade and pulse on and off about 20 times, until the pieces of food are quite small but not a mush. Transfer to a bowl. **Alternatively**, grate the malanga and onion on the fine side of a grater and place in a bowl.

2. Add the remaining ingredients **except** the oil and mix well.

3. Heat about 1 inch of oil in a frying pan or deep fryer until very hot, about 375°F.

4. Drop the mixture by teaspoon into the hot oil. Fry until golden on each side.

5. Drain on paper towel.

6. Serve immediately with *mojo* sauce (see recipe on the following page), sour cream, and applesauce, or purchased salsa.

Yield: 6–8 servings

TINA'S TIDBITS

- *The addition of a small amount of vinegar prevents the fried food from absorbing excess oil.*
- *For a crispy coating, use this malanga mixture on floured fish before frying.*
- *Garlic should never be allowed to brown, as it becomes very bitter.*
- *Crumble paper towels to have more surface area to absorb oil from fried foods.*

Mojo Sauce

Sour orange juice is a common ingredient in Cuba, confirming its roots in Spanish and possibly Jewish cooking. The ubiquitous orange trees in Andalusia are not the sweet variety that we associate with Valencia, and these oranges must have been brought to this region with the Spanish conquistadores.

¼ cup olive oil
6 large cloves garlic, finely minced
½ cup sour orange juice or ¼ cup orange juice and
   ¼ cup lime juice

½ teaspoon ground cumin
Salt and freshly ground black pepper to taste

1. Heat a 1-quart saucepan for 20 seconds. Add the olive oil and heat for 10 seconds over medium heat.

2. Add the garlic and cook for 20 seconds or until it just starts to get lightly golden. Do **not** let the garlic brown or the sauce will be bitter.

3. Add the remaining ingredients; be careful, as the sauce may steam. Bring to a rolling boil and cook for 3 minutes. Remove from heat, adjust the seasonings if necessary, and chill until ready to serve with the fritters or on top of vegetables, meats, or fish.

Yield: 6 servings

LATKES
(POTATO PANCAKES)

Latkes are traditionally served for Chanukah because they are cooked in oil (to commemorate the vial of oil lasting for 8 days). However, since they are pareve when served without sour cream, they are also a perfect accompaniment to a beef or chicken entrée. For an elegant appetizer, prepare as small rounds and top with sour cream and caviar.

6–8 large thin-skinned potatoes, California long whites or Yukon Gold
3 eggs, beaten well
1 tablespoon salt
½ teaspoon freshly ground pepper
½ cup matzah meal or cracker meal
1 large onion, cut into 8 pieces
Oil for frying
Applesauce (optional)
Sour cream (optional)

1. Grate the raw potatoes using the large grating disk on a processor or the largest holes on a grater if doing it by hand. Place the grated potato in a colander, rinse with cold water. Set aside to drain.

2. Combine eggs, salt, pepper, and matzah meal or cracker meal in a 3-quart bowl. Mix thoroughly.

3. Change to the cutting blade on your processor. Add the onions to the work bowl. Pulse on and off 5 times. Add ¼ of the grated potatoes to the onion and pulse on and off to make a coarse paste. Add to the egg mixture and stir to combine.

4. Add the drained potatoes to the bowl and mix thoroughly, using a large spoon or your hands.

5. Heat a large frying pan or large skillet for 20 seconds. Add enough oil to cover the pan to a depth of ¼ inch and heat for an additional 10 seconds. Drop mounds of potato mixture into the pan. Fry on both sides until golden. Drain the fried latkes on a platter covered with crumpled paper towels. Serve with applesauce and sour cream.

Yield: 2–4 dozen depending on size

TINA'S TIDBITS:

- *Grated potatoes turn black when exposed to air. Rinsing the potatoes under running water washes away excess starch, the discoloring culprit.*
- *Always grate the potatoes separately from the onions so that you don't lose any of the flavorful onion juice when you drain the potatoes.*
- *The best way to drain fried foods is on a plate covered with crumpled paper towels. Crumpling them yields more surface area for absorption.*

LEMON RICOTTA PANCAKES

In deference to the heroine Judith, who saved the Jews from annihilation by feeding salty cheese and wine to General Holofernes, getting him drunk enough so she could behead him and scare off his troops, I have created this updated version of classic kaese latkes. *A delicious treat all year long, not just for Chanukah.*

1 tablespoon unsalted butter
1 cup whole milk ricotta
2 eggs
2 tablespoons light brown sugar
Zest of $\frac{1}{2}$ medium lemon, finely minced
$\frac{1}{2}$ teaspoon vanilla extract

$\frac{1}{8}$ teaspoon ground nutmeg
$\frac{1}{4}$ teaspoon salt
2 tablespoons whole-wheat flour
2 tablespoons all-purpose flour
Unsalted butter for frying

1. Place the 1 tablespoon of butter in a $1\frac{1}{2}$-quart glass bowl and microwave on high for 40 seconds or until the butter is melted.

2. Add the ricotta and eggs and mix well with a whisk to thoroughly combine.

3. Add the brown sugar, lemon zest, vanilla, nutmeg, salt, and the two flours and stir well.

4. Heat a griddle over medium-high heat and rub the end of a stick of butter all over the surface of the pan to coat it well.

5. Drop heaping tablespoons of batter onto the griddle and cook for 3 minutes or until the underside of the pancake is golden brown and the top is slightly dry.

6. Gently flip the pancakes over (it might be easier to use 2 small spatulas to do this), and cook for another 2 minutes until the edges are barely crisp and both sides are golden brown.

7. Serve drizzled with additional melted butter, honey, or a dollop of sour cream, if desired.

Note: Recipe may be doubled if desired.

Yield: About 20 silver-dollar-sized pancakes, 4–6 servings

TINA'S TIDBITS

- *These pancakes are as light as air and delicate, so turning is best achieved using two spatulas, one in each hand, to evenly brown both sides.*
- *Whole-wheat flour contains more gluten than white flour, so less is needed in delicate foods to bind ingredients together.*
- *A rasp-type grater is perfect for creating fine shards of lemon zest that will flavor the batter evenly without any bitter white pith from the inner peel.*

STUFFED KIBBEH

Kibbeh is a popular national dish of Syria, Lebanon, Jordan, and Iraq. Kurdish Jews call this dish kubba, *and in Egypt it is called* kobeba. *A woman was judged on her prowess in forming the kibbeh into long, torpedo-shaped, shelled dumplings. If a baby girl was born with a long finger, she was considered blessed. Making the crust is much easier now that a food processor can be used to make the paste. However, all the hard work of pounding the bulgur with the meat and shaping the crust into a thin shell to be stuffed has been alleviated by the more modern technique of layering the cooked filling in between the crust layers and baking the entire kibbeh instead of frying individual pieces. As a result, this dish can be made by hand without the use of electrical equipment.*

In the Middle East, dishes made with bulgur always graced the Chanukah table.

CRUST:
1¼ cups bulgur
2 cups water
1 cup coarsely chopped onion (about one 3-inch onion)
1 pound ground beef or lamb
½ teaspoon salt
10 grindings of black pepper
1 teaspoon cinnamon

FILLING:
2 tablespoons extra virgin olive oil
2 cups finely chopped onion (about ½ of large sweet onion)
¼ cup pine nuts
½ pound ground beef or lamb
½ teaspoon salt or to taste
12 grindings of black pepper
¼ teaspoon allspice
½ teaspoon cinnamon
1–2 tablespoons extra virgin olive oil for coating

1. To make the crust, combine bulgur and water in a 1-quart glass bowl and microwave on high for 2 minutes. Let the bulgur soak for 10–15 minutes. Drain in a mesh sieve, pressing out most of the liquid. Set aside.

2. Place the 1 cup of onion in a processor work bowl with the metal blade and pulse the machine to chop the onion fine.

3. Add the rest of the crust ingredients (meat, salt, pepper, and cinnamon) and turn the machine on for 10 seconds to form a paste. Add the drained bulgur and process until a smooth paste is formed.

4. Spread half of this meat mixture ½ inch thick over the bottom and up the sides of a 10-inch glass pie plate. Set aside while you make the filling.

5. Heat a 10-inch sauté pan on high for 20 seconds. Add the olive oil and heat for another 10 seconds. Reduce the heat to medium high and add the finely chopped onions. Sauté the onions until they are soft and lightly golden.

6. Add the pine nuts and sauté until they are lightly golden.

7. Add the meat to the pan along with the remaining filling ingredients. Break the meat up with a fork or the back of a large spoon. Cook the meat until it loses its pink color, but do not overcook or the meat will be tough and rubbery.

8. When the mixture is cooked, pour into the center of the meat shell.

9. Wet your hands with cold water and gently spread the remainder of the crust meat mixture smoothly over the top, covering the filling completely.

10. Spread 1–2 tablespoons of olive oil over the top of the kibbeh. With the tip of a sharp knife, lightly score the meat on the diagonal every $1\frac{1}{2}$ inches to create a diamond pattern.

11. Place in a 400°F oven and bake for 30–35 minutes, until the top is golden brown and slightly crisp.

12. Cut the kibbeh in wedges and serve as a main course, or cut along the scored lines and serve little diamonds as an appetizer.

Yield: 4–6 servings

TINA'S TIDBITS

- *A food processor is not necessary to make this recipe if fine bulgur is used and you chop the onion very small.*
- *Bulgur is wheat that has been steamed, dried, and crushed. It comes in coarse, medium, and fine grain. If you are not using a processor, make sure you use medium- or fine-grain bulgur.*
- *Bulgur (or bulghur) should not be confused with cracked wheat, which has not been previously treated.*

Moroccan Sweet Couscous with Mixed Dried Fruits

This dish is now a staple on my buffet table for all fall Jewish holidays, since I like to incorporate a new fruit (pomegranate) or fall fruits (raisins, apples, pears in their dried form) for Rosh HaShanah and Sukkot. In reality, this traditional Moroccan dish is served for Chanukah, but I can't relegate it to just that one holiday. I have streamlined the preparation time by using dried fruit that is already chopped, and you can use any combination of dried fruit that you want. This is a very kid-friendly recipe and a great way to get those iron-packed fruits into their diet.

1 cup Israeli couscous
2 tablespoons unsalted butter or pareve margarine
1/4 cup sugar
1/2 teaspoon cinnamon
One 7-ounce package of chopped mixed dried fruit
 or 1 1/2 cups assorted dried fruits

1/3 cup whole almonds, roasted and coarsely chopped
2 tablespoons pine nuts, lightly roasted
1/3 cup milk with 3 drops of almond extract added
Cinnamon, pitted Medjool dates, pomegranate seeds, and/or apricot slivers for garnish

1. Cook couscous in a large pot of boiling salted water for 7 to 10 minutes or until tender but still firm. Drain, but do not rinse, and place in a large mixing bowl.

2. Melt the butter or margarine in a 1-cup bowl in the microwave for 35 seconds. Add the sugar and cinnamon and stir to combine. Pour the mixture over the couscous to coat thoroughly.

3. Add the dried fruit and roasted nuts.

4. Mix the 3 drops of almond extract into the milk. Add just enough of the milk to the couscous to moisten it. Do not add too much or the mixture will be runny. Reserve excess milk in case the couscous is dry. Remoisten before you garnish.

5. Pile the couscous into a mound or pyramid shape on a serving platter. Sprinkle with additional cinnamon and garnish with Medjool date halves, pomegranate seeds, and/or apricot slivers.

Yield: 10 or more servings as part of a holiday buffet

DUTCH HUTSPOT

History often gets transformed into a culinary creation and people often use a recipe to symbolize a part of that historical event. Although all countries have a favorite fried recipe for Chanukah, Dutch Jews also serve this rich mixture of vegetables at Chanukah to recount a Dutch tale. During the Spanish siege of Leyden in 1574, the Dutch made a surprise attack on the Spanish camps at dinnertime, and the soldiers were forced to flee, leaving their simmering pots of stewed vegetables and meat behind. This stew is symbolic of that siege and its parallel to the Maccabean fight.

1 tablespoon rendered chicken fat or vegetable oil
2 medium-large onions, diced
3 large Yukon Gold or California white potatoes, peeled and cut into eighths
2 large carrots, peeled and cut into eighths
2 cups water or chicken broth

Salt and freshly ground black pepper to taste
Additional tablespoon chicken fat (optional)
Cayenne pepper (optional)
1 garlic-flavored Polish sausage or knockwurst, finely diced (optional)

1. Heat a 3-quart saucepan over high heat for 20 seconds. Add the chicken fat or oil and heat for 10 seconds. Add the onions and sauté for 5 minutes or until golden brown but not dark.

2. Add the potato chunks and carrots to the saucepan. Add the water or broth, which should not cover the vegetables more than halfway.

3. Bring the vegetable mixture to a boil, and then cover and reduce the heat to a simmer. Cook the vegetables until they are very tender.

4. Remove the pan from the heat and carefully drain the liquid from the pot. Reserve the liquid for another use, if desired.

5. Mash the drained vegetables until they form a fairly smooth mass. (Carrots and onions may be pureed in a processor, but mash the potatoes by hand—do **not** use a processor for the potatoes.) If the mixture appears too watery, return it to the stove and cook over moderate heat until the excess moisture evaporates. Stir occasionally to prevent scorching.

6. Add seasonings and an additional tablespoon of chicken fat if desired. Stir to combine. Add the diced sausage, if using. Reheat just before serving.

Yield: 1$\frac{1}{2}$ quarts or 8 or more servings

TINA'S TIDBITS

- *Never use a processor to mash white potatoes. You will always get a consistency akin to wallpaper paste if you do!*
- *Yukon Gold and California whites are more dense varieties of potato that create a creamier consistency and less water in the finished mash. They are also thin-skinned and do not require peeling unless specifically called for in a recipe.*
- *Browning onions caramelizes the natural sugars in the onion and brings out the sweetness that enhances most dishes.*

FRITTELLE DI RISO
(ITALIAN RICE PANCAKES)

According to the Italian Jewish culinary authority Edda Servi Machlin, these rice pancakes are traditionally served for Chanukah. I have adapted her recipe so that the pancakes are not saturated in oil and the use of eggs is decreased. I have also roasted the nuts first to enhance their flavor and crispness.

Served with cinnamon and sugar or honey, these frittelle *make a very acceptable dessert or breakfast. However, because they are pareve, they would make a welcome side dish to any main course. Recipes that call for raisins and pine nuts in Italian cuisine strongly suggest the influence of the Jewish émigrés from Spain in the fifteenth century.*

1 cup arborio rice
2¼ cups water
1 teaspoon salt
½ cup slivered almonds or pine nuts
1 cup dark raisins

Finely grated zest of 1 lemon
4 large eggs or 2 whole eggs and 3 egg whites
3–5 tablespoons extra virgin olive oil
¼ cup sugar mixed with 1 teaspoon cinnamon or honey (optional)

1. Place the rice, water, and salt in a 2-quart saucepan and bring to a boil. Cover the pan and lower the heat. Simmer for 20–25 minutes, until the water is absorbed.

2. Roast the nuts on a cookie sheet in a 350°F oven for 5 minutes or until lightly golden.

3. Add the nuts, raisins, and lemon zest to the rice and stir well to combine. Let the mixture sit for 20 minutes to cool.

4. Lightly beat the eggs in a bowl and add them to the rice mixture.

5. Heat a large, nonstick frying pan over high heat for 20 seconds. Add 3 tablespoons of olive oil and heat for 15 seconds. Reduce the heat if the oil begins to smoke.

6. Drop about 2 tablespoons of the mixture into the hot pan. Repeat with more rice mixture until the pan is full but not crowded.

7. Cook the pancakes on one side for 3 minutes or until golden. Flip them over and cook for another 2 minutes or until crisp and golden. Transfer the pancakes to a pan lined with paper towels.

8. Add additional tablespoons of oil to the pan as needed, and make the remaining pancakes.

9. Serve the pancakes immediately with the optional cinnamon and sugar or honey.

Yield: 24 pancakes

TINA'S TIDBITS

- *Converted rice or "minute" rice cannot be used in recipes that require the mixture to bind together, because they do not contain enough starch.*
- *Arborio rice is a short-grain, highly starchy rice. When not available, any short- or medium-grain rice that has not been polished will suffice as a good substitute.*

Halvah de Semola
(Sephardi Semolina Pudding)

Halvah refers to any Middle Eastern or Asian sweet that is made with sweetened cooked grain. Originally a staple of the Sephardic repertoire, halvah gained popularity in this country in the Ashkenazic community as a confection made from ground sesame seeds and sugar. Even the comprehensive Food Lover's Companion *dictionary defines halvah as a sesame seed treat. This recipe is actually much easier to make and is probably the ultimate Sephardic comfort food. This recipe is served for Chanukah by Bulgarian Jews and is a nice alternative to fried pastries.*

1 stick unsalted butter
1½ cups semolina (or cream of wheat cereal), *not* semolina flour
3 cups water
1 cup granulated sugar (honey may be substituted, although not traditional)

1 teaspoon vanilla extract
½ cup finely chopped walnuts (chopped finely, but *not* a paste)
Cinnamon for sprinkling on top (optional)

1. Melt the butter in a 2-quart saucepan over moderate heat.

2. Add the semolina and stir to completely coat the grains of wheat with the butter.

3. Continue to cook and stir the semolina until the mixture is light brown, about 10 minutes.

4. Meanwhile, combine the water and sugar in a small saucepan and bring to a boil. Boil for 3 minutes.

5. Stir the semolina mixture constantly while you carefully pour the boiling syrup into the pot. Avoid burning yourself with the spattering liquid.

6. Remove the pan from the stove and continue to stir for about 4 minutes until the mixture becomes thick.

7. Gently stir in the vanilla and the finely chopped walnuts until well combined.

TINA'S TIDBITS

- *Cream of wheat is a good substitute for semolina but will not create as fine a grain as semolina.*
- *For a more Middle Eastern flavor, substitute 1 1/2 teaspoons rose water for the vanilla, and add 1/2 teaspoon ground cardamom. Finely ground pistachios may be added to the mixture instead of the walnuts.*
- *For a more Indian influence, add the zest of 1/2 orange to the hot sugar syrup, and substitute 1/4 cup raisins and 1/4 cup grated coconut for the walnuts.*

8. Cover the pot with a double layer of dishtowel and let the mixture set for about 30 minutes or until thick and all the moisture has been absorbed.

9. Lightly butter an 11 × 7-inch glass casserole or six to eight 4-ounce ramekins. Stir the mixture one more time and spread the semolina mixture evenly in the chosen container, smoothing out the top.

Sprinkle with cinnamon. Let mixture set for $\frac{1}{2}$ hour or chill. Cut into diamond shapes and serve warm or at room temperature.

Note: If using ramekins, chill and then unmold before you sprinkle with some cinnamon.

Yield: 2–3 dozen pieces

TU BISH'VAT

For the Eternal your God is bringing you into a good land,
a land with streams and springs and fountains issuing from plain and hill;
a land of wheat and barley, of vines, figs, and pomegranates,
a land of olive trees and honey.

DEUTERONOMY 8:7-8

Tu BiSh'vat, the fifteenth of Sh'vat, is the celebration of the Jewish new year for trees. The holiday occurs in late January or early February, four months after the holiday of Sukkot. Sukkot marks the beginning of the rainy season in the Land of Israel, and after four months, the rain-soaked ground is ready to support the young roots of trees to help them flourish in the parched Israeli desert.

Originally a celebration coinciding with the tithing of agricultural products, in Talmudic times Tu BiSh'vat became a minor holiday celebrating God's blessings on the community and its fields. A quick look at the Jewish calendar and you can see that major holidays center around the agricultural harvests. Pesach coincided with the barley harvest, wheat and the first fruits and vegetables were harvested at the time of Shavuot, and on Sukkot we celebrate the final wheat, grape, and vegetable harvests of the year.

Sixteenth-century kabbalists instituted the custom of having a Tu BiSh'vat seder, similar to a Passover seder. This seder had no specific order but included the blessing and enjoyment of at least the seven species of agricultural products listed in the Bible. In modern times, with Jews dispersed throughout the world, it is a celebration of our connection to the actual Land of Israel; congregations encourage families to plant trees in Israel through the Jewish National Fund, and many fruits and grains indigenous to the region are eaten as part of the celebration. As a child, I remember being given a piece of *bokser*, or carob, to chew on. In this country, we mainly consider carob a healthy substitute for chocolate. However, in ancient times, exiles of the region would take carob with them because it was one of the few agricultural products from Israel that could survive the long voyage to a foreign land.

On Tu BiSh'vat it is customary to eat foods containing the seven species and to bless them. These are wheat, barley, grapes, figs, pomegranates, dates, and olives. Although not mentioned in Deuteronomy, almonds also figure prominently in this celebration, as they are the first tree to flower in Israel at that time of year.

❧ ALMONDS ❧

Their father Israel said to them,
". . . Take from among the land's choice products in your bags,
and bring the man [Joseph] an offering—
a bit of balm, a bit of honey, some laudanum,
mastic, pistachios, and almonds."

GENESIS 43:11

Almonds are seeds of the fruit *Prunus dulcis*, which is an inedible fruit closely related to peaches and plums. Almond trees resemble peach trees, but their fruit cracks open, revealing the seed (or nut) when it is ripe.

There are two kinds of almonds—sweet, the almond we commonly eat, and bitter. The bitter almond contains poisonous prussic acid and must be roasted to be consumed as a nut. In small amounts this bitter almond was used for medicinal purposes and as a flavoring agent. Our modern almond extract is a mixture of bitter almond oil, water, and alcohol.

Almonds are considered to be the oldest cultivated nut, dating back ten thousand years. Some feel that the first documentation of almond cultivation was in the Torah, Numbers 17:23: "There the staff of Aaron of the house of Levi had sprouted: it had brought forth sprouts, produced blossoms, and borne almonds." Almonds and pistachios are the only nuts cited in the entire Torah.

The almond originated in the mountains of western China and was brought along the Silk Road to be cultivated in western Asia, Greece, Turkey, and ancient Persia. Its popularity extended to Rome, where it was often served sugar-coated at festivities. These sugared nuts were considered to be one of the first sweetmeats, or desserts, in history. Almonds were seen as a sign of fertility, probably because they were the first tree in the Mediterranean region to flower each spring. Roman and then European tradition included serving almonds to wedding guests and/or throwing almonds at newlyweds to wish them fecundity.

The route of the almond mirrored, in many ways, the route of the olive and grape. From the Middle East, almond production eventually centered in Italy and Spain. Conquistadors from Spain brought the trees to the New World, and Franciscan monks planted almond trees around their missions up the Pacific coast of California. Today, California is the only state in the union to produce almonds on a commercial scale.

Spanish Jews first introduced the use of almond meal, or finely ground almonds in cakes such as *pan d'Espanya*, a technique used especially at Passover. In Toledo, where there was a large Jewish population, it was the Jewish confectioners who perfected the art of making marzipan, a mixture of almond paste and sugar, bitter almond, and sometimes egg white.

◦⌇ FIGS ⌇◦

Then the eyes of both of them were opened,
and, realizing that they were naked,
they sewed fig leaves together
and made themselves skirts.

GENESIS 3:7

Figs were one of the first fruits to be cultivated over five thousand years ago. Grown predominantly in the Arabian Peninsula and the Mediterranean, they were brought to Northern Europe in the early sixteenth century and to Mexico by Cortez at approximately the same time. Franciscan monks introduced the fig throughout the California missions, and that variety of fig came to be known as the mission fig.

Figs are mentioned in Genesis 3:7, as the first addition to Adam and Eve's wardrobe. The fig appears often in the Bible and was revered by many cultures and religions. The founders of Rome, Romulus and Remus, were said to be nurtured by the she-wolf under a fig tree, which was later declared a sacred tree. Arabs regarded figs as their most esteemed fruit. Athenians, who were enamored of figs, were dubbed sycophants (*syke* means "fig eaters"). This word took on a new meaning after some Athenians informed authorities about illegal fig exportation in order to gain favor with the leaders of the community. Next to wine and olive oil, figs were the most important crop of Greece.

Figs were primarily eaten when they were succulent and fresh. However, the best-quality figs were also dried individually or strung on thread. Lesser-quality figs were also mashed into cakes, which became invaluable during long winters or long sieges. Remnants of first-century fig cake were found in the storehouses on top of Masada, the last remaining Jewish stronghold against the Roman invasion in 73 C.E.

Aside from their nutritive value and wonderful flavor, figs were purported to have medicinal powers as well. In II Kings 20:7, the prophet Isaiah healed Hezekiah by telling his aides, "'Get a cake of figs.' And they got one, and they applied it to the rash, and he recovered." Evidently, there is historical evidence that using fig paste as a poultice was an ancient

Assyrian practice. Pliny of Rome, in the first century C.E., thought that figs were restorative and suggested that people who were suffering from long illness would recover if they ate figs. He also said that figs would "preserve the elderly in better health and make them look younger with fewer wrinkles." Does that mean they should eat them or put cakes on their faces, like Hezekiah?

Although figs were popular with the Greeks and Romans, it was the Arabs' cultivation of the trees and irrigation skills that produced superior figs in the lands they inhabited.

Figs ripen between July and September. They should be purchased when firm but have some give to them when pressed. Varieties of figs can range in color from green to brown to mottled purple. If a fig is hard and green, it is immature, regardless of the variety. Figs can be eaten raw (skin and all), poached, stewed, dried, pureed, used for jam, or made into a strong beerlike drink.

❧ GRAPES AND WINE ❧

The fig tree has put forth its green figs,
and the vines with their tiny grapes have given forth their fragrance;
arise, my beloved, my fair one, and come away.

SONG OF SONGS 2:13

Grapes are mentioned throughout the Torah as one of the symbols, along with olives and figs, of the fertility of God's Promised Land to the Israelites. The first mention of grapes, and their by-product, wine, takes place in Genesis 9:20–21, which records Noah's planting of the first vineyard and his subsequent drunken state. The more beautiful references to grapes, however, appear in Solomon's moving verses in Song of Songs.

Wine was used as a drink offering in the Temple, and in Exodus 29:40–41 specifics are given for the quantity and frequency of its use during the consecration of Aaron and the priests.

In order for a wine to be considered kosher, only Jewish hands could be involved in the planting, cultivating, and pressing of the grapes for the purpose of producing wines. These laws stem from the reality that in ancient biblical times wine was used in many pagan rituals and was a product of idolatry. The only way to guarantee that the wine hadn't been prepared for less honorable use than as a drink offering in the Temple was to have every aspect of its production supervised by a rabbi and Sabbath-observant Jewish workers.

There are two types of kosher wine, non-*mevushal*, which is the wine described above, and *mevushal*, which are kosher wines that go through an extra process of flash pasteurization. This process subjects the wine to very high heat for a few seconds—it is not boiled, as often thought—and renders the wine unfit for idolatrous worship. Today this technique allows the wine to be certified kosher even when served at a banquet by non-Jewish servers, which conforms to the needs of the Orthodox community.

Because Jews were generally not allowed to own their own land and were often uprooted from their homes with little notice, wine production has taken on different definitions in different parts of the world. Raisins and other fruits and vegetation helped create many ceremonial kosher wines. Necessity was the mother of invention.

Many people think that kosher wine is synonymous with the very sweet Concord grape wine produced in upstate New York. Of course, nowadays this isn't the only source of kosher wine, and many grape varietals are used to produce excellent drinking wines. However, when Jewish émigrés came to this country in the mid-1800s, they needed to make ritual wine, and the only grapes available were the big, plump grapes growing near Concord, Massachusetts. When the grapes produced extremely bitter wine, our resourceful ancestors added sugar to the liquid and a new Passover icon was born!

Jewish tradition and custom mandate the ceremonial and medicinal drinking of wine, and on Purim we are commanded to imbibe enough wine so that we get confused between the names of Haman and Mordecai. What you will not find amid Jewish customs is traditional Jewish food preparation containing wine (other than *charoset*). This practice is not prohibited, it just wasn't done. Until now . . .

ᨶ POMEGRANATES ᨷ

On the hem of the robe they made pomegranates
of blue, purple, and crimson yarns, twisted.
They also made bells of pure gold,
and attached the bells between the pomegranates,
all around the hem of the robe, between the pomegranates.

EXODUS 39:24–25

Pomegranates have been around the Middle East and the Mediterranean region for thousands of years. King Solomon cultivated large groves of pomegranates and likened the beauty of his love to the fruit in his sensual Song of Songs.

The beauty of the fruit inspired the use of its design in the High Priests' robes as well as the columns in the holy Temple. Muslims called it the "fruit of paradise" in the Koran. The Moors were so enamored of the fruit that they renamed their fortress city in Andalusia Granada (Spanish for "pomegranate"). The Spanish missionaries brought pomegranates as well as figs and almonds to the missions of California and its central valley.

The pomegranate is traditionally eaten on the second night of Rosh HaShanah as a symbol of the new fruit of the season. Sephardim connect the supposed 613 seeds that are found in a pomegranate to the 613 mitzvot we are to fulfill every day.

When buying a pomegranate, look for a bright red or pink fruit with firm shiny skin that feels dense for its size.

Although Cleopatra was purported to use the juice of the pomegranate as "lipstick," the fruit's ability to stain often becomes a culinary liability. Separating the seeds from the inedible white pith in a bowl, under water, is the best way to seed a pomegranate without turning your fingers red. The seeds sink to the bottom of the bowl, and any loose pith floats to the surface, making it very easy to remove. Pomegranate seeds are used to garnish dishes, the juice is used in sauces, and a concentrate of the juice, often referred to as pomegranate molasses, is used in marinades and sauces that require a tart-sweet component.

❧ DATES ❧

The date palm is thought to have originally grown in the Persian Gulf region, and in biblical times it was growing densely in the areas around the Nile River in Egypt and the Euphrates River in Mesopotamia. The earliest records of its presence in the Land of Israel were found near the site of Jericho.

The migration of the date plant can be traced to the nomads who planted saplings whenever they came to an oasis. The Moors brought the date palm to Spain when they came from North Africa in the eighth century.

The date got its name from the Greek *daktulos*, "fingers," because the growth of dates on the tree resembles a cluster of fingers.

The date palm is important to Jewish tradition as well as to everyday life in the countries where it is grown. The fronds of the tree are used as part of the *lulav* during Sukkot, and syrup made from crushed and boiled dates is considered the "honey" referred to in Leviticus 20:24, "a land flowing with milk and honey." The fronds were also used for thatching, and the bark was used for its fibers to make ropes and baskets. Pakistani syrup made from ripe dates is used to make a viscous coating for pipes to prevent leaks. This is not to be confused with delicious *halek* or *hullake*, date syrup made in India or the Middle East, which is used as a sweetener or as a base for *charoset* during Passover.

Prior to the 1991 war, Iraq was the number one producer of dates in the world, growing over twenty-two million date palms and exporting over six hundred thousand tons of dates annually. Dates also come from other countries in the Middle East and are grown very successfully in the Central Valley of California.

Rarely can you buy a fresh date in North America. The first time I ate a fresh date was in Israel. Its consistency was reminiscent of a ripe plum, and it was not as sweet as the dried, but plump Medjool date I was used to in the United States. When buying dried dates, look for dates that are slightly wrinkled but not hard. The drier the date, the sweeter it will be because of the concentration of sugar. I prefer to buy pitted whole dates and chop them myself to avoid the excessive sugar that commercially chopped dates contain.

WHEAT AND BARLEY

Wheat and barley have been growing in the Land of Israel for thousands of years. Barley is indigenous to this region. The original wild strains of wheat were very hard and difficult to grind. The grains were consumed at every meal but rarely in the form of bread; the production of flour, being very laborious, required hours of pounding, grinding, and sifting. Any bread made from this grain was dense and dark, and all were produced without using yeast. The bread of display brought to the Temple was more like pita bread than like our modern-day challah. Lighter loaves were produced when more tender strains of wheat, higher in gluten and easier to mill, were cultivated, and yeast—developed by the Egyptians—was incorporated into the dough.

In biblical times, most grains were heartily consumed in the form of porridges, pilafs, soups, salads, and even beverages. Today whole barley is regaining its popularity on the dinner table, but the major portion of the modern barley crop is used for making beer.

Tuscan Biscotti

If this recipe looks similar to mandelbrodt, *it could be the coincidence that Jews were sea traders, and sea traders took these hard, dry biscuits on board their ships for long voyages, knowing they would remain edible for months.*

$3\frac{1}{2}$ cups flour
3 tablespoons cornstarch
1 teaspoon baking powder
$\frac{1}{4}$ teaspoon baking soda
$\frac{1}{2}$ teaspoon salt
$\frac{1}{3}$ cup finely ground almonds
1 cup sugar
1 cup vegetable oil, preferably corn oil

3 eggs
Zest of 1 lemon, grated
$\frac{1}{2}$ tablespoon vanilla extract
$\frac{1}{2}$ teaspoon almond extract
$\frac{1}{2}$ cup toasted almonds, chopped into large pieces
1 tablespoon sugar
$\frac{1}{2}$ teaspoon cinnamon

1. Combine the flour, cornstarch, baking powder, baking soda, salt, and ground almonds in a 1-quart bowl and set aside.

2. Cream 1 cup sugar and the oil in a 2-quart bowl on high speed until light and fluffy. Add the eggs, zest, vanilla, and almond extract and mix until thoroughly combined.

3. Stir in the flour mixture and mix well. Add the toasted chopped almonds and combine.

4. Line 2 cookie sheets with parchment paper. Divide the dough into 4 portions. Lightly oil your hands and gently form each portion into a log 10 inches long and 2 inches wide. Place 2 logs on each prepared sheet. Gently shape the soft dough into a uniform log that is now probably 12 inches long.

5. Sprinkle the tops of the loaves with the cinnamon and sugar mixture. Bake at 350°F for 20 minutes or until the edges are golden brown.

6. Remove the loaves from the oven. Let cool for 5 minutes. Slice each loaf crosswise into $\frac{1}{2}$-inch cookies. Place cookies cut side up and bake for another 5 minutes. Turn slices over and bake for another 5 minutes. Cool and store in an airtight container for 2 weeks or freeze.

Yield: 3–4 dozen

TINA'S TIDBITS

- *Sixteenth-century Italian sailors would bring these twice-baked cookies on long sea voyages because their dry consistency prevented the cookies from getting soft or moldy.*
- *The addition of cornstarch gives the cookie a dense, but smoother consistency.*
- *Ground almonds and oil make this cookie very hard, which is perfect for dipping into hot coffee or tea.*

ALMOND HONEY STICKS

Nut confections "glued" together with honey are prevalent in most cultures. One of the most common candies for Passover is individually wrapped sesame bars from the Middle East. Almond candies are also prevalent in that region so I created this recipe as a special treat all year round. Any shape can be created as the mixture is malleable until it hardens. One end of each bar could be dipped in chocolate for a truly decadent treat.

15 ounces slivered almonds
½ cup honey

1. Toast the almonds in a 325°F oven until golden, about 5–9 minutes. **Do not burn!**

2. In a large skillet, bring the honey to a boil. Add the almonds. Stir the almonds for 2 minutes until they start to stick together. **Note:** If you don't cook the honey long enough, the mixture won't hold together when cool.

3. Lightly oil a board, your hands, and a metal spoon, and then chill your hands by grabbing a bag of frozen vegetables in your freezer.

4. Pour 1 tablespoon of the mixture out onto the board in a small mound. Repeat with 4 or 5 more mounds at a time. Working quickly, shape the mounds into compact 2-inch sticks. Repeat with the remaining honeyed almonds until all sticks are formed.

5. Cool completely before storing in airtight containers.

Yield: 2–3 dozen pieces

TINA'S TIDBITS

- *Boiling the honey reduces its moisture content so that when it cools it will be hard and bind the almonds together.*
- *Hot honey and sugar mixtures both reach a very high temperature (over 350°F) so caution must be taken when making these candies, especially if working with children.*
- *If the mixture gets too hard before you get a chance to shape the sticks, place the cookie sheet in a 300°F oven for a minute or so until the mixture is more pliable. If you are too late then you just serve little mounds. They are still delicious and better tasting than burnt honey.*

FRESH FIGS WITH GOAT CHEESE AND HONEY

Upscale restaurants and caterers are serving this combination of fruit and cheese that Middle Easterners enjoyed thousands of years ago. Although this is a simple preparation, the quality of each component must be very high for it to taste fantastic. It is best when figs are at the height of ripeness.

12 ripe Mission or Brown Turkey figs, cut in half
4 ounces good-quality chèvre goat cheese

3–4 tablespoons wildflower or berry honey
French bread or crackers (optional)

1. Place figs on a plate cut side up.

2. Spread some of the goat cheese on each fig.

3. Drizzle with some honey and serve with bread or crackers.

Yield: 6 or more servings

TINA'S TIDBITS

- *Alternatively, serve a plate with all of the ingredients and allow your guests to prepare their own. You can also serve them on a bed of lettuce as a first course.*
- *Mission figs are named for the California Franciscan missions where they have been cultivated since 1770.*

Moshe's Stuffed Figs

I ate at Moshe Basson's Jerusalem restaurant Eucalyptus while attending an HUC-JIR board meeting a number of years ago. I had heard about his knowledge of biblical foods but was not prepared for the breadth and depth of his information. He was personable, relaxed (hard to believe for a man who had evaded an intifada against him), a great cook, and an incredible teacher. Ten of us sat around a large round table while Moshe brought dish after dish to our table and explained about this vegetable and that herb. We were all so thrilled to have had the opportunity to experience Moshe's expertise. After the meal, however, one fellow diner said that he couldn't decide which he enjoyed more, the food on the table or the rapturous look on my face! The following is an adaptation of Moshe's creative genius for the home cook.

One 8- or 9-ounce package dried calimyrna figs
   (about 24 figs)
2 cups water
2 tablespoons extra virgin olive oil
2 small onions (about 6 ounces), finely diced
8 ounces boneless chicken breast, finely diced
$\frac{1}{8}$ teaspoon ground cardamom
$\frac{1}{4}$ teaspoon ground allspice
$\frac{1}{4}$ teaspoon ground cinnamon
Kosher salt and freshly ground pepper to taste

SAUCE:
3 tablespoons tamarind paste
Additional water as needed
3 tablespoons brown sugar
$\frac{1}{8}$ teaspoon ground cardamom
$\frac{1}{4}$ teaspoon ground allspice
$\frac{1}{4}$ teaspoon ground cinnamon
Kosher salt and freshly ground pepper to taste

1. Place dried figs in a glass bowl and cover with 2 cups water. Microwave on high for 3 minutes, and set aside while you make the filling.

2. Heat a 10-inch sauté pan over high heat for 20 seconds. Add the oil and heat it for another 10 seconds. Reduce the heat if the oil is beginning to smoke.

3. Add the diced onions to the pan and sauté until golden brown.

4. Add the finely diced chicken breast, the spices, and the salt and pepper to the onions. Sauté the chicken over medium-high heat until the chicken has lost its color and the spices are evenly distributed. Remove the contents to a small mixing bowl to cool while you prepare the sauce.

TINA'S TIDBITS

- *If using fresh figs, cut the upper half of the figs in half and scoop out most of the seeded flesh. (Reserve the flesh to make jam if you like.) Proceed with stuffing the figs, and cook for 10 minutes or until the figs are soft but not overcooked.*
- *Some adaptations of this recipe use onions and eggplant along with the figs for stuffing. If you find yourself with excess stuffing, then consider adding other vegetables to the pot.*
- *Although a food processor can be utilized to finely chop the chicken, I find it pulverizes it into a mass that is hard to separate when cooked. Using ground turkey or veal instead of chicken, with the onions and spices used for the filling, would work well.*
- *Using the soaking liquid from the figs helps impart the fig essence to the sauce without overcooking the figs and yields the same result.*

5. Drain the figs, reserving the soaking water. Measure the liquid and add enough water to make a total of 2 cups.

6. Add the tamarind paste, water, and sugar to the used, unrinsed frying pan. Add the spices and the salt and pepper to the sauce, and bring the mixture to a boil. Stir to dissolve the tamarind concentrate, and cook until the mixture is smooth and slightly thickened. Set aside while you stuff the figs.

7. Insert your forefinger into the opening at the top of the fig to enlarge the opening for stuffing.

8. Using your fingers, stuff the figs with the chicken mixture, and place the figs in the pan with the sauce.

9. When all the stuffed figs are placed in the pan, turn the heat on and bring the sauce to a boil. Cover the pan, reduce the heat, and simmer for 15 minutes.

Note: Moshe suggests serving with rice or couscous.

Yield: 4–6 servings as an entrée

Herbal Grape Sorbet

Anya Von Bremzen is an expert on Spanish culture and cuisine. I was intrigued by a recipe in her book, The New Spanish Table, *for a grape granita. Since Mexican mint marigolds were thriving in my garden, I thought I would play around with this food concept. Here is my adaptation.*

1 pound seedless green or red grapes
5 small leaves of Mexican mint marigold, tarragon, or basil
4 ounces sweet dessert wine—Riesling, Moscato d'Asti, or Gewürztraminer

Juice of ½ medium lemon
2 or more tablespoons of simple syrup (see recipe below)

1. Cut the grapes in half and place them in a processor work bowl. Pulse the machine on and off until most of the grapes are pulverized.

2. Add the herbs and process the mixture until it is fairly smooth. Let the mixture sit and the flavors steep for 15 minutes.

3. Place the grape-herb mixture in a fine-mesh strainer over a 2-quart mixing bowl. Press on the grape pulp to extract as much juice as possible.

4. Add the wine and lemon juice and 2 tablespoons of simple syrup to the grape liquid. Taste to see if more syrup is needed (this will depend on the sweetness of the grape). Chill.

5. Place in the container of an ice-cream maker, and follow the manufacturer's directions to make the sorbet. The sorbet may be served immediately or stored in an airtight container in the freezer until ready to serve.

Yield: 1½ pints

Simple Syrup

1 cup granulated sugar
1 cup water

2 teaspoons orange blossom water (optional—but terrific!)

1. Combine the sugar and water in a 1-quart saucepan. Bring the mixture to a boil, stirring until the mixture begins to clear.

2. When the mixture is clear and all the sugar is dissolved, remove from heat, add the orange blossom water, and pour into a jar. Store in the refrigerator indefinitely. Use in sorbets or drinks, or pour some over fresh berries just before serving.

TINA'S TIDBITS

- *Using a simple syrup ensures that your sorbet won't be grainy and gives a little more body to the frozen product than using undissolved granulated sugar.*
- *Orange blossom water hints of the Moors' influence in Andalusia, the region that had a very large Jewish population before the expulsion.*
- *Simple syrup must be very cold or sorbet won't freeze in an ice-cream maker.*

SOPI DI BINA (CURAÇAO WINE SOUP)

The Jewish community of Curaçao was established over 350 ago years and its Mikvé Israel-Emanuel is the oldest continuously operating synagogue in the Western Hemisphere. As in all Jewish communities in the Diaspora, cooking traditions from countries of origin mingled with the foods readily available to create new preparations that conformed to the Jewish dietary laws. The following is adapted from their community cookbook, Recipes from the Jewish Kitchens of Curaçao.

3 cups water
6 ounces pitted prunes (about 20)
1 cinnamon stick
4 tablespoons cornstarch

½ cup water
One 750 ml bottle of Zinfandel or Shiraz wine
⅓–½ cup sugar, depending on sweetness of prunes

1. In a 3-quart saucepan, bring the 3 cups water to a boil and add the prunes and cinnamon stick. Reduce the heat and simmer until the prunes are soft.

2. Using a slotted spoon, remove the prunes from the pot and reserve them in a bowl. Discard the cinnamon stick, and return the saucepan with the liquid to the stove.

3. In a small dish, combine the cornstarch with the ½ cup water to make a smooth paste. Slowly add the cornstarch to the prune liquid, stirring constantly to combine.

4. Reheat the liquid over moderate heat. Stir constantly until the liquid thickens.

5. Increase the heat to bring the liquid to a boil, and add the wine and the sugar. Stir constantly until the sugar is dissolved. Add a little more water if the soup is too thick. Return the prunes to the soup. Serve warm or refrigerate until ready to serve cold.

Yield: 6–8 servings

TINA'S TIDBITS

- *Cinnamon stick adds flavor to liquid without adding the grittiness that results from using the powdered version.*
- *Cornstarch requires the mixture to come to a boil in order for it to thicken properly. Its use makes the mixture thicken clear, compared to flour, which thickens a mixture opaque.*
- *Add 2 or more tablespoons of curaçao liqueur to the soup after it is cooled to add a touch of orange, and the signature liqueur of the island, to your soup.*

SANGRIA DE CURAÇAO

This recipe is unique for sangria since it has a minimal amount of fruit juice added to the wine. However, the cinnamon-scented syrup, plus the limes and nutmeg, highlight the versatility of wine and the resulting beverage is very refreshing.

1 cup water
3/4 cup sugar
2 cinnamon sticks
One 750-ml bottle red wine (Shiraz, Zinfandel, or Burgundy)

2–3 limes
1/4 teaspoon nutmeg

1. Combine the water, sugar, and cinnamon sticks in a 1-quart saucepan. Bring to a boil and cook over moderately high heat for 5 minutes or until the bubbles get larger and slower. Remove from the heat and cool until room temperature.

2. Remove the zest from two of the limes in long thin strips. Cut away all of the white pith and peel, and discard.

3. In a large pitcher, combine the sugar mixture, wine, two peeled whole limes, zest, and nutmeg. Let it steep, covered, for a number of hours or overnight.

4. To serve, remove the limes, and add 1 cup hot water and the juice from one of the limes. Taste and add more lime juice if necessary (this will depend on the fruitiness of the wine you use).

5. Serve in 4- to 6-ounce glasses.

Yield: 8–10 servings

TINA'S TIDBITS

- *If you prefer a more Spanish variation, oranges may be used instead of the limes.*
- *Boiling sugar and water puts the sugar into solution, and it will stay that way, refrigerated, for months. This is called a simple syrup.*
- *Simple syrups are used in liquid recipes because they distribute throughout the beverage and do not make the drink grainy.*

WINE JELLY

I first learned about wine jelly when I was in graduate school at NYU. Exploring foods from around the world, Mr. Tarantino exposed us to new preparations (at least new for the early 1970s!). Serve this as an addition to a cheese platter or with a scoop of the pear-wine sorbet from the poached pear recipe that follows.

2 cups red wine (I prefer Shiraz or Zinfandel)
4 whole allspice berries
One 3-inch stick of cinnamon

3 cups of sugar
One 3-ounce pouch of liquid fruit pectin

1. Combine the wine with the spices in a 2-quart saucepan. Heat the wine until it is warm. Turn off the heat and allow the wine and spices to steep for 30 minutes.

2. Add the sugar to the spiced wine and heat to a rolling boil. Stir constantly for 1 minute or until the sugar is totally dissolved.

3. Add the pectin and return the mixture to a rolling boil. Stir for 1 minute and pour into clean glass jars or a decorative mold.

4. Allow the jelly to cool at room temperature before covering and refrigerating. Unmold before serving.

5. If desired, decorate with frosted grapes (see recipe below).

Yield: 1 two-cup mold or 16 small servings

FROSTED GRAPES

1. To frost the grapes, either rinse them under water or toss them in slightly beaten egg whites.

2. Place a few tablespoons of sugar in a small dish, and roll the moist grapes in the sugar.

3. Place the sugared grapes on a plate or rack, and allow the sugar to dry completely before using as an edible decoration.

TINA'S TIDBITS

- *If you plan to serve the jelly with cheese and crackers, pour it into a mold or a shallow container that will easily release the jelly.*
- *Using liquid pectin prevents any chance of lumps from forming or having to heat the wine too long while waiting for a powder to dissolve.*
- *Frosting grapes with egg white helps the sugar adhere better and longer. However, if you are uncomfortable with using raw eggs, water will do the trick.*

POACHED PEARS IN RED WINE

It was hard to decide in which section of the book this recipe should appear, but it was easy to decide to include it. This is a perfect use for sweet pears, and here I have taken the flavorful cooking syrup, redolent with spice and pear essence, and turned it into a delicious sorbet to serve with the pears and/or wine jelly.

1½ cups water
Juice and zest of ½ lemon
1 cup red wine, preferably Zinfandel or Shiraz
1 cup sugar

½ teaspoon vanilla
3 medium Anjou pears or 4 small Seckel pears, peeled and halved if large

1. Place the water, lemon juice, lemon zest, wine, sugar, and vanilla in a 2-quart saucepan. Bring to a boil for 5 minutes.

2. If the pears are small and you are keeping them whole, use a long corer to remove the seeds and core from the bottom of the pear upward. Keep the stem intact on top. If you are using larger pears, cut the pears in half lengthwiseand remove the core with the seeds using a melon baller to scoop out the center of the core. As you finish preparing each pear, put it into the pan with the wine mixture.

3. Bring the pears and the liquid to a boil. Reduce the heat, cover, and simmer for 10 minutes or until a knife easily pierces the fruit. Turn off the heat and allow the pears to soak in the poaching liquid until ready to eat. Mixture may be refrigerated for up to a week. Once the poaching liquid is cold you may proceed to make the following sorbet, if desired.

Yield: 6 servings

SPICED PEAR INFUSED WINE SORBET

2–3 cups poaching liquid from Poached Pears recipe (see above)
1 ice-cream maker, preferably 1- to 2-quart size

1. Chill the poached pears in the wine poaching liquid for 2 or more hours or until the liquid is quite cold.

2. Remove the pears from the liquid and set aside in a glass or plastic bowl.

3. Pour the liquid into the frozen container of a small ice-cream maker and follow the manufacturer's directions until a soft, but thoroughly frozen mixture is formed. Store the sorbet in a sealed plastic container and serve when ready to use.

TINA'S TIDBITS

- *Alcohol will lower the freezing point of the sorbet so that the mixture will never get rock hard.*
- *If you don't have an ice-cream maker, freeze the liquid in a tray and use a fork to shave off portions. This is called a granita and is just as delicious.*

MUSHROOM BARLEY SOUP

One of the best Jewish delis and caterers on Long Island was Andel's in Roslyn, New York. Estelle Areman, the owner, was a fantastic cook and a good friend of my family. Knowing that I was pursuing a career in foods and education, she always took the time to teach me some new culinary tricks and some great recipes. I think that this is one of the all-time best soups that I have ever tasted. The secret to the thickness of this soup is the lima beans. They are peeled and therefore disintegrate into the stock when fully cooked. Do not panic—they peel very easily if soaked long enough and you use large beans.

1 cup dried large lima beans
0.5 ounces dried imported mushrooms, preferably porcini
2 slices of flanken (short ribs cut into long thin slices)
2 quarts water
2 tablespoons oil

1 onion, finely diced
1 stalk celery, finely diced
8 ounces fresh mushrooms, diced
Salt and pepper to taste
1 carrot, diced
1/4 cup medium pearl barley

1. Cover the lima beans with 1 inch of water. Microwave on high for 3 minutes, and let them soak for 1 or more hours or until the skins easily slide off.

2. Cover the dried mushrooms with water. Microwave for 2 minutes, and let them sit for 1/2 hour.

3. Place flanken in a soup pot and cover with the 2 quarts water. Bring to a boil and cook for 1/2 hour, skimming off the foam periodically.

4. Meanwhile, remove the skins from the lima beans by gently squeezing on one end; the bean will just slide out.

5. Carefully lift the dried mushrooms out of the water, and gently squeeze them over the bowl to save the juices. Dice the soaked, dried mushrooms and set aside.

6. Add the beans and the diced, dried mushrooms to the soup pot. Strain the mushroom liquid into the pot as well.

7. Heat a 10-inch skillet for 20 seconds, add oil, and heat for another 10 seconds. Sauté the onion in the oil for 2 minutes. Add the celery and fresh mushrooms, and cook until wilted and translucent. Add to the soup pot.

8. Add the diced carrot and salt and pepper to taste. Cook for 1 hour, stirring occasionally so that the mixture does not stick.

9. Add the barley and cook for 1/2–1 hour longer or until the meat is tender, the lima beans disintegrate, and the soup is thick. Check the seasoning.

Yield: 10–12 servings

TINA'S TIDBITS

- *Because the lima beans and barley make this soup thick, additional water might be necessary to give the soup the proper consistency.*
- *Do not make the mistake of buying small lima beans. It will take you forever to peel them!*
- *Always initially cook your meat in the water alone so that you can remove any coagulated impurities (foam) from the water first, before it adheres to any of the solid foods added to the broth later. This is true for chicken soup as well.*
- *Sautéing your vegetables in oil caramelizes the natural sugars in the vegetables and produces a far superior soup.*

1654 BARLEY SALAD

I created this salad for Reform Judaism *magazine in celebration of the 350th anniversary of Jews in America. The method of gardening in Plymouth, Massachusetts, inspired this salad. Small squares of land were cultivated next to the house to provide food for the family. The Native Americans taught the pilgrims how to commingle different crops in one square bed to enhance the growth of all. A fish head was buried in the center of a three-foot square. Corn was planted directly on top to absorb the nitrogen from the decomposing head. Pole beans were planted around the corn to protect and fertilize the corn as well. Cucumbers or squash were planted around the perimeter because their rough leaves kept animals and playful children away from the vegetation. Tomatoes were native to the Americas but not necessarily used in salads until much later, but I have included them for the modern palate.*

4 large cloves of garlic, finely minced
$\frac{1}{4}$ cup finely chopped parsley
24 red grape tomatoes, cut in half horizontally
1 teaspoon minced fresh rosemary or $\frac{1}{4}$ teaspoon
   dried rosemary
$\frac{1}{2}$ teaspoon cinnamon
Pinch of cloves
1 jalapeño pepper, seeded and finely diced
$\frac{1}{4}$ cup extra virgin olive oil
$\frac{1}{2}$ teaspoon coarse kosher salt

Freshly ground black pepper to taste
2 cups frozen yellow corn, defrosted
1 cup frozen cut green beans, defrosted
4 cups water
$\frac{3}{4}$ cup barley
3 scallions, finely sliced
$\frac{1}{4}$ cup roasted red pepper, jarred or fresh, diced
One 15-ounce can black beans, drained and rinsed
Additional salt and freshly ground pepper to taste

1. Combine the first 10 ingredients in a large, glass serving bowl. Let marinate for at least $\frac{1}{2}$ hour at room temperature.

2. Defrost the corn and green beans. Discard any accumulated liquid.

3. Bring the 4 cups water to a rolling boil. Add a pinch of salt and the barley. Stir to combine, cover, and reduce the heat to low. Cook the barley for 40 minutes or until tender but not mushy.

4. Prepare the remaining ingredients while the barley cooks.

5. When the barley is done, quickly drain it and pour it over the tomato mixture. Toss with the remaining ingredients. Add more salt and pepper if needed.

Yield: 10–12 servings

TINA'S TIDBITS

- *The easiest way to peel a clove of garlic is to lightly smash it under the flat side of a knife. The peel then easily pulls away.*
- *Small grape and cherry tomatoes do not need to be seeded; large ones do because the seeds are slightly bitter.*
- *When working with hot peppers, place your hand in a plastic bag before holding the pepper to slice.*
- *For a great additional flavor to salads, roast cobs of corn over a fire, and cut the kernels off the cob using a large knife.*

PURIM

Sweet foods, filled foods, and an abundance of alcohol are prescribed for the joyous celebration of Purim. All are rich in symbolism. Filled foods are served because they represent the secrets and intrigue of Esther and Mordecai as they uncovered Haman's wicked plot to destroy the Persian Jews. It has also become

the custom to consume sweet foods, much like on Rosh HaShanah, to convey the wish for a sweet future. One theory suggests that making all the sweets to give as gifts, *shalach manot*, was a great way to rid the home of flour before Passover. Finally, while it is true that Jewish tradition says one should drink enough on Purim so as to be unable to distinguish between Haman and Mordecai, it is also true that giving charity to the poor is a mitzvah associated with the holiday.

Sephardic Jews tend to eat cookies that are fried or baked in the shape of Haman's ear. Ashkenazic Jews eat cookies that are filled with fruit or nut filling and shaped in triangles. This shape has been referred to as Haman's hat or pocket or even as representing the three Patriarchs, Abraham, Isaac, and Jacob.

Poppy seeds are often used in Purim confections. Aside from their widespread popularity in Eastern Europe and the Middle East, they are symbolic of the many lots cast by Haman and the promise God made to Abraham to spread his seed throughout the world, the very antithesis of the annihilation Haman planned. If you've ever dropped a spoonful of poppy seeds, then you know how quickly they disperse! In Israel, many Purim foods are prepared with poppy seeds in keeping with this promise.

Poppy seed filling is called *mohn* in Yiddish. *Mohn*-filled triangle cookies were very popular in

medieval Central Europe. These confections were called *mohntaschen*, "poppy seed pockets." *Mohntaschen* sounded enough like *hamantaschen*, "Haman's pockets," that these cookies were adopted as the first unofficial Purim treat in the eleventh century.

Prune filling, the other widely popular filling for these triangular cookies, became traditional in 1731. David Brandeis, a plum preserve merchant, was acquitted after being charged with poisoning some plum preserves. He was released from prison just before Purim. In order to celebrate his freedom, the townspeople of Jungbunzlau in northeastern Bohemia (now part of the Czech Republic) filled the hamantaschen with *povidl*, plum preserves, and referred to the holiday as Povidl Purim.

When Rhineland Jews moved east to Poland, Russia, and Hungary, they brought the hamantaschen tradition with them. The Jews remaining in Western Europe, however, made gingerbread men to represent Haman and enjoyed gobbling off his head!

Today you can buy prepared poppy seed (*mohn*) filling as well as prune (lekvar) and other fruit fillings for hamantaschen. Hamantaschen cookies can often be found in bakeries throughout the United States all year round, another example of a traditional Jewish food going mainstream in America.

Left: *Easy Palmiers, page 306*

HAMAN'S EARS

This recipe is a variation of fried Italian dough, which was commonly prepared in Italian kitchens but had no association with Purim. It is a perfect example of one ethnic holiday custom infiltrating general society. The Italian flavoring of choice was anisette for some of the brandy in this recipe. The addition of finely grated lemon zest is a more "Jewish" variation. In European countries, pastries were often shaped like parts of Haman's body so that people could "eat him into oblivion."

2 cups all-purpose flour plus additional for rolling
2 tablespoons sugar
1/4 teaspoon salt
1/2 teaspoon baking powder
Finely grated zest of 1/2 small lemon
1/3 cup milk
1 egg

1 egg yolk
2 tablespoons olive oil
2 tablespoons brandy
1 1/2 teaspoons vanilla
Vegetable oil for frying
Confectioners' sugar

1. Combine the first 5 ingredients in a mixing bowl. Set aside.

2. Combine the remaining liquid ingredients for the dough in a small bowl and whisk together until well combined. Proceed immediately to add this mixture to the flour, and stir by hand or machine until a soft, slightly sticky dough is formed.

3. Turn out the dough onto a generously floured board and gently knead for 15 strokes to form a soft ball of dough. Cover with the inverted used mixing bowl and let the dough rest for 1/2 hour.

4. Divide the dough in half and roll one half on a moderately floured board until it is very thin (1/16 inch) and almost transparent.

5. Pour 3 inches of oil into a deep pot or fryer and heat to 375°F.

6. Cut strips of dough that are about 4 inches in length by 1 inch. As you lift up each strip, the dough will stretch a little, which is OK. Bring the two ends of the dough together and lightly press them to form a sagging O.

7. Fry the dough 3 or 4 pieces at a time until golden. Drain on crumpled paper towels.

8. When all the dough is fried, place on a serving tray and sprinkle liberally with confectioners' sugar while still warm. Serve.

Yield: 3–4 dozen pieces

TINA'S TIDBITS

- *Dough made with oil will always appear to be sticky, even when its consistency is correct. Use a little more flour than usual on your board when rolling out the dough to prevent it from sticking.*
- *It is important to keep the temperature of the frying oil consistent so that the dough does not get soggy. Never add too much food to the oil at once or the temperature will drop and change the quality of your finished product.*
- *Whenever a recipe calls for draining food on paper towels, always crumple the paper into loose balls first before putting them on a tray. The crumpling creates more surface area for the excess oil to be absorbed, resulting in less greasy foods and fewer used towels.*
- *Confectioners' sugar will adhere much better when it is sprinkled on food that is warm rather than cool.*

MOHNBRODT

As early as the Middle Ages, cookies for Purim were made in stick shapes to denote the finger of accusation pointed at the Jews by Haman. Children would use the cookie to represent a character in the M'gillah and act out the story with their pastry. The addition of the poppy seeds, or mohn, *to this sweet is very common in Israel, as are other dishes using this seed. The seeds represent God's promise that the seed of Israel would spread throughout the world, rather than Haman's wish to obliterate the Jews.*

3¾ cups flour
2 tablespoons cornstarch
1 teaspoon baking powder
¼ teaspoon baking soda
1 teaspoon salt
2 tablespoons poppy seeds
1 cup sugar

1 cup peanut oil
3 eggs
Zest of 1 lemon, grated
2 teaspoons lemon juice
1½ teaspoons vanilla
1 tablespoon sugar
½ teaspoon cinnamon

1. Preheat oven to 350°F.

2. Combine the flour, cornstarch, baking powder, soda, salt, and poppy seeds in a bowl and set aside.

3. Cream the sugar and oil on high speed until light and fluffy. Add the eggs, zest, juice, and vanilla and mix until thoroughly combined.

4. Stir in the flour mixture and mix well.

5. Line 2 cookie sheets with parchment paper. Lightly oil your hands, and divide the dough into 4 portions. Lightly handle each portion as you form a loose log that is about 10 inches long and 2 inches wide. Place 2 logs on each cookie sheet. Gently shape the soft dough into a uniform log that is now probably 12 inches long.

6. Sprinkle the tops of the loaves with the cinnamon and sugar mixture.

7. Bake for 20 minutes, or until the edges are golden brown.

8. Remove the loaves from the oven. Let cool for 5 minutes. Slice horizontally into ½-inch cookies. Place cut side up and bake for another 5 minutes. Turn the cookies over and bake for another 5 minutes. Cool and store in an airtight container for 2 weeks or freeze.

TINA'S TIDBITS

- *The use of cornstarch in this recipe creates a dough that is more compact and smooth. This type of dough is much easier to cut into uniform cookies after it is partially baked.*
- *Whenever a recipe for a baked good calls for a large amount of oil, it is imperative that the oil, eggs, and sugar be beaten together well to form an emulsion. If this step is followed properly, you will never have a greasy cake or cookie. Your finished product will be light and airy instead of dense and greasy.*
- *This type of "bread," or biscotto, was invented in Italy, probably by Jewish seamen. The double baking process rendered the finished pastry very dry, so it could withstand the humidity of the ocean air for long periods of time without becoming rancid.*

Yield: 3–4 dozen cookies

HAMANTASCHEN DOUGH (DAIRY)

Here's another dough that is firm but lighter, because of the baking powder.

1 stick unsalted butter
½ cup sugar
2 large eggs
½ teaspoon vanilla extract
½ teaspoon pure almond extract

2 cups all-purpose flour
1 teaspoon baking powder
¼ teaspoon salt
Confectioners' sugar (optional)
Filling of your choice, canned or homemade

1. Preheat oven to 350°F. Line cookie sheets with parchment paper.

2. Using an electric mixer, cream the butter and sugar together until thoroughly combined.

3. Add the eggs, vanilla, and almond extract, and beat until lighter in color and fluffy.

4. Add the flour, baking powder, and salt, and mix just until the mixture starts to hold together.

5. Very gently knead the dough on a lightly floured surface about 10 strokes or until the dough is smooth and holds together. Cover with plastic wrap and refrigerate for at least 15 minutes.

6. Roll the dough out on a board that is lightly covered with flour or confectioners' sugar. **Note:** The sugar will slightly glaze the baked cookie and make it a little sweeter.

7. Cut the dough into 2½-inch circles, and place 1 scant teaspoon of filling in the center of each circle.

8. Shape into triangles by using your thumbs to push up from the bottom of the circle and your forefingers to pull down from the top sides. Pinch the top seams of the dough well to securely enclose almost all of the filling. A little should peek through the top of the opening. See diagram on page 302.

9. Pinch the dough together so that the filling is exposed only at the top of the cookie.

10. Bake the hamantaschen in the preheated oven for 10 minutes or until golden. Store in a plastic bag or container when cool, or freeze for later use.

Yield: 1½–2 dozen hamantaschen

TINA'S TIDBIT

• *Do not overwork the dough when kneading it or you will toughen it and the hamantaschen will be heavy.*

HAMANTASCHEN DOUGH (PAREVE)

Another version of dough when you want your pastry to be dairy-free.

2 sticks unsalted pareve margarine
1½ cups sugar
2 large eggs
1½ teaspoons vanilla extract
Zest of ¼ of a large orange
5½ cups all-purpose flour

1¼ teaspoons baking powder
¼ teaspoon salt
½ cup orange juice
Filling of your choice, canned or homemade (see
    recipes on the following page)
1 egg plus 1 tablespoon water for glaze

1. Cream the margarine and sugar until well combined. Add the eggs, vanilla, and orange zest, and mix until light and fluffy.

2. Combine the flour, baking powder, and salt in a 1-quart bowl. Add half the flour mixture to the mixing bowl, and stir until almost incorporated. Add half the orange juice and combine.

3. Repeat with the remaining flour mixture and the remaining orange juice until a soft, smooth dough is formed. Refrigerate the dough for 15 minutes or longer before rolling out.

4. Roll out the dough to ¼-inch thickness on a lightly floured board, and cut into 2½-inch circles.

5. Place 1 scant teaspoon of filling in the center of each circle. Shape into triangles by using your thumbs to push up from the bottom of the circle and your forefingers to pull down from the top sides. Pinch the top seams of the dough well to securely enclose almost all of the filling. A little should peek through the top of the opening. See diagram on page 336.

6. Combine the remaining egg with the 1 tablespoon of water, and brush the egg wash on the tops of the hamantaschen.

7. Bake at 350°F on parchment-lined cookie sheets for 12 minutes or until lightly golden.

Yield: 3–4 dozen hamantaschen

TINA'S TIDBITS

- *The addition of orange juice not only adds flavor, but the acid breaks down some of the gluten in the flour. This will make your cookie tender.*
- *Never use whipped or diet margarine. You will add too much air and water to the dough and change its consistency, making it harder to roll out and shape.*

Hamantaschen Fillings

Although there are many good canned fillings on the market, it is good to know how to make the fillings from scatch.

Prune Filling (Lekvar)

1 pound soft pitted prunes
¼ cup sugar
1 teaspoon lemon juice
Grated zest of ½ lemon

¼ teaspoon cinnamon
½ teaspoon vanilla
⅓ cup finely chopped walnuts

1. Combine the prunes, sugar, lemon juice, lemon zest, cinnamon, and vanilla in a processor work bowl. Process the mixture until smooth.

2. Transfer the mixture to a bowl and fold in the finely chopped walnuts. Cover and refrigerate until ready to use.

Mohn Filling

1 cup poppy seeds (about 4 ounces)
¼ cup sugar
⅓ cup honey
Grated zest of ½ lemon

⅔ cup raisins
1 teaspoon vanilla
½ cup finely chopped walnuts

1. Place the poppy seeds in a 1-quart bowl, and pour boiling water over to 1 inch above the seeds. Set aside for 15 minutes and drain thoroughly.

2. Place the poppy seeds, sugar, honey, lemon zest, raisins, and vanilla in a processor work bowl. Process until well ground.

3. Transfer the mixture to a bowl and fold in the finely chopped walnuts. Cover and refrigerate until ready to use.

Yield: About 2 cups each

HOW TO SHAPE HAMANTASCHEN

1. Roll the dough out to $\frac{1}{8}$-inch thickness, and cut into 3-inch circles.

2. Place a teaspoon of filling in the center of each circle. Regular fruit preserves with lots of fruit pieces can be used, but **don't** use jelly, as it will melt and dissipate, leaving you with an empty cookie.

3. Hold your hands so that the tips of your thumbs touch and your forefingers are straight up in the air, so that the left hand makes an L and the right hand makes a J. Place your thumbs at the bottom of the circle (B) and slightly lift up the dough. Bring your forefingers down at an angle (between A and C and between A and D) and gently push up the dough from all sides until the dough forms an equilateral triangle. Gently pinch the top edges together and you will have a perfect, professional-looking hamantaschen.

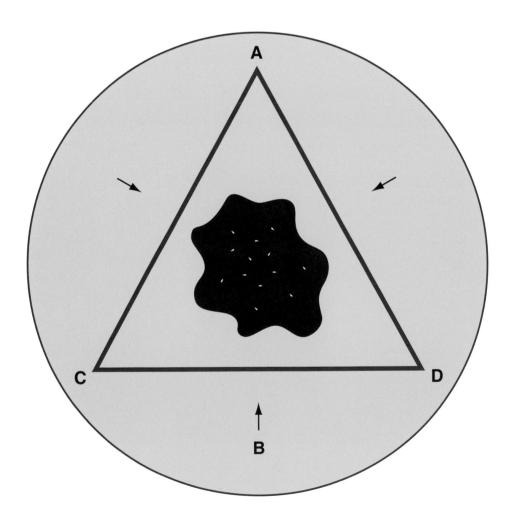

HAMENTASCHEN DE PANAMA

The following recipe epitomizes the transformation of a Jewish recipe due to immigration. I received the cookbook of the Panama chapter of the Women's International Zionist Orgranization from a friend of mine in Mexico City. The recipes were all in Spanish, but my high school teacher would have been proud! I came across a recipe titled Orejas de Haman para Purim *(Haman's Ears for Purim). But instead of a recipe for fried dough, the ingredients and diagram were for hamantaschen. To blur the lines of transition even further, many of the ingredients (including the brandy) were more typical of Middle Eastern fried dough than the Eastern European pastry* murbeteig *or* pâte sucrée. *There is a large Sephardic population from Syria and Lebanon in Latin America, and of course there is a substantial Ashkenazic community as well. Their traditions were commingled probably through shared celebrations to produce the following dessert.*

Enjoy this dish, adapted from a recipe by Rita Sasso, for its taste as well as for its history.

3¼ cups flour
½ cup sugar
½ teaspoon salt
Zest of 1 small lemon
1 stick margarine, cut into eighths
1 stick unsalted butter, cut into eighths
1 egg yolk

1½ teaspoons vanilla
2 or more tablespoons of brandy or rum
Milk (optional)
Confectioners' sugar
Commercially prepared poppy seed, prune, or apricot filling

1. Place the flour, sugar, salt, and lemon zest in the work bowl of a food processor fitted with the metal blade. Pulse the machine on and off to combine the ingredients.

2. Add the margarine and butter, and pulse on and off about 20 times or until the dough resembles a coarse meal.

3. Quickly combine the egg yolk, vanilla, and brandy or rum in a small bowl.

4. Immediately add the liquid mixture to the processor while it is running, and mix only until a ball of dough starts to begin to form. Do not overmix. If the dough looks very dry, you may add another tablespoon of brandy or some milk. The dough should not be too moist or the cookie will be heavy.

5. Turn the dough out on a lightly floured board and lightly knead into a ball. Divide the dough into 2 or 3 portions and refrigerate, covered, for 20 minutes.

6. Remove the dough and roll out to ⅛-inch thickness on a surface that has been liberally coated with confectioners' sugar.

7. Cut the dough into 3-inch circles, and place a small amount of prepared filling in the center of each circle. Shape the dough into triangles, pinching the edges together.

8. Place the cookies on parchment-lined cookie sheets, and bake for 12–15 minutes in a preheated 350°F oven until golden brown.

Yield: 3 dozen or more, depending on size

TINA'S TIDBITS

- *Pastry that contains alcohol or fruit juice will taste even better the next day, as the flavors need time to mellow.*
- *Liquid is necessary, even in small amounts, to bind the flour and fat in pastry together. A processor is so efficient that dough could be formed without it, but it will fall apart when rolled or baked.*
- *Always roll sweet pastry in confectioners' sugar instead of flour. The cornstarch in the sugar prevents sticking, and the sugar creates a light, glistening glaze over the finished product..*

YOLANDA'S MOTHER'S BEST COOKIES

When Yolanda first gave me this recipe it was all in pounds and ounces. That is tricky when you are weighing flour, so I made the recipe user-friendly. This makes a great hamantaschen dough as well as a rolled-out cookie dough or even a log, coated in sugar and then cut into slices. All-purpose!

1 pound unsalted butter
$\frac{1}{2}$ pound minus 1 tablespoon confectioners' sugar
1 tablespoon corn syrup
2 teaspoons vanilla

$\frac{1}{2}$ teaspoon salt
$4\frac{1}{2}$ cups all-purpose flour
Confectioners' sugar if rolling cutout cookies

1. Cream the butter, sugar, and corn syrup together on high speed until light and fluffy.

2. Add the vanilla and salt, and mix until incorporated.

3. Add the flour and mix only until the dough starts to come together.

4. Remove the dough from the bowl and lightly knead the dough into a ball.

5. Divide the dough in half and either flatten it into disks (for rolling out) or shape it into two logs (for slice and bake). Cover with plastic wrap and refrigerate until ready to use, at least 1 hour.

6. Preheat the oven to 300°F.

7. Roll the dough out in confectioners' sugar, and cut into desired shapes. For hamentashen, cut dough into 2–3 inch circles. Place a teaspoon of prepared filling in the center of the circle. Shape into triangles by using your thumbs to push up from the bottom of the circle and your forefingers to pull down from the top sides. Pinch the top seams of the dough well to securely enclose almost all of the filling. A little should peek through the top of the opening. See diagram on page 302.

8. For slice and bake, roll the logs in colored sugar, and slice into $\frac{1}{8}$-inch slices. Place flat on parchment-lined cookie sheets.

9. Bake the cookies for 15–20 minutes, until light golden brown.

Yield: 4–5 dozen cookies

TINA'S TIDBITS

- *Confectioners' sugar makes the dough very firm and smooth, ideal for shaping cookies.*
- *The addition of corn syrup enhances the golden color of normally pale cookies.*
- *Never mix scraps of dough (second-generation dough from cutouts) with dough that has not been rolled (first-generation dough). The cookie won't lie as flat and might brown unevenly.*

Easy Palmiers

This light, crunchy pastry is often referred to as "pig's ears" in America. However, the French Jews serve these "ears" at Purim, attributing their shape to Haman's misshapen ones. Ears are often associated with the villain Haman because medieval Europe had a ritual of cutting off a villain's ear prior to execution.

This is a very easy recipe, especially because you don't have to make the dough from scratch. I have given you detailed steps, but the cookies can be prepared in very little time.

Purchased puff pastry sheets are pareve, so this can be served with tea after a meat meal.

One 17.3-ounce box of puff pastry sheets
Granulated sugar

1. Remove the two frozen sheets of dough from the box and defrost at room temperature for 20–30 minutes.

2. Spread about $\frac{3}{4}$ cup of sugar over a pastry board or countertop, and press the sugar into both sides of one sheet of dough.

3. Roll the sheet lengthwise on the sugar surface until the dough is slightly thinner and about 16 inches long. Do not change the width of the sheet.

4. Find the center of the dough on the long side and make a little mark with a knife.

5. Starting from each short end, tightly roll up the dough so that each side meets in the middle. Wrap with plastic wrap and freeze for 30 minutes. Repeat the procedure with the other sheet of dough.

6. When ready to bake, line a cookie sheet with parchment paper or use foil, dull side up, which you have lightly sprayed with cooking oil.

7. Slice the dough into $\frac{1}{2}$-inch slices.

8. Sprinkle additional sugar on your board or counter. Using a rolling pin, gently roll each slice, cut side down, in the sugar until the dough is about $\frac{1}{8}$ inch thick. Turn the dough over, and coat the other cut side with sugar. Place it on the cookie sheet, with about $1\frac{1}{2}$ inches between pastries.

9. Place in a preheated 400°F oven and bake for 12–15 minutes, until the bottom and sides of the cookies are caramelized.

> ### TINA'S TIDBITS
>
> - *Because the pastry consists of many fine layers of dough, it is important when working with any leftover pieces that the scraps be layered and not just bunched into a ball.*
> - *This recipe often calls for confectioners' sugar instead of granulated. I prefer the extra crunch one gets from the granulated.*
> - *Another alternative is to cut the dough into circles, cut the circles in half, and pinch the dough in the middle of the straight edge to resemble an ear.*
> - *When cutting shapes from puff pastry, never twist the cookie cutter. This motion will stretch the dough out of alignment, and the pastry will bake slanted.*

10. Remove the cookie sheets from the oven, and gently turn the cookies over, using two spatulas.

11. Return them to the oven and bake for another 3–5 minutes, until the bottoms are golden.

12. When thoroughly cool, remove the cookies from the sheets. Store in an airtight container for a week or freeze until needed.

Yield: 3–4 dozen

PASSOVER

I renovated part of my house for Passover. Really! I tore down the archway between the living and dining rooms to create a large, open space. Each year I remove all the furniture from the living area, put up five long folding tables, and transform the space so the seder can be shared with forty people. You see, my family knows that I take to heart the command in the Haggadah, "Let all who are hungry come and eat." Aside from my husband and children, none of the forty are relatives, but they are all family.

Passover is a time when I feel steeped in my heritage and have fond memories of my mother's kitchen. I still take out the wooden bowl and hand chopper that I used as a child to make the *charoset*. With the acquisition of a food processor, these utensils are obsolete; I no longer need to chop by hand, but my daughter prefers it. She also prefers—no, I take that back—she demands that we must **always** be home for Passover so that we can have at least one seder at our house. She loves the way her father conducts the seder, the way each person has a sound to make while singing *"Chad Gadya,"* and the constancy of familiar faces. She is not alone in her feelings. Passover is celebrated by over 77 percent of Jewish households in America, making it the most observed Jewish holiday, according to the most recent National Jewish Population Study.

Julius Lester, in the CCAR Haggadah *The Open Door,* describing his preparation for Passover, says, "Passover is a blending of history and religion, of celebration and commemoration, a drama of remembering, of transforming history into personal memory so that it is I who am emerging from bondage in Egypt." Our memories connect us to our past, and the seder opens our hearts and minds to our people's suffering and triumph over persecution. The possibility of creating memories for our children and grandchildren is very enticing. Maybe this is the true explanation for Passover's popularity.

---

* Sue Levi Elwell, ed. (New York: Central Conference of American Rabbis, 2002), p. 6.

MINA DE MAZA

Although it is common to see recipes for matzah lasagna or pies in cookbooks, it is not an invention of the American Jewish kitchen. Throughout the Mediterranean, Turkish minas, Italian scacchi, and Greek pitas have been prepared for at least a thousand years with matzah used for dough during Passover. The following is a variation of the classic Turkish mina and a meatless scacchi.

2 tablespoons pine nuts
2 tablespoons butter
1 medium onion, finely diced
One 10-ounce package frozen chopped spinach, defrosted
½ pound feta cheese, crumbled
7.5 ounces dry curd farmer cheese (pot cheese)
2 eggs, lightly beaten
Salt and freshly ground pepper to taste
¼–½ teaspoon nutmeg, to taste
1 tablespoon minced fresh dill

2 tablespoons unsalted butter
1 large clove garlic, finely minced
8 ounces sliced mushrooms
8 ounces defrosted artichoke hearts
Salt and freshly ground black pepper to taste
2 cups warm mushroom or vegetable broth
6 plain matzah squares
1 egg
¼ cup grated Parmesan cheese
Additional butter for greasing pan

1. Preheat oven to 350°F.

2. Lightly grease a 13 × 9-inch pan with some additional butter. Set aside.

3. Toast pine nuts in a 350°F oven for 4–6 minutes until lightly golden brown.

4. Melt 2 tablespoons of butter in a 2-quart pan. Sauté the onion until golden.

5. Squeeze out all of the excess moisture from the spinach. Add the spinach to the onions and cook over low heat until most of the moisture has evaporated. Stir occasionally. Add the feta, farmer cheese, eggs, seasonings, and dill and combine. Set aside.

6. Melt the remaining 2 tablespoons of butter in a small sauté pan. Add the garlic and cook for 20 seconds over medium-high heat. Add the mushrooms and sauté until they have given up most of their moisture.

7. If the artichoke pieces are large, cut them in half. Add to the mushroom mixture and stir to heat through. Add the toasted pine nuts and season with salt and pepper. Set aside.

8. Heat the 2 cups of broth in the microwave for 1½ minutes. Pour into an 8-inch square casserole or a deep dish that will hold the liquid, and soak 2 sheets of matzah until soft and pliable. As they become soft, fit them into the bottom and sides of the 13 × 9-inch buttered dish. Repeat with 2 more sheets so that the entire bottom and some of the sides of the pan are covered with matzah.

9. Spread the spinach mixture over the matzot, and top with the mushroom mixture.

10. Soak the remaining 2 sheets of matzah in the broth and cover the filling. Trim or tuck the sides in to make it look neat.

11. Add the remaining egg to the remaining broth in the dish. (Note: If no broth is left, combine 1/2 cup of additional broth with the egg.) Pour it evenly over the entire casserole.

12. Sprinkle the Parmesan cheese over the top and bake for 30–35 minutes until golden brown and bubbling. Serve hot or at room temperature.

Yield: 10–12 servings

TINA'S TIDBITS

- *Nuts will continue to roast even after removing them from the heat of the oven. They fry in their own oils so do not let them get too brown in the oven.*
- *Onions must always be sautéed alone for part of their cooking time to caramelize the natural sugars that make fried onions sweet.*
- *One 10-ounce package of frozen chopped spinach is equal to 1 pound of fresh spinach (minus all the large stems), and you don't have to wash, de-stem, or chop the frozen variety.*

Capsouto Frères Potato Mina

When the Capsouto brothers make this recipe in their New York City restaurant, Capsouto Frères, for their annual charitable community seder, they usually start out with more than forty pounds of potatoes and ninety eggs. I have adapted the recipe to make a deep 13 × 9-inch casserole that will be sure to please many hearty eaters. The flavor is delicate, more southern France than eastern Poland.

4 pounds russet potatoes (4 large)
1 tablespoon kosher salt for cooking potatoes
8 large eggs
1 cup finely grated Parmesan cheese
1 tablespoon kosher salt or to taste
15 grindings (or ½ teaspoon) black pepper

7 boards of matzah
2 eggs
½ cup milk
3 tablespoons extra virgin olive oil, divided use
½ cup grated Parmesan cheese for topping

1. Wash and cut potatoes into eighths, and place in a large pot. Cover with water, add about 1 tablespoon of salt, and bring to a boil. Cook for 20 minutes or until a knife inserted into the potatoes comes out easily.

2. Drain potatoes, peel when cool, and mash in a 4-quart bowl.

3. Add the eggs and stir with a flat whisk or fork until thoroughly combined. Add the 1 cup Parmesan cheese, salt to taste, and the pepper, and mix well. Set aside.

4. Preheat oven to 350°F.

5. Place 3 inches of water in a glass dish wide enough to hold a board of matzah. Microwave the water for 3 minutes or until very warm.

6. In another bowl or dish large enough to hold a board of matzah, combine the remaining 2 eggs, milk, and 2 tablespoons of oil with a pinch of salt.

7. To assemble the *mina*, grease a 13 × 9-inch glass dish with 1 tablespoon of olive oil. Place in the oven for 2 minutes.

8. Meanwhile soak 2 boards of matzah in the warm water until slightly soft. Lift from the water and dip each board in the egg-milk mixture. Remove the baking dish from the oven, and lay the 2 boards of matzah in the bottom of the dish. They will lie flat and be slightly narrower than the pan. That's OK.

TINA'S TIDBITS

- *Because potatoes absorb a great deal of salt, it is necessary to add more salt to this dish than you normally would.*
- *If you are salt restricted, add a seasoning from one of the variations to enhance the flavor.*
- *Because this dish already contains a milk product, you may choose to enrich the dish by using butter.*
- *When cooking with butter, **always** use unsalted butter.*

9. Place half of the potato mixture over the matzot and spread evenly. Repeat step 8 and then cover with the remaining potatoes.

10. Repeat step 8 again with the last three boards of matzah, using the third matzah to fill in on the sides if necessary. Pour the remaining egg mixture, if any, over the matzot, and sprinkle with the remaining ½ cup Parmesan cheese.

11. Bake for 35–40 minutes until the top is golden and a knife inserted into the center comes out hot.

12. Serve hot or at room temperature.

Note: This tastes even better reheated the next day!

Yield: 12–15 servings

VARIATIONS

Here are three variations on this recipe:

Add 1 small grated onion to the potato mixture.

Add 2 tablespoons finely chopped basil.

Sauté 1 cup chopped onion until lightly golden. Add 8 ounces chopped mushrooms and cook until the mushrooms are done. Layer half of this mixture over each potato layer. Follow the remaining instructions.

CARROT TZIMMES WITH DUMPLINGS

When I was young, I loved Mrs. Adler's jarred carrot tzimmes. I created this recipe in Texas when it was no longer available. It's great for Passover too!

1 pound carrots, steamed and sliced, or 1 pound
   cooked frozen carrots
⅓ cup chicken stock (or pareve bouillon)
⅓ cup orange juice
¼ teaspoon ginger
⅓ cup honey

1 tablespoon pareve margarine
1½ teaspoons potato starch dissolved in 3 tablespoons
   water
Leftover matzah balls, quartered, or 12 miniature
   matzoh balls prepared according to instructions in
   step 1.

1. Make matzah ball mixture according to your favorite recipe. Use part of the mixture to make miniature balls by shaping ½ teaspoon of dough into a ball in your oiled hands and adding it to the boiling water. Cook and reserve matzah balls for later.

2. Place sliced cooked carrots, stock, orange juice, ginger, and honey in a saucepan and heat to boiling.

3. Reduce heat and add margarine.

4. Give potato starch mixture a stir to recombine and add to the carrots. Stir constantly until mixture thickens.

5. When mixture has thickened, add the reserved matzah balls and gently combine until the dumplings are coated and heated through.

Yield: 8–10 servings

TINA'S TIDBITS

- *If you want to make a portion of carrots look larger, slice them on the diagonal.*
- *Always stir a hot mixture as you add a potato starch-water mixture to it. Potato starch will congeal instantly if not stirred rapidly.*
- *An easy way to make little matzah balls is to put the mixture in a pastry bag fitted with a number 6 tip. Squeeze out 1/2 inch of dough and cut it off with a knife over the pot of boiling water.*

Deluxe Matzah Kugel

This kugel is moist and flavorful and can be adapted to any assortment of vegetables or fruit to re-create your bubbe's (unless hers was rock hard and dry—then you'd better write to me!). It can be made in advance and briefly warmed in the microwave, but do not reheat it for a long time in the oven.

¾ cup plus 1 tablespoon oil or chicken fat
1 cup diced onion
1 cup diced celery
1 cup diced fresh mushrooms, crimini or portabella preferred
1 box matzah farfel
1¼ teaspoons salt or to taste

½ teaspoon freshly ground black pepper
½ teaspoon garlic powder
3 garlic cloves, finely minced
1 tablespoon paprika
2 eggs, well beaten
3 cups canned chicken broth or more if needed

1. Sauté the onion in a 4-quart saucepan using ¾ cup of the oil or chicken fat until golden brown. Add the celery and mushrooms and sauté some more, until the celery is translucent. Add a little more oil if the vegetables appear to be sticking to the pan.

2. Add the farfel and toss thoroughly so that all the farfel is coated with the vegetables and fat and lightly toasted. Place mixture in a large bowl.

3. Combine the seasonings, eggs, and broth and pour over the farfel mixture. The mixture should be loose. If needed, add more broth.

4. Grease a 9 × 13-inch roasting pan with 1 tablespoon of shortening (preferably chicken fat). Pour in farfel mixture and bake at 350°F for 45 minutes or until golden brown.

Yield: 12–15 servings

TINA'S TIDBITS

- *Scrape the fins away from the underside of a portabella mushroom with a teaspoon before using. This will prevent the mushrooms from turning the mixture inky black when they are sautéed.*
- *A box of matzah can replace a box of farfel. Place broken sheets of matzah in a plastic bag and use a glass or rolling pin to break them into smaller pieces.*
- *Always sauté onions alone until lightly golden before adding other vegetables. The moisture in the other vegetables will stew the onion if you add them all at once and will change the flavor of the mixture markedly.*
- *For a sweeter kugel, use 3/4 cup onion, 1 1/2 cups apple chunks, and orange juice for all or part of the broth.*

AFTER-THE-SEDER FRITTATA

While I was researching for this book, it became clear that our forebears utilized every bit of food that was available to them to create nutritious, satisfying meals. Frittata-style pancakes were common in Iraq and Persia as well as in southern France and Italy. I must have inherited this cooking philosophy, because one year I took a look at all of the leftover ingredients in my refrigerator that were a result of overzealous Passover shopping and created this recipe.

¼ cup extra virgin olive oil
1 medium onion, cut in half lengthwise and sliced
  very thin
10 baby redskin new potatoes, unpeeled, thinly sliced
5 large eggs
1 tablespoon finely minced parsley

1 teaspoon (or more) prepared horseradish in the jar
Salt and freshly ground pepper to taste
10 cooked asparagus, cut into 1-inch lengths
¼ cup Passover mayonnaise
1 tablespoon Passover ketchup
1 teaspoon Concord grape wine, or to taste

1. Heat an 8- to 10-inch nonstick pan over high heat for 20 seconds. Add the oil and heat for another 10 seconds.

2. Add the onions to the pan and cook for 2 minutes. Add the sliced potatoes to the pan, reduce the heat to medium, and cook until potatoes and onions are golden. Remove from the heat.

3. Whisk the eggs, parsley, horseradish, salt, and pepper in a 2-quart bowl until well combined. Add the asparagus and all of the contents of the frying pan. Gently mix together so that the egg is evenly distributed.

4. Place the empty frying pan back on the burner over medium-high heat. Pour the egg mixture into the pan and flatten slightly.

5. Cover the frying pan and cook the egg-potato mixture over medium heat for 6–7 minutes until the sides are golden and most of the center is cooked.

6. Remove the frying pan from the heat. Cover the pan with a large plate and flip the pan over so that the frittata goes onto the plate.

7. Return the pan to the heat and gently slide the frittata back into the pan, cooked side up.

8. Cook the frittata for an additional 3–4 minutes until the bottom is golden and the frittata is cooked through.

9. Meanwhile, combine the last three ingredients to make a sauce. Serve with the frittata.

Yield: 4–6 servings

TINA'S TIDBITS

- *Adding salt to eggs serves two purposes: in addition to flavoring the eggs, the salt breaks down the egg white so it will uniformly blend with the other ingredients, eliminating those tough white strands throughout your frittata.*
- *Obviously any leftover vegetable such as broccoli, spinach, cauliflower, or sautéed mushrooms may be used in this recipe. Just make sure that the size of your vegetable is no larger than 3/4 inch thick so that it will be properly encased by the egg.*

Braised Lamb Shanks in Merlot

Since leg of lamb is technically not kosher (because the sciatic nerve runs through it), lamb shanks are the meat of choice when you want a flavorful lamb dish on your seder table. Slowly braising the shanks in an aromatic liquid flavored with kosher wine yields a moist, tender, fall-off-the-bone delicacy.

2–4 lamb shanks
2 tablespoons mixed fresh herbs (basil, rosemary, oregano, or mint), finely minced
1 cup of orange juice or the juice of 2 oranges
Grated zest of 1 orange

$2\frac{1}{2}$ cups full-bodied Merlot
4 large or 6 medium cloves of garlic, minced
Salt and freshly ground black pepper
2 tablespoons of extra virgin olive oil
1 cup low-salt chicken stock or water

1. Rinse the lamb shanks and place them in one layer in a wide glass dish.

2. Combine the mixed herbs, orange juice, orange zest, Merlot, and garlic and add to the shanks. Turn the shanks over so they are coated with the marinade.

3. Cover with plastic wrap and let the shanks marinate at room temperature for 2 hours or overnight in the refrigerator. Every half hour, turn the shanks to coat well.

4. Remove the shanks from the marinade, and pat them dry with a paper towel. Reserve the marinade.

5. Preheat the oven to 450°F.

6. Lightly season the shanks with freshly ground black pepper and a pinch of salt. Heat a large skillet over high heat for 20 seconds. Add 2 tablespoons of olive oil and heat for 10 seconds. Reduce the heat to medium-high and add the lamb shanks.

7. Cook each side for approximately 2 minutes, until the shanks are brown on all sides.

8. Place the shanks in a single layer in an ovenproof casserole. Pour the chicken stock into the hot pan. Scrape up any meat particles, add them to the reserved marinade, and pour over the shanks in the casserole. Cover with a lid.

9. Put the casserole in the preheated oven, and immediately reduce the temperature to 350°F. (The hot oven will sear the meat initially, but the

TINA'S TIDBITS

- *Because the shanks are cooked for a long time, it is important to use a wine whose flavor won't be lost after prolonged heating. Full-bodied reds like Cabernet Sauvignon, Merlot, and Syrah/Shiraz fit the bill and balance the strong flavor of lamb.*
- *In general, avoid using white wines in dishes with acidic ingredients such as orange juice. Wine flavors tend to grow stronger during cooking, and white wines tend to reduce to a more acidic finish, which may throw your more acidic recipe off balance.*

mixture needs to cook at a lower temperature or the meat will toughen.)

10. Roast the shanks for 45 minutes. Remove from the oven and baste with the sauce. Return the casserole to the oven and roast for an additional 1–1½ hours, or until the meat is very tender and easily pulls away from the bone. If the liquid has reduced greatly, add ½ cup of water to the pan.

11. Remove the meat from the pot and put on a serving platter and keep warm. If the gravy is too watery, boil the liquid down for about 5–10 minutes or until it has thickened to the consistency of tomato sauce. Drizzle some of the sauce on each shank and serve.

Yield: 4 servings

PASSOVER GRANOLA

This recipe will make your Passover week! It is delicious with milk for breakfast, and a healthy snack for school or work. If you must satisfy your sweet tooth further, make the chocolate candies at the end of this recipe.

3 cups matzah farfel
⅔ cup slivered almonds
½ cup sweetened or unsweetened coconut
⅔ cup pecans, broken into large pieces
¼ teaspoon salt
1½ teaspoons cinnamon

¼ teaspoon nutmeg
6 tablespoons unsalted butter or pareve kosher for Passover margarine
⅓ cup wildflower or clover honey
1½ cups chopped dried mixed fruit of your choice including raisins or 7-ounce bag of dried fruit pieces

1. Preheat oven to 325°F.

2. Combine the farfel, almonds, coconut, pecans, salt, cinnamon, and nutmeg in a 3-quart mixing bowl.

3. Melt the butter and honey in a small glass bowl in a microwave for 1 minute until butter is melted and honey is more fluid.

4. Stir the butter mixture into the farfel mixture until all farfel is lightly coated with the butter.

5. Spread the mixture over a large jelly roll pan with 1-inch sides and bake for 15 minutes until deep golden brown. Halfway through baking, stir to brown evenly.

6. Remove from oven. Cool completely and toss with the dried fruit.

7. When totally cooled, store in a ziplock bag or airtight storage container for all eight days of Passover—if it lasts that long!

Yield: 1–1½ quarts

VARIATION: CHOCOLATE GRANOLA TREATS

1. Melt 8 ounces of Passover chocolate chips and mix them with 1½ or 2 cups of the prepared granola. Stir to coat well.

2. Drop by teaspoonful onto parchment paper, and allow the mounds to firm up before you devour them!

3. These can be stored in a sealed container at room temperature or frozen. Chocolate might appear chalky after freezing, but this does not alter the taste.

Yield: 2–3 dozen pieces

TINA'S TIDBITS

- *To prevent burning, never pre-roast nuts if they will be baked in the oven.*
- *This recipe can be made with old-fashioned oatmeal when Passover ends.*
- *Salt should always be added in a small quantity to a sweet mixture to bring out the flavors of the individual foods but not lend a salty taste to the dish.*
- *If making ahead, leave out fruit until the day you want to use it so farfel doesn't get soggy.*

LEFT: *Passover Granola*

PASSOVER LINZER TORTE

This is my signature Passover dessert. Debby Stahl's German mother-in-law gave the two of us this recipe over thirty years ago. Many students have told me that their families love this so much they make it year-round.

Spanish Jews were the first to use ground nuts in place of some or all of the flour to make their tortes, especially for Passover, when flour was prohibited.

½ cup cake meal
½ cup potato starch
1 cup unsalted pareve kosher for Passover margarine
½ cup sugar
1 cup unpeeled, finely ground hazelnuts, almonds, or a combination

½ teaspoon cinnamon
2 large eggs, separated
½ cup kosher for Passover raspberry jam, preferably seedless

1. Combine the cake meal and the potato starch in a processor work bowl.

2. Using the cutting blade, add the margarine and pulse on and off until the mixture is well combined.

3. Add the sugar, hazelnuts or nut mixture, cinnamon, and egg yolks, and mix until smooth and well blended.

4. Take ⅔ of the dough and press it over the bottom and 1 inch up the sides of an ungreased 9-inch springform pan. Leave a 1-inch-wide rim of dough around the top.

5. Spread with ½ cup or more of raspberry jam.

6. Gently squeeze egg-sized balls of remaining dough between your fingertips over the top of the jam to simulate weaving ropes for the lattice top.

TINA'S TIDBITS

- *Springform pans often leak butter during baking, so always place the filled pan on a rimmed cookie sheet to avoid burnt oil spills on the bottom of your oven.*
- *When grinding nuts in a food processor, always pulse the mixture on and off rather than just turning the machine on. This will prevent nut butter from forming on the bottom of the bowl and your nuts will be more uniform in size.*
- *This recipe should be made with preserves or jams, not jelly, so that its volume will remain intact after baking.*
- *Nuts do not have to be pre-roasted if they are contained in pastry that is baked for over 40 minutes.*
- *The recipe can be increased 1 1/2 times to cover a 13 × 9-inch pan, which can be cut into 2-inch squares.*
- *If you are planning to make more than one torte and/or want to freeze it after baking, tightly line the base of the springform pan with aluminum foil. Freeze the torte in the pan, remove the cake with the foil attached, and put it back in the freezer in a freezer bag. You must place the frozen cake back on the springform base or directly on the serving plate **while still frozen**. This cake is delicate.*

This dough cannot easily be handled, but don't worry because the ropes don't have to be perfect, as they become smooth during baking.

7. Fasten the dough rope to the rim of dough, and smooth it out with your fingertip, pressing lightly.

8. Beat the egg whites slightly and brush over the top of the lattice. As you brush, the ropes will get smoother and more uniform.

9. Place the springform pan on a cookie sheet that has very low sides and bake at 325°F for 1 hour and 15 minutes.

10. Partly cool before removing the rim of the pan. Do not attempt to remove the base of the pan. Serve the cake from the base.

Yield: 12 or more servings

SABAYON FOR PASSOVER

Earlier in this book there is a recipe for zabaglione. It is very similar to this one. However, geographic region and Jewish culinary custom dictate how a dish is prepared. This recipe is a perfect example. Sabayon is the French name for the Italian egg custard sauce that is served with fruit or cake. The French chefs use the local sparkling white wine from the Champagne region of France to flavor their custard instead of the Italian fortified Marsala wine. Passover dictates what liqueur can be used, so a different combination of flavors might result in a variation. This is ultimately how Jewish food developed throughout the Diaspora, keeping tradition and using the foods locally available.

4 egg yolks
¼ cup sugar
¼ cup dry white wine or Champagne

1 tablespoon fruit liqueur (see note below)
1 pint fresh berries or other fruit

1. Place the egg yolks and the sugar in the top of a double boiler or in a 1-quart saucepan and whisk together until a thick ribbon of mixture pours off the whisk.

2. Place the pan with the sugar-egg mixture over another pan containing hot, but not boiling water. The mixture shouldn't be so hot that it will cook the yolks.

3. Add the wine and liqueur to the sugar-yolk mixture and whisk constantly over the hot water for 3–4 minutes until a nice thick custard is formed.

4. When the custard has thickened, **immediately** remove from the heat or you will have fancy scrambled eggs!

5. Have your fresh berries or other fruit divided into 4 or 5 serving dishes or glasses. Pour the sabayon over the fruit and serve.

Note: Use the following brandies or liqueurs with the appropriate fruit:
   · Amaretto with raspberries or strawberries
   · Orange-flavored liqueur with oranges or any berry
   · Rum (if using) with almost all fruits

Yield: 8 servings

TINA'S TIDBITS

- *Israel has recently started to produce liqueurs that are kosher for Passover. Some companies in the United States are also producing some fruit-flavored brandies that can be used during Passover as well.*
- *It is important to cook the yolks slowly so that they will incorporate air as you whisk. As the structure of the yolk firms up around the air, a light, foamy sauce will be created.*
- *The trick with this sauce is not to undercook the yolks or they won't retain the air. However, at the first sign of solidification, get it off the heat. It is better to have a sauce that is runny than one that is firm and with lumps!*
- Sabayon *does not hold for long periods of time. However, if you must make it before the meal, keep its consistency stabilized by placing the pan over warm water so that the sauce doesn't liquefy and settle to the bottom.*

IRENE'S PASSOVER STRAWBERRY FLUFF CAKE

This recipe is not difficult—no spending hours baking—but this cake is a hit with my guests every year that my good friend Irene makes it. Try other fruits that can break down easily, like raspberries or frozen mixed berries, which are softer.

²/₃ of a can Passover almond macaroons
2 egg whites
2 pints or 2 cups sliced strawberries

1 tablespoon fresh lemon juice
1 cup sugar
1 teaspoon vanilla extract

1. Press the macaroons evenly into the bottom of a 9-inch springform pan.

2. Place the remaining ingredients in the bowl of an electric mixer.

3. Beat on high for 15–20 minutes or until the mixture has significantly increased (tripled) in volume and is light and foamy.

4. Carefully pour the strawberry mixture into the prepared pan. Decorate with some additional sliced strawberries and freeze uncovered for at least 2 hours or until firm. If not serving immediately, cover with plastic wrap and place in the freezer.

Yield: 15 or more servings

TINA'S TIDBITS

- *Any crust can be used as the base for this dessert. However, if you have to bake your crust first, make sure it and the pan are completely cool before adding the filling.*
- *Normally egg whites are beaten only with sugar to achieve a high volume. In this recipe it would be impossible to incorporate the strawberries if they were added at the end, so the long beating time is necessary to achieve a uniform consistency.*
- *If you want to serve more people with the same amount of filling, use the entire can of macaroons and press into the bottom of a 13 × 9-inch pan.*

Passover Pecan Biscotti

One Passover season there was a nationwide shortage of kosher for Passover pareve margarine. This hampered baking because most desserts for the holiday do not contain dairy products so that they can be served at the end of the seder. I developed the following recipe using oil instead of margarine and the cookies came out great!

1 cup pecans
$1\frac{1}{4}$ cups Passover cake meal
4 tablespoons potato starch
$\frac{1}{4}$ teaspoon salt
$\frac{1}{2}$ teaspoon cinnamon

3 eggs
1 cup sugar
$\frac{3}{4}$ cup vegetable oil
$1\frac{1}{2}$ teaspoons vanilla extract
2 tablespoons orange juice

1. Place the pecans in a processor work bowl and pulse the processor on and off until the nuts are finely ground.

2. Place the nuts in a small bowl and add the cake meal, potato starch, salt, and cinnamon. Stir well to combine.

3. Beat the eggs, sugar, and oil together until an emulsion is formed and no streaks of oil are visible. Add the vanilla and orange juice and mix to incorporate.

4. Add the dry ingredients to the egg mixture and stir to thoroughly combine.

5. Divide the dough into three strips on parchment paper and bake in a 350°F oven until golden brown.

6. Remove from the oven and cut each log crosswise into $\frac{1}{2}$-inch slices. Place slices on their sides and bake for 5 minutes.

7. Remove from the oven and turn the cookies over. Bake for an additional 5 minutes to brown.

8. Cool and store in an airtight container.

Yield: 3–4 dozen

TINA'S TIDBITS

- *It is very important to thoroughly combine the eggs and oil together to make an emulsion before adding the dry ingredients. The end result is a cookie that is crisp and light without any greasy consistency.*
- *Twice baking the cookies not only browns them beautifully, but dries them out sufficiently so that they will stay fresh for a week or more.*
- *Adding potato starch creates a dough that is less rough than one made with just matzah cake meal, and it slices well.*

SHAVUOT

On the third new moon after the Israelites had gone forth
from the land of Egypt, on that very day, they entered the wilderness of Sinai.

EXODUS 19:1

Shavuot is the holiday that celebrates the giving of the Torah on Mount Sinai. It is called the Feast of Weeks because it occurs seven weeks after the end of Passover. It is also called Yom HaBikurim, "Day of the First Fruits." In biblical times Shavuot marked the end of the grain harvest (end of counting the Omer) and

the beginning of the harvest of the first fruits of the year. Two loaves of leavened bread were brought to the Temple to signify the conclusion of the counting of the Omer, and Jews brought the first fruits of the new crops as an offering to the Temple as well. Actually, the first fruits of a crop could be brought anytime between Shavuot and Sukkot. Once the Temple was destroyed in 70 C.E., there was no place to bring the harvest offerings. Since the giving of the Torah at Mount Sinai was in the month of Sivan, the holiday became more associated with the giving of the Torah than as one of the three harvest festivals.

Many symbolic customs and food traditions surround Shavuot. Greenery and flowers are placed in synagogues and homes to commemorate the lush, green fields surrounding Mount Sinai. Spices and roses are also used for decorative purposes, possibly because one interpretation of the Bible was that the Israelites fainted when they heard the voice of God and they had to be revived with the smell of spices. In Eastern Europe, beginning in medieval times, a young boy was brought to the *cheder* (schoolroom) to begin his studies. To make the start of his education sweeter, a drop of honey was placed on each letter of the *alef-bet*. As he learned the letter, he was encouraged to lick off the honey.

Eating dairy foods instead of meat to celebrate the holiday is the most prevalent Shavuot food association. Although there is no definitive explanation for its origin, theories abound. These

Left: *Deluxe Noodle Kugel, page 338*

include that the laws of kashrut were given at Sinai, and the Jews knew their utensils were not kosher, so they ate uncooked dairy foods; the cattle were grazing on fresh grass, so their milk was rich and plentiful; God was bringing the people to the land of "milk and honey." Whatever the interpretation, dairy recipes are prepared for the holiday. Enjoy!

BLINTZES

It is not clear why blintzes are associated with Shavuot. Some say it is because they contain cheese and others because two blintzes on a plate side by side look like a Torah scroll. Whatever the theory, blintzes are great to eat anytime.

DOUGH:
2 large eggs
²/₃ cup milk
¹/₃ cup water
Pinch of salt
1 cup flour
Butter for frying
Sour cream

FILLING:
7.5ounce package farmer cheese
8 ounces cream cheese
3 tablespoons sugar
2 eggs
¹/₂ teaspoon cinnamon
1¹/₂ teaspoons vanilla

1. To make the dough, beat the eggs until slightly mixed. Add the milk, water, and salt and beat until smooth.

2. Using a wire whisk, gradually beat the flour into the mixture until each addition is totally incorporated and the mixture is smooth.

3. When the batter is the consistency of heavy cream, stop adding the remaining flour. Tap the bowl on the table to remove air bubbles, and set the mixture aside for ¹/₂ hour while you make the filling.

4. To make the filling, beat the cheeses with a mixer or processor until smooth. Add the remaining ingredients and mix thoroughly to combine. Set aside.

5. To make the blintz crepes, lightly butter a 6- or 8-inch frying pan. When the butter is sizzling, pour in 2 or more tablespoons of batter (the amount depends on the size of the pan), and swirl it around in the pan to make a uniform pancake. Alternatively, you could add ¹/₄ cup batter, let it set for 5 seconds, and then quickly pour out the excess.

6. When the pancake top is glistening and dry, flip it out onto a plate. Proceed with the remaining batter.

7. Place the pancakes brown side up and put 1 tablespoon of filling on each center. Fold up the bottom, fold in the sides, and roll up the blintz until the filling is sealed. Place seam side down on a plate until ready for frying.

8. Heat some butter in a pan, and when sizzling, add a few blintzes, seam side down. Fry on both sides until golden brown all over. Serve with sour cream.

Yield: Approximately 12 blintzes

TINA'S TIDBITS

- *If you allow the batter to rest for 1/2 hour, the flour will hydrate, which will make the batter smoother and thicker.*
- *Always put the filling on the side that was initially browned when making the crepe. That way the uncooked side is on the outside of the blintz when it is baked or fried and no side of the dough will be cooked twice, which would make it tough and rubbery.*

DELUXE NOODLE KUGEL

My friends call this "killer kugel." Joan Nathan ran this recipe in her New York Times *column one year, and, as a result, I received many e-mails thanking me for sharing this recipe. I joke that this is a poor excuse for a cheesecake. Rich, creamy, and utterly delicious, a kugel in a 13 × 9-inch baking pan should serve twenty-five people. However, one reader said she made two kugels for fifteen people and almost all of it was gone!*

½ pound medium or extra-wide noodles (see note under Tina's Tidbits)
1 pound cream cheese
½ pound unsalted butter
1 cup sugar
1 pint sour cream
1 teaspoon vanilla

8 eggs
1 small can mandarin oranges, drained
1 small can crushed pineapple, drained
4 ounces walnuts
⅓ cup sugar
1 teaspoon cinnamon
2 tablespoons butter

1. Cook the noodles according to package directions. Drain and place in a 4-quart bowl.

2. Combine the cream cheese and butter in a processor work bowl and blend until smooth. Scrape down the sides of the work bowl. Add the sugar and process until well combined. Add the sour cream, vanilla, and eggs and process until well mixed. Pour into the 4-quart bowl with the noodles.

3. Stir the fruits in by hand, and pour the mixture into a buttered 13 × 9-inch baking dish. The mixture will almost overflow. Cover with plastic wrap and refrigerate overnight.

4. When ready to bake, uncover and place in a preheated 350°F oven and bake for 50 minutes.

5. Combine the walnuts with the sugar and cinnamon and sprinkle on top of the kugel. Dot with the 2 tablespoons of butter and bake for 15 minutes more. Serve warm or at room temperature. This could be made totally in advance, but it won't be as light.

Yield: 15 or more servings

TINA'S TIDBITS

- *Large noodles will be more visible in this kugel but will provide a more cheesecake-like consistency in some areas. Medium noodles will be distributed more uniformly. Either way this is delicious.*
- *The easiest way to dot butter is to freeze a stick of butter and then grate it over the top of your casserole.*
- *Refrigerating the mixture overnight allows the butter and cream cheese to solidify around the eggs and sour cream. This creates a mixture that will trap the air and puff up better when baked.*
- *If you don't want to use nuts, try crushing cocoa crisp cereal, sprinkling it on top of the kugel, and then dotting it with butter. The original recipe, given to me over forty years ago, used this topping, but I can't teach it or I would lose my credibility!*

RIGATONI CON QUATTRO FROMAGGI (RIGATONI PASTA WITH FOUR CHEESES)

My students call this "adult macaroni and cheese"; I call it a perfect example of Italian cuisine at its richest, with a little tweaking to substitute the smoky pancetta ham with the substance and earthy character of porcini mushrooms. This is a very rich cheese entrée that needs only some crusty bread and a salad to round out the meal.

½ cup butter, divided use
8 ounces crimini or domestic mushrooms, cubed
1 ounce dried porcini mushrooms
½ cup mushroom broth prepared from bouillon cube or bought ready-made, boiling
1½ cups chopped onions
½ cup flour
1 quart milk

½ pound rigatoni
¾ cup cubed fontina cheese (about 3 ounces by weight)
¾ cup cubed Gruyère
¾ cup cubed Emmenthaler or Jarlsberg cheese
¾ cup cubed Bel Paese cheese
¼ cup freshly grated Parmesan cheese

1. Melt 1 tablespoon of the butter in a large sauté pan and sauté the mushrooms until lightly golden and soft, about 7 minutes.

2. Crush the dried porcinis in your hand and add to the fresh mushrooms. Add the boiling liquid and simmer for 5 minutes. Set aside.

3. Melt the remaining butter in a 3-quart saucepan and sauté the onions until soft and translucent.

4. Put the sautéed onions in a processor work bowl and pulse until the onions have been pureed. Return the onions to the saucepan.

5. Add the flour to the onion mixture and stir constantly with a wire whisk until smooth.

6. Heat the milk until scalded (little bubbles form around the edges). Put the milk in the processor work bowl and pulse on and off 2 or 3 times to "clean" the bowl. Add the milk to the onion-flour mixture and whisk until smooth and thick.

7. Cook the rigatoni according to package directions, and preheat the oven to 350°F.

8. Place half of the rigatoni in the bottom of a 2-quart casserole. Cover with half the mushroom mixture and then half of all the cheeses **except** the Parmesan. Spoon half of the sauce over all. Repeat the process using the remaining ingredients and topping the last layer of sauce with the Parmesan cheese.

9. Bake at 350°F for 30–35 minutes or until golden and bubbly.

Yield: 8–10 servings

TINA'S TIDBITS

- *Necessity is the mother of all inventions, and just as Jewish cooks had to make adjustments to local recipes centuries ago, so too did I have to find a good substitute for pancetta, Italian cured and spiced bacon. Dried, earthy porcini mushrooms add a smoky spice taste as a substitute.*
- *Rigatoni increases in size when boiled so that little shelves of pasta are distributed throughout the casserole.*
- *The rich onion-cream mixture created for the base of this sauce is called a soubise.*

MEDITERRANEAN CHEESE TORTA

All the flavors of the Mediterranean in one layered dish! I created this recipe after seeing a prominent department store advertise a cheese mold that was extremely expensive. This recipe made six molds for the price of one! As part of your dairy meal, serve this as an appetizer or accompanied by a warm pita or bagels.

10 sun-dried tomato halves
3.5 ounces jarred roasted red peppers, drained
20 pitted Calamata olives
8 ounces cream cheese
4 ounces unsalted butter
6 ounces Gorgonzola or other blue-veined cheese
8 ounces mascarpone
8 ounces cream cheese

1 cup firmly packed fresh basil leaves
2 large cloves garlic
3 tablespoons extra virgin olive oil
½ cup grated Parmesan cheese
2 tablespoons pine nuts
8 ounces cream cheese
4 ounces unsalted butter

1. Lightly grease one 4-cup mold or 5–6 six-ounce ramekins. Line the mold(s) with plastic wrap or cheesecloth and set aside.

2. Combine the first five ingredients in the processor work bowl and process until a smooth paste is formed. Pour the mixture into the 4-cup mold or divide evenly among the ramekins. Rinse the work bowl.

3. Combine the Gorgonzola with the mascarpone and cream cheese in the processor and process until smooth, stopping to scrape down the sides of the bowl if necessary. Pour the mixture evenly over the sun-dried tomato mixture in the mold(s). Rinse out the bowl.

4. Combine the basil with the garlic and oil in the processor work bowl and process until a fairly smooth paste is formed. Add the remaining ingredients and process until well combined and smooth, stopping to scrape down the sides of the bowl if necessary. Pour this mixture over the other layers and smooth evenly. Cover with plastic wrap until firm.

5. When ready to serve or package for gifts, unmold and carefully remove plastic wrap.

Yield: 8–10 servings per 1 mold

TINA'S TIDBITS

- *Cheese and cheese mixtures may be frozen as long as they do not have high moisture content. Freeze these tortas first in their molds, and then remove them with the plastic wrap and freeze in airtight freezer bags.*
- *Put a straw into an almost sealed freezer bag and suck out all the air. Remove straw and seal quickly. This stops the formation of ice crystals.*

ICONS OF JEWISH COOKING

CHICKEN SOUP

Chicken soup has been an icon of the Jewish table since early medieval times. Its presence defined the Shabbat table, and a Jewish wedding feast symbolically started with the soup. At a wedding, chicken soup was served to draw the parallel between the fecundity of chickens and the wish that the new couple be fruitful and multiply. The golden droplets of chicken fat that pooled on the top of the soup also demonstrated the wealth of the host of the wedding. In those days, the rendered chicken fat in the soup was never discarded; on the contrary, it was a prized addition to the bowl.

In keeping with the imperative of Shabbat to perform *hidur mitzvah*, "glorifying the Sabbath," even the poorest of Jews would save their funds for a chicken to be the highlight of the Friday night meal. Our ancestors were resourceful and utilized as much of the chicken as possible. Imagine a poor family living in the Pale of Settlement in Eastern Europe—one chicken could provide three courses! The liver was cooked with onions and mixed with some of the *schmaltz* (chicken fat) to start the meal with some chopped liver. Then the chicken was boiled in water with some meager vegetables and became the wonderful soup course. Finally, the meat was eaten, and the bones were probably reserved to provide a base for a bean soup later in the week! My father-in-law had an interesting custom of eating the soup after the entrée. He did it because that was how it was always done in his house. There is a Lithuanian tradition, according to Rabbi Gil Marks, that Jews saved the soup for last in case Elijah the prophet knocked on their door in the middle of dinner to take them to Jerusalem. This way they would have eaten enough to sate them on their long journey.

As far as the curative powers of chicken soup, recent studies conducted at the University of Nebraska Medical School (see www.unmc.edu/chickensoup/article.htm) identified some properties in chicken soup with vegetables that suggests it has an anti-inflammatory effect on our bodies that helps lessen the symptoms of the common cold. Moses Maimonides, the great scholar and physician of the twelfth century, prescribed chicken soup to the weak and the infirm in one of his medical writings, and this was thought to be based on earlier Greek texts.

LEFT: *Basic Chicken Soup, page 346*   345

BASIC CHICKEN SOUP

This is the way my mother taught me to make chicken soup. She always used fresh dill. My friend Leslie's mom always used thyme. Neither one was wrong. Each had her own tradition. In this section I will not tell you the "right" way to make a dish. Consider these recipes as building blocks, so you can tweak the recipe to your own personal memory.

One 4- to 5-pound fowl or yearling (soup chicken)—a roaster will do
5 quarts water or water to cover
1 parsnip, peeled and cut into thirds
1 large onion, peeled but left whole
1 turnip, peeled and cut into quarters
2 stalks celery with leaves, cut into thirds

3 or more carrots, peeled and sliced into 1-inch lengths
Fresh dill, 3 or more sprigs to taste
Fresh parsley, 2 sprigs or more if parsnip isn't being used
Salt and pepper to taste
Kreplach or matzah balls (optional; see recipes)

1. Cut the chicken into pieces. Place the pieces in a large soup pot and cover with water.

2. Bring the water to a boil and simmer for 30 minutes, skimming the top of the liquid to remove all of the brown foam.

3. Add the remaining ingredients and cook over low heat until the chicken is quite tender and the vegetables are soft, about 2–3 hours.

4. Remove the chicken with a slotted spoon. Discard the dill and parsley. Remove the vegetables to nibble on, and save the carrot for later use in the soup. Strain the soup so that it is nice and clear.

5. Place the soup in a clean pot, and add the carrots. Cooked kreplach or matzah balls may be added at this point. Heat until nice and hot. Serve.

Yield: 3 quarts soup

TINA'S TIDBITS

- *Always cut up your chicken before making soup. This will expose more of the interior of the meat to the water and will produce a much richer-flavored soup.*
- *Even if you don't keep kosher, use kosher chickens or organic chickens to make the soup. I once made this recipe in a friend's home using a well-known nonkosher chicken. The chicken shrank in half because it had been plumped with water, and the soup tasted like the chicken "ran" through it!*
- *An alternative to clear soup is to remove the vegetables and herbs from the broth and recombine the vegetables with the broth in a blender until the mixture is opaque and creamy.*
- *Another traditional way to serve chicken soup is to add the cooked vegetables and shredded chicken meat to the bowl for a hearty meal.*

CHICKEN SOUP WITH GHONDI (CHICKPEA MEATBALLS)

When I first tried to make these easy chicken meatballs, I thought that they gave new meaning to the word "sinkers." However, after consulting with Najmieh Batmanglij, one of the most renowned experts on Persian cooking, I learned a few tricks to make these toothsome morsels firm but not rocklike. Sautéing the onion adds extra flavor and more moisture to the ghondi, and using dark chicken meat from the thigh makes the balls softer. If you can't get a butcher to grind the meat for you or you don't want to grind it at home in a grinder or processor, I suggest that you try ground turkey or ground veal.

1 recipe for Basic Chicken Soup (see page 346)
1 teaspoon ground turmeric
Juice of 1/2 lemon (optional)
3 tablespoons extra virgin olive oil
1 medium onion (about 8 ounces), finely diced
8 ounces boneless chicken thighs, ground, or ground turkey

1/2 teaspoon ground cardamom
1/2 teaspoon cumin (optional)
1/8 teaspoon turmeric
1/4 teaspoon kosher salt
10 grindings black pepper or to taste
1/2–3/4 cup toasted chickpea flour

1. Prepare the basic chicken soup, but add the turmeric to the soup and the optional lemon juice after the soup is cooked and strained of all vegetables and chicken parts.

2. To prepare the *ghondi*, heat an 8-inch frying pan for 20 seconds. Add the 3 tablespoons olive oil and heat for an additional 10 seconds. Add the diced onions and sauté until they are soft and just lightly golden.

3. In a 2-quart bowl, add the ground chicken or turkey, the spices, and 1/2 cup of the chickpea flour. Add the onions and all of the oil from the pan to the bowl. Mix well with a fork at first and then with your fingers until all the ingredients are well combined. If the mixture is too moist, add some of the remaining chickpea flour. If the mixture is too dry, you can add a little bit of water.

4. Shape the mixture into balls about 1 inch in diameter. Place the balls in hot soup and simmer, covered, for 20 minutes or until they are done on the inside.

5. Serve with the soup or as a separate course with fresh herbs.

Yield: 8–10 servings

TINA'S TIDBITS

- *If you overwork ground meat by squeezing it a lot, you will toughen the meat, and ultimately your finished product will be tough and hard. Use a fork and then your fingertips to achieve a soft paste.*
- *Pamela Grau Twena's book,* The Sephardic Table, *suggests the nontraditional addition of cumin to the mixture, which tastes wonderful. She also recommends making enough to serve cold on Shabbat morning with pita and green vegetables.*
- *It is important to use toasted chickpea flour, which imparts a different taste and texture to the finished meatball than nontoasted chickpea flour.*

Sopa de Pollo con Albondigas (Chicken Soup with Meatballs)

I had the pleasure of meeting Anya Von Bremzen when she was in Dallas a few years ago. An accomplished travel and food writer, she, along with Penelope Casas, has enlightened the world to Spanish cuisine. The following is a variation of her recipe, adapted from The New Spanish Table, *that makes it easy to create a hearty soup in very little time.*

3 slices whole-wheat bread
½ cup water or chicken stock
1 large egg
½ teaspoon kosher salt
10 grindings of fresh white pepper or ⅛ teaspoon ground white pepper
10–15 grindings of fresh whole nutmeg or ⅛ teaspoon ground nutmeg
10 ounces ground turkey

⅓ cup all-purpose flour (approximately)
2 tablespoons extra virgin olive oil
Three 10.5-ounce cans of chicken broth concentrate or 64 ounces store-bought broth
7 tablespoons rice flour combined with ⅓ cup water or chicken stock
Chopped fresh chives or Italian flat leaf parsley for garnish (optional)

1. Remove and discard the crusts from the bread slices. Tear the bread into large pieces, and place in a small bowl containing ½ cup water or stock. Set aside for 5 minutes.

2. Whisk the egg in a medium bowl. Add all the spices and whisk to combine.

3. Gently squeeze the bread to remove the water, and place the bread in the bowl with the egg mixture. Stir to combine.

4. Add the ground turkey and gently mix with your fingertips until well combined. The mixture will be very loose.

5. Place the flour on a plate and drop teaspoon mounds of meat mixture onto the flour.

6. For each ball, lightly toss the meat in the flour, and then put the meat in your hand. Shake your hand with fingers slightly closed as if you were getting ready to roll dice. This method will lightly toss the meat in your hand and create a fairly uniform ball. Place the ball on the rim of the plate and proceed with the remaining meat.

7. Heat a large nonstick sauté pan over high heat for 15 seconds. Add oil and heat for 10 seconds.

8. Reduce the heat to moderate and add the meatballs. Shake the pan and gently turn the meat so that it is lightly golden on all sides.

9. Remove the meatballs from the pan and place on paper towels to absorb excess oil.

10. Meanwhile, reconstitute the canned broth and bring to a boil. Slowly whisk in the rice flour mixture and return to a boil. Cook until thickened, about 2 minutes. Add the meatballs and reheat. Serve with a garnish of chopped fresh chives or Italian flat leaf parsley.

Yield: 8 or more servings

TINA'S TIDBITS

- *Crusts of bread rarely soften the same as the interior bread and don't blend in as well. That is the main reason for slicing off the crusts.*
- *Good-quality canned or frozen chicken broth may be substituted for homemade, especially if other ingredients are added to enhance the flavor and texture of the broth. Make sure the broth is reconstituted if it is sold in concentrated form or it will have an overwhelming flavor and make your finished dish too salty.*
- *Ground turkey is moister than chicken and is readily available. If not, use ground chicken or grind your own in a processor work bowl. However, do not overprocess or meatballs will be tough when cooked.*

GREEK AVGOLEMONO SOUP

An extension of the agristada sauce, this soup is refreshing, with its lemon and dill. The use of oil points to the Jewish cook, because she had to devise a way to keep kosher and enjoy the foods of the land at the same time.

3 tablespoons extra virgin olive oil (preferably Greek oil)
1 large onion, cut into ¼-inch dice
8 cups chicken broth
½ cup long-grain rice
Salt and freshly ground black pepper, to taste

2–3 tablespoons fresh lemon juice
2 eggs
1 tablespoon chopped fresh dill
Sprig of dill for garnish (optional)
Zest of 1 lemon, cut into long, fine strips for garnish (optional)

1. Heat the oil in a 3-quart saucepan. Sauté the onions over moderate heat until soft and very lightly golden.

2. Add the chicken broth and bring to a boil. Add the rice.

3. Simmer the soup, covered, for 20 minutes or until the rice is tender. Season with salt and pepper to taste.

4. After the soup and rice are cooked, whisk the lemon juice with the eggs in a 1-quart bowl.

Whisking constantly, add ½ cup of the hot soup to the egg mixture to temper it.

5. With the soup on the lowest heat, add the lemon mixture slowly into the pot, whisking constantly until the mixture is thoroughly incorporated.

6. Add the chopped dill, and garnish with the thin strips of lemon zest and an additional sprig of dill.

Yield: 8–10 servings

TINA'S TIDBITS

- *Do not mix the egg yolk and lemon juice together if you are not prepared to finish the soup right away. The acid in the juice will curdle the egg yolk if they are combined for a long time.*
- *Adding some hot soup to the eggs before adding the eggs to the soup will temper the eggs and allow them to thicken the soup rather than seize and curdle and make the soup lumpy.*

Italian Stracciatella Soup

Stracciatella *means "little rags" in Italian, and it is descriptive of the egg-cheese mixture once it is cooked by the heat of the soup. Traditionally, the base of this soup is either chicken or beef broth. However, in order for the laws of kashrut to be observed, the broth needs to be pareve.*

2 eggs
2 tablespoons freshly grated parmesan cheese
2 tablespoons finely chopped fresh parsley
   (preferably Italian flat leaf)

Pinch of freshly ground nutmeg
Pinch of salt (optional)
1 quart high-quality imitation chicken broth or
   vegetable stock

1. In a small bowl, beat the eggs until they are just blended, and mix in the cheese, parsley, nutmeg, and salt.

2. Bring the stock to a bubbling boil in a heavy 2-quart saucepan.

3. Pour in the egg mixture, stirring gently and constantly with a whisk. Simmer for 2–3 minutes. The egg and cheese mixture will form tiny flakes in the stock.

4. Taste for seasoning. Ladle the soup into a tureen or individual soup bowls and serve at once.

Yield: 4 servings

TINA'S TIDBITS

- *There are many high-quality vegetarian "chicken" broths on the market today.*
- *Similar to egg drop soup, the cheese creates a more ragged appearance when it is melted in the egg mixture, and that's how it received its name.*

CHINESE HOT AND SOUR SOUP

Not exactly what you had in mind for Shabbat dinner? Well, the thousands of Jews who have lived in China over the last thirteen hundred years probably weren't eating kreplach soup. Actually they might have . . . and just called it "wonton soup"! Using chicken soup as the base, hot and sour soup is not only iconic for Chinese cuisine, but it is representative of China's contribution to the chicken soup category.

4 large dried shitake mushrooms
6 tree ear mushrooms
6 dried tiger lily buds, stem (hard end) removed
1 tablespoon oil
¼ pound finely julienned veal scaloppine
1 tablespoon light soy sauce
½ cup finely shredded bamboo shoots
5 cups chicken broth
Salt to taste

2–3 tablespoons Chinese black vinegar or red wine vinegar
1 teaspoon dark soy sauce
2 tablespoons cornstarch
3 tablespoons water
1 block firm white bean curd, cut into thin strips
1 tablespoon sesame seed oil
1 teaspoon freshly ground pepper
1 egg, slightly beaten
2 tablespoons chopped scallions

1. Place the black Chinese mushrooms, tree ears, and tiger lily buds in a glass bowl and cover with water. Microwave for 2 minutes, allow the dried vegetables to sit for 15 minutes or longer until soft, and drain.

2. Cut off and discard the stems of the mushrooms. Cut both the mushrooms and the tree ears into thin slices. With your fingers, shred the tiger lily buds, and if they are long, cut them in half.

3. Heat a wok or 3-quart saucepan for 20 seconds. Add the oil and heat for another 10 seconds. Add the julienned veal and stir-fry for 10 seconds. Add the light soy sauce and stir-fry for another 20 seconds or until the meat is about done.

4. Add the mushrooms, tree ears, tiger lily buds, and bamboo shoots. Stir-fry quickly for 30 seconds, and add the broth and salt to taste. Stir in the vinegar and dark soy sauce.

5. Combine the cornstarch and water, and stir into the simmering broth. When the mixture is slightly thickened, add the bean curd and bring to a boil.

6. Turn off the heat. Add the sesame seed oil and the pepper, and stir to blend.

7. Pour the soup into a hot tureen or keep it in the pot with the heat still turned off.

8. Add the lightly beaten egg in a steady stream as you slowly stir in a circular motion. Sprinkle with the scallions and serve at once.

Yield: 6 servings

TINA'S TIDBITS

- *The distinctive musty flavor of this soup comes from the tiger lily buds. These dried buds are from the tiger lily flower and are considered vegetarian and kosher.*
- *For an authentic taste, veal is the perfect substitute for pork in any Chinese dish. Similar in color and texture to pork, it does not alter the flavor or the look of the dish one iota.*
- *Cornstarch must be exposed to boiling liquid for it to thicken properly. If your soup doesn't look thick enough, combine another tablespoon of cornstarch with 2 tablespoons of cold water and stir it into the hot soup. The beauty of cornstarch is that it doesn't immediately swell and clump together when added to a hot liquid, so adjustments to the soup are easy to make.*

INDIAN MULLIGATAWNY SOUP

This soup hails from the Tamil region of southern India (the first Indian region inhabited by Jews). The name means "fire water," but this soup is not that spicy. It is loaded with flavor and packed with protein from the chicken as well as the chickpeas. It is very easy to make and fun to eat, especially if you serve it over rice, with peanuts, coconut, and raisins sprinkled on top.

One 3-pound chicken, cut up
6 cups chicken stock or water
1 onion stuck with 6 cloves
1 stalk of celery
1 carrot, coarsely chopped
1 bay leaf
2 sprigs of parsley
Salt to taste
15 whole peppercorns
1 cup packaged coconut
One 15-ounce can chickpeas, drained
6 tablespoons flour
1 tablespoon turmeric

½ teaspoon powdered ginger
1 tablespoon ground cumin
1 tablespoon ground coriander
⅛–¼ teaspoon cayenne pepper
4 tablespoons margarine
2 cloves garlic, minced
1 cup soy creamer or water
Salt and pepper to taste
Basmati rice (optional)
Coconut (optional)
Raisins (optional)
Peanuts (optional)

1. Cook the chicken in a 4-quart pot with the next 8 ingredients for 1 hour or until the chicken is tender. Strain the broth, and remove the skin and bones from the meat.

2. Put 2 cups of the strained broth into a blender and add the cup of packaged coconut. Blend until the coconut is pulverized. You have now created fresh coconut milk. Strain this coconut milk over a bowl through cheesecloth or a double-mesh strainer to remove all the solid particles of coconut. Throw away any coconut solids.

3. If the blender is gritty, rinse out the container. Add the coconut milk and chickpeas to the blender and blend until smooth.

4. Combine all of the dried spices with the flour in a small bowl. Set aside. Melt the margarine in a 3-quart saucepan. Whisk in the flour mixture and the garlic, and stir for 1 minute.

5. Whisk in the coconut milk mixture and the remaining broth until smooth and thickened.

6. Add the creamer (or water) and the chicken pieces, and season to taste with the salt and pepper. Serve.

Yield: 8 servings

TINA'S TIDBITS

- *To make this soup into a meal, place a scoop of cooked basmati rice (very fragrant rice) in the bottom of the soup bowl. Pour the soup over the rice, and pass dishes of the optional condiments for guests to sprinkle on top of their soup.*
- *Coconut milk is not milk at all but the white liquid derived from grinding coconut with water and then squeezing the pulp to extract as much flavor as possible.*

Tom Kah Gai
(Thai Chicken in Coconut Curry Soup with Rice Stick Noodles)

At present there are three hundred Jews living in Thailand, all in Bangkok. Although the first documented Jew in Thailand was in the early seventeenth century, the present Jewish community established its earliest roots in 1890 when the Rosenberg family migrated to Thailand and established modern hotels in the country. There are three synagogues in Bangkok—one Sephardic, one Ashkenazic, and a Chabad house that is frequented by thousands of Jewish tourists every year. This chicken soup-based Thai soup is my homage to the tolerant, accepting Thai people, who have always welcomed our people.

4–6 ounces *Chantaboon* noodles or any flat, wide, rice stick noodle
2 tablespoons peanut oil
4 cloves garlic, finely minced
1 scallion, finely minced
Two 3-inch pieces of dried lemongrass or 1 fresh stalk of lemongrass, cut into 4 pieces
$\frac{1}{4}$ teaspoon freshly ground black pepper
1 teaspoon Thai red curry paste
$\frac{1}{2}$ serrano pepper, seeded and chopped
4 Kaffir lime leaves

1 piece dried galangal root or $\frac{1}{2}$-inch slice of fresh ginger root
4 cups water
$\frac{1}{2}$ pound boneless chicken breast, sliced into $\frac{1}{4}$ × 3-inch pieces
2 tablespoons cornstarch
One 14-ounce can coconut milk
One 15-ounce can straw mushrooms, drained
2 tablespoons light soy sauce or *nam pla* fish sauce
Juice from $\frac{1}{2}$ lime
$\frac{1}{4}$ cup chopped fresh cilantro

1. Bring 3 quarts of water to a boil. Add the noodles and stir constantly for 1 minute to prevent sticking together. Drain in a colander and rinse with cold water. Set aside.

2. Heat a 4-quart saucepan or soup pot over high heat for 20 seconds. Add the oil and heat for another 20 seconds. Reduce the heat to medium high, and add the garlic, scallion, lemongrass, black pepper, curry paste, serrano pepper, Kaffir leaves, and galangal root. Stir-fry for 2 minutes, until the seasonings are fragrant. Add the water and bring to a boil.

3. Place the chicken in a small bowl and lightly toss with the cornstarch to coat well. Add the chicken to the pot of soup. Reduce the heat to medium and simmer the chicken in the soup for 4 minutes or until the meat is thoroughly cooked.

TINA'S TIDBITS

- *Most, if not all, of the ingredients are available in local supermarkets throughout the country.*
- *Read the (very) fine print on the Thai red curry paste jar. Although most jarred paste is pareve, some follow the original recipe and contain 5 percent shrimp paste.*
- *The Chantaboon noodles are very wide, flat noodles of irregular shape from the Chantaboon region. They have a tendency to curl up into cylinders. If you prefer, any width rice stick noodle may be used.*

4. Add the remaining ingredients **except** the cilantro and continue cooking for another 2 minutes.

5. Add the reserved noodles and simmer for 5 or more minutes until the noodles are thoroughly swollen and the soup is slightly reduced.

6. Serve in soup bowls garnished with some chopped cilantro.

Yield: 8 servings

KNISHES, *BOREKAS*, AND FILLED PASTRIES

Little "pies" of dough filled with meat, cheese, or vegetables are ubiquitous in every region of the Jewish Diaspora. I think that this genre of food is illustrative of the history of the Jews. With the laws of kashrut and Shabbat dictating what ingredients could be used and what time was appropriate to cook the food, little

packets of food encased in dough could be made in advance and served at will. To those dictates add the extra burden of poverty and long hard toil in the fields and one can see why a food that provides sustenance, is portable, and relies more heavily on vegetables than meat would be popular among the Jewish community. Add symbolism and superstition to the equation and you have the ultimate Jewish finger food.

The Radenites, ninth-century Jewish traders along the Silk Road, are thought to be the original importers of Asian pocket foods. With their rise in popularity in the West, many of these filled pastries took on folkloric meaning. Hamantaschen were symbolic of the hated enemy of the Persian Jews, and the actual consumption of the baked good was a metaphor for "devouring our enemies." Kreplach, originally worn around the neck as an amulet at the time of the New Year, might not ward off evil decrees, but the superstitious medieval German Jews weren't taking any chances and hoped that their well-being would be "sealed" for good in the coming year. Some pockets of dough were shaped in half moons to represent political regimes that were at times hated, and thus consumed like hamantaschen. One interpretation of triangular shaped pastries is that

the points represent the three Patriarchs, Abraham, Isaac, and Jacob. Many celebrations included filled pockets of dough to symbolize that God surrounds us and protects our goodness from evil.

In North America, we have been exposed to the many names and permutations of these dishes. Due to the largest migration of Jews to the United States at the beginning of the twentieth century, the cooking of Eastern European and Russian Jews has left the most indelible mark on our culinary memories. Dense crusty dough filled with potato, kasha, or liver is known by all Americans as a knish. Today knishes are four-inch square pillows of dough bursting with popular potato-onion filling. Long ago they were bite-sized morsels served as part of a Russian *zakuski* (appetizer plate) or served at special events like a bris (*b'rit milah*), bar mitzvah, or wedding. *Piroshkies* can be sweet or savory, fried or baked. The Polish immigrants called them pierogis, and these pastries were often boiled instead of fried or baked.

If Shakespeare's Juliet could fret about "What's in a name?" the same holds true for these treasures from the kitchen. *Boyos, borekas, borekitas, sambousak, buricche, pasteles,* pierogis, *pastelikos,* empanadas, kreplach, phyllos, *cigares, bulemas, briks,* samosas, or wonton—all have made their way into the Jewish kitchen, and all

LEFT: *Grandma Gussie's Potato Knishes, pages 360–61*

can be created with the use of modern equipment or with purchased prepared dough. They are similar and yet literally worlds apart.

Fillings can be meat, fish, vegetable, or cheese. They can be baked, fried, or sometimes boiled. The dough can use oil, butter, or animal fat (chicken, goose, or beef). They can be leavened by yeast, baking powder, or air, in the case of strudel or *pâte à choux* (cream puff paste). They can be shaped in rounds, squares, half-moons, crescents, tight cylinders, triangles, or conical with the top opened to the delight of the gastronome. Flavors can be mild or spicy, sweet or tart, flavored with herbs or spices. Each little pocket tells a story of persistence and success.

EASTERN EUROPEAN POTATO KNISHES

Not quite as heavy with crust as the commercial variety, here is one of many examples of the creative use of potatoes by the Jewish cook.

DOUGH:
2 cups all-purpose flour
1 teaspoon baking powder
½ teaspoon salt
2 tablespoons water
2 tablespoons vegetable oil
2 eggs, lightly beaten

FILLING:
2 large onions, diced
2 tablespoons rendered chicken fat or oil
2 pounds russet potatoes (approximately four 5-inch potatoes)
¼ cup chopped parsley
1 large egg
Salt and freshly ground black pepper to taste
1 egg yolk mixed with 1 teaspoon water for glaze

1. Combine the flour, baking powder, and salt in a medium bowl, and form a well in the center of the flour mixture. Combine the water, oil, and eggs, and pour into the well. Mix the ingredients together to form a smooth dough. Cover the dough and let it rest while you make the filling.

2. Slowly cook the onions in the chicken fat or oil in a covered skillet over a low heat for 10 minutes. Remove the cover and fry over medium heat until golden brown.

3. Meanwhile, peel the potatoes and cut them in quarters. Put them in a pot with cold salted water to cover the potatoes and bring to a boil. Cook the potatoes until tender, about 20 minutes. Drain and cool for 5 minutes.

4. Mash the potatoes and add the parsley, egg, salt and pepper, and the sautéed onions and oil and mix thoroughly. Adjust the seasonings if necessary.

5. Preheat the oven to 350°F. Divide the dough in half, and roll each half to ⅛-inch thickness in a rectangular shape. Spread some of the filling in a line about ½ inch in from the bottom edge. Fold over the dough and roll until all of the filling is covered. Wet the edge of the dough with a little water and seal the edges of the dough. Cut the filled dough away from the remaining dough. Repeat with the remaining dough and filling, and then repeat with the other half of the dough.

6. Cut the roll into 2-inch pieces and place them on a greased or parchment-lined cookie sheet.

7. Brush with the beaten egg yolk mixed with water, and bake for 15 minutes or until golden brown.

Yield: 2 dozen

TINA'S TIDBITS

- *Flour, eggs, onions, potatoes—the most exotic item in this recipe is parsley! You may, however, choose to add any additional ingredients; just make sure they are cooked, like mushrooms, or need no cooking, like chopped fresh dill.*
- *It is easier to roll out two large rectangles and create two or three rolls of filled dough from each piece of dough than to roll out six small rectangles and fill them individually.*
- *These may be made in advance and refrigerated or frozen after baking until ready to use.*

Grandma Gussie's Potato Knishes

In my family, knishes weren't the large, square, hard cushions of dough with potato on the inside. They were a soft patty of potato dough with fried onions encased in the center. No family function at my grandmother's house was without this treat, and you had to act fast or you didn't get to grab more than one. When she was recovering in the hospital from a heart attack, everyone centered their conversation on Grandma's knishes. Subliminally everyone knew that the precious recipe had not been written down. No one was able to comprehend "a bissel" (little) of this and "a shiterein" (handful) of that until one day I came across a recipe that reminded me of Grandma's knishes, and with a little tweaking, I now pass the recipe on to the next generation!

4½ cups dry mashed potato (no liquid or fat added)
3 eggs, lightly beaten with a fork
½ cup or more flour or matzah meal
¼ teaspoon freshly ground black pepper

3 teaspoons salt, divided use
¼ cup olive oil or chicken fat
3 large onions, finely diced
Additional olive or vegetable oil for frying knishes

1. Mix the potatoes, eggs, flour or matzah meal, pepper, and 2 teaspoons of salt together to form a smooth, but slightly sticky dough. Set aside for 20 minutes while you fry the onions.

2. Heat a 10-inch skillet over high heat for 20 seconds. Add the oil or chicken fat and heat for another 10 seconds, turning down the heat if the oil begins to smoke. Add the onions and sauté until the onions are dark golden brown but not burnt. Remove from the heat and stir in the remaining teaspoon of salt.

3. Heavily flour a board and your hands with flour or matzah meal. Take about 1 tablespoon of dough and, using your fingertips, flatten it in your palm or on the board until it is about a 2- to 3-inch circle. If dough is too sticky, roll in additional flour or matzah meal.

TINA'S TIDBITS

- *Cooked mashed potatoes tend to hydrate when they sit out for a long time. To prevent excess moisture, use within an hour of mashing or leave the potatoes whole until ready to proceed with a recipe.*
- *These knishes are perfect for Passover if you eliminate the flour. However, the dough will be smoother if flour is used.*
- *Matzah meal acts like a sponge, absorbing excess moisture in dough. To allow for this, the mixture must rest for 15-20 minutes before using.*
- *Sometimes tossing the dough very lightly on a floured board will make the dough less sticky and the process of shaping will be easier.*

4. Place a scant teaspoon of the onion mixture in the center of the circle, and fold the dough edges over the filling to meet in the center to create a smaller, filled circle of dough.

5. Place on a floured plate until ready to fry or fry immediately. **Note:** These should not stand too long or they will get soggy.

6. Heat a clean frying pan for 20 seconds. Add the additional oil to a depth of $1/4$ inch and heat for 15 more seconds.

7. Place the knish seam side (the side where the dough came together) down in the hot oil and fry over moderate heat for 4 minutes or until golden brown. Flip the knish over and fry until the other side is golden, about 2 minutes. Remove with a slotted spatula to paper towels to drain. Let cool for a minute or so.

8. Serve as soon as they are not too hot to handle. Enjoy!

Yield: 2–3 dozen

AUSTRIAN POTATO-MUSHROOM STRUDEL

Making strudel is much easier now that we have quality phyllo dough available in the supermarket. The lowly shtetl knish goes upscale with mushrooms, parsley, and Yukon Gold potatoes!

2 pounds Yukon Gold potatoes (approximately 4 potatoes)
½ ounce dried porcini mushrooms
4 ounces crimini or baby bella mushrooms
2 tablespoons vegetable oil
2 medium onions, diced
1½ teaspoons truffle-scented flour or all-purpose flour

2 tablespoons parsley
1 large egg, lightly beaten
1½ teaspoons salt
Freshly ground black pepper to taste
½ pound phyllo dough
1 stick unsalted butter, melted

1. Cook the whole, unpeeled potatoes in boiling salted water to cover for 25 minutes or until a knife easily pierces the potato. Drain and cool until easy to handle.

2. Place the porcini mushrooms in a 16-ounce bowl and cover with water. Microwave on high for 3 minutes. Allow the mushrooms to soak for 10 minutes or until soft. Gently squeeze some of the excess moisture out of the mushrooms and reserve the liquid for later. Chop the mushrooms into fine pieces. Set aside.

3. Chop the crimini or baby bella mushrooms into ¼-inch dice. Set aside.

4. Heat a 3-quart saucepan over high heat for 20 seconds. Add the oil and heat for 10 seconds. Add the diced onions and stir to coat with oil. Cover and cook over low heat for 10 minutes. Remove the cover and sauté over medium heat until golden brown.

5. Add the crimini or baby bella mushrooms to the onions and cook for 2 minutes. Add the chopped porcini mushrooms and ¼ cup of the soaking liquid. Be careful to remove the liquid from the top of the bowl to prevent inclusion of sediment from the bottom of the bowl. Cook for 2 minutes and add the flour. Stir to combine and cook for 1 minute more. Remove from the heat.

6. Peel the potatoes and mash until smooth. Add the onion-mushroom mixture, parsley, egg, salt, and pepper, and mix until thoroughly combined. Check for seasonings.

7. Place one sheet of phyllo dough, short side facing you, on a clean, large towel, and brush with some melted butter. Place a second sheet of dough to the right of the first but overlapping the first sheet by 2 inches. Brush the second sheet with butter.

8. Place a third sheet of dough directly below the first sheet but overlapping it by 2 inches. Brush with melted butter. Place the fourth sheet to the right of the third sheet, overlapping the bottom of the second sheet and the right side of the third. Brush with melted butter.

9. Place a 1-inch-thick line of the potato mixture 1 inch above the bottom of the dough and 2 inches in from each side. Brush the edges with some

butter. Fold the bottom up over the filling, and fold the sides in over the filling to conceal.

10. Tightly roll the dough up from the bottom, and place the log of strudel on a parchment-lined, rimmed cookie sheet. Brush the top with some melted butter.

11. Lightly score the dough in 1-inch intervals, and liberally sprinkle water all over the dough so that some of the water pools in the bottom of the pan.

12. Place in a 375°F oven and bake for 20 minutes or until the strudel is golden brown.

13. When ready to serve, cut the log into 1-inch pieces and serve.

Yield: 30 pieces

TINA'S TIDBITS

- *Oil or margarine can be used in place of butter to make this recipe pareve.*
- *Phyllo dough can be cut into 2-inch-wide strips, brushed with melted butter, and then folded like a flag into filled triangles.*
- *These knishes are delicious served with some sour cream to which some chopped chives have been added.*

TUNISIAN BRIKS

These wonderful pastries might be reminiscent of knishes, but they are literally worlds apart. Briks are the iconic street food of Tunisia. Street vendors sell these savory fried turnovers of dough filled with meat, fish, or vegetable stuffing all over Tunisia. Their popularity is similar to the sale of hot dogs in our country or falafel in Israel. Normally, briks are served with harissa, but here I have used some of the spicy relish to enhance the flavor of the sweet potato filling. In the sixteenth century, sweet potatoes were brought by the Portuguese from the New World to Africa, where they have been continuously cultivated to this day.

The following is a sweet potato adaptation of a brik *recipe from Pamela Grau Twena's book* The Sephardic Table.

1 tablespoon extra virgin olive oil
½ cup finely chopped onion
1 large clove garlic, finely minced
1 tablespoon finely chopped flat leaf parsley
1 medium sweet potato, about 8 ounces after cooking and peeling, preferably with pale flesh if available, or Yukon Gold potatoes

2 teaspoons harissa, or more to taste
1 egg, separated
Salt to taste
12–15 regular-sized (8-inch square) *lumpia* shells or thin spring roll skins
1 or more cups of vegetable oil for frying *briks*

1. Heat an 8-inch skillet over high heat for 20 seconds. Add olive oil and heat for 10 seconds more. Reduce the heat if the oil is smoking, and add the onion.

2. Sauté the onion until golden. Add the garlic and sauté another minute until the mixture is fragrant; do not let the garlic get too dark.

3. Remove the skillet with the onion mixture from the heat, and add the parsley and potato. Mash the potato well to mix all of the ingredients together. Add the harissa, egg yolk, and salt to taste, and stir to combine.

4. Combine the remaining egg white with 1 teaspoon of water.

5. Lay one *lumpia* shell or spring roll skin on a board or countertop. Place 1 heaping tablespoon of the potato mixture in the center. Using your finger, rub some egg white on the bottom and top edges of the shell or skin.

    (See next page.)

TINA'S TIDBITS

- *Burnt garlic will impart a bitter taste to food. Always add the garlic after the onions are golden to add flavor and prevent burning.*
- *Egg white cooks immediately when exposed to high heat. It is a perfect sealant for that reason and will not splatter in the hot oil the way pure water would.*
- *Crumpling paper towels provides a larger surface area to absorb oil from fried foods and makes the food less greasy.*
- *Although* briks *are meant to be eaten right after cooking, these are good warm or at room temperature. Reheat in a 425°F oven until crisp if you want to serve them hot.*

LEFT: *Tunisian Briks*

6. Fold the bottom edge over the filling, and lightly press down along the long edge. Do the same with the top edge, bringing it down to the long edge, creating a rectangle.

7. Rub some egg white on the left and right edges of the formed rectangle. Fold the right edge over the filled section and gently press down to seal the edge. Repeat with the left edge, creating a packet that looks almost square. Place seam side down on a plate while you form the other packets.

8. Pour the oil into a flat-bottomed wok or a small saucepan so that the oil is 1 inch deep.

9. Heat the oil to 350°F on a frying thermometer until hot but not smoking.

10. Place the packets, 2 or 3 at a time, into the hot oil, seam side down. Fry until lightly golden and the tops begin to puff up a little. Turn the *briks* over and fry just until lightly browned. Immediately remove from the oil with a wire spatula or slotted spoon.

11. Drain on crumpled paper towels and serve. Additional harissa may be used for a dip, if desired.

Yield: 12–15 servings

Indian Samosas

Is it possible that potatoes are the number-one culinary choice for stuffing, or does the choice of filling have more to do with the cost of food and being frugal? Whatever the answer, potatoes show up in India as well for wonderful little packets of spicy potato and pea filling. There is no need to make your own dough when wonton skins are readily available. Serve with some raw mango chutney.

2 tablespoons vegetable oil
1 teaspoon crushed red pepper
1 teaspoon chopped fresh ginger
1 teaspoon chopped fresh garlic
1 medium onion, cut into 1/4-inch dice
1/2 teaspoon salt

3 medium Yukon Gold, California whites, or russet potatoes, peeled and cut into 1/4-inch cubes
2 cups water
One 10-ounce package frozen peas, thawed
2 teaspoons curry powder
1/2 pound wonton skins
Oil for frying filled dough

1. Heat the 2 tablespoons oil in a large frying pan, and add the red pepper, ginger, garlic, and onion.

2. Sauté for 5 minutes or until the onion is golden. Do not burn the garlic.

3. Add the salt, potatoes, and water, and stir to combine. Cover and cook for 20 minutes over medium heat, until the potatoes are tender.

4. Add the peas and the curry powder, and cook until the peas are hot and any excess water is evaporated.

5. Brush the edges of the wonton skin with a little water. Place a teaspoon of the filling in the center and fold over into a triangle, sealing the edges well. Continue with the rest of the dough and filling.

6. Heat the oil to 375°F in a frying pan or wok to a depth of 2 inches. Do not let the oil smoke.

7. Fry a few samosas at a time in the hot oil until golden. Drain on paper towels and serve.

Yield: 1–2 dozen

TINA'S TIDBITS

- *Stir potato mixture occasionally, using a rubber spatula so that the potatoes don't break up. Yukon Golds or California long whites break up less than russet potatoes, which are the traditional choice.*
- *Do not use too much filling or the wontons will open in the hot oil and lose their contents.*
- *Use only enough water to dampen the edges so that they stick together. Too much water will cause steam when the samosas go into the oil and the wonton skins will open.*
- *Do not try to fry too many samosas at a time. If the samosas are not crowded when they are frying, the temperature of the oil won't drop and the dough won't absorb excess oil. The finished product will be light, crisp, and not greasy.*

Hungarian Mushroom Turnovers

Using dough similar to rugelach dough, these mushroom turnovers are rich and savory. You won't miss the cinnamon and sugar!

DOUGH:
4 ounces unsalted butter
4 ounces cream cheese
Pinch of salt
1 cup all-purpose flour

FILLING:
4 tablespoons butter
1 onion, finely chopped
1/2 pound fresh mushrooms
Salt and freshly ground pepper to taste
1/4 teaspoon nutmeg
1 tablespoon cream sherry
1 egg yolk mixed with 1 teaspoon water for glaze
Sesame seeds

1. Cream the 4 ounces of butter, cream cheese, and salt in a mixer at high speed until well combined, light, and fluffy.

2. Add the flour. Mix on medium speed only until the flour is incorporated and the mixture just begins to hold together. Divide the dough into 4 equal pieces, and form each piece into a ball, flatten to 1 inch, and refrigerate for 20–30 minutes.

3. While the dough is chilling, sauté the onion in the 4 tablespoons of butter until lightly golden.

4. Wash and pat dry the mushrooms and place them in a processor. Pulse the processor on and off until the mushrooms are in uniform, fine pieces.

5. Add the mushrooms to the onions and sauté until they give up their juices and begin to appear dry.

6. Add the seasonings and the sherry.

7. Roll a ball of dough 1/8-inch thick on a lightly floured surface and cut into approximately six 2-inch circles.

8. Place a teaspoon of filling in the center of each circle. Dip your finger in water and brush the edges of the circle with it. Fold the circle in half. Pinch the edges together and use the tines of a fork to crimp the edges. Place on an ungreased cookie sheet and proceed with the rest of the dough in the same manner.

9. Brush the tops of the turnovers with the egg yolk glaze and sprinkle with some sesame seeds. Bake at 400°F for 15 minutes or until light and golden. Serve hot. Freeze leftovers only after turnovers have completely cooled.

Yield: 2 dozen turnovers

TINA'S TIDBITS

- *Beating the cream cheese and butter together helps to thoroughly combine the two ingredients and incorporates air into the dough to help make it light and flaky.*

- *Although the ancient city of Byzantium (now Istanbul) adopted the crescent shape as its symbol to honor the goddess Diana long before the Ottoman Empire was established, the crescent remained a symbol of that empire and the present country of Turkey. Legend has it that in 1793 when the Austrians defeated the Ottoman advance into their country, they celebrated by making pastries in the shape of a crescent so that they could symbolically devour their enemy. Although the symbolism is long forgotten, many countries that bordered or were a part of the empire have crescent-shaped pastries in their repertoire.*

Boston Chremslach (Stuffed Matzah Balls)

These little balls or pancakes can be filled with fruits and cinnamon and sugar or with meats. They are perfect for dinners the rest of Passover.

DOUGH:
1 recipe for matzah balls, yours or a prepared mix
¼ teaspoon ground ginger

FILLING:
2 cups cooked meat, finely chopped (meat shreds from your sliced brisket are perfect!)

½ medium onion, finely grated
1 tablespoon chicken fat
Salt, pepper, and cinnamon to taste
3 quarts water with 2 good-quality chicken bouillon cubes
2 tablespoons oil or chicken fat for frying (optional)
1 onion, sliced (optional)

1. Make the dough for matzah balls, adding the ginger to the recipe, and set aside until ready to form the balls.

2. Combine the meat, grated onion, chicken fat, salt, pepper, and cinnamon for the filling.

3. Shape 2 tablespoons of the matzah ball mixture into a flat, thick disk.

4. Place a teaspoon of meat mixture into the center of the disk and pull up the sides of the dough over filling to shape the dough into a ball. Make sure no filling is exposed or it will open in the water. Repeat with the remaining dough and filling.

5. Combine the 3 quarts of water and two bouillon cubes in a large pot and bring to a boil.

6. Add the filled balls, cover the pot, reduce the heat, and simmer for 20 minutes.

7. To serve, fry the sliced onion in 2 tablespoons of oil or chicken fat and then lightly fry the cooked, stuffed matzah balls in the pan with the onions until golden. If necessary, more oil and more onion may be added to fry all of the stuffed matzah balls.

Yield: 12 servings

TINA'S TIDBITS

- Chremslach *are generally pancake-shaped and fried or baked. My version lets you use leftover matzah ball mixture and all the shreds from your sliced brisket!*
- *Leftover prepared matzah balls can be fried in a pan with the onions, too, and served with leftover meat and gravy days after the seder.*
- *Never lift the lid on the pot when the* chremslach *are boiling or they will shrink and be tough and raw on the inside. Boil for 20 minutes and* **don't peek!**

EASTERN EUROPEAN KREPLACH

The kreplach represent our fate being "sealed" for the coming year. They are often served in chicken soup on Rosh HaShanah or before sundown the evening Yom Kippur begins. Wonton dough makes it very easy to make kreplach, but they will be floppy and thin. Homemade dough or purchased ravioli dough will give the thickness reminiscent of your grandmother's.

½ pound homemade dough (see below), fresh ravioli
    dough, or wonton skins
2 cups cooked meat, finely chopped, or hamburger
    lightly sautéed
1 medium onion, finely chopped

1 teaspoon chicken fat
Salt and pepper to taste
1 egg, slightly beaten
Oil for frying (optional)

1. Cut the dough into 2-inch squares.

2. Combine the meat, onion, chicken fat, and seasonings in a small bowl. Beat the egg in a glass dish and add to the meat mixture. Add a little water to the dish used for the beaten egg.

3. Place a teaspoon of filling on each square.

4. Brush the top edges of the dough with the egg-water wash.

5. Fold the dough in half on the diagonal to make a triangle. Pinch the edges together to seal.

6. Cook in boiling salted water for 10 minutes or until done. Serve in the chicken soup or fry in a little oil.

KREPLACH DOUGH

2 large eggs
1 tablespoon olive oil
2 tablespoons ice water
2 cups bread flour

1. Place eggs in the food processor work bowl. Add the olive oil and the water and mix by turning the processor on and off twice.

2. Add 1 cup of the flour and turn the processor on for 5 seconds. Scrape the sides of the bowl.

3. Add the other cup of flour and process for 10 seconds longer. Dough will be crumbly. Pinch a little bit of dough; if it holds together it is ready to be rolled.

4. Remove the dough and divide it in half. Place it on a lightly floured surface, cover and let it rest for 10 minutes or longer if you are rolling the dough by hand.

Yield: 18 or more pieces

TINA'S TIDBITS

- *Pasta or pastry dough must be allowed to rest for at least 15 minutes after it is formed so that the gluten in the dough will relax and roll out easily without shrinking back.*
- *When slicing pot roast, shards of meat invariably fall off the slices. Although tempting to eat right then, these bits of meat make great filling for kreplach, knishes, or chremslach. Freeze the meat bits, and defrost them when you're ready to make kreplach.*
- *If you're purchasing pasta dough to make any filled pasta form, never buy sheets of lasagna noodles. They are too thick when folded over and will be quite chewy. On the other hand, maybe that's the way your bubbe made them!*
- *Salt should never be used in pasta dough, as it will toughen the dough and make it very difficult to roll out. Always add the salt to the water when cooking the filled dough.*

SPANISH SPINACH EMPANADAS

Empanadas are sealed pockets of dough filled with a myriad of fillings. Here we see the classic Jewish Sephardic filling using spinach, pine nuts, and raisins.

2 tablespoons raisins
¼ cup water
1½ tablespoons extra virgin olive oil
One 10-ounce package frozen chopped spinach, thawed and squeezed very dry
Salt and pepper to taste

3 anchovies, mashed, or 1 teaspoon anchovy paste
2 cloves garlic, finely minced
3 tablespoons pine nuts
1 package frozen puff pastry sheets (preferably one containing butter, but not necessary), thawed
1 egg mixed with 1 teaspoon water for glaze

1. To make the filling, cover the raisins with the water in a small bowl and microwave for 1 minute. Set aside and soak until needed.

2. Heat the oil in a skillet and sauté the spinach until it gives up its juices. Add the salt, pepper, anchovies or anchovy paste, and garlic and cook for a minute.

3. Drain the raisins and finely chop them with the pine nuts in a food processor or by hand. Stir into the spinach mixture.

4. Defrost the dough according to package directions. Roll the puff pastry out on a lightly floured surface to a thickness of ⅛ inch. Cut the dough into 2- to 3-inch circles. Lightly brush the edges of the circle with a little bit of the egg-water mixture.

5. Place a teaspoon of the filling on each dough circle and fold it in half. Seal the edges by crimping with the tines of a fork, and brush the top with the egg glaze.

6. Line a cookie sheet with parchment paper. Preheat oven to 350°F. Place the empanadas on the cookie sheet and then bake for 15 minutes or until golden. Serve hot or at room temperature.

Yield: 18 pieces

TINA'S TIDBITS

- *Ten ounces of frozen chopped spinach is equivalent to one pound of large leaf spinach before cleaning off the sand and removing the stems.*
- *To avoid having the spinach turn green-gray from long cooking, squeeze small amounts of the defrosted spinach in your hand until no liquid can be seen. This will let you sauté the ingredients fast without having to spend time sautéing, so the excess water in the vegetables evaporates.*
- *Egg is needed to seal puff pastry because the egg will cook and seal the dough when exposed to the heat in the oven, whereas water might just evaporate and then the puff pastry dough would open up, exposing the filling.*

French Stuffed Brie en Croûte

I used to make my own brioche dough to wrap Brie, and then I discovered that prepared frozen pastry sheets are much easier to use and available in supermarket freezers. There are no potatoes here as in so many other stuffed pastries, but I suppose sautéed slices of potato and onion with chives could taste great on the inside. Create your own filling, or use one of the recipes below.

One 14-ounce wheel of Brie cheese
One 10 × 10-inch sheet of prepared frozen puff pastry (half of 17.3-ounce package)

1 egg
1 tablespoon water

1. Thaw the sheet of dough for 30 minutes, and preheat the oven to 400°F. Prepare your choice of filling (see recipes below).

2. Roll out one sheet of dough into a 14 × 14-inch square. Combine the egg and water, and brush over the sheet of dough.

3. Evenly cut the Brie in half horizontally. Place one half of the cheese, cut side up, on the egg-brushed dough. Place filling over the cheese and top with the other half of the cheese, cut side down.

4. Fold up the sides of the dough over the cheese, brushing the dough with extra egg wash to "glue" the dough edges together and trimming any excess dough. Press the edges to seal. Flip the covered Brie over and place seam side down on a parchment-lined cookie sheet.

5. Brush the top and sides of the dough with the egg wash, and use any remaining dough to decorate the top. Brush decorations with egg wash as well.

6. Either freeze at this point for later gift giving, or bake in the preheated oven for 20 minutes or until golden brown. Allow the cheese to sit at least ½ hour before serving. Serve alone or with toasted French bread or crackers. Serves 12–15.

Apple-Cranberry Filling

⅓ cup sweetened dried cranberries
2 tablespoons orange juice
1 small Gala apple, peeled
1 teaspoon unsalted butter

1 tablespoon applejack or Grand Marnier
¼ teaspoon cinnamon
¼ cup chopped toasted pecans

1. Place the dried cranberries in the orange juice and microwave on high for 1 minute. Let the mixture rest while you prepare the rest of the filling.

2. Thinly slice the peeled apple, and sauté in a nonstick pan in the butter until slightly golden and soft. Add the soaking cranberries and the juice to the pan, and gently sauté until the juice is absorbed.

3. Add the applejack or Grand Marnier and the cinnamon. Reduce the mixture over high heat until the liquor is incorporated into the fruit. Add the chopped pecans, stir, and set aside while preparing the dough.

Mushroom-Chive Filling

½ tablespoon unsalted butter
1 clove garlic, finely minced
8 medium mushrooms, thinly sliced

Salt and freshly ground pepper to taste
1–2 tablespoons cream sherry
Six 8-inch stalks of fresh chives, finely chopped

1. Melt the butter in an 8-inch nonstick frying pan. Add the garlic and sauté over medium heat for 30 seconds or until the garlic is soft. **Do not brown** the garlic or it will be bitter.

2. Add the mushrooms and salt and pepper to taste, and sauté over medium heat until soft and lightly browned.

3. Add the cream sherry and increase the heat to incorporate the sherry and reduce the sauce to less than ½ tablespoon.

4. Turn off the heat and add the chopped fresh chives. Stir and set aside while you prepare the dough.

Yield: 25 servings

TINA'S TIDBITS

- *If you have leftover dough, you can patch it together, but you must keep the dough with its layers going in the same direction rather than just squeezing it into a ball. Once the dough is layered, it may be folded over and rolled out. This technique keeps the layers intact so the dough will puff up instead of spreading out in all directions.*
- *Fillings may be made in advance and refrigerated until ready to use.*
- *Each filling should be good for 2 to 3 small Brie. Use one and freeze the rest for a later date.*
- *Cut a decorative piece of dough for the top that will describe the filling inside.*

GREEK SPANAKOPITA

The best filling in my estimation. I used to make a thousand of these at a time for a large kosher caterer in Philadelphia. Worth the effort, I promise.

1 medium onion, finely diced
2 tablespoons unsalted butter
One 10-ounce package frozen chopped spinach, defrosted
½ pound feta cheese, crumbled
7.5 ounces farmer cheese (pot cheese)

3 eggs lightly beaten
Salt and freshly ground pepper to taste
Nutmeg, to taste
¼ cup dry bread crumbs, unseasoned
½ pound phyllo dough
¾ cup melted unsalted butter

1. Preheat the oven to 425°F.

2. Sauté the onion in the 2 tablespoons butter until golden. Squeeze out all of the excess moisture from the spinach. Add the spinach to the onions, and cook over low heat until most of the moisture has evaporated, stirring occasionally. Add the feta, farmer cheese, eggs, and seasonings and combine. Add the bread crumbs and cook, stirring constantly, for 3 minutes.

3. Cut through the roll of phyllo dough 2 inches from the end. Return the rest of the dough to its plastic sleeve and cover with plastic wrap and a damp towel. Unroll the cut phyllo and lay out 3 or 4 strips at a time. Cover the unused strips with plastic wrap and a damp towel to prevent them from drying out before using.

4. Brush the unrolled strips of dough with melted butter. Put 1 teaspoon of filling at the far right end of the strip. Fold the dough over the filling to form a right triangle. Continue folding the dough over and over to make a triangle (as if you were folding a flag). Make sure that one of the edges is always lined up with the top or bottom of the strip of dough.

5. Arrange the triangles on a baking sheet, seam side down, and brush with melted butter. Bake 15–20 minutes or until golden.

Yield: 5–6 dozen

TINA'S TIDBITS

- *May be frozen before or after baking.*
- *If freezing unbaked, do not brush with butter before freezing. Place foil between layers to prevent them from sticking together. Take them from the freezer and immediately proceed to step 5.*

Spinach and Cheese Filled Ravioli

Here, again, is the wonderful combination of spinach and cheese whose roots go back to Spain. The pasta dough is an easy, processor dough, and the filling could be poached in salted water without the dough. This is a modern dish called gnudi *(pronounced "nudey"), I guess because it is devoid of its pasta.*

FILLING:
One 10-ounce package frozen spinach
2 large eggs
¼ cup finally minced fresh parsley or 1 tablespoon dried
1 pound ricotta cheese, whole milk or part skim
¾ cup freshly grated parmesan cheese
2 teaspoons sugar
¼ teaspoon grated nutmeg

Salt and freshly ground black pepper to taste
Cornmeal for dusting

PASTA:
2 large eggs
1 tablespoon olive oil
2 tablespoons ice water
2 cups bread flour

1. To make the filling, thoroughly thaw the spinach and squeeze out all of the liquid. Add the remaining ingredients and mix thoroughly. Set aside while you make the pasta.

2. Place the eggs in the food processor work bowl. Add the olive oil and the water, and mix by turning the processor on and off twice.

3. Add 1 cup of the flour and turn the processor on for 5 seconds. Scrape the sides of the bowl.

4. Add the other cup of flour and process for 10 seconds longer. The dough will be crumbly. Pinch a little bit of dough; if it holds together, it is ready to be rolled. If it doesn't hold together then add water a teaspoon at a time to the dough while the processor is running.

5. Remove the dough and divide it in half. Place both halves on a lightly floured surface, cover them with an inverted bowl, and allow them to rest for 10 minutes or longer if you are rolling the dough by hand.

6. Prepare the pasta according to machine directions.

7. Fill the sheets of dough at intervals with a teaspoon of the filling.

8. Brush the area of dough around each filling mound with a little bit of water.

9. Cover the sheet with the filling with another sheet of dough, and press down with the sides of your pinkies around each mound of filling. Cut with a knife or fluted pastry cutter, or use a ravioli form and follow the manufacturer's directions.

10. As the ravioli are made, place them on a towel lightly sprinkled with cornmeal.

11. Bring a large pot of salted water to a boil and drop the ravioli in the pot. When the ravioli come to the surface, partially cover the pot and cook for 5 minutes or until done.

12. Serve with butter and parmesan cheese or casserole style with tomato sauce.

Yield: 4–6 servings

TINA'S TIDBITS

- *Bread flour has a higher gluten content than regular flour, so it mimics the semolina flour used in Italy.*
- *Italians always add a touch of sugar to counteract any bitterness that might be in the vegetable.*
- *Nutmeg should always be added in small quantity when working with cheese and/or spinach. It enhances the flavor of the filling. Don't use too much, however, or your ravioli will taste like egg nog!*

BULGARIAN POTATO-CHEESE BOREKAS

As one moves closer to the Ottoman Empire and the Middle East, the dough and choice of cheese change. The finished result is flavorful but slightly different from the Ashkenazic preparation.

DOUGH:
½ cup extra virgin olive oil
1 cup water
½ teaspoon salt
1 tablespoon sugar
2¼ cups all-purpose flour

FILLING:
1 cup mashed potato (½ pound potato cooked in salt water and mashed)
½ cup grated *Kashkavel*, Jarlsberg, or Gouda cheese
¾ cup crumbled feta cheese
⅛ teaspoon nutmeg (or 2 good pinches)
4 grindings of black pepper (or to taste)
1 egg mixed with 1 tablespoon water for glaze
Sesame seeds for topping

1. Place olive oil, water, salt, and sugar in a 2-quart saucepan and bring to a boil. Remove from heat.

2. Immediately add the flour and stir with a wooden spoon or rubber spatula until the flour is thoroughly combined with the liquid. Turn the dough out onto a board or countertop, and gently knead about 8–10 times until the mixture is a smooth ball of dough (be careful, the dough is hot!). Turn the empty saucepan over to cover the dough on the counter for 15 minutes or until the dough can be handled.

3. While the dough is cooling, combine all of the filling ingredients together in a bowl.

4. Preheat the oven to 400°F.

5. Roll the dough out on a board or counter (no need to flour) to ⅛-inch thickness. Cut into 2½-inch circles. Pat each circle with your fingertips to make the dough thinner and the circle slightly wider.

6. Place 1 teaspoon of filling in the center of each circle. Fold the dough over to make a semicircle. Touch your pinkies together to make an arch, and press the sides of your pinkies down around the edge of the dough to seal in the filling.

7. Place on a parchment-lined cookie sheet. Continue with the rest of the dough and filling (you might have some extra filling, which can be refrigerated or frozen for later use). Gently curve each *borekas* to make a crescent, and press the tines of a fork around the edges to seal. Brush with the egg mixture, and sprinkle with sesame seeds.

8. Bake for 18–20 minutes or until golden. Serve warm or at room temperature. May be frozen and reheated for 10 minutes at 350°F.

Yield: 2–3 dozen

TINA'S TIDBITS

- *The American palate is not familiar with the lower-salt, lower-sugar dough of Europe. Those ingredients may be adjusted to accommodate your preferences.*
- *Using the tines of a fork to crimp the edges of the dough not only provides a decorative accent, but actually seals the dough as well.*
- *No amount of egg wash or crimping will compensate for overfilling the pastry. The steam created by the filling when baked will push open the dough if too much filling is used in one crescent pastry.*

BOLEMAS WITH PUMPKIN-CHEESE STUFFING

Bolemas are small, snail-shaped filled pastries that are part of the Turkish culinary repertoire. Here the dough of choice is yeast dough. You may use your favorite yeast dough recipe; however, to save time, I use frozen bread or challah dough and it works beautifully.

1½ pounds frozen bread dough, rolls, or the equivalent of your favorite bread recipe
1 small pie pumpkin or 1 cup canned pumpkin puree
1 large egg
½ cup shredded Monterey Jack or Jarlsberg cheese
⅓ cup feta cheese, crumbled
1 tablespoon grated Asiago or Parmesan cheese

1 tablespoon sugar
½ teaspoon salt
¼ teaspoon cinnamon
1 tablespoon fine semolina flour or cream of wheat cereal
1 egg mixed with 1 teaspoon water for glaze

1. Thaw the bread dough or rolls, and divide into 24 equal pieces. If you're making your own bread dough, weigh the dough to find the right amount (1½ pounds will probably be half your recipe), and divide it into 24 pieces. Set it aside while you make the filling.

2. If you're using fresh pumpkin, bake the whole pumpkin on a rimmed cookie sheet in a 350°F oven for 45–60 minutes. When it's cool enough to handle, split it open, remove the seeds and stringy membrane, and scoop out the soft flesh. You will have more than you need for this recipe, but the rest can be refrigerated or frozen for later use.

3. Combine the filling ingredients and set aside.

4. Roll out each piece of dough on a lightly floured board to approximately 4 × 7 inches. Place 1 tablespoon of filling in the center of the long edge, and use your fingers to create a line of filling about ½ inch wide parallel to the long edge. Roll the dough up tightly like a jelly roll and then coil the roll, pinching the end of the dough under to secure it while baking. Place it on a parchment-lined cookie sheet, and repeat with the remaining dough and filling. Set aside to rise for 15 minutes.

5. Brush the tops of the coils with the egg wash and bake in a preheated 350°F oven for 20 minutes or until the rolls are nicely browned. Serve warm or at room temperature.

Yield: 24 bolemas

TINA'S TIDBITS

- *The filling is not sweet, like pumpkin pie. You may add a little more spice or sugar if you think it is warranted, but use caution because the feta and Jarlsberg are very strong in flavor.*
- *Semolina or cream of wheat absorbs the excess moisture in fillings and swells up. The quality of the dough is intact, and the filling is moist.*

THAI VEGETARIAN SPRING ROLLS

No frying or grease, just the fresh, clean tastes of green herbs and sweet vegetables to delight your guests.

1 teaspoon sugar
2 tablespoons soy sauce
Juice from 1½ limes (approximately 3 tablespoons)
2.25 ounces thin rice stick noodles (rice vermicelli)
1 large carrot, peeled
½ cup roasted peanuts or cashews
½ teaspoon crushed red pepper flakes
1 English seedless cucumber, about 1 pound, peeled
Bunch of fresh Thai basil or fresh mint
Bunch of fresh cilantro
¼ pound extra firm tofu (optional)
8 rice paper disks, about 8 inches in diameter

DIPPING SAUCE:
¼ cup chunky peanut butter
¼ cup hoisin sauce
¼ cup water
1 tablespoon Thai chili sauce with garlic or Thai sweet chili sauce
1 tablespoon vegetable oil
Additional water as needed

1. Combine the sugar, soy sauce, and lime juice in a small bowl and set aside.

2. Bring 2 quarts of salted water to a boil and add the rice noodles. Cook for 4 minutes or until noodles are very tender. Drain and rinse with cold water to stop the cooking. Drain and combine the cooked noodles with 2 tablespoons of the soy-lime mixture. Set aside.

3. Cut the carrot into 3-inch lengths. Using the finest grating disk on your processor, lay the carrot down in the feed tube and process. The finished result will be the finest julienne of carrot. Another way to do this is to draw a 5-hole zester in long strokes down the sides of the carrot.

4. Pulse the nuts in a processor work bowl until nuts are chopped small but still have a coarse texture. Combine the carrot with the nuts. Add the crushed pepper flakes and 1½ tablespoons of the soy-lime mixture and set aside.

5. Cut the cucumber into 3-inch lengths. Using a large grating disk in the processor, lay the cucumber lengthwise in the feed tube and process to get a medium to thin julienne. You can also do this by slicing the sections of cucumber lengthwise into a fine julienne. Toss the cucumber with the remaining soy-lime mixture and set aside.

6. Tear off about 48 small leaves of cilantro or tear larger leaves in half so you have about 48 pieces. (This may be done in advance to make assembly faster.) Prepare the Thai basil in the same way,

7. To assemble the spring rolls, fill a large pie plate or casserole with very warm tap water. Place a damp towel on your counter.

8. Place one rice paper disk in the warm water for about 20 seconds or until it is pliable. Remove to the damp towel. Sprinkle 6 basil or mint leaves and 6 cilantro leaves all over the wrapper.

9. Place 1 tablespoon of cucumber horizontally 2 inches from the bottom of the wrapper. Place 1 stick of tofu over that, if using.

10. Spread 1 tablespoon of the carrot mixture over the cucumber. Place approximately 2 tablespoons of noodles over the carrots.

11. Fold the bottom up over the filling. Fold in the left and right sides of the wrapper to enclose all of the filling. Starting from the bottom, tightly roll up the wrapper, and place the finished roll on a lightly greased platter or on a bed of lettuce leaves. Continue with the remaining wrappers.

12. Cover the rolls with plastic wrap and keep refrigerated until ready to serve. They will hold for a number of hours, but they get watery as they sit. They may be made 4–5 hours in advance.

13. To make the sauce, combine all of the ingredients by hand or in a small processor work bowl. Thin with additional water if needed.

Yield: 15 rolls

TINA'S TIDBITS

- *If all ingredients are prepared in advance, assembly is very easy. You could have your guests put their own together if the party is informal.*
- *Leftover dipping sauce can be tossed with pasta, cooked vegetables, and cooked chicken or fish for an easy meal.*
- *If there are any seeds in the cucumber, use the tip of a teaspoon and scrape them out before proceeding with the julienne.*
- *Rice paper gets its distinguishable design because it is made on bamboo woven mats and the design of the mat shows when it is dry.*

CHINESE DEEP-FRIED WONTON

Who knows which came first, the Russian and Middle Eastern Jewish traders bringing their kreplach and borekas to China or the Chinese teaching the Jews how to make wontons? It doesn't really matter—they are all delicious to eat.

2 tablespoons oil
½ pound ground veal
2 tablespoons light soy sauce
1 tablespoon cream sherry
½ teaspoon salt
6 canned whole water chestnuts, finely chopped

1 scallion, finely chopped
1 teaspoon cornstarch dissolved in 1 tablespoon water
½ pound prepared wonton skins
3 cups oil for frying
1 jar plum sauce

1. To prepare the filling, set a 12-inch wok over high heat for 30 seconds. Pour in the 2 tablespoons of oil, swirl it about in the pan, and heat for another 30 seconds. Turn the heat down if the oil begins to smoke.

2. Add the veal and stir-fry for 1 minute or until it loses its pink color.

3. Add the soy sauce, sherry, salt, water chestnuts, and scallions, and stir-fry for 1 minute.

4. Give the cornstarch mixture a stir to recombine, and pour it into the pan. Stir constantly until the mixture thickens. Transfer the contents to a bowl and cool to room temperature before assembling the wonton.

5. Lay a wonton square so that the point is on top and looks like a diamond. Place 1½ teaspoons filling on each wonton center.

6. Wet your finger with a little water, and brush the upper left and lower right edge with your wet finger.

TINA'S TIDBITS

- *Veal is a perfect substitute for pork. Its color, consistency, and flavor mimic those attributes of pork, allowing cooks to maintain the original flavor as well as the laws of kashrut.*
- *Because the filling is already cooked, all you need to do is focus on the color of the dough as it is frying. When golden, they are done!*
- *Crumpling up the paper towel creates more surface area for the oil to be absorbed.*
- *Because frying in deep oil often leaves those brown sticky lines all over the pan, it is advisable to keep one inexpensive steel wok on hand for frying in this manner. Woks are meant to be cleaned but left with that dark patina, so cleanup is much easier, with no hard scrubbing.*

7. Pretend that the diamond is like the points of a clock. Folding the dough in half, bring the point of dough at 6 o'clock up to just left of 12 o'clock. You now have a slightly off-center triangle. Wet the bottom left point of the dough with a little water.

8. Hold the bottom points in your left and right hands and pull down on the points so that the point in your right hand overlaps the wet point in your left hand. Pinch the dough together. Set aside while you fold the remaining wonton. This may be done an hour or so in advance. If the wontons have to sit longer, they should be covered with plastic wrap and refrigerated. Remove from the refrigerator at least ½ hour before cooking.

9. To cook, place 3 cups of oil in a deep fryer or a clean 12-inch wok and heat the oil until it registers 375°F on a frying thermometer.

10. Deep-fry the wontons 6 at a time until they are golden. Transfer to crumpled paper towels to drain while you fry the rest. Serve with plum sauce.

Note: Fried wontons can be kept warm for an hour or so in a 250°F oven or reheated for 5 minutes in a 450°F oven.

Yield: 2–3 dozen

GEFILTE FISH

Gefilte fish is so much a part of the Jewish culinary psyche that we take it for granted that everyone loves it and eats it. But you know that statement is false if you have ever invited a non-Jewish friend for a Passover seder (for that matter, it's not always popular with every Jew around the table either). Gefilte fish is often approached by the uninitiated in the same way as haggis or headcheese—hesitantly. This simple ball of ground fish says volumes about the medieval Jewish world, Jewish laws, and rabbinic interpretations of those laws.

Gefilte fish was created in late medieval Germany. The Mishnah reinforced the rule of no work on Shabbat by including the prohibition of removing any inedible parts of a mixture from our food. This would include the bones of a fish. To enable fish consumption on Shabbat, the raw fish meat was removed, the bones were discarded, and the fish meat was mixed with eggs and seasonings and stuffed back into the whole fish carcass to be cooked. *Gefullte* means "stuffed" in German!

Over time, the recipe for stuffed whole fish became one for balls of ground fish mixture poached in a large pot of fish heads and skin accompanied by some onion, celery, and carrot and then cooked for about 1½ hours until the smell in the house was definitely going to ward off Elijah when he came to the seder door! This process existed for the sole purpose of creating the jelly for the chilled fish. If you don't want the jelly, then gefilte fish is as easy to make as meatballs without the spaghetti!

Aside from the strong smell in the house, the worst aspect of making gefilte fish the "old" way is that coagulated blood from the bones (the brown scum on the broth's surface) and some of the fish scales would stick to the fish, and that wasn't pleasant.

The following recipes take you from the classic preparation to a modern interpretation without losing the gestalt of the dish but lessening the time and odor in the kitchen significantly.

LEFT: *Gefilte Fish and Horseradish Mold, page 385*

GEFILTE FISH AND HORSERADISH MOLD

*This could be the **only** time you will see flavored gelatin in one of my recipes! That said, an argument can be made for this easy, beautiful presentation. Making this recipe means you don't have to have those twenty glass plates with a leaf of lettuce, piece of carrot, and ball of gefilte fish precariously balancing on top of each other in your refrigerator taking up room. It also takes less time to serve, since it can be prepared on one platter that can be passed.*

One 3-ounce box of lemon gelatin
1 cup boiling water
1 cup fish broth from jar
One 6-ounce jar red horseradish, drained of excess
   liquid

1 or 2 jars gefilte fish
1 carrot for garnish (optional)
Scallion or chives for garnish (optional)

1. Remove gefilte fish from the jar, pat dry, and put in a large, shallow, slightly rimmed serving dish.

2. Place gelatin in a medium-sized bowl. Add boiling water and stir until dissolved. Add fish broth and horseradish, and stir until well blended.

3. Pour the liquid mixture around the gefilte fish pieces.

4. Slice the carrot into $\frac{1}{8}$-inch circles, and cut with a teeny flower-shaped cutter or with a knife to resemble a flower. Cook in boiling salted water until tender. Drain.

5. Cut thin curved slices from the green part of the scallion. Set aside.

6. Lightly dip the bottoms of the carrot flowers in some of the gelatin mixture and strategically place the carrot shapes on the gefilte fish pieces. Do the same with the curved slices of scallion to resemble the leaves. Chill and serve when firm.

Yield: 12 servings

TINA'S TIDBITS

- *Some prepared horseradish has such a high level of acid that it impedes the gelatin from setting completely. That's OK—just make sure that you arrange the gefilte fish and jelly in a rimmed platter and everything will still look and taste good.*
- *If you heat up the jelly in the jar until it is liquid, it will set the mixture better because the jelly is formed by the collagen in the fish bones and this will firm when chilled.*

GEFILTE FISH

Making gefilte fish is just like making chicken soup and meatballs, especially if you follow my recipe below. So don't be afraid to try it!

   Here's the classic preparation for you to "doctor" to fit your memories.

4 pounds whole fish (combination of carp, whitefish, pike, snapper, or sea trout)
2 carrots, cut into 1-inch lengths on a diagonal
2 stalks celery, cut into 2-inch lengths
1 pound yellow onions
1 bouquet garni (1 bay leaf, thyme, marjoram, and summer savory or parsley) wrapped in cheesecloth
2–3 quarts water

2 medium yellow onions
1 carrot
¼ cup very loosely packed fresh parsley
2 eggs
⅓ cup water
½ cup matzah meal
Salt and pepper to taste
Garlic, ginger, sugar, dill, or whatever your bubbe used to use (regional options)

1. Fillet the fish or have the store do it for you.

2. Rinse out the head of the fish and make sure that any bloody masses are removed. Soak all of the bones and the head in cold salted water to cover for 15 minutes or longer. Drain the bones and discard the water.

3. Place the bones and the head on the bottom of a large Dutch oven, and cover with the carrots, celery, and thinly sliced onion. Add the bouquet garni and the 2–3 quarts of water to cover, and simmer for 1–1½ hours. Strain the liquid, reserve the carrots, and set aside. Discard the bones and everything else.

4. To make the fish, grind the fish fillet twice in a grinder fitted with a fine blade or process in a food processor until a fairly smooth texture. Remove the fish to a large bowl.

5. Grind or process the onions, carrot, and parsley and add to the fish.

TINA'S TIDBITS

- *If you don't like the jelly with the fish, then you can skip the whole head and skin process! The collagen in the bone jells the liquid when it is chilled. The fish balls can be poached instead in salted water to which a little carrot, onion, and celery have been added.*
- *To grind fish in a processor, always use 1 pound of fish at a time, and always pulse (turn on and off rapidly) the machine so that you don't overgrind the fish and make it tough.*
- *Protein foods get tough when exposed to high temperatures, so keep the fish stock at a simmer when cooking the fish balls.*
- *When working with matzah meal, give the meal time to hydrate—absorb some of the moisture in the food—before you add additional matzah meal to your recipe.*
- *If you are using jarred gefilte fish, remove the liquid from the jar and reheat it with a fresh onion and cut-up carrot. When the liquid has cooled down, strain it into the jars with the gefilte fish. Add the carrot slices to the soup. This will make the broth, and subsequently the fish, taste more like homemade.*

6. Add the eggs, water, matzah meal, and salt and pepper, and mix well with a fork until light and fluffy. **Note:** To check for seasoning, cook 1 teaspoon of the fish mixture in salted water for 10 minutes. Taste and then adjust seasonings if necessary. Never taste freshwater fish raw.

7. Shape about 1/3 cup of the fish mixture in your hands to form ovals, and gently place in a frying pan to which 1 inch of prepared fish stock has been added. Poach, covered, for 20–30 minutes (depending on size) over low heat or until the center of a fish ball appears white. Drain on a cloth towel and cool in previously made fish broth. Serve with horseradish.

Yield: 8–10 pieces

ALGERIAN FISH TERRINE FOR PASSOVER

When I first came upon a variation of this recipe, I thought that it could definitely be an alternative to gefilte fish. And the fact that the hard-boiled eggs were in the loaf triggered elation that this might be the way to combine two Passover seder courses into one. But don't save it for Passover. Serve it at your next party.

1 carrot, peeled and coarsely chopped
1 stalk celery, cut into thirds
1 small onion, quartered
10 black peppercorns
2 cups water
2 cups dry white wine
2 pounds fish fillets (halibut, snapper, or tilapia)
2 large (3-inch) onions
2 roasted and peeled red bell peppers, jarred or fresh
$\frac{1}{2}$ teaspoon cinnamon
$\frac{1}{2}$ teaspoon nutmeg
Salt and freshly ground black pepper to taste
6 large eggs
$\frac{1}{2}$ cup matzah meal
Olive oil, for greasing the pan
3 peeled hard-boiled eggs
$\frac{1}{2}$ cup chopped Calamata olives

SAUCE:
$\frac{1}{2}$ cup mayonnaise
2 tablespoons ketchup
1 teaspoon prepared horseradish
1 or more teaspoons sweet vermouth or white wine for thinning sauce

1. Combine the first 6 ingredients in a large frying pan or a 3-quart saucepan. Bring to a boil. Reduce the heat and simmer for 20 minutes.

2. Strain the liquid and return the clear broth to the used pan. Bring the liquid to a simmer.

3. Rinse off the fillets and place them in the simmering broth. Cover the pan and cook the fish for 3–5 minutes or until the fish is cooked through.

4. Peel the onions and cut into quarters. Place them in a processor work bowl fitted with the metal blade. Pulse the machine on and off 20 times to create a coarse puree.

5. Rinse the red bell peppers and pat dry. Cut into eighths and add to the work bowl along with the cinnamon, nutmeg, salt, and pepper. Pulse on and off until the peppers are pureed. You may need to scrape down the sides of the bowl.

6. Drain the fish and add to the work bowl. Process until a smooth mass is formed.

7. Add the 6 raw eggs and the matzah meal, and turn the machine on long enough to incorporate all of the ingredients.

8. Lightly grease a loaf pan with some olive oil. Pour half of the fish mixture into the pan.

9. Using one of the hard-boiled eggs as your mold, make three indentations down the center of the fish mixture. Sprinkle $\frac{1}{2}$ of the chopped olives evenly into these indentations. Place the three hard-boiled eggs on top of the olives, and sprinkle the eggs with the remaining chopped olives.

10. Pour the remaining fish mixture into the loaf pan. Lightly press down on the mixture to thoroughly cover the eggs, and smooth out the top.

11. Place a paper towel in the bottom of a 13 × 9-inch pan. Set the loaf pan in the center, and pour hot water around the loaf pan to a depth of at least 1 inch.

12. Bake in a preheated 325°F oven for approximately 30 minutes or until the loaf is firm. Remove from the water bath. Cool to room temperature, and then cover and refrigerate until ready to serve.

13. To make the sauce, whisk the mayonnaise in a bowl until smooth. Add the ketchup and horseradish, and stir well. If necessary, add a small amount of sweet vermouth or wine to achieve the desired consistency.

14. To serve, remove the loaf from the pan, and slice into $\frac{1}{4}$- to $\frac{1}{2}$-inch slices. Drizzle a tablespoon or more of the sauce on a plate, and place the slice on top of the sauce.

Yield: 30 thin slices

TINA'S TIDBITS

- *Placing a paper towel in the bottom of your water bath will prevent the loaf pan or ramekins from sliding when you are removing the finished item from the hot oven.*
- *Small, individual servings can be made in 5- to 6-ounce ramekins using a few pieces of sliced egg in each ramekin instead of a whole egg.*
- *More matzah meal may be added to the mixture if you want a firmer loaf. However, make sure you allow some time for the matzah meal to hydrate before you bake the loaf.*

QUENELLES

Quenelles are to gefilte fish what mousse is to a candy bar. These are light, delicate morsels of fish and cream that deserve to be tried at least once in your life. They are not necessarily appropriate for a seder unless yours is a small, dairy affair, but basically the same concept of ground fish poached in liquid. Enjoy!

1 pound fresh halibut, sea bass, or cod fillet
1 teaspoon salt
Freshly ground pepper to taste
⅛ teaspoon ground nutmeg
1½ cups heavy cream
1 egg
3 tablespoons unsalted butter
1 small shallot, finely minced
3 tablespoons flour

Salt and freshly ground pepper to taste
Big pinch of nutmeg
1 sprig of fresh thyme or lemon thyme
1 cup court bouillon (see recipe on following page) or fish stock
1 cup half and half cream
⅓ cup freshly grated Gruyère or Emmenthaler cheese
¼ cup freshly grated Parmesan cheese
Additional Parmesan cheese for topping

1. Cut the fish fillets into cubes and place in a processor work bowl with the salt, pepper, and nutmeg. Process the fish for 30 seconds or until the metal blade has finely chopped the fish. Scrape down the sides of the work bowl, and pulse on and off a few more times until the mixture is fine.

2. With the processor running, slowly pour the heavy cream into the work bowl until all of the cream is incorporated. Stop and add the egg. Pulse 3 or 4 times to incorporate the egg completely. Transfer the mixture to a metal bowl, and place in the freezer for approximately 30 minutes until very cold but not frozen.

3. While the fish mixture is chilling, prepare the béchamel for the sauce. In a 2-quart saucepan, melt the butter and sauté the shallot for 3 minutes or until soft. Add the flour, salt, pepper, and nutmeg, and whisk for a minute to lightly toast the flour.

4. Whisk constantly as you add the court bouillon and the cream to prevent lumps. Continue stirring until the mixture is smooth and thick, about 4 minutes.

5. Strain the sauce into a 1-quart saucepan and add the cheeses. Stir over low heat until the cheeses are melted and the mixture is smooth. Turn off the heat, but keep warm until ready to use.

6. Bring a 5-quart saucepan filled with salted water to a boil. Keep the water at a low simmer while you make the quenelles.

7. To shape the quenelles, have two oval-shaped soup spoons and a glass of cold water available. Dip one spoon in the cold water, and scoop up some of the fish mixture. Dip the other spoon into the water, and shape the fish into an oval. Gently slide the quenelle into the water, and rapidly shape another fish oval. Cook 3–5 quenelles at a time in a covered pot for 2–3 minutes. Drain on paper towels, and place in a single layer in a buttered gratin dish or low-sided glass casserole. Continue with the remaining fish mixture until all the quenelles are prepared.

8. When all the quenelles have been poached, pour the reserved sauce over them and sprinkle with additional Parmesan cheese. Bake uncovered in a 425°F oven for 10 minutes. Transfer the pan to the broiler, and broil until the dish begins to lightly brown and appears to bubble on the sides, about 2 minutes. Serve immediately.

Note: The dish can be assembled up to 8 hours in advance and refrigerated. Remove from the refrigerator 1/2 hour before serving and then proceed with the baking in step 8.

COURT BOUILLON

1 carrot
1 onion
1/2 stalk of celery
1 bay leaf
1/2 teaspoon fennel seed

8 peppercorns
1 teaspoon salt (optional)
2 cups white wine
2 cups water

1. Chop the carrot, onion, and celery into coarse pieces.

2. Mix the vegetables with the remaining ingredients in a saucepan and cook at a simmer for 15–20 minutes. Strain the liquid and put it in a large frying pan or a fish poacher. Bring the poaching liquid to a boil. Proceed to poach the fish or poultry as directed in the specific recipe.

Yield: 4 servings

TINA'S TIDBITS

- *Court bouillon can be used for poaching chicken or fish. After using, strain the liquid, mark whether it was for chicken or fish, and freeze the stock for future use.*
- *Salmon imparts a strong flavor to the stock. Do not reuse the stock unless it is for salmon.*

EGGPLANT

*T*he migration of the cultivation and consumption of eggplant over the last four thousand years began in the Southeast Asian region of India and Burma. The plant was introduced to the Chinese about fifteen hundred years ago. Both societies relished (not to pun) eggplant, which is a fruit, not a vegetable.

By the fourth century c.e., the consumption of eggplant in all forms followed the path of the Silk Road from China to the Near East, and eggplant dishes became popular throughout the Middle East and especially in Egypt and Turkey. In 711 c.e., the Moors conquered Spain and introduced eggplant to that region. Many believed that the fruit of the eggplant was an aphrodisiac, and it was called *berenganas*, "apple of love," in Spain.

When the Jews residing in Spanish territories, including Sicily, were expelled during the Inquisition, they brought their culinary expertise and fondness for eggplant to the mainland Italian states. Eating eggplant became associated with the Jews, and it was over a hundred years after their arrival before Italians would begin to eat the fruit. Italians and northern Europeans were very hesitant to eat this exotic food, grown and eaten by Jews, because it was a member of the nightshade family and they thought consuming the fruit would make you go mad. Even before the influx of Spanish-Jewish immigrants to Italy, Europeans were referring to eggplant as *mala insana*, "crazy spirit," and eggplants were called "crazy apples" throughout Europe until the mid-seventeenth century. What this means is that most traditional Italian eggplant dishes originated in Jewish kitchens!

By the sixteenth century, eggplant was widely popular in Mediterranean and southern European countries.

Eggplants come in many shapes and colors, although dark purple is the color we generally associate with the fruit. When brown and white varieties were grown in Europe, the eggplant gained more popularity. As a matter of fact, the English first saw the small, white, egg-shaped variety and coined the name "eggplant."

Eggplant made the journey across the Atlantic in the mid-seventeenth century when Spaniards (or more likely Jews fleeing continued persecution) brought the plant to Brazil, and it was Thomas Jefferson who introduced the new colonies to this plant in 1806. In the United States, eggplant was used mostly as an ornament and did not gain popularity until the 1950s.

All of the following selections are listed geographically from their origin of cultivation through the routes of the Diaspora. They make excellent appetizers served with sliced pita triangles, naan bread, or crackers. Placed in a lettuce cup and garnished with a radish rose, as my mother often did, these eggplant salads make a perfect light first course to a meal.

❧ Buying Eggplant ☙

When buying eggplant, look for smooth, shiny skins with no brown spots, bruises, or indentations. Wrinkled, dull skin is a sign of age and will guarantee a bitter, spongy fruit. Smaller eggplants have fewer seeds and thinner skins—two parts of the plant that can make the cooked eggplant taste bitter. Eggplants are very perishable, so when you purchase them make sure they are very fresh. When you press your finger lightly against the skin, it should leave a subtle imprint. If the eggplant doesn't "give" at all under light pressure, it is underripe and will be bitter. If it gives too much, it is old and overripe and will not have a pleasant taste. Because of its perishability, eggplant should be cooked within 4 days of purchase and should not be stored in the cold part of your refrigerator.

Many recipes call for salting the eggplant for a half hour to remove excess water and bitterness. As it turns out, today's varieties do not require this step if they are fresh. Very large, hence old, eggplants might benefit from peeling, as much of the bitterness comes from just under the thick skin layer.

If you want to remove some of the moisture so that the eggplant doesn't sponge up oil during frying, you might try microwaving the eggplant slices on high for 4 minutes and then blotting away the excess water with paper towels before you proceed with your favorite recipe.

Because its cooked consistency resembles meat, eggplant is often used in vegetarian dishes. For the kosher cook, substituting eggplant for meat opens the door to many new recipes that normally would not be considered kosher because of the use of dairy products and meat products in the same dish.

Although the prime time to buy eggplant is August and September, eggplant is available all year round, and now might be a great time to start exploring its many uses in your favorite recipes.

Cooking Whole Eggplant

My grandmother, as well as many older cooks, used to roast their eggplants right on the top of a gas stove. I presume that either their culinary skills were great enough to know when to turn the eggplant so that no part of the skin would ever split and ooze out the eggplant's juices or they just didn't care if the stove top got messy and cleaned it up right away. In either case, the modern cook can replicate the results of stove-top broiling in an outdoor grill or in the oven. Either way, the method is easy as long as you don't get distracted and forget that the eggplant is roasting to a charred crisp inside and out!

To Grill Outside

Turn your grill on 15 minutes before using. Place the washed (don't forget to remove paper label if it is stuck to the eggplant) whole eggplant on the grill over medium-high heat, and close the lid (this also helps enhance the eggplant's smoky taste). Turn the eggplant after 10 minutes to the opposite side. Cover the grill and continue grilling for another 10 minutes. Check the eggplant and turn it on a third side if it doesn't look blackened. The goal is to have the eggplant nicely charred (can even be crisp in places) and completely deflated. If you think it needs a little more time, then lower the flame a little and let the eggplant cook another 5–10 minutes.

Remove the eggplant to a large bowl or colander, and slit the skin open on one side from near the stem all the way to the bottom. This will allow the bitter juices to run out and make your dish taste better. When cool enough to handle, peel off and discard the skin and stem, place the pulp and the seeds in a clean bowl, and proceed with your favorite recipe.

To Roast in an Oven

Preheat an oven to 425°F. Place the eggplant on a foil-lined cookie sheet that has sides (to catch any juices that might drip out). Prick the eggplant on one side with a fork to allow the steam to escape and prevent the eggplant from exploding all over your oven! Roast for about 30 minutes, turning the eggplant every 10 minutes so that all sides get exposed to the heat. The skin will appear wrinkly but might not be charred, since you are not using the broiler elements on top. When the eggplant feels soft and deflated, it is cooked. Remove it from the oven. Slit the eggplant open on one side, from stem to base, and let it drain, either in the pan or in a bowl until cool. When it is cool enough to handle, peel off and discard the skin and stem, place the pulp and the seeds in a clean bowl, and proceed with your favorite recipe.

CAPONATA

When the Jews were expelled from Spain in 1492, there were forty thousand Jews on the island of Sicily, a Spanish territory at the time. The Jews left the island with the culinary traditions of their ancestors steeped in Moorish customs. The people of northern Italy were not accustomed to eggplant. They were fearful of this fruit, which they thought had the power to make you go mad, and they also viewed eggplant as "Jew food." As a result any old eggplant dish from Italy had its roots in a Jewish kitchen.

One of the most popular Italian eggplant dishes is caponata, an eggplant relish so ubiquitous that it can be found in cans on our own supermarket shelves. Caponata is actually a Jewish Sabbath dish. The vinegar and sugar preserve the mixture so that it can be made in advance of Shabbat and served at room temperature for the s'udah sh'lishit meal Saturday afternoon.

2 eggplants, 8 inches long
1¼ cups olive oil
2 large onions, cut into ½-inch dice
One 6-ounce can tomato paste
1 ounce drained capers

2 tablespoons sugar
¼ cup red wine vinegar
1 large clove garlic, minced
Salt and pepper to taste

1. Wash the eggplants, cut off the ends, and cut into ½-inch cubes.

2. Heat a 4-quart pot for 20 seconds. Add the oil and heat for another 10 seconds. Add the eggplant cubes and fry in the oil until the cubes are soft and particles on the bottom of the pan are golden. The eggplant will absorb the oil at first and then the oil will be released. Remove the eggplant cubes with a slotted spoon and place them in a bowl. Leave the remaining oil in the pot.

3. Add the onions to the pot and fry until slightly golden and soft.

4. Return the eggplant to the pot, and add the remaining ingredients. Cook for 20 minutes over low heat, until the flavors are well blended. Stir occasionally.

5. Serve warm, at room temperature, or cold. The caponata lasts for weeks in the refrigerator and always tastes better the longer it sits.

Yield: 10 or more servings

TINA'S TIDBITS

- *Eggplant soaks up a lot of oil but will release it once it starts to cook. The best way to prevent excess absorption is to make sure the oil is very hot but not smoking.*
- *Do not cut eggplant too small or it will disintegrate. However, if you cut eggplant too thick for this recipe or for recipes that call for whole slices, the eggplant won't cook evenly and you will get undercooked eggplant that is spongy and tasteless.*
- *After the caponata is made and refrigerated, excess oil can be blotted off the top by using a paper towel.*
- *As long as a thin film of oil is covering the top of the food, this dish will last weeks or longer in the refrigerator. Oil keeps out the air that would allow bacteria to grow.*

Patragel

Every family function at my Romanian grandmother's home began with this dish, and my mother often started our dinner with a plate of lettuce topped with a scoop of patragel, *topped with a green pepper ring and a radish rose. This is my family's transliteration of her name for the dish. It is called* patlican *in Turkey; similar spellings exist throughout that part of the world. This is as simple as it gets!*

1 large eggplant
1 or more cloves of garlic, finely minced
Salt and freshly ground black pepper

1 or more tablespoons extra virgin olive oil
1 teaspoon sugar or to taste (optional)

1. Roast eggplant over a flame or in a 350°F oven until all sides of the eggplant are slightly charred and the eggplant is deflated, about 30 minutes.

2. Slit the sides of the eggplant and let it drain in a colander until cool.

3. Scoop out the eggplant pulp, and whip in the garlic, seasonings, and olive oil until smooth but not oily. Add sugar if desired. Serve with pita or crackers.

Yield: 4 servings

TINA'S TIDBITS

- *The "or more" of garlic in the recipe is there not to scare the faint of heart; Romanians eat **lots** of garlic on their food and often sweeten their dishes, even if it has an abundance of garlic in it.*
- *"Russian caviar" is basically this recipe with finely chopped onion and bell pepper in it; leave out the sugar, please!*

EGGPLANT SALAD WITH PINE NUTS KIOUPIA

The island of Rhodes had a good-sized Jewish population before the Nazi occupation. Today there are very few Jewish families residing there, but one of the synagogues is still open for visitors, and it contains the nerot tamid, *"eternal lights," from all of the destroyed synagogues on the island.*

On a recent visit I drove four miles inland to a restaurant called Kioupia. Here we ate in a farmhouse courtyard, surrounded by whitewashed terraced walls whose ledges housed hundreds of votive candles twinkling in the night air, as we ate a twenty-five-course meal of assorted little mezes. Their eggplant dish was reminiscent of my Romanian grandmother's, but there was an added ingredient. I was informed that it was yogurt. Here is my version of that wonderful eggplant dip. Drizzle it with a little extra olive oil and serve it with some Greek olives and feta cheese and you could make it a meal.

2 large eggplants (about 2 pounds)
2 tablespoons extra virgin Greek olive oil
Juice of 1 small lemon
2 cloves of garlic, chopped

¼ cup Greek yogurt
Salt and freshly ground black pepper
2 tablespoons pine nuts

1. Wash the whole eggplants and pierce with a small, sharp knife in one or two places.

2. Place the eggplants on a rimmed cookie sheet and broil under the broiler in the oven or cook directly on an outdoor grill, turning every 10 minutes, until the eggplants are deflated and their skins are charred.

3. Remove the eggplants to a colander placed in the sink, and slit the skins open. Allow the eggplants to drain for at least 10 minutes or until they are cool enough to handle. If there is a large clump of seeds, remove some of it (you don't have to get all of them), and discard the stem and the skin. Place the pulp of the eggplant into a processor work bowl.

4. Add the olive oil, lemon juice, and garlic to the eggplant, and pulse on and off 7 times until the mixture is fairly smooth but still a little chunky. Pour the mixture into a bowl.

5. Whisk the Greek yogurt and salt and pepper into the mixture. Add more olive oil or lemon juice if the mixture appears too dry. Adjust the seasoning if necessary.

6. Toast the pine nuts on a cookie sheet in a 350°F oven for 5 minutes or until lightly golden. Do not burn.

7. Just before serving, fold the toasted nuts into the eggplant, reserving a few to garnish. Serve at room temperature or cold with crackers or wedges of pita.

Yield: 6–8 servings

TINA'S TIDBITS

- *Greek yogurt has the consistency of sour cream, and even the fat-free variety tastes richer than most sour creams on the market. Domestic yogurt is not as thick. It can be squeezed in some cheesecloth, but it won't have the same consistency. It is easier to just locate some good Greek or Bulgarian yogurt.*
- *Greek olive oil is pressed from Calamata olives and has a distinctive, slightly stronger flavor than Italian olive oil. Extra virgin olive oil of any variety should be used for a clean taste and a higher smoking point.*
- ***Never*** *use lemon juice from a bottle. It is not "real" in taste because of all the preservatives added to it.*
- *Lemons will give off more juice if they are stored at room temperature.*

Imam Bayaldi

One of the most famous Turkish dishes, the name says it all. Translated it means "the imam fainted." Small eggplants are slit, stuffed with sautéed onion, tomato, and spices, and slowly cooked in a lemon and olive oil sauce until the eggplants have absorbed most of the sauce and are luscious and soft. Some say this dish got its name because the dish is so wonderful; others suggest the great amount of oil used in the recipe caused the imam to assess the expense of this dish, which overwhelmed him, and he fainted. You be the judge.

10 small, round eggplants (2–3 ounces each)
2 quarts salted water for soaking eggplant, or enough to cover
$\frac{1}{3}$ cup extra virgin olive oil

FILLING:
2 tablespoons extra virgin olive oil
1 large onion, thinly sliced in semicircles (about 3 cups)
4 large cloves of garlic, finely minced (about 2 tablespoon)
One 14.5-ounce can diced tomatoes, drained
One 5.5-ounce can tomato juice (about $\frac{3}{4}$ cup)
Juice of $\frac{1}{2}$ medium lemon
Kosher salt and freshly ground black pepper
1 tablespoon sugar, or to taste

1. Remove the leaves around the stem of the eggplant, keeping the stem attached.

2. Using a bar zester or vegetable peeler, cut away 4 strips of peel from around the eggplant to create a striped effect. Cut a slit down the middle from the stem to the bottom, being careful not to cut completely through to the other side. Place in the bowl of salted water.

3. When all of the eggplants are in the bowl of salted water, let them soak for 10 minutes. Drain and pat dry.

4. Heat a 10-inch frying pan for 20 seconds. Add the $\frac{1}{3}$ cup olive oil and heat for another 10 seconds. Add all of the eggplants and cook over low heat for 5 minutes, turning occasionally to cook all sides.

TINA'S TIDBITS

- *Small baby eggplants are hard to find outside of Asian markets. However, small Italian eggplants can be used in the same manner. Portion size will be slightly larger but not significantly.*
- *When a recipe calls for sliced onions, it never means onion rings. Slice the onion in half from top to bottom, and then thinly slice with the grain (top to root end) or across to create half moons.*
- *A bar zester has a little notch on one side to deeply peel one strip of lemon for a "twist." This notch will also give you uniform lines on the eggplant.*
- *To avoid burning garlic and destroying the subtle flavor of the filling, add garlic to the pan when more moisture has accumulated from the onions. This will allow the flavors to meld without jeopardizing the garlic's flavor.*

5. Set the pan with the eggplant aside to cool while you make the filling.

6. To make the filling, heat a 10-inch skillet for 20 seconds over high heat, and add the remaining 2 tablespoons of olive oil. Heat the oil for 10 seconds, and add the sliced onions.

7. Sauté the onions over low heat for 7 minutes or until soft and very lightly golden. Add the garlic and sauté for 1 minute. Add the drained diced tomatoes and cook for 2 minutes. Set aside.

8. Fill each eggplant with some of the onion mixture and return to the oily pan in which they were fried, cut side up.

9. Combine the remaining ingredients and pour around the eggplant. Cover and simmer for 30 minutes or until the eggplants are soft to the touch but still hold their shape. Baste with the tomato-oil mixture. If there is too much sauce, simmer uncovered until the sauce is reduced.

10. Transfer the cooked eggplants and their liquid to a shallow-rimmed serving dish and cool to room temperature. Serve.

Note: Eggplants may be refrigerated for a few days for later use, but bring to room temperature before serving.

Yield: 5–10 servings

CHEESECAKE

The cheesecakes Judith fed to Holofernes bore no resemblance to the modern-day icon of Jewish cuisine. Her cakes were salty, to induce a thirst for wine and an eventual drunken stupor; these cheesecakes just induce high cholesterol!

For centuries Jews produced all the dairy products they needed. The family cow provided the milk products needed to produce cheese, cream, and butter, and ultimately her supervised slaughter could take care of the meat needs. She could be considered a walking cheesecake factory.

We don't need to have a cow in our backyard to provide us with the provisions to make a great cheesecake, just good recipes.

ITALIAN CHEESECAKE

It is rare that we can re-create a food memory from our childhood. Time and experience color our thoughts and palate. However, I was able to re-create the delicious, light cheesecake from Debold's Bakery in Hempstead, New York. They might not have considered it Italian, but with the ricotta instead of cream cheese and sour cream, it definitely hails from close to the Mediterranean.

CRUST:
1 cup plus 2 tablespoons flour
3 tablespoons sugar
6 tablespoons unsalted butter
1 egg
1/2 teaspoon vanilla

FILLING:
1 pound ricotta cheese
1/2 pound cream cheese
3 tablespoons flour
1/2 teaspoon salt
1 teaspoon vanilla
Grated zest of 1/2 lemon
2 eggs
4 egg whites
3/4 cup sugar
3/4 cup crushed pineapple, drained

1. Preheat the oven to 300°F, and butter the bottom and sides of a 10-inch springform pan.

2. Place the flour and sugar in a processor and pulse on and off to combine. Cut the butter into 6 pieces and add to the work bowl. Pulse the machine until the mixture looks like coarse meal.

3. Combine the egg and vanilla in a small dish, and add it to the work bowl with the processor running. As soon as a ball of dough begins to form, stop the processor and remove the dough.

4. Roll the dough 1/4 inch thick between two sheets of plastic wrap or wax paper, and using the bottom of the pan as a pattern, cut out a 10-inch circle. Place the dough in the pan, prick it all over with a fork, and bake for 15 minutes. Cool.

5. Drain the ricotta, and place the 2 cheeses in the processor work bowl and process until the mixture is smooth. Add the flour, salt, vanilla, lemon zest, and 2 eggs, and process until smooth. Pour into a bowl.

6. In another bowl, beat the egg whites with the sugar until stiff, but shiny. Fold into the cheese mixture.

7. Spread the drained, crushed pineapple over the crust, and gently pour the cheese mixture over the pineapple. Bake for 45 minutes or until the cake is fairly set. Cool and serve.

Yield: 8–10 servings

TINA'S TIDBITS

- *The crust for this cake is a murbeteig, or German short crust. A firm cookie dough is needed so that the pineapple doesn't dissolve it during baking.*
- *Use whole-milk ricotta for a rich taste and lower water content.*
- *If cream cheese is at room temperature, it will blend well with other ingredients and no lumps will be apparent.*
- *Creating a meringue before adding to the cheese mixture not only incorporates air into the mixture but also ensures that the sugar will be completely dissolved.*

RICH SOUR CREAM CHEESECAKE

It doesn't get much richer than this! Firm but light because there is less cheese and more eggs and sour cream, this is a dessert to make any person living within the Pale feel rich!

CRUST:
10 double crackers of graham crackers (1 paper packet), broken in pieces
1/4 cup sugar
4 tablespoons unsalted butter

TOPPING:
16 ounces cream cheese
1 cup sugar
5 large eggs, separated
1 teaspoon vanilla extract
2 teaspoons lemon juice
1 pint sour cream

1. Place the broken pieces of graham crackers in a processor work bowl with the 1/4 cup sugar. Pulse the machine on and off until the crackers are completely pulverized.

2. Add the butter and pulse on and off again until the butter is incorporated. Butter the sides of a 10-inch springform pan, and press the crumb mixture into the bottom of the pan, reserving 1/2 cup of crumbs for later.

3. Bake in a preheated 400°F oven for 8 minutes or until lightly golden. Set aside.

4. Reduce the oven temperature to 300°F.

5. In a clean processor work bowl, combine the cheese and the sugar until smooth. You might have to stop and scrape down the sides of the bowl once. Add the egg yolks and process for 5 seconds or until combined.

6. Add the vanilla, lemon juice, and sour cream and pulse for 20 seconds or until the mixture is very smooth. Pour the mixture into a 2-quart bowl.

7. Using a handheld mixer, beat the egg whites until firm peaks form. Stir 1/2 cup of these whites into the cream cheese to "lighten" the mixture a little. Add the remaining egg whites and fold gently but swiftly to produce a lighter but not streaked mix.

8. Pour the batter into the prepared pan with the crust. Smooth out the top and bake for 1 hour. Turn off the oven, but keep the cake in the oven for another 1/2 hour. Open the oven door and let the cake cool in the oven for an hour or so.

9. Run a sharp knife along the edge of the pan and remove the springform sides. Gently press the reserved crumbs around the side of the cake. Refrigerate until serving. Serve plain or with a fruit topping of your choice.

Yield: 10–12 servings

TINA'S TIDBITS

- *Low heat and little air in the batter will do the most for preventing cracks in a cheesecake.*
- *The cake might seem a little soft at first, but it will firm up when cold.*
- *Eggs act like flour in this cake; they bind the ingredients together.*

NEW YORK STYLE CHEESECAKE

As much as I love my childhood Italian cheesecake, nothing sends me into rapture more than an ultrasmooth, ultrarich New York style cheesecake. I want it so smooth that you would be tempted to spread it on a bagel if it wasn't so rich and sweet. Here is my version, which I taught so long ago that I found it in my files printed in dot matrix!

CRUST:
1 cup flour
¼ cup sugar
1 teaspoon finely grated lemon zest
1 stick cold unsalted butter
¼ teaspoon vanilla extract
1 egg yolk

FILLING:
24 ounces good-quality, full-fat cream cheese
¾ cup sugar
Finely grated zest of ½ orange
Finely grated zest of 1 small lemon
1 teaspoon vanilla
3 eggs plus 2 egg yolks
¼ cup heavy cream

1. Place the flour, sugar, and teaspoon of lemon zest in a processor work bowl and pulse on and off 3 times to combine.

2. Cut the butter into 8 pieces and distribute in the work bowl. Pulse the machine for 5 seconds or until the mixture looks like coarse meal.

3. Combine the egg yolk and the vanilla and add to the work bowl while the processor is running. Mix only until the dough begins to clump together and starts to form a ball. Refrigerate for 15 minutes or longer, if necessary.

4. Preheat the oven to 400°F.

5. Pat the chilled dough over the bottom and 2 inches up the sides of a 9-inch springform pan. Bake for 10 minutes in the preheated 400°F oven. Cool while you make the filling.

6. Reduce the oven temperature to 275°F.

7. Using an electric mixer, beat the cream cheese until it is very smooth with no lumps. Scrape down the sides of the bowl if necessary. Add the sugar slowly and mix well to incorporate.

8. Add the remaining ingredients to the work bowl and mix thoroughly.

9. Pour the cheese mixture into the springform pan with the partially baked crust. Lightly tap the pan on the counter to bring any trapped air to the surface.

10. Bake the cake for 1 hour. Cool thoroughly before refrigerating or covering with a topping. Keep chilled in the refrigerator until ready to serve.

Yield: 12–15 servings

TINA'S TIDBITS

- *Processors generate a lot of heat, so it is best to have your butter cold when making dough.*
- *Never let the dough form a ball. At that stage, the gluten has been activated, and the dough could be tough and hard to roll.*
- *When egg or egg yolk is the only liquid except flavoring, make sure that the two ingredients are combined first so that they will be uniformly distributed without overworking the dough.*
- *Cream cheese must be smooth before other ingredients are added or the mixture will retain any lumps.*

CANNOLI CHEESECAKE

I developed this cheesecake after making mini cannoli for a Rosh HaShanah open house. With so much filling left over, I decided to transform the leftovers into a cheesecake. This is slightly grainy because it is based on ricotta and not cream cheese, but if you like cannoli you will be very happy with this alternative. Obviously, if you do not have any store-bought shells at your disposal, you can use one of the previous crust recipes for your base.

CRUST:
4 ounces of prepared cannoli shells (about 12 mini shells)
4 tablespoons unsalted butter
½ cup sugar
¼ teaspoon cinnamon

FILLING:
3 large eggs
1 cup sugar
1 teaspoon vanilla
5 cups leftover prepared cannoli filling (see recipe below)

1. Preheat the oven to 350°F.

2. Combine the cannoli shells with the butter, sugar, and cinnamon in a small processor work bowl and process until fine crumbs.

3. Press the crumbs into the bottom of one 9-inch springform pan or five 4½-inch mini springform pans. Place the prepared pans on a rimmed cookie sheet.

4. Bake the crust for 10 minutes at 350°F. Remove from the oven while preparing the filling.

5. Combine the eggs, sugar, and vanilla with a wire whisk. Add the cannoli filling and blend well.

6. Pour the filling into the prepared pan and place in the oven. Immediately reduce the temperature to 300°F and bake for 50 minutes or until the mixture is set but not dry.

7. Cool and then refrigerate until serving.

CANNOLI FILLING

1½ pounds whole-milk ricotta
8 ounces cream cheese, softened
1 tablespoon vanilla extract
1½ cups confectioners' sugar

½ teaspoon cinnamon
¾ cup mini chocolate chips
¼ cup finely chopped candied citron (optional)

1. Place the ricotta and the softened cream cheese in a large mixing bowl and beat with an electric mixer until smooth.

2. Add the vanilla, confectioners' sugar, and cinnamon and beat until the sugar is dissolved and the filling is smooth. Add the chocolate chips and the citron if using and stir by hand to combine.

Yield: 10–12 servings

TINA'S TIDBITS

- *To make the cake more dense, drain the ricotta cheese in a sieve or cheesecloth to extract some of the excess moisture.*
- *Confectioners' sugar is 3% cornstarch, which helps absorb excess moisture in the ricotta as well.*
- *To achieve a smoother cake consistency, do not add chocolate chips and citron to the batter; sprinkle the mini chips and citron over the top of the cake right after it is removed from the oven.*

Praline Cheesecake

Many years ago I freelanced for the largest kosher catering company in Philadelphia. I was asked to make sixteen of my praline cheesecakes for a bar mitzvah. Commercial mixers are identical to stand mixers in a home kitchen, just bigger. They also "attack" in the same way if you are not careful. When I added four dozen eggs to the cream cheese in the bowl and turned the mixer on, two eggs shot out into the room in opposite directions and they splattered on the floor fifteen feet away! The mixer does an excellent job of combining ingredients, but you need to turn the machine on slowly or you could repeat my performance. Here's the recipe I used that day, but only for one cake!

CRUST:
1 cup graham cracker crumbs
$\frac{1}{4}$ cup finely ground pecans
3 tablespoons sugar
$\frac{1}{2}$ stick unsalted butter

FILLING:
24 ounces cream cheese (3 packs)
$1\frac{1}{4}$ cups dark brown sugar
1 tablespoon cornstarch
3 large eggs
2 teaspoons vanilla
$\frac{1}{4}$ teaspoon cinnamon
Pure maple syrup
2 tablespoons large pecan halves, lightly toasted in the oven (at 350°F) for 4 minutes

1. Preheat the oven to 325°F.

2. Combine the crust ingredients in a bowl and work the mixture into a dough with your fingertips. Pat this dough into the bottom of a 9- or 10-inch springform pan. Bake for 6–8 minutes and remove from the oven.

3. In a processor work bowl, combine the cream cheese and sugar and pulse until the sugar is mixed in well and the cream cheese is smooth. Scrape down the sides of the bowl.

4. Add the cornstarch, eggs, vanilla, and cinnamon, and when the mixture is smooth, pour into the prepared crust.

5. Gently tap the cake pan on the counter to remove any excess air. Place the pan in the middle of the oven and bake for 40–50 minutes. Remove from the oven and let the cake cool completely.

6. Run a knife around the sides of the cake before removing the springform. Brush 1–2 tablespoons of pure maple syrup over the top of the cake, and place the toasted pecan halves in a decorative pattern on top. Chill before serving.

Yield: 8–10 servings

TINA'S TIDBITS

- *The shape of the springform pan sometimes leaves a depression in the cheesecake running parallel to the sides of the pan. This actually looks attractive and provides a rim for any topping you might add.*
- *If the top cracks, use the pecans to creatively cover those cracks with an interesting design. No one will know.*
- *Toasting nuts brings out their flavor, so it is an especially good idea to toast the pecans so that their rich flavor will complement the strong maple flavor of the syrup.*

CHAROSET

The Passover seder begins with the description of the items on the seder plate, and the anticipation mounts to the time in the "order" of this ceremony when participants will be eating their Hillel sandwich of matzah and bitter herbs. The first bite is plain and hot, but then they get a chance to eat those little shards of matzah with something special: the mixture called *charoset*, symbolizing the mortar that was used by the Jewish slaves in Egypt to hold the pyramid stones together.

What are the requirements for making *charoset*? Nothing, except a desire to have it look dark and muddy like cement. Any special ingredients? None, but creative cooks have always managed to find something indigenous to the area where they live to create this symbol. Whether a lumpy mixture of fresh and dried fruit, a smooth paste, a liquid, or a firm ball, charoset is an expression of the diversity of Jewish cultural backgrounds tied together by the single root planted firmly in the story of continuity and survival.

The following is a small sampling of *charoset* recipes from throughout the Diaspora, representing the bounty of the lands of their origin.

ASHKENAZIC CHAROSET

My job when I was a child was to chop the charoset *in the wooden bowl with a mezzaluna that looked more like a handheld guillotine than a moon-shaped chopper. Making the mixture gray to represent the mortar that was used to hold the bricks of the pyramids together was no problem, since it took a long time to chop the apples and they oxidized during the process.*

Before food processors the task was arduous, but the mixture held together while still being a little lumpy. Today, using the processor, the charoset *can be as smooth as paste, if you want it to be that way.*

Here is the classic Ashkenazic charoset *made in the United States over the last century.*

2 McIntosh apples, peeled and cored
1 cup walnut pieces
1½ teaspoons cinnamon or to taste

Sweet Concord grape or Malaga Passover wine
Matzah meal, if necessary

1. Combine the apples and walnuts in a wooden bowl, and chop to a fine consistency with a curved chopper or mezzaluna.

2. Add the cinnamon and wine to bind, and set aside, covered, in a glass bowl in the refrigerator until ready to use.

3. If the apples give up a great deal of juice, add a few tablespoons of matzah meal to bind the mixture together. Don't add too much matzah meal, as it swells and the mixture could become too thick.

Yield: 1½ cups

TINA'S TIDBITS

- *Since walnuts and soft McIntosh apples were most abundant in the states with the most Jewish immigrants, these ingredients were most often called for in printed recipes.*
- *The sweet wine most associated with Jewish ritual was a result of the availability of tart grapes that could only be made palatable by adding copious amounts of sugar to them while making the wine.*
- *Matzah meal can absorb excess liquid in the* charoset. *Use a little at a time because it will take about 15 minutes for the liquid to absorb, and if you add too much, you will have a dry mass that tastes like matzah instead of apples.*

TRADITIONAL CHAROSET TEXAS STYLE

For over twenty years our family has been spending the first night of Passover at the Friedlanders' home. Lynn is a native Texan with Ashkenazic roots. How does this lineage manifest itself in her charoset? The basic Ashkenazic formula is augmented with native Texas pecans and sugar. Migration changes recipes to conform to what is readily available . . .

8–10 sweet apples (Fuji, Gala, Honeycrisp, or Jonagold)
8–10 ounces pecans, toasted

1 tablespoon cinnamon, or to taste
⅓ cup sugar, or to taste
1 cup sweet Concord grape Passover wine

1. Peel, core, and cut the apples into 8 pieces.

2. Place ½ of the apples in a processor work bowl and pulse until the pieces are about ¼ inch. Remove to a large glass bowl, and repeat with the remaining apples.

3. Toast the pecans at 350°F for 5 minutes. Cool slightly and add them to the work bowl. Pulse the machine on and off until the pecans are finely chopped. Add the pecans to the apples.

4. Add the cinnamon and sugar to the apple mixture and stir to combine.

5. Add the wine and mix well.

6. Cover and refrigerate at least overnight, but preferably 1–2 days.

7. If the mixture is watery, drain off the excess liquid and adjust the cinnamon, sugar, and wine as desired.

Yield: About 1½ quarts

TINA'S TIDBIT

- *The choice of nut used in making charoset has more to do with availability than anything else. Walnuts were readily available in eastern Europe and parts of the Middle East; Texas has an abundance of pecans. Necessity opens the door to creativity. In this case there is no bitterness in pecans as there is in walnuts and the resulting mixture has a much sweeter, more well-rounded flavor.*

JAROSET
(PANAMANIAN HALEK)

This recipe comes from Rita Sasso, a Panamanian whose roots go back to Spain via Amsterdam and Curaçao, which had a significant Jewish population in the seventeenth and eighteenth centuries. Rita and I became pen pals when I published a recipe in my Reform Judaism *column that was given to me by a friend in Mexico. She recognized the recipe as her own. We have shared recipes ever since, and here is one she gave me with her permission to publish.*

4 ounces dried figs
4 ounces raisins
4 ounces prunes
4 ounces pitted dates
1½ cups peanut butter or almond butter

2–3 cups brown sugar, according to taste
½ cup sweet Passover wine, as needed
Cinnamon, enough to cover the balls of *charoset*
   (approximately 1½ ounces)

1. Place the dried fruits in a processor work bowl and process until a relatively smooth paste is formed.

2. Add the peanut butter and brown sugar to the processor work bowl and pulse on and off a few times to begin to combine the ingredients. The machine will only begin the process, as the mixture will be thick.

3. Remove the mixture to a bowl, and continue to combine the ingredients, kneading with your hands.

4. Little by little add the wine to the mixture until you obtain a firm ball of fruit. This mixture will be quite sticky. If necessary, refrigerate for ½ hour until the mixture firms up a little.

5. Wet your hands periodically with cold water and form small balls of *charoset* about the size of a small walnut.

6. Place the balls on a parchment-lined cookie sheet and put them in the freezer until frozen.

7. Once the balls are hard, you can remove them to a freezer bag until needed.

8. Just before serving, defrost and roll each ball in cinnamon. Serve.

Yield: 4 dozen balls

TINA'S TIDBITS

- *Do not double this recipe unless you have a very large food processor or the mixture will be too difficult to combine thoroughly.*
- *Because of the strong Sephardic influence in Central America, peanuts are often found in foods for Passover. Observant Ashkenazic Jews will not eat peanuts during Passover so almond butter makes a good substitute in this recipe.*

Garosa
(Charoset from Curaçao)

Here's a recipe from modern-day Curaçao, whose Jewish roots go back over four hundred years.

2 ounces pitted dates, preferably Medjool
2 ounces pitted prunes
2 ounces dark raisins
2 ounces dried figs
2 cups unsalted peanuts
½ cup cashew nuts
Grated zest from 1 medium lemon

½ cup dark brown sugar
2 tablespoons honey
2 teaspoons cinnamon plus additional for coating
1–2 tablespoons sweet Passover wine
1 tablespoon orange juice
1 teaspoon lemon juice

1. Combine the dates, prunes, raisins, figs, peanuts, and cashews in a processor work bowl and pulse on and off until the contents are fairly small.

2. Add the zest and the remaining ingredients, and continue to process until the mixture is moist and relatively smooth and firm.

3. Roll the mixture into 1-inch balls, and roll each ball in cinnamon to coat well. Place in 1 layer on a flat plate until ready to serve.

Yield: 15–20 balls

TINA'S TIDBITS

- *One of the noticeable differences between Eastern European* charoset *and Middle Eastern or Sephardic* charoset *is that in the latter, the basis for the mixture is dried fruit, using what grew abundantly all around the Jews.*
- *Probably because the dried fruit is so sticky, most* charoset *from the Mediterranean are shaped into balls.*

ITALIAN CHAROSET

This recipe really tells a story. The Ottoman influence is seen with the dates, walnuts, and spices. The apples represent the immigrants from the north of Italy. The citrus fruits signal the presence of Jews in the citrus industry in Italy, and the cocoa and vanilla have to come from the Jewish traders who lived in South and Central America and traded with their brethren in Italy. The fact that this recipe, adapted from Edda Servi Machlin, incorporates the use of the processor shows that our traditions continue to adapt to the times and equipment readily available to us.

½ pound pitted dates
½ pound walnuts
3 large apples, peeled and cored
1 large whole seedless orange, washed and cut into
    chunks
3 large ripe bananas
⅓ cup sweet wine

½ teaspoon cinnamon
⅛ teaspoon cloves
1 tablespoon lemon juice
Matzah meal as needed
¼ cup unsweetened cocoa
¼ cup vanilla-flavored sugar

1. Place the dates, walnuts, apples, and orange chunks in a processor and process until very fine. Spoon into a medium bowl.

2. Peel and mash the bananas, and add to the other mixture in the bowl.

3. Add the wine, spices, and lemon juice and mix well. If the mixture is too moist or soft, then add a few tablespoons of matzah meal to the fruit mixture. Wait 10 minutes before proceeding so that the matzah meal can hydrate and absorb any excess moisture.

4. Mix together the cocoa and sugar.

5. Make little balls out of the paste, and roll them in the cocoa-sugar mixture.

Yield: 3–4 dozen balls

TINA'S TIDBIT

- *Because cocoa will hydrate easily, make the paste balls in advance, and roll them in the cocoa just before serving.*

Rhodesian Charoset

On the island of Rhodes, the charoset exemplifies its place in the Eastern Mediterranean by the use of only oranges and dates as the base, augmented with the spices from the nearby spice trade route and almonds. The addition of Concord grape wine (a wine commercially made only in the northeastern United States) shows the migration of the tradition across the Atlantic.

1 medium orange
Zest of ½ medium orange
18 pitted large dates, preferably Medjool
½ cup honey

½ teaspoon ground cinnamon
¼ teaspoon ground cloves
¼ cup sweet Concord grape Passover wine
⅓ cup toasted, finely chopped almonds

1. Zest half of the orange and put the peel in a processor work bowl.

2. Cut off the top and the bottom of the orange to reveal the fruit inside. Starting from the top, place your knife just under the peel and cut it away, following the curve of the orange. The first slice is the hardest, and then you can easily see how deep to cut to remove the peel without cutting into the fruit.

3. Cut the orange into 3 or 4 slices crosswise and place in the processor work bowl with the zest.

4. Pit the dates if necessary and add to the orange pieces. Process the mixture until a fairly smooth paste is formed.

5. Scrape the mixture into a 2-quart saucepan. Add the honey to the pot and cook over medium-low heat until the mixture thickens and the bubbles are so thick they can hardly come up through the paste. This will take about 10 minutes. Stir often to prevent scorching.

6. Remove from the heat and add the spices and wine. Stir over low heat until all the ingredients are well combined and the mixture begins to thicken again.

7. Remove from the heat, stir in the toasted finely chopped almonds, and place in a bowl. Cover and refrigerate for at least a few hours or longer to allow the flavors to meld.

Yield: 1½ cups

TINA'S TIDBIT

- *This recipe uses heat to reduce the liquid content of the* charoset *rather than adding matzah meal, which has only been in existence commercially for the last 150-plus years.*

Israeli Charoset

This recipe is an adaptation of the California-influenced Israeli charoset of the well-known kosher cooking instructor and cookbook author Judy Zeidler. This recipe truly tells a story since the ingredients are an amalgam of both Ashkenazic and Sephardic culinary traditions. Flavorful, intriguing, and a big hit at the seder.

⅔ cup pistachio nuts
2 apples (Gala or Empire), peeled, cored, and cut into chunks
15 pitted dates
2 bananas, peeled and cut into 1-inch pieces
1–2 tablespoons fresh lemon juice (depending on sweetness of fruits used)

Zest of ½ lemon
¼ cup fresh orange juice
Zest of ½ orange
1 teaspoon cinnamon
¼ cup sweet Concord grape Passover wine
4 tablespoons matzah meal

1. Place the pistachio nuts in a processor work bowl and pulse on and off until the nuts are ground fine but not forming butter.

2. Add the apples and dates, and pulse until the fruits are fairly well chopped.

3. Add the bananas, lemon juice and zest, orange juice and zest, and cinnamon, and pulse until the mixture is a coarse but combined mass.

4. Remove the mixture to a glass bowl, and stir in the wine and matzah meal. Chill, covered, until serving time.

Yield: 10–15 servings

TINA'S TIDBIT

- *Here the banana is used again, with its great ability to impart both sweetness and a dark brown color when the mixture oxidizes.*

EGYPTIAN CHAROSET

The Capsouto brothers left Cairo for Lyon when the lives of Jews became difficult in Egypt after the creation of the State of Israel. Their little synagogue in Lyon was gifted a Torah by the synagogue in Istanbul so that they could conduct services. They later settled in New York. In 1987, after a dramatic massacre that occurred at the Neve-Shalom Synagogue in Istanbul, Turkey—the brothers' parents were from Turkey—the Capsouto brothers began their tradition of holding a Passover seder at their New York City restaurant for charity. At first their efforts helped raise funds to rebuild the Istanbul synagogue, and now they donate the proceeds to a cause that the American Joint Distribution Committee feels is in need.

The following recipe, adapted from the Capsouto Frères menu, is the charoset served at these charitable seders.

8-ounce package of Medjool dates, pitted
2 Fuji or Gala apples

1 cinnamon stick (optional)

1. Place the dates in a 2-quart saucepan with water to cover and cook, covered, on medium high while you prepare the apples. The water should be reduced to below the level of the dates, and the dates should begin to soften.

2. Peel, core, and dice the apples into ½-inch chunks. Add the apples and cinnamon stick (if using), and cook over low heat until the apples are soft. Do not let the water completely evaporate. It is rare that this happens, but if it does, add ¼ cup water to the pan.

3. Remove the cinnamon stick, if using. Pass the dates and apples through a food mill using the medium disk or use a processor, pulsing the machine on and off to get a rough puree of the ingredients. If the mixture is too watery, return it to the pan and cook on low heat until the desired thickness is achieved.

Yield: 2 cups

TINA'S TIDBITS

- *A food mill will puree mixtures while separating the skin from the pulp of the food. It is a hand-cranked, nonelectric utensil and a valuable tool to have in your kitchen.*
- *Apples may be left with their skin on prior to cooking, because the food mill will separate the skin from the fruit pulp. However, the pectin in the skin will create a thicker* charoset *when cooled, so don't let the water evaporate while cooking or your final, chilled mixture will be too thick.*
- *Cinnamon stick is my addition for the modern palate, but it bridges the gap from traditional Ashkenazic* charoset *to this Middle Eastern variety.*
- *This is actually a much easier and less labor intensive method of making* halek *(see page 433).*

NONTRADITIONAL TOMATO CHAROSET

OK, so sometimes creativity gets the best of us, but when I thought about creating this recipe, I knew I wanted it to be a paste that was dark like mortar and incorporated some of the foods of Israel. Everyone loved it, and I didn't tell them what they were eating until after the seder. Let's keep it our little secret, shall we?

1½ pounds small grape tomatoes
6 tablespoons granulated sugar, divided use
8 ounces whole almonds
¼ cup honey

Zest of ¼ medium orange
1½ teaspoons cinnamon
½ teaspoon ground ginger
¼ teaspoon ground cloves

1. Preheat the oven to 350°F (325°F for convection oven).

2. Line a large rimmed cookie sheet with parchment paper. Cut the tomatoes in half lengthwise and place cut side up on the cookie sheet.

3. Sprinkle 2 tablespoons of the sugar over the tomatoes and place in the oven for 15 minutes.

4. Remove the tomatoes from the oven and sprinkle them with another 2 tablespoons of sugar. Return to the oven and roast for 30 minutes or until the tomatoes are beginning to brown and the sugar is caramelizing. Do not let the sugar burn.

5. Remove from the oven and allow the tomatoes to cool.

6. Meanwhile, toast the almonds in the oven for 7–8 minutes, until fragrant. Do not let the almonds get too dark. Cool the almonds and finely grind them in a nut mill or food processor, using short pulses so that the nuts are ground fine without forming a butter. Place the nuts in a 1-quart bowl and set aside.

7. Place the tomato mixture in the processor work bowl and process until coarsely chopped. Add the honey, orange zest, spices, and remaining 2 tablespoons of sugar. Process to a smooth paste.

8. Add 1½ cups of the ground almonds to the tomato mixture and pulse on and off until the mixture is well blended. Transfer to a storage container and place in the refrigerator for 3 days.

9. When ready to serve, either serve in a dish with a spoon or shape into ¾-inch balls and roll in the remaining ground almonds. Serve cold.

Yield: 20 balls

TINA'S TIDBITS

- *Roasting the tomatoes serves two purposes: the flavor is enhanced by the caramelized sugar and juices, and it helps the tomato dry out so that the mixture won't be too thin and wet.*
- *One tablespoon of sugar and some cinnamon may be added to the remaining nuts for the coating.*

APPLES AND HONEY

$\mathcal{A}$pples and honey. The words are bound together like peanut butter and jelly and are rife with memories. Ask Jewish preschoolers what these words bring to mind and they will shout out gleefully, "Rosh HaShanah!" Dipping sliced apple in honey in the Ashkenazic world and eating a sweet apple conserve with bread

in the Sephardic world are universal traditions to express our hope for a sweet and fruitful year. These apple traditions are not based on law or dictates but customs. Jewish customs often originate as a way of reinforcing Jewish identity and history and serve to bind Jews throughout the Diaspora to their heritage and homeland. The question is, why apples and honey?

Although most associate the apple with Adam and Eve's mishap in the Garden of Eden, the Bible never states what fruit was picked from the Tree of Knowledge—apples are most often used as metaphor for affection and association with God.

In the traditional interpretation of Song of Songs, the Jewish people are compared to an apple: "As the apple is rare and unique among the trees of the forest, so is my beloved [Israel] among the maidens [nations] of the world" (2:3). In medieval

times apples were considered so special that prayers were etched into the skin of the apple before it was eaten. Could this have led to the custom of using the apple as a symbol of our "wishes" for a fruitful year? Even the *Zohar*, a thirteenth-century Jewish mystical text of kabbalistic writings, states that beauty "diffuses itself in the world as an apple."

The use of honey seems obvious; it is sweet and therefore symbolically represents our hopes for a sweet year. Consuming honey during the High Holy Days was an old custom followed by Jews throughout the world. This custom was referenced in writings in the seventh century by Babylonian Talmudic scholars, although its practice is presumed to predate the writings. Eating apples and honey connects us to our ancient past and brings sweetness and hope for each new year and each new generation.

HALEK
(DATE HONEY)

This recipe is worth trying when you have a little time, because the resulting liquid has many culinary uses all year long. This is the honey referred to in the Torah when Israel is called the "Land of Milk and Honey."

2 cups pitted dates
5 cups water

1. Combine the dates and water in a 2-quart saucepan and bring to a rolling boil.

2. Remove from the heat and cover. Let the dates steep in the water for 4 hours or overnight. They will get very soft, and their skins will begin to peel off.

3. Cut out a 10-inch square of triple-layered cheesecloth, and place it in a small colander over a clean 1-quart saucepan.

4. Carefully pour the date-soaking liquid through the cheesecloth into the pan.

5. Working with ½ cup of dates at a time, place the dates in the cheesecloth, and bring up the corners so that the dates are encased in the cloth.

6. Twist the cheesecloth over the pot, as tight as you can until the dates give up some more juice. Keep squeezing until it appears that the dates have been wrung dry.

7. Discard the used pulp and repeat with another ½ cup of dates. Continue this process until all the dates have been used.

8. Return the pot to the stove and cook over moderate heat until the liquid is reduced to a syrupy consistency.

9. Pour this liquid into a 1-pint jar and refrigerate until ready to use.

Yield: 1½–2 cups

TINA'S TIDBITS

- *This amount of dates makes about a pint of* halek. *Some people make 5-6 quarts at a time, but I assume friends come to help, because it could take all day to make that large a quantity.*
- *Because there is so much natural sugar in the dates, the boiling creates syrup as the water evaporates.*
- *The syrup will get thicker as it chills and will last for many months in the refrigerator.*

HONEYED CHERRY-PECAN BRIE

The ultimate Jewish mother feeding the masses is Ina Pinkney, the owner of Ina's in Chicago. Warm, loving, and nurturing, she can serve up the best stories with the best food while you dine in her casual eatery. Ina gave me the idea for this Brie. I've adapted it using Texas pecans and dried cherries, but sweetened dried cranberries or dried apricots, finely diced, would be delicious, too.

One 15-ounce wheel of Brie
²⁄₃ cup pecan halves, coarsely chopped
¹⁄₃ cup dried cherries, coarsely chopped if large
¹⁄₄ cup honey

1 tablespoon unsalted butter, melted
¹⁄₄ teaspoon cinnamon
¹⁄₄ teaspoon ground cardamom

1. Place the Brie on a large sheet of foil or a decorative disposable cake pan (if you're giving this as a gift).

2. Combine the remaining ingredients in a small bowl, and pour the mixture on top of the Brie.

3. When ready to bake, preheat the oven to 350°F. Bake the Brie, uncovered, for 15–20 minutes, until the cheese puffs slightly on the sides. Let rest for 15 minutes.

4. To serve, cut out a small wedge of cheese with a sharp knife; the cheese will ooze out. Serve with crackers or thinly sliced French bread.

Yield: 12–15 servings

TINA'S TIDBITS

- *Always place Brie on a pan with a slight rim (such as a pizza pan) when baking. Brie is considered a double crème cheese with a relatively high butterfat content. When it bakes, some oil often oozes out, so a pan with a rim is a good idea.*
- *This is enough topping for two 5-inch Brie wheels. One of these smaller wheels would serve 8-10 people if you had other hors d'oeuvres to serve.*
- *Refrigerate the Brie until the topping is firm and then cover it if you are transporting it to a friend.*

"Waldorfed" Spinach Salad

Much of fall's bounty finds its way into this salad bowl. This is a great salad to take to a friend's house for Rosh HaShanah, with the apples and honey already in it. Or bring this salad out to the sukkah for entertaining your own ushpizin (guests).

2 large Jonagold apples, peeled, cored, and sliced ¼ inch thick
Juice of 1 large lemon
Zest of ½ lemon
4 small scallions, thinly sliced
2 stalks of celery, finely diced
½ cup dark raisins

⅓ cup mayonnaise
¼ cup almond butter or peanut butter
2 tablespoons maple syrup or honey
5 cups baby spinach leaves
¼ cup toasted slivered almonds or peanuts
(depending on which butter you are using)

1. Combine the apples with the lemon juice, zest, scallions, celery, and raisins in a large bowl.

2. In a small bowl, whisk together the mayonnaise, almond or peanut butter, and maple syrup or honey.

3. Toss this mixture with the apple mixture and chill until serving.

4. When ready to serve, toss the apple mixture with the spinach, and garnish with the toasted nuts.

Yield: 6–8 servings

TINA'S TIDBITS

- *When buying a lemon, lightly scratch the rind with your fingernail. The aroma that is given off will tell you if the zest will be sweet like a lemon lollipop or tart and if the flavor of the juice will be full-bodied and tart or tasteless and astringent.*
- *To remove the strings from a stalk of celery, just bend the large, white end back and pull down; a number of strings should pull away.*

SOUTHWESTERN HONEY CHICKEN BREAST

I served this adaptation of a deep-fried chicken recipe, to two hundred women at a Dallas Akiba Academy luncheon to demonstrate that keeping kosher did not keep us out of the forefront in culinary trends.

1–2 pounds boneless chicken breast
½ cup honey
⅓ cup apple juice or cider
2 tablespoons applejack or brandy

½ cup whole-wheat flour
Salt and pepper to taste
4 tablespoons olive oil and/or butter

1. Remove the fillet from the chicken breast and lightly pound the breast for uniform thickness. Marinate the chicken in the honey, juice, and brandy for a few hours or overnight.

2. Combine the flour with the salt and pepper on a large plate.

3. Remove the meat from the marinade but **do not dry**. Dip in the seasoned flour and sauté in the hot olive oil until golden on both sides (about 3 minutes per side). Serve with black bean sauce and avocado-tomatillo relish (see recipes below).

BLACK BEAN SAUCE

1 can black beans, rinsed and drained
1 cup chicken broth
1 teaspoon minced garlic
3 serrano chilies, seeded and deveined
1½ tablespoons chopped tomatillo
1 tablespoon chopped cilantro
1 tablespoon chopped onion
Lime juice to taste
Salt to taste

1. Combine all of the ingredients, except the lime juice and salt, in a medium saucepan and cook for 5 minutes.

2. Blend the mixture in a blender until smooth.

3. Season with the lime juice and salt. Serve warm with the chicken breasts.

AVOCADO-TOMATILLO RELISH

1 avocado, diced into ½-inch cubes
2 tablespoons diced tomatillo
1 tablespoon diced red bell pepper
1 tablespoon diced green bell pepper
½ teaspoon minced jalapeño pepper
1 tablespoon chopped scallions
3 tablespoons olive oil
Lime juice to taste
Salt to taste

1. Combine all of the ingredients in a bowl.

2. Season with lime juice and salt to taste. Chill until ready to serve.

Yield: 6–8 servings

TINA'S TIDBITS

- *Boneless chicken breast does not need tenderizing; marinating is purely for enhanced flavor.*
- *This flour coating is delicate, because there is no egg to adhere to. However, if your pan is sufficiently hot and there is enough oil in the pan, the delicate whole-wheat flour coating will adhere.*

German Apfelpfannkuchen (Apple Pancake)

German bakers used apples in many of their recipes. Jewish cooks were no exception. Apples were plentiful in Europe and Eastern Europe, but to the poor they were a delicacy that made a simple dish a special occasion food. Here, an oven-baked pancake is topped with a luscious apple topping. The really good news is that the topping can be made in advance and just reheated, and the pancake takes almost no time to prepare and cook.

1 Jonathan or Winesap apple, peeled and cored
1 tablespoon unsalted butter
¼ cup apricot preserves
½ teaspoon vanilla
Pinch of cinnamon
2 tablespoons sugar
2 eggs

½ cup milk
½ cup flour
Pinch of nutmeg
Zest of ¼ orange
1 stick unsalted butter
Confectioners' sugar for dusting

1. Prepare the topping by thinly slicing the peeled and cored apple.

2. Melt the 1 tablespoon butter in a frying pan and add the apples, apricot preserves, vanilla, cinnamon, and sugar. Sauté over low heat until the apples begin to give off some of their juices. Turn the heat up to medium and continue sautéing until the mixture becomes a little more syrupy. Cover and keep warm while you prepare the pancake **or** cover and refrigerate for up to 5 days until needed.

3. To make the pancake, preheat the oven to 475°F.

4. Combine the eggs, milk, flour, nutmeg, and orange zest in a blender and blend until smooth and well combined.

5. Place the butter in a 10-inch ovenproof frying pan, cast-iron skillet, or heavy metal pie pan that holds 2 quarts.

6. Heat the butter in the pan **in the oven** until the butter is melted.

7. Immediately add the batter to the hot pan. Return the pan to the oven and bake for 12 minutes or until golden. Remove from the oven and transfer to a hot pad or place the pancake on a plate.

8. Reheat the apple mixture in the sauté pan or in the microwave (if the mixture was made in advance and refrigerated), adding a little water, apple juice, or applejack if the mixture is too thick.

9. Place the apples on top of the pancake. Dust with confectioners' sugar and serve.

Yield: 4–6 servings

TINA'S TIDBITS

- *It is important to use a large, heavy frying pan or a rimmed pan for this recipe so that the batter will immediately sear when it comes in contact with the hot pan, and it will puff up enormously as a result.*
- *The choice of apple is really up to you in terms of taste, but make sure your choice is a firm, crisp apple, so that it will retain its shape after sautéing.*
- *The blender works better than a processor for this recipe because the liquid batter is drawn into the blade and will be rendered smooth. Liquid in a processor tends to hydroplane over the blades, and small particles escape, resulting in a lumpy or coarse-textured product.*

APPLE BROWN BETTY

The major connection to Jewish cooking in this recipe is the desire to create something wholesome and wonderful for our families. Actually this is my dessert of choice for Sukkot and for Erev Yom Kippur. This recipe is easily made pareve by substituting pareve margarine for the butter.

2 pounds or 4 cups chopped pared apples, about ¾-inch chunks
¼ cup orange juice
1 cup brown sugar
½ cup all-purpose flour

¼ cup whole-wheat flour
½ teaspoon cinnamon
¼ teaspoon ground nutmeg
1 stick unsalted butter

1. Butter a 9-inch pie plate or a 2-quart casserole. Place the apples in it and sprinkle with the orange juice.

2. Combine the remaining ingredients thoroughly with your fingertips or in a processor and crumble the sugar mixture on top of the apples.

3. Bake at 375°F for 45 minutes or until the apples are tender and the topping is crisp. Serve warm.

Yield: 6–8 servings

TINA'S TIDBITS

- *The whole-wheat flour not only adds more nutrients to this dessert, but also makes the topping extra crunchy.*
- *Overhandling flour with butter makes the flour tough and hard when baked; this is exactly what you want to do with this recipe! So let your kids help. They can't harm the finished product.*
- *The orange juice prevents the apples from turning brown, flavors the dish, and combines with some of the flour in the topping to create a subtly thickened sauce.*

APPLESAUCE

You will never want to buy applesauce again after tasting this. No sugar is needed for taste or consistency. And if you own a food mill, no peeling is required! Start to finish, this takes 15 minutes to prepare.

4–6 medium apples
¼–½ cup water

2-inch cinnamon stick or ½ teaspoon ground
    cinnamon
¼ cup sugar (optional)

1. Wash the apples, core, and cut them into eighths. Do not peel.

2. Combine the apples, water, and cinnamon in a saucepan. Cover the pot and simmer for 10 minutes or until the apples are very tender.

3. Remove the skins. Mash the apples until smooth and add sugar if desired.

Yield: 2–3 cups

TINA'S TIDBITS

- *It is not necessary to peel the apples before you cook them. If the apples are unpeeled, the natural pectin in the skins will thicken the sauce, and the skin will give the sauce a rosy color.*
- *To remove the apple skins, pass the apples through a food mill or just remove the skins by hand with a spoon.*
- *The flavor cells of an apple are just below the skin. Cooking the apple with the skin only enhances its flavor.*

LEKACH (HONEY CAKE)

Nothing says Rosh HaShanah or Shabbat Kiddushim more than the iconic honey cake. Moist and delicious, this cake definitely tastes even better when made a day in advance. The coffee and spices meld with the honey and brandy to give full flavor. Made with oil, the traditional way, this cake is pareve.

1 cup wildflower honey
½ cup strong coffee or 1 teaspoon instant espresso and ½ cup water
1 tablespoon brandy
2 eggs
1 tablespoon oil
¼ cup brown sugar
1¾ cups flour

Pinch of salt
½ teaspoon baking soda
1 teaspoon baking powder
½ teaspoon allspice
¾ teaspoon cinnamon
¼ teaspoon ground ginger
⅓ cup raisins (optional)
Whole blanched almonds for topping (optional)

1. Preheat the oven to 325°F.

2. Grease 2 loaf pans, 48 mini muffin pans, or 1 tube pan with cooking spray, or use paper liners in the muffin tins.

3. Bring the honey to a gentle boil and cool slightly. Add the coffee and brandy and set aside.

4. In a large bowl, beat the eggs until light and lemon-colored. Add the oil and gradually beat in the sugar.

5. In a separate bowl, combine the dry ingredients. Add the dry ingredients alternately with the honey mixture to the egg-sugar mixture. Mix well after each addition to thoroughly incorporate the ingredients.

6. If you are using raisins, dust them with a little additional flour so that they will not sink to the bottom of the cake. Fold the raisins into the cake batter, and pour the mixture into the prepared pans. If using, place one almond in the center of each muffin or in a line on the top of the cake.

7. Bake the muffins for 15–18 minutes or until a tester comes out clean. Loaf pans take up to 45 minutes and tube pans will take a little longer. Test with a toothpick. If you insert the toothpick in the cake and it comes out without any batter adhering to it then the cake is done. Muffins may be served with ginger-orange cream cheese spread.

GINGER-ORANGE CREAM CHEESE SPREAD

8 ounces cream cheese
1 tablespoon frozen orange juice concentrate
2 tablespoons milk
1 tablespoon brown sugar
1 tablespoon crystallized ginger, chopped

1. Combine all of the ingredients in a processor work bowl and process until smooth.

2. Serve alongside sweet quickbreads, such as honey cake or pumpkin bread, or pipe individual rosettes on top of the mini muffins of the above sweet breads.

Yield: 20 servings or 48 mini muffins

TINA'S TIDBITS

- *This cake is aromatic and tasty warm from the oven, but because of the brandy and spices, it tastes even better if it's allowed to sit a day or so wrapped in foil.*
- *Because the batter is high in sugar and relatively thin, the cake may have a tendency to sink in the middle if the pan is too deep. I recommend a tube pan because the open center can heat the cake more evenly.*
- *Mini muffins are great for a big party. Everyone wants a spiritual taste of the honey cake but only a small bite when many foods are offered.*

QUICK HONEY CAKE

When I was creating my honey cake bread pudding recipe, it was July and no prepared honey cakes were available. I didn't have the time or desire to make a honey cake from scratch just to cut it up for an experiment, so I devised this simple way to make the base for my recipe. Turns out, this cake was good on its own—just as sticky on top and balanced with the coffee flavor and honey.

3/4 cup warm coffee or 1 teaspoon instant espresso and 3/4 cup water
1/4 cup honey

One 14.5-ounce box gingerbread mix
Eggs, as needed in the mix
Oil or margarine, as needed in the mix

1. Microwave the coffee with the honey for 30 seconds. Stir to combine.

2. Prepare the cake following the package directions **except** substitute the warm coffee and honey for all of the liquid in the recipe. Use the appropriate amount of oil and eggs called for on the package.

3. Bake the cake according to the package directions. Cool completely and serve, or use in the Apples and Honey Cake Bread Pudding recipe (see page 444).

Yield: 8 servings

TINA'S TIDBITS

- *It is not always easy to find, but I keep a jar of Medaglia D'Oro instant espresso in my freezer for all the times a recipe calls for strong coffee or espresso. It dissolves immediately and is not bitter.*
- *Although most honey on the market is clover honey, I love wildflower honey. The floral undertones are terrific and are really pronounced in mild-flavored dishes.*

APPLES AND HONEY CAKE BREAD PUDDING WITH BUTTERSCOTCH SAUCE

I created this recipe when I had too much leftover honey cake. Moist and rich, this "bread" pudding is not overly sweet. Serve with some vanilla ice cream or whipped cream if you like, but I promise you the spiked butterscotch sauce is delicious over the warm dessert (see the recipe on the following page).

1 loaf honey cake (approximately 9 × 5 inches), store-bought or homemade
3 Jonagold, Fuji, or Gala apples
2 ounces (½ stick) unsalted butter
¼ cup sugar
½ teaspoon cinnamon

4 eggs
⅓ cup brown sugar
1 teaspoon vanilla
1 cup half-and-half cream
3 cups milk (whole or 2% preferred)

1. Butter a 13 × 9-inch glass pan. Preheat the oven to 350°F.

2. Cut the honey cake into ¾-inch cubes. Place in a 4-quart bowl and set aside.

3. Peel, core, and slice the apples into eighths. Cut each eighth crosswise into 3 or 4 chunks.

4. Heat a 10-inch skillet for 15 seconds. Add the butter and melt. Sauté the apples in the butter over medium-high heat until the apples give up some of their juice.

5. Add the sugar and cinnamon to the apples, and continue sautéing until the sugar is dissolved and the apples begin to brown and get softer. Remove from the heat and set aside until needed.

6. In a 2-quart bowl, whisk the eggs until lightly beaten. Whisk in the brown sugar and vanilla until thoroughly incorporated. Pour in the cream and milk and whisk to combine.

7. Place half of the honey cake cubes in the prepared pan. Cover with the reserved apples and then with the remaining honey cake cubes.

8. Pour the egg-milk mixture through a sieve directly over the entire surface of the honey cake. Lightly press down on the cake to make sure it is covered with the custard.

TINA'S TIDBITS

- *Because honey will absorb moisture in a baked product, it is important that there be enough liquid in the bread pudding to allow the cake to swell and soften.*
- *Bread puddings in general are best made with dry or dense bread so that they absorb more of the egg-milk mixture, creating a light, airy product. If your grandmother's recipe for honey cake is dry and hard, you can salvage your efforts with this recipe.*
- *Evaporated milk is often used in sauces because it provides the smooth consistency of cream and doesn't curdle easily.*

9. Place the pan in a larger pan, and pour hot water into the larger pan to a depth of 1 inch.

10. Bake in the preheated oven for 45 minutes or until a sharp, thin knife inserted into the center of the pudding comes out wet, but clear. Serve warm with optional sauce on the side.

Yield: 12–15 servings

HOMEMADE BUTTERSCOTCH SAUCE

1 cup light or dark brown sugar (see note below)
⅔ cup light corn syrup
2 ounces (½ stick) unsalted butter

⅔ cup evaporated milk
1 teaspoon vanilla extract
1–2 tablespoons Scotch or dark rum (optional)

1. In a medium saucepan, combine the sugar, syrup, and butter. Stir only until the butter is melted and the mixture comes to a full boil. Adjust the heat to medium high and boil without stirring for 1 minute. Remove from the heat.

2. Combine the milk with the vanilla and add to the pan. Stir only to combine. Add liquor, if using, and pour into a glass jar. Use immediately or refrigerate until ready to serve. May be warmed in the microwave or served cold.

Note: Light brown sugar is standard for butterscotch flavor, but dark brown sugar may be used for a stronger molasses flavor, if desired.

PICKLES AND PRESERVING

Originally cultivated in India and later in Mesopotamia and the Tigris Valley, the cucumber goes back to biblical times (Numbers 11:5 and Isaiah 1:8). And so does the art of pickling. During the age of exploration, Christopher Columbus brought cucumber plants to the New World on his voyages, and the pickles that were aboard ship prevented the seamen from getting scurvy. For the Jews who lived in Eastern Europe before the great immigration to America, pickling served two purposes: it preserved, for future consumption, the meager amounts of produce and fish that were available, and it enabled women of the shtetl to earn a few extra kopeks so that their husbands could spend more time studying Talmud.

Is it any surprise that pushcarts with pickles found their way to the New World?

In the early 1900s, Jewish immigrants began New York City's first commercial pickle district. Many vendors started out with a rented pushcart to haul homemade pickles. In 1920, there were more than eighty pickle vendors in the vicinity of Hester Street. One of the most successful was Izzy Guss. That year he bought his own pickle store, which he named Guss' Pickles. Over time, with the decline in the economy and tougher immigration and pushcart laws, most of the pickle men went bust. Today, only one pickle store on Essex Street remains, and its owner, Alan Kaufman, learned the business from his mentor, Izzy Guss. He continues to pickle by hand, the old-fashioned way, using the original Eastern European recipe. He can tell you why it's preferable to use salt (the shtetl way) instead of vinegar— vinegar will brown the pickle faster and sour it more quickly. And if you ask him the difference between a Polish pickle and a kosher dill pickle, he'll tell you that the Polish has more dill and the dill more garlic. Go figure.

For the home cook, there's more to pickling than pickles. All kinds of foods can be preserved through this process. Our Sephardic ancestors, for example, would roast produce and then preserve it in vinegar and olive oil. As far back as Roman times, mushrooms, zucchini and other squash of all shapes and sizes, turnips, eggplant, citrus fruits, and many other fruits and vegetables were seasoned and then immersed in a vinegar/salt bath. They were then allowed to marinate and cure. Not only did this save the food for future consumption, but it allowed the household to enjoy delicious foods on Shabbat without any last-minute preparation that was forbidden by Jewish law.

LEFT: *Relish Assortment*

PICKLED CUCUMBERS

If you follow the recipe in one popular American cookbook, making pickles can take countless hours. Instead, I followed the advice of Alan Kaufman (the owner of The Pickle Guy, the only privately owned pickle store on the Lower East Side) and tried the following recipe—the pickles take about twenty minutes to make and need only two days of waiting time. And the addition of the ginger, cardamom, and cinnamon renders a subtle touch of the Middle East to these pickles.

12–16 small cucumbers, about 5 inches long
4 large cloves of garlic, cut in half, green stem
   removed
⅛ teaspoon coriander seed
2 bay leaves, crushed
½ teaspoon black peppercorns
¼ teaspoon mustard seed

8 whole allspice berries
1-inch piece of crystallized ginger
½ stick cinnamon
6 cardamom pods
4 cups of water
½ cup distilled organic white vinegar
3 tablespoons coarse kosher salt

1. Slice the cucumbers crosswise into ¼-inch pieces and discard the ends.

2. Place the cucumbers in two 1-quart wide-mouthed jars. (I use leftover gefilte fish jars!)

3. Combine all of the spices and lightly crush with a mortar and pestle or the back of a spoon. (For a more Eastern European pickle, you can eliminate the allspice, ginger, cinnamon, and cardamom and replace with dried hot pepper, more garlic, and dill or dill seed.) Divide the spice mixture evenly between the two jars.

4. Bring the water to a boil in a stainless steel, glass, or enamel saucepan.

5. Add the vinegar and salt, and stir with a rubber spatula until the salt dissolves.

6. Pour the hot liquid evenly into the jars.

7. Let cool on the counter for about an hour, and then cover with the jar lids.

8. Shake the jars, turning over 2 times to distribute the spices in the water.

9. Place the jars in a closet or another cool dark place for 2 days to pickle and flavor the cucumbers properly. Then refrigerate until ready to eat.

10. Serve and enjoy! (The pickles may be stored in the refrigerator for up to 6 weeks or longer.)

Yield: 12–16 servings

TINA'S TIDBITS

- *Pickling in vinegar hastens the process of souring, but your vegetables will discolor faster.*
- *If fresh garlic turns blue/green in the pickling jar, the garlic is very fresh or there is not enough salt in the brine.*
- *Placing the pickles in the refrigerator immediately without waiting the two days will yield pickles that are bright green and crispier.*

ITALIAN MARINATED ROASTED RED BELL PEPPERS

The following recipe is based on the technique described in Classic Italian Jewish Cooking *by Edda Servi Machlin. My use of balsamic vinegar imparts a sweet taste to the peppers. Jewish cooks have been preparing peppers this way for centuries.*

3 very large sweet red peppers
½ cup balsamic vinegar
1 teaspoon salt

2 very large cloves of garlic, cut into quarters
Salt and freshly ground black pepper to taste
About ¾ cup extra virgin olive oil, enough to cover

1. Preheat the oven to 450°F.

2. Place the whole peppers on a baking sheet and roast them for 15 minutes or until the peel is blackened in spots.

3. Meanwhile, fill a large bowl with water and 8 ice cubes.

4. When the peppers are done, immediately plunge them into the bowl of ice water.

5. When the peppers are cool enough to handle, peel them under water. Remove the stem and seeds and any interior membrane.

6. Cut the peppers lengthwise into ½-inch strips. You may wish to cut the strips in half crosswise if the peppers are very long.

7. Bring the vinegar and salt to a boil in a stainless steel or enameled pan. Add the sliced peppers and cook for 3 minutes, stirring with a soft spoon or spatula.

8. Remove the peppers from the heat and allow the mixture to cool to room temperature.

9. Drain the peppers. Stir in garlic and salt and pepper to taste.

10. Place the mixture in a 1-quart wide-mouthed glass jar. Pour olive oil over the peppers to cover. Bang the jar on the counter to force any air bubbles to the surface; this will help prevent mold from forming inside the jar.

11. Close the lid tightly on the jar and refrigerate. The peppers may be eaten right away, but their flavor will be greatly enhanced after a day. They will last about 1–2 weeks in the refrigerator before spoiling, or you may freeze for later use. (If freezing, transfer to a freezer safe container or make sure there is enough room in the jar for the liquid to expand.)

Yield: 6 servings

TINA'S TIDBITS

- *Roasting peppers in a hot oven causes the peppers to blister, but the "meat" of the vegetable does not burn. You'll preserve the flesh of your peppers far better this way than roasting them on a grill.*
- *By far, the easiest way to peel peppers is immediately after water submersion.*
- *Any time you are boiling vinegar and salt, it must be in a nonreactive pan. Stainless steel, glass, or enamel is okay. Copper, brass, and aluminum will react with the liquid and ruin your recipe.*
- *Balsamic vinegar will impart a dark mahogany hue to the peppers. If you want them more natural looking, use apple cider vinegar or white wine vinegar instead.*

Harissa

Harissa is to Tunisia what ballpark mustard and ketchup are to America . . . don't set the table without it! There are more variations in the recipe than there are cooks in Tunisia, but you can be assured that all harissas will contain a lot of heat and that caraway seed will find its way into the mix. Although harissa is readily available in many markets, I wanted to include a recipe for you to enjoy.

2-ounce package dried poblano or other hot chilies
3/4–1 cup water
2 large cloves of garlic, peeled and crushed
1 1/2 teaspoons coriander seed, lightly crushed

1 teaspoon caraway seed, lightly crushed
1 teaspoon salt
3 tablespoons extra virgin olive oil plus 1 tablespoon for topping paste in jar

1. Carefully remove the stem and seeds from the chilies, and place the chilies in a glass bowl. Cover with the water and microwave on high for 2 minutes. Set the bowl aside and let the chilies soak and get soft, about 20 minutes.

2. Drain the chilies, reserving 1/4 cup of the water.

3. Add the garlic, crushed coriander, and caraway seeds to a small processor work bowl, and process until a coarse mixture is formed.

4. Add the drained chili peppers and salt, and process to break up the peppers. You will need to stop the machine and scrape down the sides of the bowl a few times.

5. Add 2 tablespoons of the reserved chili water, and process until a coarse paste is formed. Scrape down the sides of the bowl again.

6. With the processor running, slowly add 3 tablespoons of the olive oil to the paste, and process until all the oil is incorporated and the mixture forms a spreadable, coarse paste.

7. Place the mixture in a clean 8-ounce jar, and pour the remaining tablespoon of olive oil over the top of the mixture to prevent it from drying out and spoiling. Refrigerate until needed.

Yield: 3/4 cup

TINA'S TIDBITS

- *Some small processors can't quite grind the whole spices and chili peppers into a smooth paste. That is OK. However, if you don't want to sit with a mortar and pestle and pound your way to smoothness, you might want to try an immersion blender or a regular blender to get a smoother consistency. If you double the recipe, you will find it easier to puree in a big blender.*
- *When storing a prepared paste in the refrigerator, cover the top of the paste with 1/4 inch of oil before putting on the lid. The oil creates a barrier between the paste and the air, and mold is less likely to form.*

AMBA
(IRAQI PICKLED MANGO)

Mangoes are the most popular fruit in the world and the third most popular fruit, after apples and bananas, in the United States. Although they are grown in many tropical and subtropical climates, the Middle East counts on the height of the growing season in India and Pakistan to get the best fruit. When they are plentiful, they can be eaten out of hand or used in preparing many dishes. When they are not reliably available, the mango aficionado has to rely on the fruits that were pickled to enjoy their taste. Here is one such favorite.

1 teaspoon turmeric
2 teaspoons curry powder
1/4 teaspoon fenugreek seeds (optional)
10 grindings of black pepper (approximately 1/2 teaspoon)
2 tablespoons kosher salt

1 teaspoon citric acid
Zest of 1/4 lemon
1 teaspoon ginger
1 1/3 cups water (preferably filtered)
2 ripe unblemished mangoes

1. Combine the spices together with the water in a 2-quart bowl. Set aside while you cut the mangoes.

2. Mangoes are oval with two somewhat flat sides. A large flat seed is in the center. Slice the mango lengthwise along the flat side, running your knife along the seed. Repeat the same procedure on the other side. You now have two sides with pulp attached to the skin.

3. Cut lengthwise and crosswise lines 1/2 inch wide through the flesh to the skin, making a grid through the fruit. Turn the fruit "inside out" so the flesh sticks up. Carefully cut the cubes off into a small bowl.

4. Using a rubber spatula, stir to recombine the pickling solution. Carefully fold in the mangoes and coat with the spices.

5. Transfer the mixture to a clean 1-quart jar or two 1-pint jars, evenly distributing all of the ingredients. Screw the tops on tightly, and place in a cool dark place for 3 days. Gently turn the jars upside down periodically to disperse the spices.

6. *Amba* will last in the refrigerator for a month or more.

Yield: 1 quart

TINA'S TIDBIT

- *If you love mangoes, then you should invest in a mango slicer. It looks like an apple corer that slices apples into eighths, but it has two curved blades that core out the pit. You wind up with two perfect halves and enough fruit still attached to the pit to munch on before discarding.*

ENGLISH TOMATO CHUTNEY

I love chutney. The juxtaposition of the sweet and tart, the mild and hot, intrigues my palate. When I was in England, I was treated to a taste of this variety of chutney and couldn't wait to get home and re-create it.

2 medium-large tomatoes, seeded and chopped into ½-inch dice (approximately 3 cups)
1½ medium onions, cut into ½-inch dice (approximately 2 cups)
1¼ cups dark raisins
1¼ cups brown sugar
1 cup apple cider vinegar
¼ teaspoon salt

1½ teaspoons mustard seeds, slightly crushed
Dash of cayenne pepper
1 yellow or red bell pepper, cut into ½-inch dice
1½ teaspoons chopped candied ginger root
1 small clove of garlic, minced
¼ teaspoon turmeric
¼ teaspoon celery seed

1. Combine all of the ingredients in a heavy 3-quart saucepan.

2. Bring the mixture to a boil over high heat. Reduce the temperature until the mixture starts to simmer.

3. Simmer uncovered over low heat for approximately 2 hours or until most of the liquid has evaporated and the mixture has thickened. Stir periodically to prevent the mixture from sticking.

4. Pour into jars that have been sterilized (washed in a dishwasher and filled while still hot). Seal and store in the refrigerator.

5. Serve with meats or cheese or on a buttered baguette.

Yield: 1 quart

TINA'S TIDBITS

- *If you want slightly less "bite" to your chutney, try using unflavored rice wine vinegar or champagne vinegar instead of the apple cider variety.*
- *Two 1/4-inch slices of peeled fresh ginger may be used instead of candied ginger if that's not readily available. You can mince them or leave them whole for discarding later.*

THAI BASIL–JALAPEÑO PESTO

You might question the inclusion of an herb paste with pickling, but the Italians knew that the addition of acid and oil would preserve the fresh taste of the herbs long after the frost had arrived. I created the following pesto recipe out of necessity: I had a bumper crop of Thai basil in my garden and wanted it to last. The pesto contains no butter or cheese, is sharp and tangy, and has a subtle Asian flavor. Toss with pasta or a favorite vegetable. It's also a great spread on a turkey sandwich.

3/4 cup macadamia nuts or almonds, lightly toasted
3 jalapeños, seeds and membrane removed
2 large cloves of garlic, cut into quarters
2 cups firmly packed Thai basil leaves (Italian basil may be substituted)

3 tablespoons unseasoned rice wine vinegar
1/3 cup extra virgin olive oil
Salt and freshly ground pepper to taste

1. Add the nuts to the processor work bowl and pulse the processor on and off until the nuts are fairly fine.

2. Add the jalapeño and garlic and pulse 5 times. Scrape down the sides of the bowl with a spatula.

3. Add the basil and pulse about 10 times or until a coarse paste is formed.

4. Add the rice wine vinegar and pulse on and off a few times to combine.

5. Turn the processor on and slowly drizzle the olive oil into the pesto until the mixture looks creamy and fairly smooth.

6. Scrape into a bowl and season to taste with salt and pepper.

7. Refrigerate or freeze.

Yield: 1 1/4 cups

TINA'S TIDBITS

- *The "heat" in a jalapeño derives mostly from the seeds and the **white** interior membrane. The more seeds and membrane you leave, the hotter your dish will be.*
- *Pesto means "to pound." Traditionally, the basil leaves and nuts were pounded into a paste. Using a processor is much easier.*
- *Macadamia nuts are the hardest nuts in the world. Use almonds if you are making this pesto by hand.*
- *Be careful not to overprocess green herbs—you'll bring out the chlorophyll in the leaf and your mixture will taste more like grass than basil.*

SPICY BLUEBERRY VINEGAR AND BLUEBERRY CHUTNEY

When I was Chef Field years ago, it was my job to experiment with foods and demonstrate their uses to the customers at Marshall Field's department store. I loved jarred blueberry chutney and its accompanying vinegar, but after a few years the product was no longer being sold. The following two recipes are good on their own, in salads and sandwiches, with cheese and with meats. The chicken recipe uses both these products to tenderize and flavor the meat. My creation of these recipes is no different than what our ancestors did when they arrived in a new country: take what's locally available, add personal preference and experience to the mix, and make sure it conforms to kashrut.

SPICY BLUEBERRY VINEGAR

2 cups fresh blueberries, rinsed and dried with
   paper towel
2 whole sticks cinnamon
1¼ cups unseasoned rice vinegar

1. Place the blueberries and the cinnamon in a clean pint jar.

2. Heat the vinegar in a microwave for 2–3 minutes until hot but not boiling.

3. Pour the vinegar into the jar with the blueberries, leaving ½ inch headroom.

4. Cover and store in a cool dark place for 10–14 days before using.

Yield: 1 ½ cups vinegar

BLUEBERRY CHUTNEY

2 cups fresh or frozen blueberries
1¼ cups sugar
½ cup white vinegar
½ teaspoon cloves
1 teaspoon cinnamon

1. Combine all of the ingredients in a stainless steel 2-quart pot, and cook over medium heat for 10–15 minutes or until slightly thickened.

2. Cool and place in clean jars. Keep refrigerated.

Yield: 2 cups

BAKED CHICKEN WITH BLUEBERRY CHUTNEY

½ cup spiced blueberry vinegar (see recipe above)
1 chicken, cut into 8 pieces
¾ cup or more blueberry chutney (see recipe above) or preserves

1. Marinate the chicken in the blueberry vinegar for at least 30 minutes.

2. Preheat the oven to 350°F.

3. Drain the chicken and place it in a foil-lined roasting pan.

4. Coat the chicken pieces on all sides with the blueberry chutney. Place the chicken pieces, skin side up, in the roasting pan.

5. Roast for 45 minutes or until the chicken is golden and the juices run clear when the meat is pierced with the sharp end of a knife. Serve.

Yield: 4–6 servings

TINA'S TIDBITS

- *Although chicken doesn't need tenderizing, marinating the meat in a vinegar solution will yield a more moist and tender finished product, much the same as brining.*
- *Blueberry chutney is sweet and tart at the same time. It is a perfect accompaniment to cheese. Try it poured over a wedge of Gorgonzola Dolce or even over a brick of cream cheese.*

INDEX

Numerals in italics signify pages of photographs

A

Abayudaya Jews, 41
Africa
    diaspora communities, 29–30, 31
    East African Groundnut (Peanut) Soup, 31
    Ethiopian Black-Eyed Peas, 221
    Ethiopian Shabbat Stew, 36
    Ugandan Fall Harvest Fruit Salad, 41
After-Seder Frittata, 323
Agristada, 86
Algeria
    culinary traditions, 40, 389–390
    diaspora community, 27, 28, 29
Algerian Festive Stew, 40
Algerian Fish Terrine for Passover, 388–389
Almond bread (Mandelbrodt), 214
Almond Honey Sticks, 282
Almond Macaroons (Hadgi Badah), 232
Almond(s)
    Honey Sticks, 282
    Hadgi Badah (Almond Macaroons), 232
    Mandelbrodt (Almond Bread), 214
    Miniature Chocolate Tortes, 278–279
    Moroccan Couscous with Mixed Dried Fruits, 262, 263
    Mustacchioni, 188
    Nontraditional Tomato Charoset, 429
    Passover Granola, 326, 327
    for Tu BiSh'vat, 270–271
    Tuscan Biscotti, 280, 281
    Yemenite Fruit and Nut Chicken, 207
Amba, 451
Anchovies, 60
Appetizers. See also Tapas

Autumn Pâté, 238–239
Baba Ghanoush, 399
Chanukah Radish Salad canapés, 252, 253
Crostini with Tapenade, 49
Dill Puffs with Caviar, 142, 147–148
Dolmas, 242–243
Gougere, 149
Latkes, 256, 257
Manchego Cheese with Quince Preserves, 50
Nirvana Chicken Wings, 98, 104
North African Eggplant with Honey, 402–403
Patragel, 406
Smoked Salmon with Melon, 59
Tortilla Española, 48
Apple Brown Betty, 440
Apple-Cranberry Filling, 372
Apple Pancake (German Apfelpfannkuchen, 439
Apple Preserves, 220
Apples
    Applesauce, 441
    Ashkenazic Charoset, 421
    Bukharan Shabbat Chicken Palov, 200, 206
    Butternut–Apple Soup, 237
    Dulce de Manzana, 220, 430
    Egyptian Charoset, 428
    French Stuffed Brie en Croûte, 372
    Fresh Apple Cake, 233
    German Apfelpfannkuchen, 439
    High Holy Days, 217
    and Honey Cake Bread Pudding, 444–445
    iconic status, 431
    Israeli Charoset, 427
    Italian Charoset, 425
    Maple-Glazed Chicken Breasts, 227
    Mixed-Fruit Cranberry Relish, 240, 241

    Rosh HaShanah Noodle Kugel, 228
    with Sweet and Sour Red Cabbage, 159
    Traditional Charoset Texas Style, 422
    "Waldorfed" Spinach Salad, 436, 437
Applesauce, 441
Apricots
    Baked in Orange Blossom syrup, 23
    Syrian Compote in Rosewater Syrup, 14, 15
Arabian Olives, 19
Artichokes
    with Lime (Artichaud au Citron), 32
    Mina de Maza, 316–317
Artichokes with Lime, 32
Arugula Salad with Dates and Chèvre, 196, 197
Ashkenazi Jews
    apples and honey, 431
    Charoset, 421
    in China, 117
    culinary traditions, 266
    in England, 146
    High Holy Days, 217
    in Latin America, 303
    Purim ingredients, 295
    in Russia/Central and Eastern Europe, 130, 131, 132
    Shabbat recipes, 201
Ashkenazic Charoset, 421
Asian Spinach Salad with Candied Walnuts and Fried Tofu Croutons, 116, 119
Asparagus
    After-Seder frittata, 323
    with Maltaise Sauce, 20
Asparagus with Maltaise Sauce, 20
Austrian Potato-Mushroom Strudel, 362–363
Autumn Pâté, 238–239

B

Baba Ghanoush, 399
Bagels, Passover, 312
Baghdadi Jews, 99–100, 117
Baigan bharta (Indian Spice Eggplant), 398
Baked Apricots in Orange Blossom Syrup, 23
Baked Chicken with Blueberry Chutney, *454*, 455
Baker, Edith, 315
Baklava, 92–93
Bamboo shoots, 351
Bananas
    Israeli Charoset, 427
    Italian Charoset, 425
    Ugandan Fall Harvest Fruit Salad, 41
Barley
    Bulgarian Baked Chicken, 85
    Mushroom Barley Soup, 292
    1654 Barley Salad, 293
    Tu BiSh'vat, 270, 275
Basic Chicken Soup, *344*, 346
Basson, Moshe, 5, 284
Batmangli, Najmieh, 347
Bean curd, 351
Beef. *See also* Ground beef
    Algerian Festive Stew (Tabikha), 40
    Boston Chremslach (Stuffed Matzah Balls), 369
    Classic Pot Roast, 155
    Easy Sauerbraten, 158
    Grilled Steak with Chimichurri Sauce and Orange Slices, *168*, 177
    Lentil Soup, 133
    Mushroom Barley Soup, 292
    Prune Tzimmes, *128*, 134
    Russian Cabbage Borscht, 132
    Steak with Cellophane Noodles, 126
Beets, 218
Bene Israel, 99, 102, 201, 396
Berry, Elliot, 218
Bestilla, 29, 34
Beta Israel, 29–30
Biscotti, Tuscan, *280*, 281
Black-Eyed Peas (Lubiya), 221
Blintzes, 337
Bloom, Morris, 145
Blueberries, *454*, 455

Blueberry Chutney, *454*, 455
Bohemia, 295
Bokser, 269
Boneless Chicken with Port, 52–53
Book of Jewish Food (Roden), 188, 278
Borekas (filled pastries), 357–358, 376
Borekitas (filled pastries), 357–358
Borekitas kon Kalavasa, 96–97
Bortnick, Rachel Amado, 73–74, 84, 226
Boston Chremslach, 369
Bouillabaisse, 156
Boyos (filled pastries), 357–358
Braised Lamb Shanks in Merlot, 324–325
Brandy/liquor
    Crème Brûlée, 194–195
    Dacquoise, 166–167
    Greek Psari Saganaki, *88*, 89
    Haman's Ears, 297
    Hamentaschen of Panama, 303
    Honey Cake, 442
    Hungarian Mushroom Turnovers, 368
    Mustacchioni, 188
    Rum Sauce, 183
    Sabayon for Passover, 331
    Southwestern Honey Chicken Breast, 438
    Zabaglione, *56*, 71
Brazil
    culinary traditions, 52, 169, 393
    diaspora community, 169
Brazilian Cheese Puffs (Fao de Queijo), 176
Bread
    Challah, 201, *216*, 219
    Chanukah Radish Salad Canapés, *252*, 253
    Sopa de Pollo con Albondigas (Chicken Soup with Meatballs), 348
Bread Stuffing, 209
Briks (filled pastries), 357–358
Briks, Tunisian, 29, *364*, 365–366
Budino Cioccolato (Italian Chocolate Pudding), 185
Bukharan Shabbat Chicken Palov, *200*, 206
Bulemas (filled pastries), 357–358
Bulgaria, 85, 266
Bulgarian Baked Chicken with Barley, 85
Bulgarian Matzah Puffs, 315

Bulgarian Potato-Cheese Borekas, 376
Bulgur, 8
Bulgur wheat, 260–261
Buricche (filled pastries), 357–358
Burma, 17, 393
Burmolikos, 315
Butternut squash
    Borekitas kon Kalavasa, 96–97
    Butternut–Apple Soup, 237
    Moroccan Meatball Tagine with Couscous, *26*, 39
    Pumpkin Ravioli from Mantua, 61
    Winter Squash Gnocchi with Spinach and Pine Nuts, 62–63
    Zucca Gialla in Agrodolce (Squash in Sweet and Sour Sauce), 70
Butternut–Apple Soup, 237

C

Cabbage
    Russian Cabbage Borscht, 132
    stuffed, 244–245
    Sweet and Sour Red Cabbage with Apples, 159
Cacao trade, 183–184
Cakes/cookies
    Borekitas kon Kalavasa, 96–97
    Cannoli Cheesecake, 416
    Chocolate Chip Cappuccino Brownies, *182*, 192
    Croquembuche, *164*, 165
    Cuban Rugelach, 181
    Dacquoise, 166–167
    Fresh Apple Cake, 233
    Hadgi Badah (Almond Macaroons), 232
    Haman's Ears, 297
    Hamantaschen, 299–302
    Hamentaschen de Panama, 303
    Honey Cake, 442
    Irene's Passover Strawberry Fluff Cake, 332
    Italian Cheesecake, *410*, 413
    Jaffa Cakes, 24–25
    Mandelbrodt, 214
    Mohnbrodt, 298
    Mustacchioni, 188
    New York Style Cheesecake, 415
    Passover Linzer Torte, *328*, 329–330
    Passover Pecan Biscotti, 333
    Praline Cheesecake, 417

for Purim celebrations, 295
Quick Honey Cake, 443
Rich Sour Cream Cheesecake, 414
Roulage Leontine, *186, 187*
Rugelach, *140, 141*
Tunisian Guizada, 42
Tuscan Biscotti, *280, 281*
Yolanda's Mother's Best Cookies, *304,* 305
Zimsterne Cookies, 215
Candy
  Almond Honey Sticks, 282
  Chanukah Chocolate Truffles, 190–191, 250
  Mexican Dark Chocolate Bark, 189
Cannoli Cheesecake, 416
Caponata, *404, 405*
Capsouto Frères Potato Mina, 318–319
Careme, Antoine, 165
Carob, 269
Carrot Tzimmes with Dumplings, *320, 321*
Carrots
  Basic Chicken Soup, *344, 346*
  Dutch Hutspot, 264
  Gefilte Fish, 386–387
  High Holy Days, 217
  Maple-Glazed, 222
  Tunisian Spiced, 33
  Tzimmes with Dumplings, 320, 321
Casas, Penelope, 348
Catalan Bread with Tomato Spread (Tostada con Salsa Tomaquet), 51
Cauliflower, 66
Caviar
  with Dill Puffs, *142,* 147–148
  and Latkes, *256, 257*
Central Europe, 129
Challah
  for the High Holy Days, *216,* 219
  for Shabbat, 201
Chantaboon Noodles, 124, 354
Chanukah
  celebration, 251
  Chocolate Truffles, 190–191, 250
  Dutch Hutspot, 264
  Frituras de Malanga, 254
  Halvah de Semolina, 266
  Italian Rice Pancakes, 265
  Latkes, *256, 257*
  Lemon Ricotta Pancakes, *258, 259*
  Mojo Sauce, 255

Moroccan Couscous with Mixed Dried Fruits, *262, 263*
Radish Salad Canapés, *252, 253*
Stuffed Kibbeh, 260–261
Charoset, 418–430
  Ashkenazic, 421
  assortment, *418*
  from Curaçao, 424
  Egyptian, 428
  Garosa (Charoset from Curaçao), 424
  Israeli, 427
  Italian, 425
  Jaroset (Panamanian Halek), 423
  Nontraditional Tomato, 429
  Rhodesian, 426
  Traditional Texas Style, 422
Cheder, 335
Cheese
  Arugula Salad with Dates and Chèvre, *196, 197*
  Blintzes, 337
  Bolemas with Pumpkin-Cheese Stuffing, 377
  Bulgarian Potato-Cheese Borekas, 376
  Cannoli Cheesecake, 416
  Coulibiac, 137–139
  Fiori de Zucca Ripieni (Stuffed Zucchini Blossoms), 60
  Five-Onion French Onion Soup, 152–153, *154*
  Fondue, 151
  French Stuffed Brie en Croûte, 372–373
  Fresh Figs with Goat Cheese and Honey, 268, 283
  Gougere, 149
  Greek Spanakopita, 374
  Honeyed Cherry Pecan Brie, *434,* 435
  Italian Cheesecake, *410,* 413
  Lemon Ricotta Pancakes, *258, 259*
  Liptauer, 75
  Manchego with Quince Preserves, 50
  Mediterranean Cheese Torta, *340, 341*
  Mina de Maza, 316–317
  Pasta with Salsa Cruda, 64, 65
  Quenelles, 390–391
  Rigatoni con Quattro Fromaggi (Rigatoni Pasta with Four Cheeses), 339

Spinach and Cheese Filled Ravioli, 375
Three-Potato Cheese Gratin, 150
Cheese Fondue, 151
Cheesecakes
  Cannoli, 416
  iconic status, 411
  Italian, 410, 413
  New York Style, 415
  Praline, 417
  Rich Sour Cream, 414
Chelo, 5–6
Cherries
  Dried with Orzo, 78
  Honeyed Cherry Pecan Brie, *434,* 435
Chicken
  Baked with Blueberry Chutney, *454,* 455
  Basic Soup, *344, 346*
  Bene Israel Shabbat Chicken Curry, 102–103
  Bukharan Shabbat Chicken Palov, *200, 206*
  Bulgarian Chicken with Barley, 85
  Chilean Pastel de Choclo, 172–173
  East African Groundnut (Peanut) Soup, 31
  Ethiopian Shabbat Stew, 36
  Fesenjan with Walnuts and Pomegranate Syrup, 10
  Grilled with Basil-Garlic Tomato Sauce, 212–213
  Grilled Breasts with Sofrito, 174–175
  Grilled with Spice Rub, 114
  High Holy Days, 218
  Hot and Sour Soup, 351
  Indian Mulligatawny Soup, *352,* 353
  Iraqi with Rice, Chickpeas, and Raisins, 12
  Maple-Glazed Breasts with Apples, 227
  Moroccan Kebabs, 37
  Moroccan Pigeon Pie, 34–35
  Moshe's Stuffed Figs, 284–285
  Nirvana Wings, *98,* 104
  Not So Basic Salad, *210, 211*
  Orange, 22
  Pechuga de pollo con Porto (Boneless Chicken Breast with Port), 52–53

Schmaltz, 203
Soup with Ghondi, 347
Southwestern Honey Breast, 438
Spice Route Nasi Goreng, 111
Stir-Fried in Hoisin Sauce, 277
Syrian Spiced with Rice, 11
Szechuan Cold Spicy Noodles,
    120–121
Tom Kah Gai, 354
Yemenite Fruit and Nut Stuffed,
    207
Chicken Fesenjan with Walnuts and
    Pomegranate Syrup, 10
Chicken livers
    Autumn Pâté, 238–239
    Chopped Liver, 204, 208
Chicken Soup
    Basic Preparation, *344*, 346
    East African Groundnut (Peanut),
        31
    with Ghondi, 347
    Hot and Sour, 351
    Greek Avgolemono, 349
    iconic status, *344*, 346
    Indian Mulligatawny, *352*, 353
    with Meatballs (Sopa de Pollo con
        Albondigas), 348
    Tom Kah Gai, 354
Chickpea(s)
    flour, 347
    Indian Mulligatawny Soup, *352*,
        353
    Iraqi Chicken with Rice and
        Raisins, 12
    Vegetarian Couscous, 247
Chile, 172
Chilean Pastel de Choclo, 172–173
China
    culinary traditions, 22, 277, 351,
        380, 393
    diaspora community, 117–118
Chinese Deep-Fried Wonton, 380–
    381
Chocolate
    Budino Cioccolato (Italian
        Chocolate Pudding), 185
    Cannoli Cheesecake, 416
    Chanukah Truffles, 190–191, 284
    Flan, 185
    Mexican Dark Chocolate Bark, 189
    Miniature Almond Tortes, 278–
        279
    Mustacchioni, 188
    Roulage Leontine, *186*, 187

Tahitian Croissant Bread Pudding,
    162–163
Chocolate Chip Cappuccino Brownies,
    182, 192
Chocolate Chip Meringues, 161
Chocolate Flan, 185
Chopped Liver, 204, 208
Chremslach, 143
Chutneys. *See* Relishes/chutneys
Cigares (filled pastries), 357–358
Classic Italian Jewish Cooking (Machlin),
    449
Classic Pot Roast, 155
Cochin Jews, India, 99
Coconut, 233
Coconut milk, 102–103
Coffee, 442
Conversos, 45–46
Corn
    with Millet Pancakes, 7
    1654 Barley Salad, 293
    Sopa de Elote (Mexican Corn
        Soup), 171
Corn meal, *72*, 80–81
Coulibiac, 137–139
Court Bouillon, 390, 391
Couscous
    Maghreb region, 29
    with Moroccan Meatball Tagine,
        26, 39
    Moroccan Sweet with Mixed Dried
        Fruits, *262*, 263
    Vegetarian, 247
Cranberries
    French Stuffed Brie en Croûte, 372
    Mixed-Fruit Relish, *240*, 241
Cream cheese
    Cannoli Cheesecake, 416
    Ginger Orange Spread, 442
    Hungarian Mushroom Turnovers,
        368
    New York Style Cheesecake, 415
    Praline Cheesecake, 417
Crème Brûlée, 194–195
Croquembuche, *164*, 165
Crostini with Tapenade, 49
Crusades, 18, 143, 144, 145
Cuba
    culinary traditions, 169, 180, 181,
        254
    diaspora community, 174
"Cuban Rugelach," 181
Cucina Ebraica (Goldstein), 61, 70,
    81

Cucumber Yogurt Dip, 79
Cucumber(s)
    cultivation of, 447
    Ottoman tsatsiki, 79
    pickling, 448
    Thai Vegetarian Spring Rolls,
        378–379
    Yogurt Dip, 79
Curaçao, 184, 287, 288, 423, 424
Curried Lentils and Vegetables,
    106
Curried Turkey and Rice, 105
Curry
    Bene Israel shabbat chicken,
        102–103
    Lentils and Vegetables, 106
    Tamarind Marinated Grilled
        Salmon with Thai Sauce on
        Rice Flake Noodles, 124–125
    Tom Kah Gai, 354
    Turkey and Rice, 105
Custards/puddings
    Apples and Honey Cake Bread
        Pudding, 444–445
    Budino Cioccolato (Italian
        Chocolate Pudding), 185
    Crème Brûlée, 194–195
    Flan, *54*, 55, 185
    Halvah de Semola, 266
    Indian Coconut Rice, 107
    Koliva (Sweetened Wheat Berry
        Pudding), 229
    Pumpkin with Spiced Coconut
        Custard, 127
    Sabayon for Passover, 331
    Tahitian Croissant Bread Pudding,
        162–163
    Zabaglione, *56*, 71

D

Dacquoise, 166–167
Daktulos, 274
Date honey, 433
Date(s)
    Arugula Salad with Chèvre, *196*,
        197
    Egyptian Charoset, 428
    Garosa (Charoset from Curaçao,
        424
    Honey, 433
    Israeli Charoset, 427

Italian Charoset, 425
Jaroset (Panamanian Halek),
423
Koliva, 229
Moroccan Sweet Couscous with
Mixed Dried Fruits, *262*,
263
Rhodesian Charoset, 426
Tu BiSh'vat, 270, 274
"Day of the First Fruits," 335–336
Deluxe Matzah Kugel, 322
Deluxe Noodle Kugel, *334*, 338
Desserts. *See also* Custards/puddings,
Pastry
Baked Apricots in Orange Blossom
Syrup, 23
Baklava, 92–93
Chocolate Chip Meringues, 161
Dacquoise, 166–167
Herbal Grape Sorbet, 286
Honeyed Cherry Pecan Brie, *434*,
435
Kataifi with Cream Filling, 90–91
Mermelada de Guayaba (Guava
Marmalade), 180
Miniature Chocolate Almond
Tortes, 278–279
Pumpkin Mousse, 249
Sesame Halvah, 13
Spiced Angel Pecans, *108*, 115
Syrian Apricot Compote in Rose
Water Syrup, *11*, 15
Vanilla Custard Ice Cream, 193
Wine Jelly, 289
Zabaglione, *56*, 71
Zimsterne Cookies, 215
Diaspora communities
African, 29–30, 31
East and Southeast Asia, 117–118
India, 99–100
Italy, 57–58
Levant, 3–5
Maghreb, 27–39
New World/Latin America, 169
Orange trade, 17–18
Ottoman Empire/Turkey, 73–74
Persia/Iran, 5–6
Russia/Central and Eastern
Europe, 129–130
Spain, 44, 45–46
Spice route traders, 109–110
Vanilla/Cacao traders, 183–184
Western Europe, 143–146
Dill Puffs with Caviar, *142*, 147–148

Dips/spreads
Ginger Orange Cream Cheese
Spread, 442
Ottoman Tsatsiki, 79
Dolmas, 242–243
Dressings
Mango Salad Dressing, 101
Pomegranate and Vanilla
Vinaigrette, *196*, 197
Dulce de Manzana (Apple Preserves),
220, *430*
Dutch
culinary traditions, 106, 222, 251,
264, 423
diaspora community, 109–110, 183
Dutch Hutspot, 264

E

East African Groundnut (Peanut)
Soup, 31
East/Southeast Asia
Asian Spinach Salad with Candied
Walnuts and Fried Tofu
Croutons, *116*, 119
Pumpkin with Spiced Coconut
Custard, 127
Soba Noodles with Shiitake
Mushrooms and Tofu, *122*, 123
Steak with Cellophane Noodles,
126
Szechuan Cold Spicy Noodles,
120–121
Tamarind Grilled Salmon with
Thai Curry Sauce on Rice Flake
Noodles, 124–125
Eastern Europe
culinary traditions, 135, 201, 224,
345, 447
diaspora community, 129–130
Eastern European Kreplach, 370
Eastern European Potato Knishes,
359
Easy Palmiers, *294*, 306–307
Easy Rouille, 156, 157
Easy Sauerbraten, 158
Egg Lemon Sauce, 86
Eggplant Bharta, 396–397
Eggplant Salad with Pine Nuts
Kioupia, 407
Eggplant(s)
Baba Ghanoush, 399
Bharta, 396–397

buying, 384
Caponata, 404, 405
cooking whole, 395
iconic status, 393
Imam Bayaldi, 408
Indian Spice Eggplant, 398
Moroccan Eggplant Salad, 401
North African with Honey,
402–403
Patragel, 406
Salad with Pine Nuts Kioupia,
407
Syrian with Pomegranate Molasses,
400
Syrian Spiced Meat with Prunes,
112
Vegetarian Couscous, 247
Eggs
After-Seder Frittata, 323
Agristada, 86
Algerian Fish Terrine for Passover,
388–389
Chocolate Chip Meringues, 161
Italian Rice Pancakes, 265
Rich Sour Cream Cheesecake,
414
Sabayon for Passover, 331
Tortilla Español, 48
Vegetarian Chopped Liver,
205
Egypt
culinary traditions, 90, 260, 393
diaspora community, 32
Egyptian Charoset, 428
Einbrenne, 132
Empanadas, 371
England
culinary traditions, 161
diaspora community, 145–146
English Tomato Chutney, 452
Ethiopia
culinary traditions, 36, 221
diaspora community, 29–30
Ethiopian Shabbat Stew, 36
Etrog, 17, 235

F

Fao de Queijo, 176
Fasting recommendations, 218
Fattoush Salad, 9
Feast of Weeks, 335–336

"Festival, The," 235
Fettiplace, Lady Elynor, 161
Figs
    Fresh, with Goat Cheese and
        Honey, *268*, 283
    Garosa (Charoset from Curaçao),
        424
    Jaroset (Panamanian Halek), 423
    Moshe's Stuffed, 284–285
    Tu BiSh'vat, 270, 271–272
Filled pastries
    Austrian Potato-Mushroom
        Strudel, 362–363
    Bolemas with Pumpkin-Cheese
        Stuffing, 377
    Boston Chremslach, 369
    Bulgarian Potato-Cheese Borekas,
        376
    Chinese Deep-Fried Wonton,
        380–381
    Eastern European Kreplach, 370
    Eastern European Potato Knishes,
        359
    French Stuffed Brie en Croûte,
        372–373
    Grandma Gussie's Potato Knishes,
        356, 360–361
    Greek Spanakopita, 374
    Hungarian Mushroom Turnovers,
        368
    iconic status, 357–358
    Indian Samosas, 367
    Spanish Spinach Empanadas,
        371
    Spinach and Cheese Filled Ravioli,
        375
    Thai Vegetarian Spring Rolls,
        378–379
    Tunisian Briks, *364*, 365–366
Fiori de Zucca Ripieni (Stuffed
    Zucchini Blossoms), 60
Fish
    Algerian Terrine for Passover,
        388–389
    Gefilte Fish, 386–387
    Gefilte Fish and Horseradish Mold,
        382, 385
    Greek Psari Saganaki, *88*, 89
    Grilled, with Spice Rub, 113
    High Holy Days, 218
    Homemade Pickled Herring in
        Cream Sauce, 131
    Huachinango Veracruz (Veracruz-
        Style Snapper), 178

Pecan-Crusted Tacos with
    Pineapple Salsa, 179
Pesce en Saor (Fish in Sweet and
    Sour Sauce), 68–69
Quenelles, 390–391
Salmon with Pink Peppercorn
    Citrus Sauce, *16*, 21
Salmone Affumicato con Melone
    (Smoked Salmon with Melon),
    59
Sautéed, with Pecan Butter, 225
Sole with Pine Nuts and Raisins,
    224
Soupe de Poissons (Bouillabaisse),
    156–157
in Sweet and Sour Sauce, 68–69
Five-Onion French Onion Soup,
    152–153, *154*
Flan, *54*, 55, 185
Fludens, 143
Food of Israel Today, The (Nathan), 36
France
    culinary traditions, 149, 151, 162,
        165, 231, 238, 331
    diaspora community, 144–145
French Stuffed Brie en Croûte,
    372–373
Fresh Apple Cake, 233
Fresh Figs with Goat Cheese and
    Honey, *268*, 283
Fritters, 254

G

Galangal root, 354
Ganache, 166, 279
Garbanzo beans. *See* Chickpeas
Garosa (Charoset from Curaçao),
    424
Gefilte fish
    Algerian Terrine for Passover,
        388–389
    basic preparation, 386–387
    and Horseradish Mold, *382*,
        385
    iconic status, 383
    Quenelles, 390–391
Gefilte Fish and Horseradish mold,
    382, 385
Gefullte (filled), 383
Gelatin, 385
German Apfelpfannkuchen, 439
German Brisket, 158

Germany
    culinary traditions, 158, 295, 383,
        439
    diaspora community, 143
Ghana, 30
Ginger Orange Cream Cheese Spread,
    442
Goldman, Rivka, 4, 12
Goldstein, Joyce, 61, 70, 81
Golishkes, 244–245
Goluptzi, 244–245
Gomel, Rachel, 32
Gougere, 149
Gourmet Jewish Cookbook, The (Zeidler),
    247
Gozlan, Simone, 29
Graham crackers, 414, 417
Grandma Gussie's Potato Knishes,
    356, 360–361
Grape leaves
    Dolmas, 242–243
    Turkish Stuffed Grape Leaves,
        82–83
Grape(s)
    frosted, 289
    Herbal Sorbet, 286
    Tu BiSh'vat, 270, 272
Greece, 89, 92, 229
Greek Avgolemono Soup, 349
Greek Lamb Stew, 87
Greek Psari Saganaki, *88*, 89
Greek Spanakopita, 374
Green beans, 205, 293
Green Lentil and Bulgur Salad with
    Hazelnuts, 8
Grilled Chicken Breasts with Sofrito,
    174–175
Grilled Chicken with Basil-Garlic
    Tomato Sauce, 212–213
Grilled Chicken with Spice Rub, 114
Grilled Fish with Spice Rub, 113
Grilled Steak with Chimichurri Sauce
    and Orange Slices, *168*, 177
Ground beef
    Chilean Pastel de Choclo, 172–
        173
    Eastern European Kreplach, 370
    Keftes de Prasa Con Carne
        (Turkish Leek and Meat
        Patties), 226
    Moroccan Meatball Tagine with
        Couscous, 26, 39
    Stuffed Cabbage, 244–245
    Stuffed Kibbeh, 260–261

Syrian Spiced Meat with Eggplant and Prunes, 112
Tomat Reynado (Turkish Stuffed Tomatoes), 84
Groundnut (peanut), 31
Guava paste, 181
"Guavalach," 181

H

HaChag, 235
Hadar tree, 17
Hadgi Badah (Almond Macaroons), 232
Halek, 274
Halvah, 13, 266
Halvah de Semola (Sephardi Semolina Pudding), 266
Haman's Ears, 297
Hamantaschen, 295
Hamantaschen
    Dough (Dairy), 299
    Dough (Parve), 300
    Fillings, 301
    shaping, 302
    symbolic meaning, 295, 357
Hamentaschen de Panama, 303
Harissa
    basic recipe, 450
    Tunisian briks, *364*, 365–366
    Tunisian condiment, 33
Havdalah, 215
Hazelnuts
    Green Lentil and Bulgur Salad with, 8
    Teiglach, *230*, 231
Herbal Grape Sorbet, 286
Herbed Crepe, 137, 139
Hidur mitzvah, 345
High Holy Days, 217–218
    Apple Brown Betty, 440
    Dulce de Manzana, 220, 430
    Fresh Apple Cake, 233
    Hadgi Badah (Almond Macaroons), 232
    Keftes de Prasa con Carne, 226
    Koliva (Sephardic Black-Eyed Peas), 229
    Lubiya (Sweetened Wheat Berry Pudding), 221
    Maple-Glazed Carrots, 222
    Maple-Glazed Chicken Breasts with Apples, 227

Rosh HaShanah Noodle Kugel, 228
Round Challah, *216*, 219
Salmon en Papillote, 223
Sautéed "Fish" with Pecan Butter, 225
Sogliola con Pinoli e Passerine (Sole with Pine Nuts and Raisins), 224
Teiglach, *230*, 231
Holipkes, 244–245
Homemade Pickled Herring in Cream Sauce, 131
Honey
    Almond Honey Sticks, 282
    with Fresh Figs and Goat Cheese, *268*, 283
    Honey Cake, 442
    Halek (Date Honey), 433
    iconic status, 431
    Nontraditional Tomato Charoset, 429
    with North African eggplant, 402–403
    Quick, Cake, 443
    Rhodesian Charoset, 426
    Southwestern Chicken Breast, 438
    Teiglach, *230*, 231
    "Waldorfed" Spinach Salad, *436*, 437
Honeyed Cherry Pecan Brie, *434*, 435
Horseradish, *382*, 385
"House of Israel," 30
Huachinango Veracruz (Veracruz-style Snapper), 178
Hullake, 274
Hungarian Mushroom Turnovers, 368
Hungary, 75, 160, 295
Hutspot, 251, 264

I

Imam Bayaldi, 408
India
    Bene Israel Shabbat Chicken Curry, 102–103
    Coconut Rice Pudding, 107
    culinary traditions, 353, 393, 396, 447
    Curried Lentils and Vegetables, 106
    Curried Turkey and Rice, 105
    diaspora community, 99–100

Mango Salad Dressing, 101
Nirvana Chicken Wings, *98*, 104
orange trade, 17
Samosas, 367
Spice Eggplant, 398
Indian Coconut Rice Pudding, 107
Indian Mulligatawny Soup, *352*, 353
Indian Samosas, 367
Indian Spice Eggplant, 398
Indonesian Fried Rice, 112
Insalada Caprese, 65
Iraq
    culinary traditions, 260, 325
    diaspora community, 4
Iraqi Chicken with Rice, Chickpeas, and Raisins, 12
Iraqi Pickled Mango, 451
Irene's Passover Strawberry Fluff Cake, 332
Irviya kon gayina, 74
Israel, 4–5
Israeli Charoset, 427
Italian Charoset, 425
Italian Cheesecake, *410*, 413
Italian Chocolate Pudding, 185
Italian Marinated Roasted Red Bell Peppers, 449
Italian Rice Pancakes, 265
Italy
    culinary traditions, 60, 61, 231, 265, 297, 331, 393, 405, 425
    diaspora community, 57–58
    Fiori de Zucca Ripieni (Stuffed Zucchini Blossoms), 60
    Pasta Riminata, 66
    Pasta with Salsa Cruda, *64*, 65
    Pesce en Saor (Fish in Sweet and Sour Sauce), 68–69
    Pumpkin Ravioli from Mantua, 61
    Salmone Affumicato con Melone (Smoked Salmon with Melon), 59
    Spinaci con Pinoli e Passerini (Spinach with Pine Nuts and Raisins), 67
    Winter Squash Gnocchi with Spinach and Pine Nuts, 62–63
    Zabaglione, 56, 71
    Zucca Gialla in Agrodolce (Squash in Sweet and Sour Sauce), 70
Izmir community, 74

J

Jackfruit, 41
Jaffa Cakes, 24–25
Japan, 123
Jaroset (Panamanian Halek), 423
Jewish Manual, The (Montefiore), 146
Jicama, 246

K

Kaparot, 218
Kasha Varnishkas, 135
Kataifi with Cream Filling, 90–91
Kaufman, Alan, 448
Keftes de Prasa con Carne (Turkish Leek and Meat Patties), 226
Khoreshes (stews), 5
Kitchen Bouquet, 52
Kneidlach, *198*, 311
Knishes
    Eastern European Potato Knishes, 359
    Grandma Gussie's Potato Knishes, *356*, 360–361
    iconic status, 357
Kobeba, 260
Koliva (Sweetened Wheat Berry Pudding), 229
Konofa (Kataifi with Cream Filling), 90–91
Kreplach, 357–358, 370
Kubba, 294
Kugel
    Deluxe Matzah, 322
    Deluxe Noodle, *334*, 338
    Potato, 136
    Rosh HaShanah Noodle, 228

L

Ladinokomunita, 73–74
Lamb
    Braised Shanks in Merlot, 324–325
    Greek Stew, 87
    Moroccan Tagine with Prunes, 38
    Spice Route Nasi Goreng, 111
    Stuffed Kibbeh, 260–261
Latin America
    culinary traditions, 169, 183, 184
    diaspora community, 303
Latkes, *256*, 257
Leeks
    High Holy Days, 218
    Keftes de Prasa con Carne (Turkish Leek and Meat Patties), 226
    Three-Potato Cheese Gratin, 150
Lekach, 442
Lemon
    Agristada, 86
    Baba Ghanoush, 399
    Greek Avgolemono Soup, 349
    with Ricotta Pancakes, *258*, 259
Lemon Ricotta Pancakes, *258*, 259
Lemongrass, 354
Lentil Soup, 133
Lentils
    Curried with Vegetables, 106
    Green Lentil and Bulgur Salad with Hazelnuts, 8
    Lentil Soup, 133
Lester, Julius, 217, 309
Levant
    diaspora communities, 3–5
    Fattoush Salad, 9
    Green Lentil and Bulgur Salad with Hazelnuts, 8
    Iraqi Chicken with Rice, Chickpeas, and Raisins, 12
    Millet Pancakes with Fresh Corn, 7
    Sesame Halvah, 13
    Syrian Spiced Chicken and Rice, 11
Lima beans, 292
Lime
    Artichokes with, 32
    Salmon with Pink Peppercorn Citrus Sauce, *16*, 21
    Thai Vegetarian Spring Rolls, 378–379
Liptauer Cheese, 75
Lithuania, 345
Lubiya (Sephardic Black-Eyed Peas), 221
Lucas, Dionne, 187
Lulav, 235, 274
Lumpia shells, *364*, 365–366
Luskey, Debby, 176

M

Macadamia nuts, 453
    Hadgi Badah, 232
Irene's Passover Strawberry Fluff Cake, 332
Machlin, Edda Servi, 265, 425, 449
Maghreb
    Algerian Festive Stew, 40
    Algerian Fish Terrine for Passover, 388–389
    Artichokes with Lime, 32
    culinary traditions, 55
    diaspora communities, 27–29
    Moroccan Chicken Kebabs, 37
    Moroccan Lamb Tagine with Prunes, 38
    Moroccan Meatball Tagine with Couscous, *26*, 39
    Moroccan Mint Tea, 43
    Moroccan Pigeon Pie, 34–35
    Shabbat recipes, 201
    Tunisian Guizada, 42
    Tunisian Spiced Carrots, 33
Maimonides, Moses, 45, 345
Mala insana (crazy spirit), 393
Malanga, 254
Mama Nazima's Jewish-Iraqi Cuisine (Goldman), 4, 12
Mamaliga (Romanian Polenta), *72*, 80–81
Manchego Cheese with Quince Preserves, 50
Mandelbrodt (Almond Bread), 214
Mango Salad Dressing, 101
Mango(es)
    Iraqi Pickled Mango, 451
    Salad Dressing, 101
    Ugandan Fall Harvest Fruit Salad, 41
Maple-Glazed Carrots, 222
Maple-Glazed Chicken Breasts with Apples, 227
Marinated Olives, *44*, 47
Marrano Jews, Spain, 45
Masa harina, 171
Massialot, Francois, 161
Matzah
    Burmolikos, 315
    Carrot Tzimmes with Dumplings, *320*, 321
    Deluxe Kugel, 322
    Matzah Brie, 313
    Mina de Maza, 316–317
Matzah balls
    Boston Chremslach, 369
    Traditional, *198*, 311
Matzah Brie, 313

Matzah farfel
    Deluxe Matzah Kugel, 322
    Passover Granola, *326*, 327
Matzah meal
    Algerian Fish Terrine for Passover,
        388–389
    Gefilte Fish, 386–387
    Grandma Gussie's Potato Knishes,
        356, 360–361
    Latkes, *256*, 257
    Matzah Balls, 311
    Mr. Wechsler's Memory Matzah
        Muffins, 314
    Passover Bagels, 312
Mediterranean Cheese Torta, *340*, 341
Melon
    Ottoman Watermelon and Olive
        Salad, *76*, 77
    Salmone Affumicato con Melone
        (Smoked Salmon with Melon),
        59
    Summer Fruit Soup, 160
Membrillo (Quince Paste), 50
Merguez (Lamb Sausage), 112
Meringue, 161
Mermelada de Guayaba (Guava
    Marmalade), 180
Mexican Corn Soup (Sopa de Elote),
    171
Mexican Dark Chocolate Bark, 189
Mikvaot, 144
Millet Pancakes with Fresh Corn, 7
Mina de Maza, 316–317
Miniature Chocolate Almond Tortes,
    278–279
Mint, 43
Mixed-Fruit Cranberry Relish, *240*,
    241
Mohn (poppy seed filling) 295
Mohnbrodt, 298
Mohntaschen, 295
Mojo Sauce, 255
Molasses, 400
Moluccas (Spice Islands), 106
Montefiore, Judith, 146
Moors, 17, 19, 37, 67, 68, 82, 96, 273,
    274, 396, 405
Moroccan Chicken Kebabs, 37
Moroccan Eggplant Salad, 401
Moroccan Lamb Tagine with Prunes,
    38
Moroccan Meatball Tagine with
    Couscous, *26*, 39
Moroccan Mint Tea, 43

Moroccan Orange and Olive Salad, 19
Moroccan Pigeon Pie, 34–35
Moroccan Sweet Couscous with
    Mixed Dried Fruits, *262*, 263
Morocco/Moroccan
    Chicken Kebabs, 37
    culinary traditions, 19, 34, 37, 43,
        47
    diaspora community, 28–29
    Eggplant Salad, 401
    Lamb Tagine with Prunes, 38
    Meatball Tagine with Couscous,
        26, 39
    Mint Tea, 43
    Orange and Olive Salad, 19
    Pigeon Pie, 34–35
    Sweet Couscous with Mixed Dried
        Fruits, *262*, 263
Moshe's Stuffed Figs, 284–285
Mr. Wechsler's Memory Matzah
    Muffins, 314
Muffins, 188, 314
Murbeteig, 303
Mushroom Barley Soup, 292
Mushroom-Chive Filling, French
    Stuffed Brie en Croûte, 373
Mushroom Duxelles, 138
Mushroom(s)
    Austrian Potato-Mushroom
        Strudel, 362–363
    Chicken Hot and Sour Soup, 351
    Coulibiac, 137–139
    Deluxe Matzah Kugel, 322
    French Stuffed Brie en Croûte,
        372–373
    Hungarian Turnovers, 368
    Mushroom Barley Soup, 292
    Rigatoni con Quattro Fromaggi
        (Rigatoni Pasta with Four
        Cheeses), 339
    Soba Noodles with Shiitake and
        Tofu, *122*, 123
    Tom Kah Gai, 354
    Winter Squash Gnocchi with
        Spinach and Pine Nuts, 62–63
Mustacchioni, 188

N

Nam pla fish sauce, 354
Nathan, Joan, 36, 338
New Spanish Table, The (Von Bremzen),
    286, 348

New World/Latin America
    Chilean Pastel de Choclo, 172–173
    Cuban Rugelach, 181
    Fao de Queijo (Brazilian Cheese
        Puffs), 176
    Grilled Chicken Breasts with
        Sofrito, 174–175
    Grilled Steak with Chimichurri Sauce
        and Orange Slices, 168, 177
    Huachinango Veracruz (Veracruz-
        Style Snapper), 178
    Mermelada de Guayaba (Guava
        Marmalade), 180
    Pecan-Crusted Fish Tacos with
        Pineapple Salsa, 179
    Sopa de Elote (Mexican Corn
        Soup), 171
New Year's holidays. *See* High Holy
Days
New York Style Cheesecake, 415
Nirvana Chicken Wings, *98*, 104
Nontraditional Tomato Charoset, 429
Noodle(s)
    Deluxe, Kugel, *334*, 338
    Rosh HaShanah, Kugel, 228
    with Shiitake Mushrooms and
        Tofu, *122*, 123
    Steak with Cellophane, 126
    Szechuan Cold Spicy, 120–121
    with Tamarind Grilled Salmon with
        Thai Curry Sauce, 124–125
    Thai Vegetarian Spring Rolls,
        378–379
    Tom Kah Gai, 354
North African Eggplant with Honey,
    402–403
Not So Basic Chicken Salad, *210*, 211
Nuts. *See also* Almonds, Hazelnuts,
    Macadamia nuts, Pecans, Pine nuts,
    Pistachio nuts, Walnuts
    almonds, 270–271
    Ashkenazic Charoset, 421
    Asian Spinach Salad with Candied
        Walnuts and Fried Tofu
        Croutons, *116*, 119
    Baklava, 92–93
    Chicken Fesenjan with
        Pomegranate Syrup, 10
    Crusted Fish Tacos with Pineapple
        Salsa, 179
    Dacquoise, 166–167
    Deluxe Noodle Kugel, *334*, 338
    East African Soup, 31
    Fresh Apple Cake, 233

Green Lentil and Bulgur Salad with Hazelnuts, 8
Hadgi Badah (Almond Macaroons), 232
Halvah de Semola (Sephardi Semolina Pudding), 266
Hamantaschen Fillings, 301
Honeyed Cherry Pecan Brie, *434*, 435
Italian Charoset, 425
Italian Rice Pancakes, 265
Koliva, 229
Mandelbrodt (Almond Bread), 214
Mina de Maza, 316–317
Moroccan Sweet Couscous with Mixed Dried Fruits, 262, 263
Mustacchioni, 188
Nontraditional Tomato Charoset, 429
for Passover, 234, 235
Passover Biscotti, 333
Passover Linzer Torte, *328*, 329–330
Pasta Riminata, 66
Pesce en Saor (Fish in Sweet and Sour Sauce), 68–69
Sautéed "Fish" with Pecan Butter, 225
Sogliola con Pinoli e Passerine (Sole with Pine Nuts and Raisins), 224
Spanish Spinach Empanadas, 371
Spiced Angel Pecans, 10, 115
Spinaci con Pinoli e Passerini (Spinach with Pine Nuts and Raisins), 67
Teiglach, *230*, 231
Thai Basil-Jalapeño Pesto, 453
Thai Vegetarian Spring Rolls, 378–379
Tunisian Guizada, 42
Turkish Stuffed Grape Leaves, 82–83
Winter Squash Gnocchi with Wilted Spinach and Pine Nuts, 62–63
Yemenite Fruit and Nut Stuffed Roasted Chicken, 207

O

Olives
Arabian, 19
Crostini with Tapenade, 49
Greek Lamb Stew, 87
marinated, *44, 47*
Mediterranean Cheese Torta, *340,* 341
Moroccan Orange and Olive Salad, 19
Ottoman Watermelon and Olive Salad, *76, 77*
Onions
Algerian Fish Terrine for Passover, 388–389
Eastern European Potato Knishes, 359
English Tomato Chutney, 452
Five-Onion French Onion Soup, 152–153, *154*
Gefilte Fish, 386–387
Grandma Gussie's Potato Knishes, *356*, 360–361
Imam Bayaldi, 408
Orange blossom water
Baked Apricots in Orange Blossom Sauce, 23
as common ingredient, 18
Kataifi with Cream Filling, 90–91
Tunisian Guizada, 42
Orange in Turkish Style, *94*, 95
Orange trade, 17–18
Orange(s)
Asparagus with Maltaise Sauce, 20
Baked Apricots in Orange Blossom Sauce, 23
Greek Lamb Stew, 87
Grilled Steak with Chimichurri Sauce and Orange Slices, *168*, 177
Italian Charoset, 425
Jaffa Cakes, 24
Mojo Sauce, 255
Moroccan Orange and Olive Salad, 19
Orange Chicken, 22
Rhodesian Charoset, 426
Salmon with Pink Peppercorn Citrus Sauce, *16*, 21
in Turkish Style, *94, 95*
Orzo with Dried Cherries, 78
Ottoman Empire
Agristada, 86
Baklava, 92–93
Borekitas kon Kalavasa, 96–97
Bulgarian Baked Chicken with Barley, 85
culinary traditions, 78, 82, 92, 425
diaspora community, 73–74
Greek Lamb Stew, 87
Greek Psari Saganaki, *88*, 89
history, 3–4
Kataifi (Konofa) with Cream Filling, 90–91
Liptauer Cheese, 75
Mamaliga (Romanian Polenta), *72*, 80–81
Orange in Turkish Style, *94*, 95
Orzo with Dried Cherries, 78
Tomat Reynado (Turkish Stuffed Tomatoes), 84
Turkish Stuffed Grape Leaves, 82–83
Ottoman Tsatsiki, 79
Ottoman Watermelon and Olive Salad, *76, 77*

P

Panamanian Halek (Jaroset), 423
Pancakes/griddle cakes
Boston Chremslach, 369
German Apfelpfannkuchen, 439
Italian Rice Pancakes, 265
Lemon Ricotta Pancakes, *258*, 259
Millet Pancakes with Fresh Corn, 7
Passover
After-Seder Frittata, 323
Bagels, 312
Boston Chremslach, 369
Braised Lamb Shanks in Merlot, 324–325
Burmolikos, 315
Capsouto Frères Potato Mina, 318–319
Carrot Tzimmes with Dumplings, *320*, 321
celebration, *308*, 309
Charoset, *418*, 419
Deluxe Matzah Kugel, 322
Granola, *326*, 327
Irene's Strawberry Fluff Cake, 332
Kneidlach, *198*, 311
Linzer Torte, *328*, 329–330
Matzah Brie, 313
Mina de Maza, 316–317
Mr. Wechsler's Memory Matzah Muffins, 314

Pecan Biscotti, 333
  Sabayon for Passover, 331
Passover Bagels, 312
Passover Granola, *326*, 327
Passover Linzer Torter, *328*, *329–330*
Passover Pecan Biscotti, 333
Pasta
  Eastern European Kreplach, 370
  Kasha Varnishkas, 135
  Orzo with Dried Cherries, 78
  Pasta Riminata, 66
  with Salsa Cruda, 64, 65
  Pumpkin Ravioli from Mantua, 61
  Rigatoni con Quattro Fromaggi (Rigatoni Pasta with Four Cheeses), 339
  Spinach and Cheese Filled Ravioli, 375
Pasta Riminata, 66
Pasta with Salsa Cruda, *64*, 65
Pasteles, 357–358
Pastelikos, 357–358
Pastry (savory). *See also* Filled pastries
  Dill Puffs with Caviar, 142, 147–148
  Fao de Queijo (Brazilian Cheese Puffs), 176
  Moroccan Pigeon Pie, 34–35
Pastry (sweet). *See also* Cakes/cookies
  Baklava, 92–93
  Coulibiac, 137
  Easy Palmiers, *294*, 306–307
  French Stuffed Brie en Croûte, 372–373
  Gougere, 149
  Kataifi with Cream Filling (Konofa), 90–91
  Teiglach, *230*, 231
Pâté à Choux, 358
Pâte sucrée, 303
Patlican, 406
Patragel, 406
Peaches, 160
Peanuts, 31
Pear Salad with Jicama and Snow Peas, 246
Pear(s)
  Mixed-Fruit Cranberry Relish, *240*, 241
  Salad with Jicama and Snow Peas, 246
  Poached in Red Wine, *290*, 291
  Spiced Infused Wine Sorbet, 291

Peas
  Indian Samosas, 367
  Lubiya (Sephardic Black-Eyed Peas), 221
  Vegetarian Chopped Liver, 205
Pecan-Crusted Fish Tacos with Pineapple Salsa, 179
Pecan(s)
  Crusted Fish Tacos with Pineapple Salsa, 179
  Fresh Apple Cake, 233
  Honeyed Cherry Brie, *434*, 435
  Passover Biscotti, 333
  Passover Granola, 326, 327
  Sautéed "Fish" with Pecan Butter, 225
  Spiced Angel, *108*, 115
  Traditional Charoset Texas Style, 422
Pechuga de Pollo con Porto (Boneless Chicken Breast with Port), 52–53
Penkar, June, 102, 107, 396
"People of Judah," 30
Persia/Iran
  Chicken Fesenjan with Walnuts and Pomegranate Syrup, 10
  culinary traditions, 223
  diaspora community, 5–6
Pesce en Saor (Fish in Sweet and Sour Sauce), 68–69
Pesto, 453
"Phyllo," 92
Phyllos, 357–358
Pickled Cucumbers, 447–448
Pierogis, 357–358
"Pig's ears," 306
Pimenton de la Vera, 401
Pine nuts
  Dolmas, 242–243
  Mina de Maza, 316–317
  Pasta Riminata, 66
  Pesce en Saor (Fish in Sweet and Sour Sauce), 68–69
  Sogliola con Pinoli e Passerine (Sole with Pine Nuts and Raisins), 224
  Spanish Spinach Empanadas, 371
  Spinaci con Pinoli e Passerini (Spinach with Pine Nuts and Raisins), 67
  Turkish Stuffed Grape Leaves, 82–83
  with Winter Squash Gnocchi and Wilted Spinach, 62–63

Pinkney, Ina, 435
Piroshkies, 357
Pistachio nuts
  Baklava, 92–93
  Israeli Charoset, 427
  Tunisian Guizada, 42
Pita, 316
Pitam, 17
Plum sauce, 380–381
Poached Pears in Red Wine, *290*, 291
Poland
  culinary traditions, 134, 244, 295, 357
  diaspora community, 129
Polenta, *72*, 80–81
Polvilho doce, 176
Pomegranate Molasses, 400
Pomegranate and Vanilla Vinaigrette, *196*, 197
Pomegranate(s)
  Chicken Fesenjan with Walnuts and Pomegranate Syrup, 10
  High Holy Days, 217
  Tu BiSh'vat, 270, 273–274
  and Vanilla Vinaigrette, *196*, 197
Poppy seeds
  hamantaschen fillings, 335
  Mohnbrodt, 298
  for Purim, 295
Port Wine Cream Sauce, 137, 139
Portugal
  culinary traditions, 106, 156, 162, 365
  diaspora community, 52, 109, 156, 162, 165, 183, 192
Potato Kugel, 136
Potato Pancakes, *256*, 257
Potatoes
  After-Seder Frittata, 323
  Austrian Potato-Mushroom Strudel, 362–363
  Bulgarian Potato-Cheese Borekas, 376
  Capsouto frères Potato Mina, 318–319
  Dutch Hutspot, 264
  Eastern European Potato Knishes, 359
  Grandma Gussie's Potato Knishes, *356*, 360–361
  Indian Samosas, 367
  Latkes, *256*, 257
  Mr. Wechsler's Memory Matzah Muffins, 314

Potato Kugel, 136
Sautéed "Fish" with Pecan Butter,
    225
Sweet Potato-Pumpkin Cazuela,
    234, 248
Three-Potato Cheese Gratin, 150
Tortilla Español, 48
Tunisian briks, *364*, 365–366
Winter Squash Gnocchi with
    Spinach and Pine Nuts, 62–63
Povidl Purim, 295
Prakkes, 244–245
Praline Cheesecake, 417
Primus dulcis, 270
Prune Tzimmes, *128*, 134
Prune(s)
    Garosa, 424
    hamantaschen fillings, 335
    Jaroset (Panamanian Halek), 423
    with Moroccan Lamb Tagine, 38
    Prune Tzimmes, *128*, 134
    Sopi di Bina (Curaçao Wine Soup),
        287
    with Syrian Spiced Meat and
        Eggplant, 112
Puddings. *See* Custards/puddings
Pumpkin, High Holy Days, 218
Pumpkin Mousse, 249
Pumpkin Ravioli from Mantua, 61
Pumpkin with Spiced Coconut
    Custard, 127
Pumpkin(s)
    Bolemas with Pumpkin-Cheese
        Stuffing, 377
    Borekitas kon Kalavasa, 96–97
    Moroccan Meatball Tagine with
        Couscous, *26*, 39
    Mousse, 249
    Pumpkin Ravioli from Mantua,
        61
    with Spiced Coconut Custard, 127
    Sweet Potato-Pumpkin Cazuela,
        234, 248
    Winter Squash Gnocchi with
        Spinach and Pine Nuts, 62–63
Purim
    celebration, 295
    Easy Palmiers, *294*, 306–307
    Haman's Ears, 297
    Hamantaschen Dough (Dairy), 299
    Hamantaschen Dough (Parve), 300
    Hamantaschen Fillings, 301
    Hamentaschen de Panama, 303
    Mohnbrodt, 298

Yolanda's Mother's Best Cookies,
    304, 305
wine, 273

Q

Quenelles, 390–391
Quick Honey Cake, 443
Quince paste, 50

R

Radenites, 133, 143, 357
Radish, 251
Radish Salad Canapés, *252*, 253
Raisins
    Dolmas, 242–243
    English Tomato Chutney, 452
    Garosa (Charoset from Curaçao),
        424
    Greek Lamb Stew, 87
    with Iraqi Chicken, Rice and
        Chickpeas, 12
    Jaroset (Panamanian Halek), 423
    Koliva (Sweetened Wheat Bread
        Pudding), 229
    Pasta Riminata, 66
    Pesce en Saor (Fish in Sweet and
        Sour Sauce), 68–69
    Rosh HaShanah Noodle Kugel,
        228
    with Sogliola con Pinoli (Sole with
        Pine Nuts and Raisins), 224
    Spanish Spinach Empanadas, 371
    with Spinaci con Pinoli (Spinach
        with Pine Nuts), 67
Rebecchine de Gerusalemme, 80
Recipes from the Jewish Kitchens of Curaçao,
    287
Red bell peppers
    Crostini with Tapenade, 49
    Eggplant Bharta, 396–397
    Italian Marinated Roasted, 449
Red zhoug, 207
Relishes/chutneys
    assorted, *446*
    blueberry, *454*, 455
    English Tomato Chutney, 452
    Harissa, 450
    Iraqi Pickled Mango, 451

Italian Marinated Red Bell
    Peppers, 449
Mixed-Fruit Cranberry Relish, 241
Rhodes, 407
Rhodesian Charoset, 426
Rice
    Bukharan Shabbat Chicken Palov,
        200, 206
    Coulibiac, 137–138
    Curried Lentils and Vegetables,
        106
    with Curried Turkey, 105
    Dolmas, 242–243
    Greek Avgolemono Soup, 349
    Indian Coconut Rice Pudding,
        107
    with Iraqi Chicken, Chickpeas and
        Raisins, 12
    Italian Rice Pancakes, 265
    in Persian cuisine, 5–6
    Spice Route Nasi Goreng, 111
    Stick Noodles, 378–379
    Stuffed Cabbage, 244–245
    with Syrian Spiced Chicken, 11
Rice flour, 348
Rice stick noodles, 378–379
Rich Sour Cream Cheesecake, 414
Rigatoni con Quattro Fromaggi
    (Rigatoni Pasta with Four
    Cheeses), 339
Roden, Claudia, 57, 90, 188, 278
Romania, 130, 406
Romanian Polenta, 80–81
Rosh HaShanah
    celebration of, 218, 273
    Noodle Kugel, 228
Rouille, 156, 157
Roulage Leontine, *186*, 187
Rugelach, *140*, 141
Rum Sauce, 163
Russia/Central and Eastern European
    Cabbage Borscht, 132
    Coulibiac, 137–139
    culinary traditions, 137, 278, 253,
        295, 357
    diaspora community, 129–130
    Homemade Pickled Herring in
        Cream Sauce, 131
    Kasha Varnishkas, 135
    Lentil Soup, 133
    Potato Kugel, 136
    Prune Tzimmes, *128*, 134
    Rugelach, *140*, 141
Russian Cabbage Borscht, 132

S

Sabayon for Passover, 331
Salad(s)
    Arugula with Dates and Chèvre, 196, 197
    Chanukah Radish Canapés, *252*, 253
    Eggplant with Pine Nuts Kioupia, 407
    Fattoush, 9
    Green Lentil and Bulgur with Hazelnuts, 8
    Moroccan Eggplant, 401
    Moroccan Orange and Olive, 19
    Not So Basic Chicken, *210*, 211
    Ottoman Tsatsiki, 79
    Ottoman Watermelon and Olive, *76*, 77
    Pear with Jicama and Snow Peas, 246
    "Waldorfed" Spinach, *436*, 437
Salmon
    Coulibiac, 137
    Dill Puffs with Caviar, *142*, 147–148
    en Papillote, 223
    with Pink Peppercorn Citrus Sauce, *16*, 21
    Smoked with Melon, 59
    Tamarind Marinated Grilled, with Thai Curry Sauce on Rice Flake Noodles, 124–125
Salmon en Papillote, 223
Salmon with Pink Peppercorn Citrus Sauce, *16*, 21
Salmone Affumicato con Melone (Smoked Salmon with Melon), 59
Salsa, 179
Sambousak, 357–358
Samosas, 357–358, 367
Sanbat Wat (Ethiopian Shabbat Stew), 36
Sangria de Curaçao, 288
Sardines, 68–69
Sasso, Rita, 303, 423
Sauces
    Agristada (egg lemon), 86
    Basil-Garlic Tomato, 212–213
    Chimichurri, *168*, 177
    Cream, 131
    Maltaise, 20
    Mojo, 255

Pesce en Saor (Fish in Sweet and Sour Sauce), 68–69
Pink Peppercorn Citrus, 16, 21
Port Wine Cream, 137, 139
Rum, 163
for Sabayon for Passover, 331
for Salmon en Papillote, 223
Thai Curry, 124–125
Velouté, 105, 139
Sautéed "Fish" with Pecan Butter, 225
Scacchi, 316
Schmaltz, 203
Semolina, 266
Sephardi Semolina Pudding (Halvah de Semola), 266
Sephardic Black-Eyed Peas (Lubiya), 221
Sephardic Jews
    culinary traditions, 96, 196, 197, 266, 371, 431
    diaspora communities, 73–74, 99, 117, 127, 145, 146, 303
    High Holy Days, 217
    New Year's celebration, 196, 197, 273
    New Year's recipes, 220, 221, 224, 226, 229, 232
    Purim ingredients, 295
    Shabbat recipes, 201
    pickling/preserving food, 447
Sesame Halvah, 13
Sesame seeds, 13
Shabbat celebration, 201–202
Shabbat
    Bread Stuffing, 209
    Bukharan Chicken Palov, *200*, 206
    Bulgarian Baked Chicken with Barley, 85
    Caponata, *404*, 405
    Chopped Liver, 204
    Ethiopian Stew, 36
    Grilled Chicken with Basil-Garlic Tomato Sauce, 212–213
    Mandelbrodt (Almond Bread), 214
    Not So Basic Chicken Salad, *210*, 211
    Roasted Turkey with Vegetables, 208
    Schmaltz, 203
    Szechuan Cold Spicy Noodles, 120–121
    Vegetarian Chopped Liver, 205

Yemenite Fruit and Nut Stuffed Chicken, 207
Zimsterne Cookies, 215
Shabbat Roasted Turkey with Vegetables, 208
Shalach manot, 295
Shatta, 207
Shavuot
    Blintzes, 337
    celebration, 269, 335–336
    Deluxe Noodle Kugel, *334*, 338
    Mediterranean Cheese Torta, *340*, 341
    Rigatoni con Quattro Fromaggi (Rigatoni Pasta with Four Cheeses), 339
Sicily, 405
Silk Road, 5, 117, 395
Simple syrup, 286
1654 Barley Salad, 293
Smoked Salmon with Melon (Salmone Affumicato con Melone), 59
Snow peas, 246
Soba Noodles with Shiitake Mushrooms and Tofu, *122*, 123
Sofrito, 174–175
Sogliola con Pinoli e Passerine, (Sole with Pine Nuts and Raisins), 224
Sopa de Elote (Meixcan Corn Soup), 171
Sopa de Pollo con Albondigas (Chicken Soup with Meatballs), 348
Sopi di Bina (Curaçao Wine Soup), 287
Sorbet, Spiced Pear Infused Wine, 291
Soup(s)
    Basic Chicken, 344, 346
    Chicken Hot and Sour, 351
    Chicken, with Meatballs, 348
    Chickpea Meatball, 347
    Curaçao Wine, 291
    East African Groundnut (Peanut), 31
    Fish, 156–157
    Five-Onion French Onion, 152–153, 154
    Greek Avgolemono, 349
    Indian Mulligatawny, *352*, 353
    Lentil, 133
    Mexican Corn, 171
    Mushroom Barley, 292
    Summer Fruit, 160

Soupe de Poissons (Bouillabaisse), 156–157
Sour cream, 414
South Africa, 30
South America
    culinary tradition, 425
    diaspora community, 169, 183, 184
Southwestern Honey Chicken Breast, 438
Spain
    Crostini with Tapenade, 49
    culinary traditions, 19, 31, 47, 48, 156, 255, 329, 375, 393, 396, 423
    diaspora community, 45–46, 52, 109, 156, 192, 396, 405
    Flan, 54, 55
    Manchego Cheese with Quince Preserves, 50
    Marinated Olives, 44, 47
    orange trade, 18
    Pechuga de Pollo con Porto (Boneless Chicken Breast with Port), 52–53
    Tortilla Español, 48
    Tostada con Salsa Tomaquet (Catalan Bread with Tomato Spread), 51
Spanish Spinach Empanadas, 371
Spice Route Nasi Goreng, 112
Spice trade route, 109–110
    Grilled Chicken with Spice Rub, 114
    Grilled Fish with Spice Rub, 113
    Spice Route Nasi Goreng, 111
    Spiced Angel Pecans, 108, 115
    Syrian Spiced Meat with Eggplant and Prunes, 112
Spiced Angel Pecans, 108, 115
Spicy Blueberry Vinegar, 454, 455
Spinach
    Asian Salad with Walnuts and Tofu Croutons, 116, 119
    and Cheese Filled Ravioli, 375
    Greek Spanakopita, 374
    Mina de Maza, 316–317
    Spanish Empanadas, 371
    with Pine Nuts and Raisins, 67
    "Waldorfed" Salad, 436, 437
    with Winter Squash Gnocchi and Pine Nuts, 62–63
Spinach and Cheese Filled Ravioli, 375

Spinach with Pine Nuts and Raisins, (Spinaci con Pinoli e Passerini), 67
Squash, 247
Squash in Sweet and Sour Sauce, 70
Sri Lanka, 106
Steak with Cellophane Noodles, 126
Stew(s)
    Algerian Festive, 40
    Carrot Tzimmes with Dumplings, 320, 321
    Dutch Hutspot, 264
    Ethiopian Shabbat, 36
    Greek Lamb, 87
    Prune Tzimmes, 128, 134
Stir-Fried Chicken in Hoisin Sauce, 277
Strawberries, 332
Stuffed Cabbage, 244–245
Stuffed Kibbeh, 260–261
Stuffed Matzah Balls, 369
Stuffed Zucchini Blossoms, 60
"Styrofoam" Noodles, 126
S'udah hamafseket, 218
S'udah sh'lishit, 405
Sukkot
    Apple Brown Betty, 440
    Autumn Pâté, 238–239
    Butternut–Apple Soup, 237
    celebration, 235, 269, 274
    Dolmas, 242–243
    Mixed-Fruit Cranberry Relish, 240, 241
    Moroccan Meatball Tagine with Couscous, 26, 39
    orange trade, 17–18
    Pear Salad with Jicama and Snow Peas, 246
    Pumpkin Mousse, 249
    Spiced Angel Pecans, 108, 115
    Stuffed Cabbage, 244–245
    Sweet Potato-Pumpkin Cazuela, 234, 248
    Vegetarian Couscous, 247
Summer Fruit Soup, 160
Sun-dried tomatoes, 49
Sweet and Sour Red Cabbage with Apples, 159
Sweet Potato-Pumpkin Cazuela, 234, 248
Sweetened Wheat Berry Pudding, 163
Switzerland, 151
Syria
    Apricot Compote in Rose Water Syrup, 14, 15

culinary traditions, 15, 90, 260
diaspora community, 3, 112
Spiced Chicken and Rice, 11
Spiced Meat with Eggplant and Prunes, 112
Syrian Apricot Compote in Rose Water Syrup, 14, 15
Syrian Eggplant with Pomegranate Molasses, 400
Syrian Spiced Chicken and Rice, 11
Syrian Spiced Meat with Eggplant and Prunes, 112
Szechuan Cold Spicy Noodles, 120–121

T

Tabikha (Algerian Festive Stew), 40
Tahini, 399
Tahitian Croissant Bread Pudding, 162–163
Tamarind Marinated Grilled Salmon with Thai Curry Sauce on Rice Flake Noodles, 124–125
Tapas
    Moroccan Eggplant Salad, 401
    Tortilla Española, 48
    Tostada con Salsa Tomaquet, 51
Taro Root Fritters, 254
Tea, 43
Teiglach, 230, 231
Tempting Kosher Dishes, 313
Thai Basil-Jalapeno Pesto, 453
Thai Chicken in Coconut Curry Soup with Rice Stick Noodles, 354
Thai Vegetarian Spring Rolls, 378–379
Thailand, 127, 354
Three-Potato Cheese Gratin, 150
Tiger Lily Buds, 351
Tikkun olam (repair of the world), 235
Tofu
    with Asian Spinach Salad with Candied Walnuts, 116, 119
    with Soba Noodles and Shiitake Mushrooms, 122, 123
Tom Kah Gai, 354
Tomat Reynado (Turkish Stuffed Tomatoes), 84
Tomatoes
    Eggplant Bharta, 396–397
    English Chutney, 452

Grilled Chicken with Basil-Garlic
	Tomato Sauce, 212–213
	Imam Bayaldi, 408
	Tomat Reynado (Turkish Stuffed
		Tomatoes), 84
	Tostada con Salsa Tomaquet, 51
Torres, Luis de, 169
Tortilla Español (Spanish Tortilla), 48
Tostada con Salsa Tomaquet (Catalan
	Bread with Tomato Spread), 51
Traditional Charoset Texas Style, 422
T'reif (nonkosher), 118
Tsatsiki, 79
Tsire, 112
Tu BiSh'vat
	Almond Honey Sticks, 282
	celebration, 269–275
	Fresh Figs with Goat Cheese and
		Honey, 268, 283
	Herbal Grape Sorbet, 286
	Koliva, 229
	Miniature Chocolate Almond
		Tortes, 278–279
	Moshe's Stuffed Figs, 284–285
	Mushroom Barley Soup, 292
	Poached Pears in Red Wine, 290, 291
	Sangria de Curaçao, 288
	1654 Barley Salad, 293
	Sopi di Bina (Curaçao Wine Soup),
		287
	Stir-Fried Chicken in Hoisin
		Sauce, 277
	Tuscan Biscotti, 280, 281
	Wine Jelly, 289
Tunisia(n)
	Briks, 364, 365–366
	culinary traditions, 29, 33, 42, 365
	diaspora community, 27–28, 29
	Guizada, 42
	Harissa, 450
	Spiced Carrots, 33
Tunisian Briks, 364, 365–366
Tunisian Guizada, 42
Tunisian Spiced Carrots, 33
Turkey's culinary traditions, 15, 377,
	393, 406, 408
Turkey [ingredient]
	Curried, and Rice, 105
	Shabbat Roasted, with Vegetables,
		208
	Sopa de Pollo con Albondigas, 348
Turkish Leek and Meat Patties, 226
Turkish Stuffed Grape Leaves, 242–
	243

Turkish Stuffed Tomatoes, 84
Tuscan Biscotti, 280, 281
Tzedakah, 218

U

Uganda, 30, 41
Ugandan Fall Harvest Fruit Salad,
	41
Ushpizin, 235, 246

V

Vanilla
	Arugula Salad with Dates and
		Chèvre, 196, 197
	Budino Cioccolato, 185
	Chanukah Chocolate Truffles,
		190–191, 284
	Chocolate Chip Cappuccino
		Brownies, 182, 192
	Crème Brûlée, 194–195
	Custard Ice Cream, 193
	Mexican Dark Chocolate Bark, 189
	Mustacchioni, 188
	Roulage Leontine, 186, 187
	trade, 183
Vanilla Custard Ice Cream, 193
Veal
	Chinese Deep-Fried Wonton,
		380–381
	Chinese Hot and Sour Soup, 351
Vegetarian Chopped Liver, 205
Vegetarian Couscous, 247
Velouté Sauce, 129
Venezuela, 184
Vinegar
	English Tomato Chutney, 452
	Italian Marinated Red Peppers,
		449
	pickling cucumbers, 448
	Thai Basil-Jalapeño Pesto, 453
Von Bremzen, Anya, 286, 348

W

"Waldorfed" Spinach Salad, 436, 437
Walnuts
	Ashkenazic Charoset, 421
	with Asian Spinach Salad and
		Fried Tofu Croutons, 116, 119

Baklava, 92–93
Chicken Fesenjan with
	Pomegranate Syrup, 10
Deluxe Noodle Kugel, 334, 338
Halvah de Semola, 266
Hamantaschen Fillings, 301
Italian Charoset, 425
Yemenite Fruit and Nut Stuffed
	Chicken, 207
Wasserman, Gladys, 211
Water chestnuts, 380–381
Watermelon, 76, 77
Western Europe
	Cheese Fondue, 151
	Chocolate Chip Meringues, 161
	Classic Pot Roast, 155
	Croquembuche, 164, 165
	Dacquoise, 166–167
	Dill Puffs with Caviar, 142,
		147–148
	Easy Rouille, 156, 157
	Easy Sauerbraten, 158
	Five-Onion French Onion Soup,
		152–153, 154
	Gougere, 149
	Soupe de Poissons (Bouillabaisse),
		156–157
	Summer Fruit Soup, 160
	Sweet and Sour Red Cabbage with
		Apples, 159
	Tahitian Croissant Bread Pudding,
		162–163
	Three-Potato Cheese Gratin, 150
Wheat, Tu BiSh'vat, 270, 275
Wheat berries, 229
Whole wheat flour, 440
Wine
	Kosher, 272–273
	Tu BiSh'vat, 272–273
Wine
	Algerian Fish Terrine for Passover,
		388–389
	Ashkenazic Charoset, 421
	Braised Lamb Shanks in Merlot,
		324–325
	Five-Onion French Onion Soup,
		152–153, 154
	Herbal Grape Sorbet, 286
	Israeli Charoset, 427
	Jaroset (Panamanian Halek),
		423
	mayonnaise-based sauce, 223
	Poached Pears in Red Wine, 290,
		291

ort Wine Cream Sauce, *137*, 139
Rhodesian Charoset, 426
Sangria de Curaçao, 288
Sopi di Bina (Curaçao Wine Soup), 287
Spiced Pear Infused Wine Sorbet, 291
Tostada con Salsa Tomaquet (Catalan Bread with Tomato Spread), 51
Traditional Charoset Texas Style, 422
Wine Jelly, 289
Winter Squash Gnocchi with Wilted Spinach and Pine Nuts, 62–63

Wonton skins, 357–358, 370
    Chinese Deep-Fried, 380–381
    Indian Samosas, 367
Wright, Clifford, 40

Y

Yemenite Fruit and Nut Stuffed Roasted Chicken, 207
Yiddish, 129
Yogurt
    Eggplant Salad with Pine Nuts Kioupia, 407
    Ottoman Tsatsiki, 79
Yolanda's Mother's Best Cookies, *304*, 305
Yom HaBikurim, 335–336
Yom Kippur, 218
Yucca flour, 176

Z

Zabaglione, *56*, 71
Zakuski, 357
Zatar, 5, 399
Zeidler, Judy, 247
Zimbabwe, 30
Zimsterne Cookies, 215
Zohar, 431
Zucca Gialla in Agrodolce, 70
Zucchini, 60, 247
Zucker, Libby, 181